STRATEGIC COMMUNICATION, MANUFACTURING OF NARRATIVES AND INDIA–ASEAN RELATIONS

A Critical Study of the Framework of ASEAN Media

STRATEGIC COMMUNICATION, MANUFACTURING OF NARRATIVES AND INDIA–ASEAN RELATIONS

A Critical Study of the Framework of ASEAN Media

Om Prakash Das

First published in 2026 by
PENTAGON PRESS LLP
206, Peacock Lane, Shahpur Jat
New Delhi-110049, India
Contact: 011-26490600

Typeset in AGaramond, 11 Point
Printed by Aegean Offset Printers, Greater Noida

ISBN 978-81-994764-1-7

www.pentagonpress.in

Contents

List of Tables, Figures and Samples of News Items

Tables

Figure

News Items

Introduction

Southeast Asia has been a region of great dynamism in world politics, with India having significant interests within. India's cultural influence and its extensive historical connections with peoples of this region since pre-modern times explain the unique and multi-dimensional nature of its engagement with Southeast Asia. Present-day India has arrived at a crossroads demanding re-appraisal of its presence within world politics at the very time that a more active presence within Southeast Asia is sought, given the prevailing economic trends and China's expansionary policies.

Media narratives, going very deep into our lives, knowingly or unknowingly shape our outlook and standpoints. In this context, we have to understand and analyse India's reach-out to the common public of Southeast Asia, utilising media narratives and trends. This study does not claim a direct role of media narratives on policymaking and the common public within Southeast Asia. Rather, this empirical work tries to probe into whether media content emerging out of India is able to influence the people effectively and to what extent it addresses India's relations with the region and its international reach. Moreover, we must understand that media operates within defined economic, social and political contexts. Media narratives are determined a lot by societal and political subtleties, and within the era of economic globalisation, capital presence and concomitant politics offer a lot of influence. Media with its ability to shape understanding is a substantial element of the economic–political order, operating within larger societal contexts.

The very essence of this book is to understand the conversion and evolution of information into news and the working of the structure of information that gives rise to cross-border media representations. In empirical studies, this study attempts to bring some understanding to these pertinent factors. In its very nature, it gives importance to the imperative role of the media to construct understanding and negotiate the dynamic and complex interaction of the political economy, media space and India's representation in Southeast Asia in general and in the five

Association of Southeast Asian Nations (ASEAN) countries in particular. It is a piece of work that studies the fine nuances of media representation and its effects on regional relations and dynamics.

Furthermore, the book discusses the complex interaction of ASEAN's political institutions, economic pressures and media liberty, with especial emphasis on threats to media independence stemming from political pressure, economic incentives and self-censoring. It discusses the salient point of how different ASEAN states cover India within their newspaper coverage, with the finding of a range of different approaches on the basis of each state's political–economic structure and media ecology. The work also discusses ASEAN states potentially seeing India's economic, geopolitical and diplomatic roles through newspaper coverage and narrative, with a further discussion of the worrisome aspect of the trend to turn to external news providers to cover India within Southeast Asia's media. It discusses the potential peril of such a trend, including constricted information diversity, diffusive myths and skewed presentations. In addition, the book discusses the international news content and its diffusiveness, especially within the confines of ASEAN media, on the establishment of region-based subscriber attitudes. It attempts to navigate the challenge of structured representation, especially within developing state contexts. Among the aims of this research is to explore the intricate interplay between media representation, political economy and foreign policy, tracing the course that the political and economic status of ASEAN states has on their media portrayals, with subsequent impacts on public sentiments and India's geostrategic location.

Representational Substructures and the Making of Perception

Within the framework of the stated propositions, a considerable degree of ambiguity persists regarding the extent to which media content originating from India effectively penetrates public consciousness across Southeast Asia. Additionally, ambiguity remains as to how prevailing media narratives construct and disseminate India's bilateral and multilateral engagements within the region and its positioning in the broader global order. Even media systems also never function with a sense of hermetic sealing but are instead constitutively embedded within and delineated by politico–economic formations. It is thus imperative to bring to critical scrutiny all the impacts that politico–institutional, economic compulsions and media system configurations have on the representation of India within each of the ASEAN national contexts.

Furthermore, the space of media usage and its correlative impact remains under-theorised, more so, with respect to the degree to which Southeast Asian media rely on external versus internal sources of news to cover India. Such dependencies also evoke pertinent queries regarding their epistemological and strategic ramifications, such that of narrative homogenisation, skewed representation or strategic omission. The way news about the world gets distributed is important, particularly in Southeast Asian (ASEAN) countries where the media has specific structural constraints. We must look closely at the language and narratives that are being used to form and repeat both the public's and the leaders' views regarding India.

The issue of media representation, particularly its constituting role with respect to public imagination and elite rhetoric begs critical review. An underlying issue is that of the operation of the representational process within the construction of India's image within Southeast Asian public arenas, and the function that such accounts occupy within, or against, hegemonic political imaginaries. An understanding of the structure and discursive nature of media milieus, and their conjoining with the region's economic politics, is a necessary prerequisite to any strategic communications initiative that India enters into within its Southeast Asian relations.

Against this background, this study tries to explore these intersecting dynamics so that a more nuanced and theory-informed addition to the understanding of India's mediated presence and path of representation within the ASEAN media region is made.

Understanding the Framework

Media texts are produced within specific, historically contingent systems that are influenced by complex interactions among nation-states, international organisations, legal institutions and cultural traditions, as well as other media corporations, technologies and economic pressures.[1] This underscores the inseparability of politics and economics, making them intertwined fields. For this research understanding this entanglement was crucial to comprehending how any society and culture operates. Moreover, the political economy approach in media understanding focusses on the interplay between the political and economic forces that influence the production, distribution and consumption of media.[2] This approach of study entailed examining the political and economic circumstances surrounding the production of media content. It encompassed the analysis of media organisation ownership structures, the influence exerted by advertisers, the role of government regulations and other relevant factors.[3] In essence, the political economy approach in media research furnished a comprehensive framework for understanding the intricate dynamics of media within society, considering both political and economic determinants. Furthermore, this approach scrutinised the systems and structures within which media operates, shedding light on the power dynamics, economic forces and cultural influences that moulded the media landscape.[4]

Central to the methodological structure was the thorough examination of primary data provided by reputable media monitoring organisations. These datasets offered invaluable insights into the evolving landscape of media freedom, access and circulation patterns across ASEAN member states. This understanding was achieved by scrutinising yearly assessments and studies conducted by these organisations. This approach of study employed a mixed-methods approach, combining quantitative analysis of numerical data with qualitative examination of craft of the media text, policy documents, constitutional provisions and media coverage. Primary data were collected from reputable media organisations, encompassing diverse indicators such as circulation figures, audience access and media ownership structures. Government documents outlining media policies and constitutional provisions safeguarding freedom of expression were systematically reviewed to discern regulatory frameworks and their implications for media independence and pluralism.

The employed sampling method was employed to select prominent newspapers from ASEAN countries that regularly featured news about India, particularly in the headlines. The duration of data collection spanned six months, from May 1, 2023 to October 31, 2023. The selection of this period followed a random method, devoid of intentional bias. The ASEAN region includes diverse member states, each with distinct cultural, political and economic characteristics. This study examined the digital versions of well-known English newspapers from five ASEAN member states: Indonesia, Malaysia, Thailand, Singapore and the Philippines. These countries were chosen because they were the top five economies in the ASEAN bloc based on their gross domestic product (GDP) rankings. Given the volatility of GDP figures across ASEAN nations because of the rapidly evolving economic landscape, this study adopted a comprehensive approach by considering data spanning from 2018 to 2022,[5] thus affording a nuanced understanding of economic trends. Consequently, Indonesia, Malaysia, Thailand, Singapore and the Philippines emerged as the focal points for examination within this temporal scope. The newspapers selected for sampling encompassed a diverse array of publications from Southeast Asia.[6] These included *The Jakarta Post*, *Tempo English* and *Indonesia expat* from Indonesia; *The Star*, *New Straits Times* and *Malay Mail* from Malaysia; *Bangkok Post*, *The Nation* and *Thaiger* from Thailand; *The Straits Times*, *Today* and *The Business Times* from Singapore; and *Philstar Global*, *Inquirer* and *ABS-CBN* from the Philippines.

In this study, headlines of news articles pertaining to India were scrutinised, with a specific focus on the framing, emphasis and tone of coverage. Coding categories were established, encompassing positive, apprehensive, negative and neutral (factual) representations. Regarding the source analysis, each news article underwent coding to ascertain whether the coverage originated internally (e.g., staff reporters, news desk, etc.) or externally (e.g., news agencies, wire services, other news publication/media organisations).

In the realm of sentiment analysis, techniques were employed to categorise the overall tone and emotional context of news articles concerning India in ASEAN newspapers. The sentiments discerned ranged from positive, to negative, to neutral. Content analysis methodologies were applied to identify patterns, themes, dominant topics/subjects and trends in the portrayal of India across ASEAN newspapers. Comparative analyses were conducted across newspapers and over time to delineate variations and similarities. For contemporary media studies, a careful perusal of news coverage goes beyond the headlines to the leading sentences. Such a holistic practice is central to understanding the whole framing of information and construction of narrative, particularly within international relations and strategic communication.

Headlines of news function as the ultimate attention-grabbers, providing a brief summary and thought-provoking preview of the respective content.[7,8] They are often what initially attract a reader to read a publication.[9] In a similar sense, a lead paragraph, or introduction, is considered to be the most important element of a publication, written to deliver reader attention through the conveyance of the most important information concisely and clearly, and also delivering the voice and direction of the publication.[10] These two entities together form the summary of the publication, delivering its semantic macrostructure and making the first impression for the reader.[11]

To effectively analyse pieces of news, researchers employ sentiment analysis, also referred to as opinion mining, to elicit the emotional tone, positive, negative, apprehensive or neutral, expressed within the narrative.[12] This involves the evaluation of written language to determine the feelings, opinions and sentiments expressed. A distinguishing characteristic of such high-level media analysis is to compare the headline's sentiment with that of the lead paragraph. This is vital since albeit the headline is unique to tempt readers with a tantalising glimpse of the tale to come, the lead paragraph provides a more detailed, albeit concise, summary of the very essence of the tale.[13,14] Discrepancies in sentiment within these two elements reveal intentional framing devices or commercial imperatives at work. Where such inconsistencies of sentiment or message occur, a detailed exploration of the underlying message within the media narrative is warranted. Sociologist Stuart Hall's framework delineates that media does not reflect reality but instead "re-presents" or "re-creates" reality, implementing a form of cultural leadership through the "politics of signification".[15,16] This equates to journalists, with their headline and lead selections, having the ability to emphasise "preferred macrostructures of mental models". Such is the analysis that aids the identification of the reality that media outlets may influence reader interpretation and potentially a public voice even if the readership does not turn a page beyond the opening elements.[17] Comprehension of such inconsistencies is relevant to pulling away the very purpose and likely effect of media tales on public perception and, subsequently, on a nation's strategic, diplomatic and geopolitical position.

It is pertinent to note that the availability and accessibility of archival data from selected newspapers may have varied, potentially constraining the comprehensiveness of the analysis. Furthermore, sports news was deliberately omitted from the analysis due to its inherently objective nature.

Imperatives of Examining ASEAN Media

Against the backdrop of a very dynamic Indo–Pacific geopolitical landscape, a proper review of media representation within ASEAN nations has now become a needed imperative to understand and fine-tune India's strategic, diplomatic and geopolitical positioning. This is also on the basis of today's reality that strategic communication is no longer a marginal function but a core component of national power equal to military power and economic potential. It is through deliberate efforts to craft and disseminate messages that states shape international opinions, promote national interests and compete against adversary narratives.

The media here is not only a passive conduit but also an active agent of the co-construction of meanings and gradual building of narratives. Strategic communicators, including state communicators, are thereby ultimately dependent on media access to impose narratives that spread their interests and build foreign opinions. Such interaction is, however, multi-dimensional, and includes internal reasoning of the media, gatekeeping based on news values and intricate political–economic dynamics. The digital revolution has also intensified this interaction, offering a wider reach and participatory engagement while simultaneously throwing challenges such as informational overload, manipulation of informational source, credibility wars and the imperative to respond in real time. Ultimately, media's selectivity, framing and dissemination is at the core of building legitimacy, framing international public opinion and achieving diplomatic objectives within the modern-day information ecosystem.

A salient factor influencing the role of media is its political economy. News, variously characterised as a 'strange commodity', has public and commercial roles and generates intrinsic contradictions that have a considerable influence on the production and reception of news. Structural biases that arise from various forms of media ownership and economic compulsions, such as profit and advertisement dependencies, can blur editorial independence, encouraging sensationalism and bias. These undermine the shared body of knowledge that is essential to communicate effectively, diplomatically. Further, active construction of the news, with the multi-dimensional character of the functionary-source media complex, leads to the construction of discourses on raw information that suit specific power relations and interests. Western agencies' dominance, with economic and editorial alignments that often dictate world discourses, tend to suppress non-Western perspectives, including those on India.

Specifically, in India's case, its coverage within ASEAN media reveals a persistent imbalance, which to a large degree is dominated by a majority of Western news agencies. Such a dependency tends to focus coverage on India's strategic and economic roles, discouraging its dynamic culture and developmental dimensions. This process has been theorised within the framework of 'strategic media regionalism', whereupon media coverage aligns with state goals rather than delivering independent or diversified coverage. India tends to be treated within a 'limited framing', whereupon it is framed as a geopolitical counterweight, economic partner or governance model, to a very high degree to suit national goals of each ASEAN state rather than a balanced coverage. Such adherence to structure gives birth to disproportionate epistemic perceptibility, whereupon prevalent narratives overwhelm more diversified or overlooked Indian realities.

Therefore, a nuanced exploration of ASEAN states' media coverage of India is not only an academic initiative but also a strategic imperative. It aids a nuanced identification of some biases, understanding of the framing of storylines through national political economies and international information flows, and a precise estimation of their impacts on India's soft power advocacy campaigns and diplomatic missions. Such a critical assessment is imperative to help India make more refined, culturally sensitive and effective media interaction policies. With the promotion of cultural narration, the advocacy of independent media and active interaction with regionally based media forums, India is able to make a more genuine and representative narration, thereby augmenting its holistic strategic, diplomatic and geopolitical presence within the Indo–Pacific.

The Structural Layout of the Book

The book is organised into ten chapters, each addressing different facets of this theme. Chapter One sets the theoretical foundation by outlining strategic communication and situating it within the broader concepts of national power. It indicates the focus of Nye's soft power framework, whereby attraction (on the basis of culture and ideas) can deliver cooperation instead of coercion. Here, states employ public diplomacy, the transparent implementation of conveying policy and values to foreign public to induce a sense of legitimacy and influence. It also surveys nation branding efforts, defined as a state's endeavour to create a favourable image abroad. Finally, Chapter One highlights the challenge of the digital age: old-style one-way propaganda is declining to interactive communication, such that governments have to not only listen, but also communicate and correct in real time. In short, this chapter argues that strategic communication is critical to the achievement of alliances, debunking misinformation and advancing foreign-policy goals within a media-saturated world.

Chapter Two discusses the role of media in narrative construction. It argues that media outlets actually do a great deal more than provide passive pipelines; rather, communicators (states, in particular) undertake efforts to reach the media to impose their preferred storylines but are constrained to work within the media's rationale and limits themselves, such as news values, news routines and gatekeeping. Describing this interplay often to be symbiotic but also tense, communicators rely on media coverage to reach their goals, while editors and journalists search for compelling content within commercial and political compulsions. The chapter identifies such phenomena as the politics–media–politics cycle, whereby coverage itself contributes to subsequent political agendas. It also identifies that digital and social media have heightened both opportunity and challenges: messages reach the broader public and evoke public reaction but also must compete with information saturation, including challenges to credibility and the challenge of instant response. Here, within this dynamic, media outlets have unprecedented power to select and shape information, thus determining what world publics consider legitimate — a central point on which to focus for any diplomat or strategic thinker.

Chapter Three analyses the political economy of news production, showing how economic and ownership structures shape strategic communication. It emphasises that news is a 'strange commodity' with both market and public good characteristics, leading to contradictions. For instance, commercial pressures (advertising revenue, conglomerate ownership) can bias content toward sensational or partisan angles, eroding the editorial independence needed for honest discourse. Such dynamics can fragment the shared facts that diplomacy relies on. At the same time, digital platforms and algorithms introduce new forms of influence: news feeds and search results are increasingly filtered by opaque algorithms (often shaped by corporate or state interests), which can inadvertently amplify misinformation or narrow the range of visible viewpoints. The chapter also discusses how some states use regulation or censorship to shape narratives, tools that may offer control but risk undermining trust and democratic norms. As geopolitical competition enters cyberspace, considerations like data infrastructure and cyber-surveillance become a part of strategic communication. In this rapidly evolving landscape, marked by fragmented information environments and even AI-driven disinformation, the chapter concludes that nations must invest in media literacy and counter-messaging to preserve public trust and national security. (As the United Nations Educational Scientific and Cultural Organization observes, promoting media and information literacy is "the first line of defence" against disinformation.)

Chapter Four examines how raw events are transformed into news stories. It shows that journalism is an active, not neutral, process: reporters and editors use gatekeeping, selection and framing to shape which facts enter the public view and how they are presented. The chapter points out that trust hinges on transparency and source credibility, when these break down, misinformation and cynicism can spread. It illustrates these concepts with historical and recent cases (e.g., wartime propaganda, the Iraq War, COVID-19 coverage), demonstrating the real-world impact of media framing. A key theme is the dominance of Western news agencies (e.g., Reuters, Associated Press (AP), Agence France-Presse (AFP)) in global news flows: by the 1980s, these wire services supplied over 90 per cent of foreign news printed worldwide. Reliance on a few international wires, especially for English-language journalism in Asia, often sideline local perspectives. The chapter argues that this concentration can perpetuate a Western-centric 'global news' narrative while reinforcing stereotypes about the Global South. To counter this, it calls for stronger local media capacity and media literacy, so that citizens can critically evaluate sources and media can provide more diverse, representative coverage.

Chapter Five turns to the specific media landscapes of five ASEAN countries. Using a political economy lens, it finds that in each case a few large conglomerates (often linked to business or political elites) dominate the media market. These ownership structures, along with legal and regulatory constraints, tend to produce self-censorship and alignment with government agendas, despite formal constitutional guarantees of press freedom. Even though digital and social media have created new forums for expression, entrenched power structures continue to shape narratives. The chapter shows that, in practice, media in these countries often functions more as an instrument of authority than as an independent forum for democratic debate. This has serious implications for governance and public trust: when the media echos ruling interests, public discourse narrows and citizens may become sceptical of the news. The analysis underscores that understanding ASEAN's media systems requires looking at who owns and controls the outlets, as well as the formal rules they operate under.

Chapter Six moves into empirical studies of India's portrayal in ASEAN's English-language media coverage. It finds that national interests and editorial contexts shape India's image in each country. For example, Indonesian media tends to portray India primarily as a major economic and diplomatic partner, often highlighting bilateral trade and cooperation initiatives while downplaying cultural or domestic political issues. Malaysian outlets likewise focus on India's economic and strategic roles, though some critical nuances appear within article texts. The chapter notes that heavy reliance on international news agency content can limit local interpretation, often reinforcing a Western oriented narrative about India. In Thailand, India is framed as an assertive strategic player in the Indo–Pacific, with headlines stressing security cooperation. Coverage in Singapore and the Philippines also centres on India's economy and foreign policy. Across these cases, a pattern emerges: media frequently uses sensational headlines to attract readers, but the substantive reporting is more balanced. These contrasts reveal the tension between commercial imperatives and journalistic thoroughness. The chapter concludes that without greater editorial freedom and context-sensitive reporting, ASEAN audiences receive a somewhat narrow picture of India — focussed on grand strategy and economics, with cultural or people-to-people aspects largely missing.

Chapter Seven presents a broader analysis of India's portrayal across ASEAN media. It documents a persistent imbalance in coverage: India is mostly visible in the region as a strategic or economic actor, whereas its cultural and social dimensions receive scant attention. The author introduces the concept of 'strategic media regionalism' to describe how media coverage tends to align with each state's foreign-policy interests, rather than reflecting an independent or nuanced view of India. The chapter also highlights that many outlets continue to depend on Western wire services and syndicated content, which imposes a top-down framing of news. Sensationalism in headlines frequently overstates or distorts India-related stories, which can undermine trust in media when the article content is more muted. Differences in coverage among ASEAN countries are traced to their varying geopolitical ties with India (for instance, defence cooperation or trade partnerships). Overall the findings align with critical media theories, suggesting that mainstream media often perpetuates elite, Western-centric narratives. The chapter ends by calling for media reforms: if ASEAN press could be more independent, transparent and locally grounded, coverage of India might become more balanced and informative.

Chapter Eight continues this empirical study of India in ASEAN news. It similarly finds that narratives are dominated by India's strategic and economic roles. The chapter reiterates the 'strategic media regionalism' idea, emphasising that most reports serve the publishing country's agenda rather than offering fresh insight. For instance, diplomacy and security issues headline the news, while cultural exchanges or India's development stories are marginal. The analysis shows once again how sensational headlines ('clickbait') can mislead readers, creating 'visibility without intimacy' — the public sees India's face on the screen, but only in narrow political terms. Variations in content across countries reflect those nations' interests, for example, India's role as a counterweight to China or as a partner in specific ASEAN initiatives will be highlighted differently depending on the outlet. In line with the previous chapter this one underscores that dependence on Western agencies and a lack of editorial autonomy limit the diversity of perspectives. It echoes the call for reforms to foster more locally informed journalism, which could enrich public understanding of India's multifaceted profile.

Chapter Nine concludes the analysis by identifying the dominant 'frames' through which ASEAN media view India. It finds a triadic framing pattern; India is cast mainly in one of three roles: as a geopolitical counterweight (security frame), as a trade and investment partner (economic frame) or as an exemplar of governance (model frame). This reduction means that India often appears in ASEAN news only when it serves those specific angles; its people, culture and grassroots innovations remain largely unseen. The chapter coins the term 'asymmetric epistemic visibility' to describe how Indian realities outside elite narratives are marginalised. In practical terms, this means that ASEAN publics know of high-level summits and crises involving India but know very little about ordinary life or softer ties. This 'visibility without intimacy' limits India's ability to build soft power in the region. To address this gap, the author suggests that India should pursue a more nuanced media engagement strategy, for example, by promoting cultural storytelling, supporting independent journalism abroad and participating in regional media forums. By doing so, India could broaden its appeal and influence in Southeast Asia beyond strategic headlines, deepening long-term partnerships with ASEAN societies.

The book weaves together theory and case studies to show that strategic communication — from state messaging to the economics of news — is a decisive factor in India–ASEAN relations. It draws on established concepts (e.g., Nye's soft power, public diplomacy, media framing and political economy) to analyse how narratives are manufactured and propagated. Each chapter builds on the last: from defining the tools of strategic communication, to examining media industries, to empirically investigating how these forces shape India's regional image. Throughout, the author emphasises that understanding the media landscape is essential for grasping contemporary diplomacy and influence in Southeast Asia.

Chapter One

Strategic Communication and the Manufacturing of Narratives

In the modern world, the definition of a powerful nation is constructed through a lexicon that includes strong political leadership, economic prosperity, military capability and access to outer space. Within this constellation of terms, the role of effective diplomatic initiatives and strategic partnerships is also profoundly consequential. In the realm of international relations, the definition of a nation's power is determined by the extent to which it can influence the perception of another nation.[18] Perception is shaped by the available information, and it leads to the subsequent relationship with the world or any entity about which the receiver obtains information. In this process of developing a perception, the availability of information is important. This availability depends on the means of communication through which the information travels. In the case of strategic communication, it is a deliberate process by any entity. In our case, that entity would be any country. This process of strategic communication shapes perceptions and influences foreign audiences. This projection of perception has to present a positive image in the world, because the projected perception eventually transforms into a narrative over a period of time. This process consists of various tools, public diplomacy, cultural media products and nation branding to build trust. It also has been used to counter propaganda from hegemonic powers, especially in the case of developing nations. Therefore, strategic communication inherently consists of using communication purposefully to reach and develop the perception that is desired by the sender of the information. At the level of a country, the desire or the goal would be the production of a message to achieve a state where its global image is enhanced and, in addition to this, to foster cooperation and advance national interests. In other words, "Strategic communication is defined as the purposeful use of communication by an organization to fulfil its mission".[19]

In both bilateral and multilateral diplomacy, military and economic instruments, commonly referred to as 'hard power', have traditionally been employed to safeguard national interests.[20] However, 'soft power' seeks to achieve similar objectives through the exchange of ideas and values, aiming to cultivate a natural acceptance or legitimacy of a particular issue or agenda. Joseph Nye conceptualised a nation's soft power as the ability to attract others through cultural and political values in such a manner that these values extend beyond national borders and contribute to the country's global identity. An appeal of such nature that "it renders the country acceptable as a legitimate and moral pillar".[21] The renowned Chinese diplomat Hu Shih once remarked that "India achieved cultural victory and exerted influence over China for twenty centuries without sending a single soldier across its borders".[22]

Joseph Nye coined the term 'soft power', which deals with "the ability to get what you want through attraction rather than coercion or payments".[23] The world realised that soft power is central to strategic communication, because this process of strategic communication promotes 'soft power' to influence others. Another significant aspect is achieving the desired perception through attraction rather than force. Again, 'soft power' is another multidisciplinary term that includes cultural appeal, political values and credible foreign policies. Nye has elaborated on the process of strategic communication, and it relies on authenticity and credibility to counter manipulative narratives from hegemonic powers. In the midst of the Cold War, few geopolitical giants used mass media to propagate a certain cultural ethos and ideology, like the U.S. through radio broadcasts and other means to countering Soviet narrative.[24,25] It is very evident that this was the propagation of soft power in the framework of strategic communication.

It seems that the dissemination of 'soft power' through various tools such as media, public engagements, etc. is one of the operational structures for strategic communication, but 'soft power' make its space through various means and public diplomacy is among them.[26]

Public diplomacy and soft power are intertwined concepts, where public diplomacy has been instrumental in exercising soft power. As we discussed earlier, soft power practices the power of persuasion through various means rather than force, relying on a nation's culture, values and policy resources. On the other hand, public diplomacy is the practice of engaging with non-official audiences to shape perceptions, build relationships and promote policy objectives.[27] Essentially, public diplomacy leverages a country's soft power to achieve desired outcomes in international relations. Therefore, we can understand that soft power contains messages to deliver, and public diplomacy provides the means of how to use it, while strategic communication works on the integration and alignment with broader objectives. In modern times, diplomacy and, moreover, foreign policy require all three working in concert to shape global perceptions, counter disinformation and advance national interests through persuasion rather than coercion.[28]

Engaging with foreign audiences is one of the keys to public diplomacy because it can build trust among nations. The University of Southern California (USC) Center on Public Diplomacy provides a relational perspective, which says, "Public diplomacy is the practice of engaging with foreign audiences to strengthen ties, build trust, and promote cooperation".[29]

Table 1: Key Theories and Their Application in Strategic Communication

Theory/Author	*Key Quote*	*Application in Geopolitics*	*Source*
Strategic Communication	"Strategic communication is defined as the purposeful use of communication by an organization to fulfill its mission"[32]	Governments use coordinated messaging to advance national interests and shape global perceptions.	—
Soft Power (Nye)	"Soft power is the ability to get what you want through attraction rather than coercion or payments".[33]	Countries promote culture and values to influence foreign audiences without force.	Nye (1990), p. 166
Soft Power (Nye)	"The best propaganda is not propaganda".[34]	Authentic messaging counters hegemonic propaganda effectively.	Nye (2004), p. x
Public Diplomacy (Britannica)	"Public diplomacy, any of various government-sponsored efforts aimed at communicating directly with foreign audiences...".[35]	Direct engagement with foreign audiences builds support for national policies.	Britannica 2025
Nation Branding (Anholt)	"Nation branding is really just a metaphor for how effectively countries compete with each other for favorable perception...".[36]	Countries craft identities to attract investment, tourism and diplomatic support.	Anholt (2007), p. 15

Strategic communication is implemented through strategy and the comprehensive purpose of this strategy is to brand a nation, where countries craft a cohesive identity to enhance their global image. Simon Anholt, a leading scholar in this field, defines it as "a metaphor for how effectively countries compete with each other for favorable perception, be it with regard to exports, governance, tourism, investment and immigration, culture and heritage, or people".[30] This perception-making process requires "strategy, substance, and symbolic actions" rather than superficial campaigns.[31] It is important to underscore that strategic communication is particularly pertinent in the realm of geopolitics. This process cultivates a favourable national image and is often viewed as a strategic asset that can enhance a state's ability to attract foreign investment and garner diplomatic support, while simultaneously mitigating the impact of adverse narratives propagated by more dominant global actors. This process also has been seen through the prism of relevancy of strategic communication in geopolitics, where a positive image can attract investment and diplomatic support, countering negative narratives from dominant powers.

Professor Dennis Murphy (U.S. Army War College) once said, "Strategic communication is an emergent concept with several definitions floating about, no doctrinal base, and a lexicon that fails to convey the desired understanding".[37]

It is significant to underline that the term strategic communication remains subject to varying interpretations and continues to evolve, with a widely accepted definition yet to emerge across different contexts and perspectives. However, despite the contested realm of exact definition, strategic communication is a coordinated effort using messaging, visuals/images and other signalling or engagement methods to inform/educate, influence or persuade specific audiences to support a national objective.[38] Strategic communication is a multi-layered process that usually denotes synchronisation and coordination with "the many different activities of an organization to communicate with and influence important audiences".[39] It is essential to consider strategic communication as a pathway towards achieving broader strategic communication goals. Furthermore, if it is for broader goals, then it also refers to "shared responsibility".[40] It (shared responsibility) is imbibed with this process, which involves many actions and utterances. It has been considered a blend of communication related to various purposes and mottos, comprising "risk communication, public relations, brand management, and corporate communication".[41]

Changing Dynamics of Strategic Communication

On September 29, 2016, India exercised its military strike power across the 'Line of Control' in Pakistan-occupied territory. After the successful surgical strike, there was a prominent display of empathy from the global public sphere towards

India's efforts to combat terrorism that was being carried out from Pakistan. Militarily this was a precise operation, but there was another operation in play as well, which was about the informational strike. This strategic informational strike was also a surgically precise operation because "the dissemination of information on the strikes, which was prompt and measured demonstrated the well-coordinated efforts of the diplomatic and defense establishments".[42] The next example is related to the China and India affair. China has been trying to transgress the Indian Line of Actual Control (LAC) and sometimes international borders despite "the Indian Armed Forces having not shown any signs of weakness since 1962".[43] It is observed that regarding strategic communication on China issues, there is often a delay and even incongruence in statements made by the Indian polity, senior bureaucracy and higher military leadership.[44]

These two episodes, as mentioned earlier, project contrary outcomes in terms of communication, especially on the issue of strategic communication and public diplomacy. The gamut of strategic communication has become more significant as the technology and structure of media organisations have changed over the last two decades, especially after the arrival of digital media.

Defence relation dialogue and public diplomacy comprise long-term strategic goals to secure national interests. Therefore, it is essential for public diplomacy efforts to reach a broader audience beyond just those who already support the national agenda. Former Ministry of External Affairs spokesperson Nirupama Rao also suggests that our strategic communication (public diplomacy) must target the region beyond our national boundary.[45] Moreover, strategic communication must be truly national. And to do that it must reflect not only government policy and an executive message but also a national narrative understood, owned and endorsed across society.[46] Information-laden airwaves of television broadcasts or beams of informational data through optical fibre often cross national boundaries and deliver a whole universe of narratives. However, unfortunately, at this juncture, these narratives have the power to project a fallacy sometimes.

Communication beyond the shores of a country and especially in the case of adversarial relationships, encoding the message cannot be only for disseminating information but also with the motive of persuasion. In addition to this, communication should not only take place with different actors of the state but with ordinary people as well. Indians have been listening to the projected idea of 'non-state actors' from one of our neighbours, especially in the case of export of terrorism. This term 'non-state actors' is an example of the projection of a narrative that does not target states but the masses. This idea is evident in the White House 2010 National Framework for Strategic Communication, which specifically emphasizes the role of information operations professionals alongside other key elements..[47]

Nevertheless, many misconceptions present strategic communication as having the ability to spin a story, which can fix real problems, instead it can be defined as a better way of telling a story. This way of communication is embedded with a more proactive posture, and it is beyond the horizon of the foreign audience. However, it starts with our people and our neighbourhood.

Strategic Communication: It Works in a System!

The evolution of strategic communication represents a relatively new framework within geopolitics and media. Diplomacy, in general, and public diplomacy, in particular, has been the primary domain of strategic communication, and refers to the deliberate and coordinated use of language and media by governments and diplomatic actors to achieve specific political and policy objectives. This involves a process of planning, executing and evaluating communication activities to "shape public opinion, influence decision-makers, and advance national interests".[48] In international relations, strategic communication is a critical tool for advancing diplomatic goals, promoting peace and stability and strengthening partnerships. In addition, effective communication strategies can help build trust and credibility, dispel myths and misconceptions and promote a positive image of one's country and its policies.[49] Besides a wide range of stakeholders, including government officials, civil society organisations' strategic communication demands engagement with the media, which is supposed to mobilise support for initiatives. Communication happens in a given scenario and context, and the media works in a system. The context may vary with the cultural and political framework, where communication requires a deep understanding. Nevertheless, the medium of communication (media) works in a system led by political–economy settings that determine the craft of the messages and selection of information with the process of 'selective attention'[50] and 'selective perception'.[51]

Face-to-face meetings, official statements, media interviews and cultural exchanges have been the tools for diplomatic communication to persuade other parties. It is self-evident that it conveys its country's positions and perspectives. In today's interconnected world, strategic communication has become an increasingly important aspect of diplomatic relations. Many countries have established specialised units or departments within their foreign ministries to coordinate and direct these efforts.[52] It is not merely limited to message making, which should be effective in terms of strength of penetration in the receiver's mind for persuasion. It is also about disseminating the message at the right time to the target receivers/ audience for the desired persuasion and through right medium. and the chosen medium. In other words, these two aspects (dissemination of the message and the selection of the medium) stress on systematic innovation, sometimes in alignment with the target audience. Strategic communication and media systems are closely intertwined, as strategic communication relies heavily on the media system to reach its target audiences. Organisations use the media system to disseminate their messages, and the media system relies on organisations to provide content. Therefore, strategic communication and media systems are both essential for effective communication.[53] One can observe the intentional attempt to make structural changes in the media system through its political–economic outlook. Content-sharing throughout Southeast Asia can be considered a covert aspect of strategic communication that is taking place through wire agencies. For example, many newspapers frequently run Xinhua (Chinese wire agency) content as part of their regular news. Moreover, a significant number of Chinese-language media outlets in Southeast Asia are now owned by Chinese companies or by individuals aligned with Beijing's interests.[54]

Manufacturing of Narratives

The word narrative refers to an account that comes after the event and describes something that has already happened. "A narrative is a story that you write or tell to someone, usually in great detail. A narrative can be a work of poetry or prose, or even song, theater, or dance".[55] Usually, it doesn't emerge from a single event or a couple of events, but is the result of a series of events. It is also the result of "any account of a series of related events or experiences".[56] It is evident that narrative, in its inherent characteristics, is somewhat removed from the truth or reality because it is the version of someone who may have witnessed the real event. One of the most important aspects of a narrative is that it is not the static transmission of information, instead it is always in a state of flux and is an iterative process embedded within the communication cycle. Manufacturing of narratives is more of a curated process than story telling or news dissemination because it takes form when carefully selected messages are disseminated, interpreted and reinterpreted by various actors over a period of time.[57]

It is important to note that strategic communication functions in a realm where politics, persuasion and storytelling intersect. In this realm, shaping a narrative is the foundation of soft power. In the age we are living in today, where information dissemination is far easier than before, multiple actors compete for legitimacy and influence. In these times of information overload, strategic communication constructs narratives that seek to define not only events but also identities, values and futures. On the part of execution, strategic communication has been seen and understood through the lens of narratology, not merely communications theory, because "StratCom continues to rely more on communications theory than narratology",[58] whereas a deeper engagement with narrative structures could significantly enhance its efficacy. Narratives can't be built without a message in the process of communication, which over a period of time ultimately shape perception. Beyond this, messages or facts themselves are not enough to achieve this state of making a narrative, the logic and resonance of stories are also critical components. As Hanska notes, "The message born in the interpretation of any activity gains prominence and surpasses the intended meaning. Thus, the narrative itself dominates the telling and not the teller or his or her organization".[59] In this given framework, eventually perception becomes the reality, and the manufacturing of a narrative becomes central to shaping political outcomes.

Political outcome is a key aspect of geopolitics, and it is the political actors and stakeholders whom the message conveyed through strategic communication aims to reach. Over time, strategic communication has moved beyond shaping perceptions and can also influence behaviour. "Strategic narratives are a means for political actors to construct a shared meaning of the past, present, and future of international politics to shape the behavior of domestic and international actors".[60]

It is quite evident that strategic communication propagates alternate ideas of social interests, values and aspirations for the international order through the shifting of the discursive environment.[61] In this state of affairs, strategic narratives serve as indispensable apparatuses through which political actors articulate and function. Policy makers and moreover statecraft cannot isolate themselves from the narratives that influence citizens' perceptions even on issues of direct concern. Moreover, "Strategic narratives play an important role in defining and reproducing collective identities. Both the formal and informal strategic culture refers to the social meaning attached to statecraft, defined as the citizens' general perception about the stature or relative power of their state in the world politics".[62]

Usually, strategic communication has a proactive nature to construct the narrative. Lawrence Freedman emphasises that it is "designed or nurtured with the intention of structuring the responses of others to developing events".[63] The underlying approach to communication can be discerned during situations of influx, as strategic communication efforts often seek to ensure that their interpretation of events attains prominence. In this state of influx, interpretation could be inclined towards the desired narrative, and "the power to shape narratives and control information can be a game-changer in international affairs".[64] There has been a significant evolution in U.S. public diplomacy, marked by a shift from one-way information dissemination to more dynamic and participatory engagement approaches. While it may appear that this process of narrative construction is one-directional, the world has seen significant change with the evolution of U.S. public diplomacy. In this "shift towards engagement" [65] of U.S., strategic communication has become a more complex process because, in such engagement, international audiences are no longer passive recipients of information.This awareness for the communication signals a deeper understanding of how audiences interact with media ecosystems, predominantly the social and digital platforms.

At this juncture, it would be significant to note how people access, interpret and respond to public diplomacy efforts. Here the understanding that "audiences are connected as networks"[66] underscores the importance of leveraging relational and participatory communication methods that align with decentralised, interactive media environments. Beyond communication and the dissemination of messages and posturing this shift in engagement in public diplomacy the focus shifts towards how narratives circulate within and across interconnected communities, where influence depends as much on resonance and credibility within peer networks as on the authority of the message source.[67] Therefore, this shift represents a strategic adaptation to the realities of a networked information age, where engagement, dialogue and reciprocity are central to effective statecraft.

Chapter Two

Strategic Communication and News Media

Strategic Communication, Media System and Values

As discussed earlier, narratives are established after the event, and it is a part of storytelling or the dissemination of information to the audience. Along with this, narratives cannot become a part of the public sphere in a short span of time, but resonate over a period of time.[68] Therefore, narrative making is also embedded with consistency in message dissemination, and mass media has been a critical tool in this process. Mass media, especially traditional news outlets and modern digital platforms, serves as a critical instrument in strategic communication, particularly in the realm of public diplomacy.[69] Access to media is crucial, and countries utilise media to craft narratives that promote their interests, policies and cultural values to foreign audiences, often to influence public opinion and advance geopolitical objectives.

Strategic communication always aligns with predetermined organisational objectives, which depend on message dissemination, where media plays a critical role. In the traditional, modernist (or prescriptive) view, organisations craft a rational, linear strategy and then disseminate it through news media in a largely top-down fashion, though critics argue that this "reduces strategic communication to asymmetrical, top-down communication from top management to employees".[70] In this given imperative, the dynamics of media functioning and systems become deterministic, wherein the roles of organisational and normative environments hold significance and context. Ironically, the postmodernist (or emergent) perspective acknowledges that strategies (and media narratives) often arise organically over time, shaped by grassroots interactions, unanticipated opportunities[71] and the feedback loops inherent in 24-hour news cycles. Moreover, modernist approach treats news media as a means to broadcast preset messages, the emergent view positions mass media–news media as dialogic spaces where strategy and communication continually evolve.[72]

Media and media organisations function within a complex interplay of normative structures, economic ecosystems, societal frameworks and cultural environments. This interconnectedness underscores the principle that media entities do not operate in isolation but rather as integral components of a larger system. It (media) also has been fundamentally characterised by "mutual dependency and competitive symbiosis".[73] The complex phenomenon is that strategic communication practices projecting selective perspectives that benefits its cause, whereas news media pursues compelling content based on its own realm of various systems including prevalent political–economic architecture. Wolfsfeld[74] explains that it is the result of dynamic representation that forms "mutual dependency",[75] with media aiming to secure the "juiciest information without having to give a free ride".[76] There are two conceptual premises to define this according to Marc Jungblut. One premise relies on the element of media logic, which dominates strategic communicators. This concept states that "the logic of the media institutions will increasingly shape politicians' publicity efforts".[77] The other premise is based on whether political actors control coverage. Jungblut ultimately positions 'political–media interdependence' as the most nuanced framework. This conceptual framework has been illustrated as a "Politics–Media–Politics (PMP) cycle",[78] which asserts that "politics always comes first".[79] If we elaborate it further, it explains this as a process, where political structure drives media coverage, but it is not absolute. The reason being that media is also reliant on its own strategic sources and organisation framework, which often align with political, economic ecosystem. In some cases, it is also acknowledged that the media "can play an independent role in political processes due to their ability to transform political realities into news stories",[80] often filtered by newsworthiness criteria and a drive towards "telling a good story".[81] This idea of a 'good story' may be defined in the context of editorial proposition and larger and given architecture political–economy.

Media itself is a part of a structure, and other than this media also carries its functional obligations. These obligations consist of various processes that take place on a day-to-day basis, and disseminated strategic messages also go through these processes. Strategic communication and mass media both operate within the framework of news values, aiming to influence audience perceptions. News media share a closely intertwined relationship. The embedded nature of media functioning has been to process the information where a selective approach in the form of gatekeeping exists. Through this processing, news stories are presented to the public, thereby signalling their importance. "Media outlets send an indirect message to audiences about a story's perceived importance through selection and how much time and exposure they give [to] the story".[82] This is a filtering process, which is usually guided by news value, and is defined as the "criteria used by media outlets to determine whether or not to cover a story and how much resources it should receive". [83] In these circumstances, a strategic message should have the ability to surpass this gatekeeping practiced in news organisations. Therefore, strategic communication must craft information that aligns messaging with these criteria to gain visibility. "The most successful public relations professionals are those who think and act like reporters".[84] This implies that a deep understanding of what drives media interest enables strategic communicators to craft stories that resonate with journalists and audiences alike, thereby increasing the likelihood of media coverage and public engagement.

Role of Media in Shaping International Narratives

With the evolution of media, technology and the flow of information across the globe have become very prevalent, along with media's overarching influence in international communication. Media in general has been emphasising its role in shaping how global audiences perceive a country's actions and policies. In the walk of deliberation on the issue of dynamics of international communication, it is significant to understand that "The media [has] emerged as a powerful force in shaping international communication and public opinion".[85] As discussed earlier in the previous chapter, the process of strategic communication doesn't take place in isolation, and there are various stakeholders as far as the role of media and its ecosystem is concerned. The reason being that media operates within a system. It is important to underline the collaborative efforts of various actors in using media to craft narratives. This suggests a coordinated approach where governments leverage media to frame issues in ways that align with their strategic objectives, influencing foreign public opinion.[86]

The media plays a crucial role in strategic communication regarding the reach or dissemination of the desired message and shaping the opinion of the public sphere. The media includes traditional outlets like newspapers, television and radio and newer platforms like social media and online news sites. Effective strategic communication involves understanding and using the media landscape to your advantage. The media can also build and maintain relationships with key stakeholders, such as customers, employees and investors. Organisations can build trust and establish themselves as thought leaders in their respective industries by providing information and engaging in ongoing conversations with these groups.

The point of contention belongs to the value of medium or media because it is not value-free. "It has much in common with another critical political economy of communication approaches in that the central focus is the structure, organization, operation, and output of the media itself".[87]

Media does not exist in isolation from individual technologies but as an interconnected system constantly evolving in response to technological innovation and political–economic changes. According to Zielinski,[88] media systems are defined by their ability to process, store and transmit information. They comprise various technologies, including print media, radio, television and digital media, as well as the institutions and practices that govern their use. Media systems are not static; they are constantly in flux as new technologies and social practices emerge and old ones fall out of use. In addition, it has been argued that media systems are not neutral tools for transmitting information but are imbued with political, economic and technological values that shape how people understand the world.

The communicated message has to be encoded in a structure with the alignment with an attitude that eventually constitutes the frame of the desired decoding of the message. It is the frame which is the story's perspective. This framing process does not occur in isolation but results from editorial policy and a given media system.[89] The output of the communication process comes through media, but its (media's) umbilical cord connection with its political–economic structure decides many crucial imperatives.[90] One of the significant imperatives is the slanting of media text as far as objectivity is concerned. It emerges from within and results from a process of gatekeeping influenced by an editorial understanding of a given organisation.

As far as the role of media in foreign relations is concerned, in broad terms, it has a dual role: media shapes how events are understood worldwide, making it essential for strategic communication in diplomacy, and the other role is to test credibility. In other words, media acts as both a messenger for governments and as a checker of their information. "The task of critical media is to test the credibility in the flow of information and argumentation from powerful social actors".[91] The flow of information is about the dissemination of a desired narrative, but another part is more important, where the projected narrative is received by other actors, where it may be reproduced and circulated in local media. This reproduction again has a dual role, because beyond narrative projection, this reproduced narrative reaches globally, where it has to compete with other narratives. "Like a debate, with nations trying to outdo each other's narratives. There is a long tradition for understanding professional communication as adversarial activity",[92] reflecting how governments use media to counter rivals and promote their own views, which is crucial for strategic communication. On the issue of a nation's media portrayal beyond borders, it becomes more complex because of the reproduction of the projected media text. During the process of reproduction, "[t]he understanding of the news value of an issue in the media and the way they angle conflict and select elements that turn the issue in a given direction is no less coloured by self-interest", [93] highlighting its importance in framing international events.

Media's Centrality in State Strategic Communication and Information Environments

Owing to communication practices and technological development, the public sphere witnessed new structural transformations, and governments have been recognising and relying on media,[94] especially mass media, for the purpose of strategic communication. When it comes to institutional change in strategic communication by the state, media outlets serve not only as passive channels but also as active agenda setters.[95] The reason being that information dissemination through the new architecture of media technology and access across the globe can determine which issues receive public attention and how they are framed. The most established and serious efforts of narrative projection have been press releases, social media campaigns and coordinated press briefings; governments craft narratives that have served the objectives of the foreign policy of any nation, but their access and acceptance in other nations have been critical. The dissemination of messages through strategic communication in foreign relations leverages the media's capacity to reach transnational publics, projecting a state's values and policy priorities beyond its borders. It is very significant to underline that even when "strategic communication from powerful actors is bound to be measured up against norms of communication",[96] this pattern of engagement with an 'independent' media system in foreign lands can enhance a government's credibility.

Consequently, it is demonstrable that sovereign states are progressively absorbing strategic communications as a core element of diplomacy, and moreover, in the new age of the global information ecosystem, "Public diplomacy has been defined in different ways"[97] and is still in the process of evolution due to technological innovation and flux in geopolitics. It remains imperative to acknowledge that all these efforts are a part of a broader strategic undertaking rather than an end in themselves. In the midst of these given premises of geopolitics and the communication ecosystem, by capitalising on media and its various technological tools, such as broadcasting, the internet and cultural exchanges, "authorities aim not only to transmit policy messages but to shape the information environment".[98] Contemporary observations indicate that governments have already departed from traditional approaches to strategic messaging, but are often described as being "stuck too often on the 'send button'",[99] which typically results in one-way messaging resembling mere 'megaphone diplomacy.' The prevalence of information flow significantly impacts outcomes. A crucial aspect of this process involves the strategic dissemination of messages aimed at either countering established narratives or addressing voids where genuine interest in the projected narrative is absent. From where the information is coming, and how it reaches newsrooms in the case of news media, and what incentives those newsrooms are receiving, these questions remain vital. While dealing with this situation, governments must embed media use within the policymaking process, treating strategic communications as both a "center-of-government" [100] concern and a "whole-of-government unifier".[101] Consequently, in this process, the crafting of the message plays a critical role, because the basic premises of any strategic message must be credible, coordinated and operationally effective.

Diplomacy has been defined as "the conduct of relations between states and other entities with standing in world politics by official agents and by peaceful means",[102] and has changed course to harness digital media's reach and immediacy. Using media, and now digital means, is being redefined as "the use of social media for diplomatic purposes". [103] This change of course essentially depends upon using media for the dissemination of information by enabling direct communication with global audiences. Moreover, through these means of media, states monitor local and global sentiment and respond to geopolitical shifts in real time, turning diplomacy into a tool to "steer change along certain pathways". [104] In this process of diplomatic practices, media gets a central position, and media's centrality to strategic communication functions lies in its ability to manufacture legitimacy and influence. New technology allows the communication architecture of any country, in the process of projecting certain perceptions, to "synthesize and analyze large amounts of data"[105] and disseminate a large amount of data, with the aim of enabling proactive policy adjustments. The change in media practices and the easy availability of information through various agencies transform communication patterns from elite-centric negotiations to a participatory process because news related to any country in foreign lands attracts "private individuals, active citizens, reporters and policymakers",[106] thus making strategic messaging a bridge between states and societies.

Media representation makes its impact at a very granular level, where the content of major media outlets has a wide range of impact through its media text not only on the public but also beyond the readers. We demonstrate a novel method to quantify inter-outlet influence using causal inference on 'quote following', where one outlet uses the same quote as another outlet at a later date".[107] At this juncture even the organisational structure of media outlets doesn't work, instead it is the information and the source of information that take advantage of their ability of dissemination and reach. These sources may be a news agency or other contributors like a social media platform, etc. that is already authenticated by media organisations and is influential enough to be used as a source of information. States have been using these non-state elements to "create and amplify conspiratorial content designed to undermine trust"[108] in state actors in foreign countries.

Earlier studies suggest that media outlets often align with national interests, especially at the time of diplomatic and security-related crises. This has been the circumstance when news stories often supported a country's diplomatic initiatives without critical scrutiny. A study on Chinese strategic communication campaign notes that media provided "largely sympathetic narratives that supported, rather than questioned, their country's diplomatic initiatives" during this period.[109] Messaging in public media by any country doesn't only convey messages to the world and spread a slanted narrative, but may also portray two nations as allies or vice versa.[110] Surowiec and Kania-Lundholm define the engagement of media for strategic messaging with nation branding as ideological narrative-building when they say, "The practice of nation branding online is an ideological construct supported by the neoliberal ideology of the free market, embracing private interests, marketing goals, and commercial techniques for self-promotion".[111]

We are going through a relatively new global information age compared to the previous digital and satellite technology era, where the dissemination of information is expeditious. In this informational ecosystem the penetration of embedded value of information is wider and more persuasive, which eventually transforms into a narrative, and "a good narrative energizes and attracts people".[112] This information ecosystem seeks to explore the persuasive capacity to build an overarching framework for "diplomacy and negotiation with the ability to harness the power and potential inherent in the new and emerging technologies that globalization has wrought.".[113]

Strategic Communication in the Digital World: A Disruption

Instead of a "communication strike" during moments of "demands for action," strategic communication is viewed as a continuous process that does not target a specific national audience. [114] Social media platforms, social networking services and micro-blogging platforms are new dimensions of technology that can connect with people from around the world, access a wide range of information and have the ability to create and share content with a global audience. Additionally, these platforms have enabled users to create and join communities of interest, allowing them to connect with like-minded individuals and content and share their ideas and experiences. Some experts[115] further suggest that technology can improve strategic planning by enabling continuous tracking in real-time and by allowing for faster goal setting. Furthermore, These platforms have allowed content creators to reach more people and interact with their audiences in new ways.[116] Therefore, it is about the construct of the message and continued dissemination to the target audience, though the frequency may be contested.

Dissemination of information through media took a sharp turn when digital technologies arrived. "The reach of digital technologies and its power to influence, monitor and manipulate global perceptions, has been significant in shaping public diplomacy for many countries while helping to construct international and domestic public opinion (PO) on major global issues".[117] In the digital world, strategic communication has become more complex due to digital communication's fast-paced and dynamic nature; this is a new landscape for communication, where messages can spread quickly and widely. As a result, organisations must communicate strategically to ensure their messages are received and understood by their target audience in the desired manner. Therefore, identifying and understanding the target audience have become significant and fundamental elements of strategic communication in the digital world.[118] Strategic communicators need to be able to identify and target specific groups, such as social media influencers, to spread their message. The characteristics of digital media for strategic communication suggest that its best to be adaptive across all channels, including social media, websites and email. Additionally, the sender of the strategic message needs to understand the pros and cons of a given technology, such as data analytics and artificial intelligence (AI), to understand their target audience and personalise their messages. Here, personalised messages do not take the individual as a unit but as a given social section in a specific geography. This (digital media) is a relatively new ecosystem of media, where information spreads quickly, and organisations need to be responsive to current events and trends.

They need to be able to react quickly and effectively to changing circumstances.[119] The additional issues include overcoming digital noise, where the challenge is to stand out and get the messages heard, and building credibility against the bombardment of unverified information.

Chapter Three

Strategic Communication, Structural Imperatives and the Political Economy of Media

The Contested Information Landscape in Geopolitics

In the age of rapid technological development, the global environment has become increasingly interconnected, where information flow has changed from its traditional role as a by-product of international relations to being at the centre stage where it becomes deterministic for power dynamics and diplomatic efficacy. Today the essence of strategic communication is delivered through various channels and media, influencing the perception of the global public, including states and non-state actors, in the complex global geopolitics and left policy nexus. In this process of persuasive messaging, the communication channel itself is elevated as a strategic actor that can shape reality and contribute to the balance of power in the realm of international relations.[120]

There are various means that determine and constitute the production, distribution and consumption of communication resources, which fundamentally consist of online, print and broadcast news.[121] Beyond these deterministic elements, it is the power relations and structural framework that negotiate between the above-mentioned deterministic elements and the values of media functioning as a whole. The political economy of media is among them, and in the context of Southeast Asia it has become even more prevalent. We will discuss the political economy of media in Southeast Asia separately in the coming chapters but will try to navigate the power relations in this chapter, which have been deterministic when it comes to strategic communication, especially in the context of diplomacy and the media portrayal of one country across the globe.

Media Systems and the Politics of Strategic Messaging

The political economic framework for media revolves around ownership concentration in the milieu of normative structure, where structural inequalities and talent management processes are fundamental for the construction of the media text and its dissemination.[122] These processes inherently apply filters,[123] which determine the reproduction of reality and push slanted narratives. Strategic communication shapes the discursive environment within the contested international security landscape[124] and according to our study, strategic communication attributes project nations' values and interests to segmented audiences and alters thought and behaviour, which eventually shapes perception on the world stage. Media channels serve as key instruments for conveying the strategic message, and these messages are produced within the structural framework of a media channel. Such channels are essentially products of specific political-economic systems. [125] This establishes that strategic communication in the context of geopolitics and diplomacy is fundamentally inseparable from the underlying political–economic ecosystem related to media structure and functioning. Building on the discussion on the structure and functioning of media from the previous chapter, strategic communication, or mass communication as a whole, operates within a given system, which may be manipulated by ownership patterns, profit motives and the state's economic and political structure.[126] This phenomenon is responsible for projecting specific messages and shaping the dissemination pattern of information. We also understand that strategic communication is not a free-floating activity but is fundamentally contingent on the characteristics of the media system, which is essentially determined by its political–economic structure.[127] This also suggests that the political economy of media is not only an element that facilitates the dissemination of strategic messages but is also one of the significant factors that determines the effectiveness of strategic communication.

In the framework of political economy, media text is considered a product, as "strange commodities" or "public goods".[128] This portrayal and consideration of media text presents an essential paradox for strategic communication in geopolitics. This paradox revolves around the very understanding of news and information, which acknowledges that these 'public goods' are not beyond economic activities and that their "consumption... does not entail its destruction",[129] and "the producer retains possession... after it has been sold".[130] Here, the role of strategic communication aims to shape public perception through these 'public goods' and 'social ties' to align with policy goals.[131] A paradox arises because the media industry functions under market logic, and public goods produced by an industry should be profitable. If it is under market logic, then another phenomenon occurs that is directly related to the alteration of media texts, aligning with sensationalism over accuracy and public service.[132] Again, it is likely that media content aligns with the ownership's interest. In these circumstances, communication navigates the media landscape and tries to work through these frameworks where commercial imperatives dominate.[133] It also explores how to curb the inherent challenges of media text production because commercial imperatives may alter strategic messages when it comes to the goals of diplomacy, making the dissemination of nuanced and accurate strategic messages challenging.

The Nexus: Political Economy of Media's Influence on Strategic Communication Efficacy

As outlined above, political–economic structural constraints limit the effectiveness of strategic communication. In addition to this, this framework also provides systematically lower proportions of public service information.[134] The multiple constraints create obstructions in the path of well-informed citizenship, where it could otherwise be possible to aim to disseminate complex policy details. Nevertheless, government- or subscriber-controlled media, which usually has a public service orientation, is supposed to be a more reliable channel for the projection of strategic messages aligned with public good objectives.[135] On the other hand, the political alignment of a media organisation is likely to lead it to pursue its own interests, whether those interests align with economic prospects or political ambitions.[136] Another issue lies with the element of credibility of the disseminated messages; enabling state-aligned strategic communication may, in fact, deflect credibility for varied publics.

Along with proprietary issues, the economic aspect significantly impacts media's functioning when it comes to prioritisation of sensationalism, bias and ideologically slanted content over objective media content.[137] The very craft of news media content has been characterized by the use of dramatic headlines and emotionally charged narratives designed to attract audience attention, a practice that may compromise the overall accuracy of information.[138]

Revenue models are a challenging realm for media functioning because critical reporting might risk financial support.[139] This eventually influences what will pass through the editorial gatekeepers in the newsroom. At this juncture, economic impediments could hurt the independence of editorial decision-making and make it susceptible to external influence.[140] This influence can potentially limit the strategic message that might disrupt the narrative of dominant forces in a political and economic ecosystem. The double blow here lies in how the credibility of the media setup itself affects its role as a channel for strategic messaging.

Limiting media content in terms of decision-making within a given political–economic ecosystem further directs or determines public opinion toward specific issues.[141] Along with this, media's concentration on a few issues leads the public to perceive those projected issues as more important than any other topic or information. Exposure of the public to limited issues further triggers a prioritisation ecosystem, wherein people prioritise those issues and narratives that are being prioritised by the media. The spiral of silence process further illustrates that the dominance of certain narratives may silence other minor or minority narratives.[142] At this juncture, for strategic communication, it becomes important to surpass the dominant narrative(s) in order to make space within the media outlook. It is certain that if a strategic message does not receive priority within a given media setup, due to economic or political challenges or structural constraints, strategic communication may become difficult,[143] thereby complicating the projection of the desired narrative.

Additionally, the given political–economic structure pushes the process of prioritising slanted media texts, and sometimes it frames media-crafted content to influence the representation of reality while embedding strategic messages.[144] It is very often the case that this may influence public discourse, because the public is receiving curated messages that originate from a structured field. Here, the repeated frames increase accessibility in people's minds and may influence the decision-making process. The frequency of certain ideological frames,[145] and the repetition of curated and selected media content, may well highlight or obscure certain features that may shape policy direction. In such circumstances, for strategic communication purposes, it is important to understand and utilise those frames that align with the existing structure or dominant frame.[146] If this is not the case, then the strategic message may not be communicated as intended. Along with this, it is important to understand that strategic messages, or strategic communicators, are not only pushing messages that align with the existing frame and designed narratives embedded in that content, but they also have the task of contending with pre-existing media frames, which may be used by competing interests.[147]

The strategic communication process is continuous in nature, which projects and spreads the essence of desired agendas and frames within an information ecosystem pre-shaped by the political economy of media. This process demonstrates that media "filters and shapes reality" and determines which issues are perceived as important.[148] Subsequently, it frames projected media text, in other words it shows how media "select[s] and emphasize[s] certain aspects of reality to influence public discourse".[149] The political economy of media dictates which issues are prioritised and how they are framed; this takes place due to market-driven prioritisation and commercial appeal over public service. This creates a dynamic where strategic communication is constantly reacting to or attempting to co-opt media narratives, rather than simply creating its own. The 'battle' is for control over the public's cognitive landscape, which is already influenced by the structural biases of the media system.

We have discussed about the conceptual framework of media content at the level of building agenda and how to frame it, subsequently. At the level of implementation especially for effective strategic communication, particularly in diplomacy, it relies on a degree of shared understanding and a common factual ground to build consensus, resolve conflicts and foster cooperation.[150] At this stage, the media ecosystem is fragmented by various "filters" and "echo chambers".[151] We have discussed the various 'filters' earlier in the context of political economy, such as ownership patterns, advertisements, etc., but 'echo chambers' are directly related to the media system. As previously discussed, a single piece of information may be circulated and published repeatedly because the source from which it was generated or supplied to various newsrooms holds a certain dominance,[152] especially in the case of international news or when news media organisations do not have a primary source and rely on dominant information providers.

Technological Transformation and the Evolving Geopolitical Information Environment

Digital means for information dissemination cover a new kind of infrastructure, including digital libraries, databases, networks, adequate communications bandwidth and supercomputers.[153] These digital infrastructures, encompassing data lakes and network connectivity, are crucial for nurturing data-driven decision-making and enhancing competitive advantage.[154] Cumulatively, these digital structures have shaped the "architects of a new global order",[155] which are subsequently reshaping alliances, disrupting traditional power dynamics and carving fresh battlegrounds in cyberspace. Even the world is witnessing a niche competition for technological hegemony, which has been regarded as a seismic shift where "data becomes the new oil, and innovation, the currency of influence".[156] In other words, the digital transformation has elevated data to a strategic geopolitical resource, akin to "new oil",[157] making its control and manipulation central to strategic communication efforts.

Digital tools have influenced the intangible domain of geopolitics, which has traditionally been grounded in the physical characteristics of territories. The arrival of the concept of the global village has blurred the boundaries between internal and external state affairs.[158] Technological advancements such as the accumulation of large datasets and their processing through new technologies like AI and digital infrastructure have emerged as new tools in global competition.[159] While digital geopolitics democratises participation, enabling individuals to influence international discourse, it also presents challenges such as misuse.[160]

In addition to this, social media ecosystems have now become central hubs for political discourse, with a significant portion of the global population actively using them. Their "democratizing potential" enables grassroots movements[161] and empowers individuals to communicate with large audiences, bypassing traditional gatekeepers. Digital algorithms create "filter bubbles" that curate content aligned with users' existing views, maximising engagement, and users form "echo chambers" that amplify pre-existing beliefs.[162] The above-mentioned dynamics cultivate "directionally motivated reasoning",[163] where individuals interpret information to support preconceptions, leading to the persistence of misinformation and increased political polarisation. These algorithms, which are persistent in nature, are fundamentally tied to the core business models of social media companies, which have built financial success on engagement-driven systems. This digital infrastructure, along with persuasive phenomena like algorithmic technologies driven by profit motives and engagement metrics, is not a neutral conduit but an active shaper of geopolitical narratives, creating "filter bubbles" and "echo chambers"[164] that profoundly impact the reception and effectiveness of strategic communication. When strategic communication operates in an information environment that is essentially not a level playing field, but one actively engineered by commercial interests to maximise user engagement, even if it means amplifying sensationalism, bias or misinformation,[165] it implies that geopolitical narratives are not just shaped by state actors or traditional media. Technology also operates on a profit-driven logic, which is increasingly influenced by opaque algorithms and monetisation strategies. This pattern makes the process challenging for strategic communicators to ensure that their messages cut through the noise and reach diverse audiences without being distorted or trapped within ideological silos.

We are witnessing a sort of ideological impact on governance in the digital world, amidst the growth of the internet, that leads to ongoing debates. Monitoring and the dissemination of information have increased in government functioning, with serious consequences for democratic values.[166] Utilising internet technologies to create extensive social credit systems in a few closed political frameworks, such as authoritarian governments, this governance system tracks and controls citizens' actions, chilling dissent.[167] Advanced surveillance systems are being used, turning media into a misleading instrument for ideological dominance. The trade in surveillance technology has become a key method for countries to grow their influence and maintain internal order, often undermining democratic ideals abroad.

At a time when cyber warfare has become a key element of geopolitical conflicts, with countries using cyber tools for disruption, espionage and influencing public opinion, cyber actions allow nations to operate without immediate consequences, thereby complicating global security.[168] Nevertheless, digital technologies are transforming diplomatic efforts, enabling real-time communication and negotiations between states, making digital diplomacy increasingly important. This transition also creates and strengthens new types of relationships between various stakeholders such as citizens, corporations and governments in international relations. Data-based and network-based realms of power are emerging, extending beyond traditional power structures. The expansion of the World Wide Web affects all areas of life, including international relations, and is transforming foreign policy concepts and practices.[169]

In this evolving stimulus of digital technology, a fundamental paradox emerges for strategic communication, where digital technologies simultaneously offer 'democratising potential' by empowering individuals and grassroots movements,[170] and provide unprecedented tools for 'tech-enabled authoritarianism' and information control by states.

The above propositions suggest that the process of strategic communication is dynamic, and its functioning is directly proportional to the normative structure, which takes leverage of mediums.[171] In a democratic framework, it might influence digital platforms for open dialogue and public diplomacy. On the other hand, authoritarian regimes can use the very same tools for propaganda, censorship and to suppress dissent, creating a highly asymmetric and contested information space.[172] However, there is a paradox in the context of the political–economic realm, which implies that the 'rules of engagement' for strategic communication are not universal; they are deeply contingent on the political–economic model of media in different regions, necessitating highly adaptive and context-specific strategic communication strategies.

Regulatory Frameworks, Censorship and the Battle for Information Control

The very definition of censorship deals with the idea of any regime or context in which the content of public expression is regulated, or where the circulation of information is controlled.[173] The given rational behind this may be for control including political (e.g., national security), moral, social or religious reasons, or even to avoid embarrassment for governments. In the case of internet censorship, it varies from selective to pervasive, with blocking access being a standard mechanism.[174] This idea also refers to a system of regulation for vetting, editing and prohibiting specific forms of public expression, overseen by a censor. Another significant method is self-censorship, which involves self-regulation by individual authors, publishers or the industry itself, often undertaken to avoid state regulation.[175]

Censorship of media policies by the government reflects a dynamic state of affairs, because while on one hand it can enable a state to control its narrative and manage perceived threats, on the other hand it can constrain free speech, erode public trust and undermine the very democratic values that many strategic communication efforts aim to project.[176] Another phenomenon of the censorship appears when it limits the flow of open dialogue, impedes the democratic exchange of dissenting ideas and creates "echo chambers" that only tolerate certain perspectives, narrowing the space for constructive arguments.[177] Ironically, censorship can enable state-level strategic communication, where it may be instrumental in "protect[ing] national security and preserv[ing] peaceful diplomatic relations with other nations" by hindering "misinformation, disinformation, and propaganda".[178]

Anlan Zhang's account of the political economy of media amidst multinational enterprises (MNEs) highlights the complex intertwinement of corporate practice with state power in the face of escalating geopolitical tensions.[179] Zhang suggests that MNEs operating amidst such volatile geopolitical contexts are subject to twin political pressures from both home and host state administrations. These are compounded further by increasing media coverage, such that corporate activity becomes a focus of discursive struggle. In this media-intensive world, the practice of framing, defined by Entman (1993) along the axes of problem definition, causal attribution, moral evaluation and prescriptive remedy, becomes a key method whereby media stations create and propagate meaning that often has a political purpose.[180]

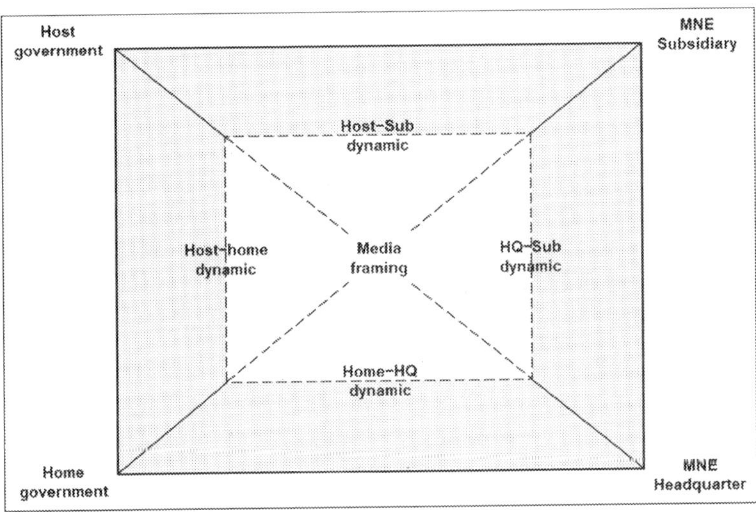

Figure 1: Dynamics of Media Coverage of Multinational Enterprises under Geopolitical Tensions[181]

Here, media accounts no longer act as abstract deliverers of information but rather as ideologically marked tools that have the potential to delegitimise MNEs within both international and national public spaces. MNEs' need to think critically about their mediated realities is all the more pressing since media structures create inequalities at a structural level.[182] In liberal democracies, while media is formally autonomous, Zhang identifies its common coordination with state agendas amidst times of geopolitical conflict. In authoritarian states, media entities are often incorporated within the state's ideological machinery as appendages of political power. This asymmetry generates a strategic challenge for MNEs that have to balance and navigate conflicting media narratives that are generated on the basis of alternative normative schemes and political agendas. Such constructions through the media are not only performative but have tangible effects on public opinion and policymaker reaction.[183] Accordingly, Zhang highlights the necessity for MNEs to develop a nuanced and situational understanding of the political economy of the media as a critical aspect of corporate strategy amidst a resurgence of geopolitical rivalry.[184]

Governmental regulatory controls such as licensing, content and ownership laws can be used by governments to control the operations of media and influence editorial autonomy.[185] The operation of media is often influenced by the interests of governments, as ruling politicians attempt to control or suppress opposing opinions. National regulatory systems are made more difficult as media systems globalise, with information flowing more readily across international frontiers while governance structures are still mainly tied to territorially based jurisdiction.[186] The negotiation and imposition of regulatory regimes, both domestic and international, are the essence of a major battleground in geopolitics, setting the boundaries within which strategic communication can function and vie to influence. The "free market"[187] of information exchange is being "altered due to manipulation by the state and special interest organizations".[188] In a globalised information environment where information flows across frontiers with increasing facility,[189] the absence of universal international regulatory regimes means that states actually compete to enforce their preferred controls and norms. This means that strategic communication is not only about message-construction but also about being active in, or fighting over, the regulatory environment to either facilitate the transmission of one's own version of realities or to restrict one's opponents'. The power to influence media policy and governance then becomes a strategic end in and of itself.

At a time when social media has become indispensable for propagation across the globe, the ability to promote government's perspective must be highly regulated or else public perception may be distorted, especially in states governed autocratically and where technological progress is employed to disseminate propaganda. The ubiquitous threat of organisational regulation or economic coercion can produce self-censorship within media outlets, imposing, quietly yet deeply, on strategic communication, limiting the scope of acceptable narratives as well as creating a culture of conformity by limiting the variety of acceptable thoughts and ideas presented in the public space. It is described as self-regulation on the part of individual author, or publisher or 'the industry', usually to escape state regulation.[190] It entails "the internal regulation of what one chooses to say in public, usually due to conformism". It results either because if they do not regulate themselves, they will be regulated by the state[191] or due to economic dependencies. For strategic communication, this renders the expectation of possible state interference or economic sanctions enough to cause media sources to screen or dilute content beforehand, thereby curtailing the variety of opinions and level of critical analysis expressed in the public space, which can subvert the effectiveness of strategic communication that is premised on open discussion, diversity of ideas or dissenting narratives. It provides, instead, a homogeneous information environment, which makes it easy, potentially, for one dominating state narrative to dominate, and also diminishes, generally, credibility and dynamism in the media space, which can ultimately rebound negatively against long-term diplomatic objectives.

Chapter Four

Strategic Communication and the Dynamics of News Media

Understanding the 'Sources of News'

Sources are not passive providers; they actively seek to 'encode their preferred agendas'. The news-making process is inherently influenced by the sources that journalists or media organisations draw upon, with those sources determining what is 'news' and how it is presented. Unequal access to platforms means that powerful individuals frequently control narratives, with few voices from marginalised communities having access to be heard. In this given context, the relationship between news sources and information sources are the pillars of journalism and strategic communication with a profound influence on how the narratives are constructed, disseminated and consumed in democracies. Not only does this dynamic determine what information reaches the public, but also whose voices are legitimised and whose are marginalised. A journalistic source refers to any source of information where a journalist gets the material to be published in a story. It includes documentary and human sources from the reporting on documents, social networks, data releases, and AI tools to eyewitnesses, experts and communication professionals.[192] However, while the theoretical pool of sources is broad, in practice not all sources enjoy equal access or influence. The assumption that "those groups which have something important to contribute... can secure access to the news media"[193] often fails under the weight of structural inequalities, economic equations and ownership architecture.

Power imbalances between sources shape the flow and framing of information. The question "Do all news sources enjoy the same degree of access and the same ability to communicate their perspectives?"[194] reveals the underlying inequality that favours elites and powerful actors in society, often at the expense of marginalised voices.[195] These disparities are compounded when media ownership becomes a vehicle for partisan or ideological influence. The candid admission, "I run the paper purely for the purpose of making propaganda, and with no other motive",[196] reflects how proprietorial control can transform the press into an instrument of influence rather than a platform for impartial information.[197]

Meanwhile, the rise of digital technologies has radically reshaped the epistemological and operating boundaries of the journalist/media organisation, source relation. Sources are no longer reliant upon traditional infrastructures of the media to articulately disseminate their accounts, but are now technologically endowed to bypass traditional gatekeeping apparatuses altogether and address audiences through direct communication pathways.[198] This paradigmatic revolution has progressively undermined the newsroom's monopolistic control as the pre-eminent arbiter and guardian of information, repositioning it simply as one amongst a proliferation of communicative nodes in an exploding media space. Publics are thus increasingly exposed to informational currents that are typically unmediated and unfiltered, without the recourse of traditional fact-checking procedures and normative safeguards of informational impartiality and accuracy.[199] "Source criticism therefore involves a more constructivist epistemological approach to knowledge claims produced by journalism since its starting point is that every source and every piece of information has a tendency and thereby a potential bias. There is no such thing as neutral, naturally occurring, objective information in the epistemology of source criticism".[200] This structure of dislocation imposes a heavy epistemic cost on publics, necessitating that they acquire intensified levels of media literacy in order to appraise the origin,[201] purpose and credibility of emergent source material. In spite of these changes, the constitutive function of source dynamics in facilitating democratic discourse is substantively unchanged.

"As for any other journalistic contexts, every role comes with normative functions. Reporters perceive their task as mainly explanatory and as a service of information provision for citizens".[202] In other words, the potential of the media to perform its normative role as a facilitator of informed citizenship is based on two interlinked conditions: affirmative access to platforms by a diversity of voices, and the equitable, accurate representation of a range of views. Yet in environments where source choice is disproportionately determined by proprietorial power or placed in secondary relation to political–economic demands, the media threatens to degenerate into tools that serve to amplify hegemonic narratives at the expense of systematically marginalisation of oppositional or subaltern views.[203] In such an environment, the press may be incapable of maintaining "the flow of ideas and information upon which choices are made",[204] thus defeating its democratic purpose as a vehicle of civic deliberation and participatory governance. Fundamentally, the legitimacy of journalism as a democratic institution is inescapably entangled with the ethics of sourcing practices and the material setups by means of which those sources are brought into the news production process.[205] As such dynamics demonstrate, today's crisis besetting journalism is not merely technological in nature but inherently normative: the need to maintain a communicative setting that protects pluralism, credibility and fair exposure to all source agents in a more commodified, ideologically polarised and decentralised information environment.

The Interplay of News and Source: A Critical Relationship

The relationship between news and the source is not a simple transmission but a rich interplay that profoundly influences the narratives made public. It is a relationship in interdependence, power relations and a profound reversal of influence in the wake of digital platforms. The existence of news production is a direct function of its sources. Newsrooms depend on sources in order to gather information and build news; without sources, news media such as it is would not be possible.[206] This creates an intrinsic and undeniable interdependence between the two. In spite of this dependence, the relationship is described as a "struggle for power over the presentation of information to the public".[207] This struggle was most famously captured by Gans (1979) in terms of both a "dance" and a "tug of war", where the source frequently manoeuvres to control the narrative.[208] This struggle typically pits the professional imperative of the press to represent the public interest through the examination of authority against the source's desire to speak to personal, commercial or politic interests and shape public opinion.[209] While this description is a simplification, since either side can be animated by public or self-interest, it serves to identify the tension inherent in the relationship.

The "tug of war"[210] and 'power struggle' that exist between sources and journalists illustrate that news accounts are not actually discovered but are instead frequently the product of a negotiation of competing interests. This makes the resulting account a product of this interaction, rather than a direct reflection of fact. This inescapable conflict of interest implies that the 'objectivity' so heralded by news outlets is continuously undermined by the inherent nature of sourcing.[211]

The pluralist view that media objectivity emerges from "self-regulating and balancing compromises"[212] may not always hold true, particularly when power imbalances exist or when sources are highly strategic in their information release. The resulting narrative is thus a mediated one, influenced by the relative power, strategic objectives and self-interests of the sources themselves. It is crucial that the audience comes to comprehend the source's motivations[213] in order to deconstruct the possible biases inherent in the story, pointing out that the 'news' itself is a creation of this complex, frequently contentious, relationship.

Sources and Journalistic Construction

Sources are the fundamental providers of the material from which a story is written.[214] These may vary in form from physical documents and computer data, including textual reports, social networking messages and dumps of data, to intangible human testimonies, such as eyewitness accounts, expert assessments and whistle-blowers' disclosures.[215] Once garnered, this raw material is typically filtered and verified by the newsroom before it is published.[216] This verification process is a cornerstone of traditional journalism, aiming to ensure accuracy and reliability.[217] The emergence of data journalism further accentuates the sources' role in terms of raw material provision, with journalists actively sourcing newsworthy points from data, in addition to information drawn from human interviews or written documents.[218] This depicts how raw, unprocessed data is now a key source in the development of narratives.

The Shift in Power Dynamics with Digital Platforms

Historically, before the advent of the internet, journalists and their "news organizations had a stranglehold on the means of publication, controlling what news appeared on people's TV screens and in newspapers".[219] This centralised control made sources heavily dependent on news organisations for the dissemination of messages. Digital platforms have revolutionised this traditional model, dissolving the lines of distinction between source and journalist and allowing sources to circumvent traditional outlets and speak directly to the public.[220] This newfound autonomy allows sources to "opt-in"[221] or "opt-out"[222] of a traditional journalist–source relationship based on their strategic communication goals and desired audience reach. For example, social media can be employed by a source to target a particular audience or mass media to reach a broader audience. Such a shift inherently challenges journalistic authority and control,[223] redistributing power in the news-making environment.

The power of sources to circumvent traditional media means a blurring of the editorial "gate",[224] creating a straighter, or possibly less filtered, path of information to the public. It affects the diversity and quality control of available narratives in a direct manner. Whilst this move seems to democratise access to information, it also results in narratives being constructed and shared without the conventional journalistic steps of filtering and authenticating, cross-checking facts meticulously[225, 226] or abiding by professional journalism standards of fairness and accuracy.[227]

This compromises the professional control over quality that traditional gatekeepers sought to deliver, resulting in an explosion of narratives that might or might not be professionally screened. The result is a much larger and less trustworthy information environment. Public critical evaluation of sources and their interests are even more necessary in discerning the truth,[228] since the greater direct access to sources is matched by a greater exposure to misinformation or fake news. Criticality of the news–source relationship is thus increased by the need for personal media literacy to navigate this difficult environment.

Source Credibility and Trust

The credibility of news stories is heavily impacted by the qualities of news sources. Public understanding and reception are influenced by the reliability, possible biases and particular types of sources. Credibility of the source is the pillar of any news story. In the absence of good sources, news becomes rumour, speculation or misinformation.[229] A source's credibility is the degree of trustworthiness and dependability of the sources through which journalists or newsroom receive information; if sources lack credibility, the entire story falls through, creating a breakdown in public confidence, the cornerstone of media text itself.[230] Determinants of source credibility are expertise, name recognition, past history of reporting fact, membership in good organisations and a good feedback from other good sources.[231] Transparency in sourcing is essential for developing a sense of trust with the public.[232] When people know where the information is coming from and how it is collected, they are more likely to read the content and come back to the publication.[233] Public confidence in mass media has decreased across the world,[234] and this is correlated with the decreased usage of established sources of information and increased usage of non-established alternatives.[235] Source attribution, or the act of attributing and referencing the source of information, is an essential technique in the development of credibility, transparency and accountability, and even in offering legal protection to journalists.[236] The reduction in public confidence in the media is influenced directly by source credibility and clarity of information.[237] If sources are not appropriately attributed or their biases are not made transparent, the reader's adoption of the story is impeded. It results in a feedback cycle: low credibility yields less consumption of conventional news, compels people towards less scrutinised alternate sources, further degrades shared narratives and enhances susceptibility to misinformation.

The prime responsibility of source attribution and transparencies is not merely an ethical requirement but a practical necessity in the preservation of public discourse and shared knowledge of reality.[238] Source bias and its manifestation bias in the press is an intrinsic feature of news production, subtly determining the presentation of news to the public.[239] It comes in different guises, such as the events and topics reported, the extent and tone of the coverage and the framing of issues.[240] Media bias can either be through omission, where major facts or opposing viewpoints are withheld, or through emphasis, where details favourable to a prevailing standpoint are weighted heavily.[241] Such editorial decisions are based on an array of motivations like politics, economic interests and public preference. This will result in a biased perception of reality, social polarisation and an ill-informed public discussion.[242] Selective reporting, whether deliberate or inadvertent, is the exclusion of data, context or adverse findings in research and reporting that ends up framing narratives that are possibly not fully truthful. Confirmation bias is where journalists identify sources in favour of their held assumptions or views, distorting information to result in an unbalanced story.[243] Also, powerful interest groups, in most cases having great financial and political power, are capable of framing and defending the status quo by framing narratives.[244] Source bias is not a shortcoming of news media but a natural problem in the construction of narratives. Where sources with a stake are giving information, and journalists/news media either consciously or unconsciously practice selective reporting/news production or confirmation bias,[245] the resulting story is a "distorted version of reality".[246] It is not only processed, but warped through a variety of biases, so that narratives confirm prevailing assumptions and not challenge them.[247] The dynamic between news and source is therefore an inescapable one in which source motivations and natural inclinations, paired with journalistic decisions, fully determine the ideological or persuasive slant of the finished story.[248]

Navigating the Global Information Landscape

News is constituted through selective processes of meaning-making, shaped by institutional discourses, ideological apparatuses and normative biases.[249] This constructivist view underscores that what is framed as 'newsworthy' is deeply contingent upon the socio-political and economic contexts[250] in which media systems operate. Furthermore, within a globally uneven media ecology, dominant actors, such as transnational corporations, powerful states or elite gatekeepers exercise disproportionate influence over content production and agenda-setting, reinforcing structural imbalances in informational sovereignty. Thus, news becomes a vehicle for reproducing hegemonic narratives rather than a disinterested or universally accessible medium of truth. News is thus understood not as a neutral commodity, but as a product deeply influenced by power dynamics.[251]

News agencies have traditionally been the "unsung heroes"[252] of the media world since the mid-19th century, and they have played an important part in shaping 'news' and informing governments, businesses and citizens all over the world.[253] Because of their foundational work in informing, their political economy is important to understand in order to grasp the world information order.

The evolution of "Third World"[254] to "Global South"[255] within academic and policy discourses marks a departure from Cold War binaries to more a nuanced acknowledgment of postcolonial disparity, structural marginalisation and geopolitical agency between countries in Latin America, Africa and Asia.[256] The history of newly independent nations' attempts to challenge Western media hegemony reflects a longstanding recognition of inherent power disparities in the production and circulation of world information. The Non-Aligned Movement (NAM) in the 1960s sought explicitly to institute channels and protocols of international cooperation and news mongering that would transcend centuries of extractive colonial dynamics.[257] A notable effort in this respect was the Non-Aligned News Agencies Pool (NANAP), founded in 1974 and in operation from 1975 to the mid-1990s.[258] Through NANAP, member states sought to supply other member states with unbiased or, at best, biased by their worldview, a counter-hegemonic report on world news regarding developing countries.[259] This concerted effort by the developing world to alter the international communication arena reflects the constant pursuit of more balanced and representative narratives, bridged directly to news patterns and the effects of Western subscriptions of the news.

Western News Agencies and Structural Imperatives

The historic pattern of world news circulation has been marked by institutionalised Western dominance of the wire service industry by Reuters, Associated Press (AP) and Agence France-Presse (AFP).[260] That dominance found roots in 19th-century cartels and since was entrenched by the commercialisation of news as commodity. That move created unidirectional north-to-south information flow, effectively shaping the world by informing it with dominant Euro–American epistemological norms. Such structural asymmetry regularly eclipsed the indigenous voices of the

Global South,[261] frequently resulting in the effacement of local epistemological systems and extending residues of colonisation to media representations. Agencies like Western-based Reuters with 2,600 staff in 165 countries[262] and AFP with 2,400 staff in 150 countries[263] traditionally commanded as much as 90 per cent of international news circulation.[264] Non-Western wire bodies are growing commercially fast, however; China's Xinhua News Agency maintained 181 bureaus by 2021.[265]

Even with the changing landscape, the Global South media continues to grapple with issues like resource constraint and political contexts, in addition to the newly emerging challenge of "digital colonialism" in which mainly US-based digital companies wield power over digital infrastructure and data.[266] Yet, this pervasive hegemonic structure is now witnessing growing contestation by the Global South's multi-faceted efforts towards exercising narrative agency. Seminal steps in this were the promotion of a 'New World Information and Communication Order (NWICO) and the MacBride Commission's report, which have recognised the hegemonic state of affairs in last century regarding flow of information and its orientation.[267] The MacBride report (1980), *Many Voices, One World*, uncovered stark imbalances in world information flow, with 80–90 per cent of international information in the hand of four Western wire services (AP, United Press International, Reuters and AFP),[268] producing an unidirectional flow from the Global North to the Global South with little recirculation between developing countries. Infrastructure disparities put poorer countries at the mercy of imported media, and commercial interests drove content with profit taking priority over cultural diversity and development imperatives. The report threatened the spectre of "cultural imperialism",[269] as Western-biased narratives often presenting the Global South in stereotypical and monolithic caricatures.[270] This narrative frequently overwhelmed the world media, posing threats to local identities. This uneven system perpetuated information dependence, circumscribing developing countries' sovereignty in their own stories.

The coming into existence of the digital age is characterised by both opportunities and limitations. On the one hand, it allows for multi-direction communication and empowers Global South actors to produce counter narratives,[271] on the other hand, it brings with it new challenges. These are the spread of fractured "splinternets"[272] and the continued existence of Western-oriented digital infrastructure, which has the potential to entrench pre-existing power asymmetry. Yet, while still clearly shaped by Western structural dominance, the new order is coming to be characterised by contestation, resistance and media sovereignty asserted by the Global South on an active and proactive basis.[273] The arrival of the digital age is accompanied by a dualistic world of potential and restriction. While it makes communication's multi-directionality possible and provides actors in the Global South with the potential to produce alternative narratives, it also introduces new challenges like the spread of splinternets and the persistence of Western-oriented digital infrastructure, thus reinforcing existing power structures.[274] Although still obviously influenced by Western structural power, such order is now more marked by contestation, challenge and the affirmative exercise of media sovereignty on the part of the Global South. Reading Western wire agencies such as Reuters, AP and AFP is key to critically understanding the world's information circulation and both the geopolitical and epistemological power relations of international news production.[275] These wire agencies are influential gatekeepers and agenda-setters who make the world's flow of news possible by choosing what to cover and what to exclude, in particular having impacts on Global South media systems. Reading Reuters, AP and AFP is therefore not simply about journalism practice but critically about the world communication's geopolitical and epistemological power relations.[276]

Although it is listed as a publicly traded organisation, the founding group of the Thomson family has significant control over Thomson Reuters Corporation (TRI) via their holding company, The Woodbridge Company Limited, with about 69 per cent of the shares.[277] This concentrated form of ownership with dominant power under the parent group profoundly influences the governance and strategic vision of the organisation in the long term.[278] Reuters provides content to various clients in the world including media houses, corporates, government bodies, banks and sporting organisations in multiple languages via text, photo, video, audio and graphics.[279] It has the largest journalist network in the world with access to 165 countries and coverage of 12 languages.[280] The Associated Press, with headquarters in New York City, is an American not-for-profit newswire in existence since 1846.[281] Its sources of revenue have shifted over time; most of its revenue is generated from international broadcast customers (37 per cent), ventures on the web (15 per cent) and foreign newspapers (18 per cent).[282] While AP's cooperative model theoretically promotes impartiality, its historical involvement in a 19th-century "press agency cartel",[283] known as the "Ring Combination"[284] with Reuters and French Havas (AFP), established a foundational power imbalance in global news flow through agreed-upon "reserved territories".[285] This historical context suggests that even without formal cartel agreements today, the established networks, infrastructure and influence persist, contributing to a "duopolistic wire service based system of global news gatekeeping"[286] with Reuters. This continued dominance means that AP, along with Reuters, continues to shape the global news agenda, potentially reinforcing a Western-centric view of what constitutes 'news' from the Global South.

Agence France-Presse, the world's oldest news agency, traces its roots to Agence Havas, which was established in Paris in 1835. AFP still has a broad international outreach. News from AFP may,[287] unwittingly, be influenced by French points of view, emphasise matters of special concern to France or portray things in a manner consistent with the goals of French foreign policy, thus advancing a particular Western version of the Global South.

Reporting Patterns and Framing of the Global South

The political economy of the Western wire agencies heavily determines their patterns of coverage regarding the Global South and tends to produce routine framing that reinforces stereotypes and impacts how this part of the world is viewed internationally. It has already been explained how a few Western wire agencies operate within a "duopolistic wire service-based system of global news gatekeeping.".[288] This consolidation results in more and more of the rest of the world being exposed to an "ever-decreasing news agenda", further exacerbated in the digital age.[289] Developing world coverage has traditionally been, and remains predominantly, skewed. The bias is in the form of disproportionate coverage of violence, conflicts, natural catastrophes and politics.[290] These imbalances are inextricably linked to historic, political and economic realities that have defined the international news agency industry from the outset.[291] Studies time and time again embrace negative coverage of Africa and Asia in the form of widespread poverty, war, hunger, illness and backwardness.[292] Africa is notably portrayed as the "Dark Continent"[293] waiting to be civilised, trying to catch up with Western societies. Familiar mental images transmitted are primeval irrationality, tribal chaos, hunger/starvation, civil strife, managerial incompetence, political upheaval, brazen corruption and inept leadership.[294] Such information is transmitted in the absence of adequate historical or analytical contexts, reinforcing a reductionist and often condescending portrayal.[295]

The pervasive negative coverage of the Global South by leading Western media perpetuates a strong "single story"[296] that is self-sustaining in world perceptions. The narrow, and sometimes de-contextualised, representation is able to directly impact international investment, policy and partnerships by reinforcing stereotypes of dependency and incompetence. The ongoing predominance of a few agencies results in their built-in values and selection processes controlling what is 'newsworthy' coming from the Global South.[297] When these values result in a pervasive coverage of conflict, disaster and poverty, it has the effect of perpetuating a deep-rooted negative narrative operating to form public opinion and policy in the Global North,[298] and influencing anything from foreign assistance to commercial relations.

Table 2: Common Framing Patterns of Western Media in Global South Coverage

Framing Category	*Description of Pattern*	*Specific Examples*	*Implied Message/ Stereotype*	*Impact/Consequence*
Crisis & Conflict	Disproportionate focus on violence, civil war, political instability and natural disasters.	General coverage of developing world.[299]	Global South is inherently unstable, chaotic and dangerous.	Shapes negative public opinion, influences foreign policy (e.g., humanitarian aid), can deter investment.[300]
Poverty & Famine	Emphasis on scarcity, hunger and lack of resources, often without historical or systemic context.	COVID-19 coverage of Africa (e.g., "starve people in low income countries", limited reserves of food/water).[301]	Global South is perpetually needy, incapable of self-sufficiency, dependent on external aid.	Justifies external intervention, cultivates misinformed readership, perpetuates "mood of hopelessness", deters investment.[302]
Incompetence & Corruption	Portrayal of weak governance, managerial ineptitude and flagrant corruption.	COVID-19 coverage linking economic challenges to corruption and poor leadership;[303] general African stereotypes.[304]	Global South leaders are ineffective, irrational and untrustworthy.	Reinforces "failing governments" stereotype, justifies external oversight, obscures colonial legacies.[305]
Humanitarian Dependency	Framing of challenges as requiring external aid and solutions from benevolent Western outsiders.	Advertisements showing white celebrities with Black children in huts, urging donations;[306] focus on foreign aid for healthcare systems.[307]	The Global South is passive, powerless and incapable of solving its own problems.	Perpetuates a cycle of dependency, deflects responsibility from global inequalities and limits perception of agency.[308]

Consequences of Western News Subscription in Developing Countries

Developing countries' subscription to and reliance on Western media organisations have several far-reaching implications,[309] including extending to the information ecosystem, public opinion and decision-making.[310,311] Continuity in the hegemony of several international news agencies, including AP and Reuters, leads to a condition where "an ever-increasing audience [is] exposed to an ever-decreasing agenda of news".[312] This is compounded by the digital age, where the Reuters–AP duopoly has developed and solidified its stranglehold on the international news market.[313] When local media organisations in developing countries subscribe and source heavily from Western wire feeds, they risk internalising the Western frame of international crises, and consequently omitting or downplaying those features of such crises that are salient locally.[314] For instance, research on Bangladesh's news coverage illustrates how the "widespread Western media's framing of the COVID-19 crisis and climate crisis" often led to the neglect of the salience of local media outlets.[315]

The economic justification of this dependency is important: it is cheaper in many cases for developing countries to subscribe to syndicated content from Western agencies than to support large international correspondent networks in-house.[316] This economic choice is part of the "diminishing need for foreign news among their consumers from alternative sources".[317] The economic efficiency and cost-effectiveness of Western wire service subscriptions make subscribing to Western wires an information dependency of vital importance to developing countries, resulting in homogenisation of the agenda in the news and the prioritising of Western viewpoints. This has the side effect of marginalising local stories, contexts and concerns and thus impairing the capability of local media to serve their communities fully and represent their specific realities. Where the local coverage of a local phenomenon (even of huge local significance) is not assigned priority or framed in a certain manner by the Western agency, it is not covered extensively or in any depth in the local media. This affects public comprehension and even policy measures since the information available to citizens and policymakers is filtered from outside.

Mass media and Western media content watched and read in the country have the power to influence public opinion and frame the agenda of public debate.[318] They exercise much influence even in government policy formulation, especially in areas of policy vacuum or rival government agenda, where media coverage serves as key sources of official policy stance and policy idea.[319] The 'CNN Effect' theory explains the media's possible role in shaping foreign policy, particularly in crisis situations of humanitarian need or the spread of disease.[320] This is the idea that media portrayals in Western media can induce government actions in poor countries, even if these actions are based on external pressure or the need to secure outside assistance.[321] In crisis humanitarian situations where there is no existing government policy, media coverage has the potential to bring in government intervention.[322] If media in poor countries are subject to Western framing, then the public opinion created by that media will be the same, and that in turn can impact government policy. If Western media frames a crisis in a poor country negatively or highlights certain parts of it, it could pressure the local government to respond in those areas that are in accordance with the outside framing or else bring in assistance with some attached strings, leading to external impact of domestic policy.

In addition, Western media's negative depiction of Africa has been found to impact how it is portrayed in local newspapers and can impact citizens' self-perceptions as well as feed into opinions that have the potential to impact domestic policy.[323] Foreign media consumption can be used to manipulate cultural perceptions, prompting discontent with native cultures and the adoption of Western ways of living.[324]

The structural deficits and challenges of independent media development and news gathering in the Global South amplify their external dependency on Western news organisations. Such challenges entail severe financial sustainability challenges, in many cases resulting in reliance on outside sources.[325] This dependency, although bringing important funding, can also be problematic in regard to editorial freedom.[326] Media in these countries also tends to have serious political risks and its journalists face physical security threats.[327]

Functional barriers further hamper the establishment of strong local digital journalism. These are poor infrastructure, poor access to the internet and poor training on digital tools, as seen in Nigerian media.[328] These are barriers that prevent local media from generating quality, original content and keeping pace with the technologically sophisticated Western outlets. The spread of false news and source credibility loss are seen as ongoing moral challenges in digital media in developing nations, further complicating the media ecosystem and making it more challenging for local media outlets to gain credibility.[329]

The structural weaknesses inherent to local media in the Global South, including financial precariousness, political interference and technological deficits, form a synergistic cycle that serves to perpetuate its reliance on Western news wire agencies. This in turn maintains an environment in which independent, locally focussed journalism is hard-pressed to survive, and the potential for self-expression on the world stage is severely restricted. The financial and logistical challenges mean that local media is not able to provide strong alternatives to Western wire services, thus perpetuating the prevailing information dependency and constraint on expressing its own stories.

Chapter Five

Framework of ASEAN Media: Political Economy Perspective

In a broader perspective, the political–economic research approach elucidates the framework of public authorities, encompassing nation-states and global governance organisations, and integrates them (the political–economic research approach) into the commercial sector. Furthermore, it serves to mitigate the distinction between public and private spheres.[330] Beyond merely mirroring corporate influence on government policies, a more expansive trans-nationalisation of political power is evident, marked by a transition from intra-national to international class divisions, especially in the case of multinational media outlets.[331] The processes of fiscal liberalisation, deregulation, privatisation and media commercialisation have become integral components of major democracies worldwide. These processes are closely linked to cross-media ownership and the rise of media conglomerates.[332] An in-depth analysis of these trends by political economists allows for the deciphering of the engagements within political and policy associations. These engagements underscore the significance of understanding the political economy of communication.

In this study, the focus is on an empirical examination of media texts within five ASEAN countries. Specifically, the case study encompasses Indonesia, Thailand, Malaysia, Singapore and the Philippines. The data collection and analysis is centred on these nations. Notably, these countries represent the largest economies in the ASEAN region,[333] as measured by Gross Domestic Product (GDP). To clarify, these five countries are considered the leading nations in ASEAN in terms of GDP.[334]

Media in Indonesia

In Southeast Asian countries, such as Indonesia, media conglomeration has advanced to consolidate economic power, ultimately evolving into a formidable political force capable of influencing communication regulations. This phenomenon extends its dominion over the regulatory framework, engaging with the political sphere and prompting amendments to government regulations.[335]

According to data from the Press Council of Indonesia, various types of mass media outlets are currently operational and active within the country. The data from 2022 reveals a diverse media landscape, encompassing approximately "436 print publications, 368 television channels, 15 radio stations, and around 865 online media platforms".[336] The aggregate figures from various sources significantly exceed the provided statistics. According to data from 2017, as reported by the Press Council, there were a total of "2,000 printed media outlets, 1,166 radio stations, 674 television channels, and 43,300 online media platforms".[337] It is noteworthy that these numbers encompass not only news and current affairs media but also extend to include general entertainment media outlets. Despite the proliferation of digital media, television continues to maintain its dominance as the most popular medium, while print newspaper circulations are experiencing a decline. The internet has a coverage rate of approximately 76 per cent in the country, and social media platforms such as Facebook, Instagram and Twitter (now referred to as X) hold significant popularity among users.[338] The Press Council itself has acknowledged a significant deficiency in professional ethics and practices within media companies. For instance, a mere "16% of print media and 0.5% of online media" are deemed to meet the standards of professionalism.[339] Few reports suggests that there are 12 major conglomerates active and they "own 60 televisions, 317 print media, 66 radios, and 9 online media outlets (2017). For example, The Jawa Pos Group has 20 television, 171 print media and 1 online media. While Kelompok Kompas Gramedia has 10 television, 12 radio, 88 print media and 2 online media".[340]

After Indonesia's transition to democracy in 1998, numerous media organisations emerged, facing the challenge and opportunity of navigating the nation's complex structure. Under President Suharto's authoritarian regime (1966–1998), press freedom was severely restricted.[341] In the present day, the media landscape is characterised by a dominance of television networks, both public and private, alongside print and other mass media outlets broadcasting in multiple languages. Indonesia, being the most populated ASEAN country with over 800 languages and dialects, presents a vast and diverse landscape, making the preservation of press freedom an ongoing and intricate struggle.[342] The daily battle involves respecting the diverse linguistic and cultural fabric while upholding the principles of a free press.

Even after the introduction of democracy, press freedom is still in disarray. In the context of legal framework, democracy ensured the end of laws promoting censorship; however, in spite of this few topics, such as issues of religious fundamentalism, have been challenging to cover and publish or broadcast.[343] A few laws (e.g., the Electronic Information and Transactions Law 2008) have even been promoting potential imprisonment for online posts, and a new Penal Code adopted in 2022 poses threats to investigative journalism due to provisions related to blasphemy and combating "fake news".[344]

The structure of Indonesia's media has undergone minimal change over the past decade, consistent with prevailing ownership patterns. Media houses are predominantly owned by conglomerates that control multiple media outlets, resulting in the dominance of a select few conglomerates.[345] This ownership pattern underscores the oligarchic nature of Indonesia's media landscape, where a few entities hold a commanding position. The economic environment further aligns with the political class, and this affiliation is occasionally evident. Another noteworthy issue pertains to the prevalence of cross-media ownership and diversified economic interests.[346] Owners of media groups also invest in various economic and business activities, thereby expanding the economic interests of media conglomerates. This significant aspect of the economic landscape intensifies the political–economic inclination, primarily aimed at securing the investments of media conglomerates by fostering a favourable environment for both political and economic interests of the oligarchic class.[347] Despite the advent of digital media, marked differences have not been established, primarily due to its inherent characteristics such as being a capital-intensive media ecosystem.[348] The influence of digital media is constrained by these financial requirements, contributing to the continuation of established patterns in the media landscape.

After 1999, the Press Law No 40/1999 and the Broadcasting Law No 32/2002 established a normative framework for media regulation, ensuring freedom of expression and its practical implementation.[349] These laws contributed to the legal structure governing the media landscape, emphasising the importance of free functioning within the established norms. The legislation aimed to safeguard and regulate the media, providing guidelines for responsible and unrestricted expression. The inherent non-media-regulating policies and laws also play a significant role in shaping or modifying the media agenda. Laws such as the

Electronic Transaction and Information Law, Pornography Law, Criminal Code, as well as ambiguous definitions and arguments related to public morality have contributed to the limitation of public opinion. This has resulted in self-censorship among media owners and professionals.[350] While various regulatory bodies such as the Indonesian Broadcasting Commission, Press Council, Telecommunication Regulatory Body, Business Competition Supervisory Commission and the Ministry of Communications exist to oversee and guide media and communication, their influence tends to align with the interests of the prevailing political class.[351] The structure of the political class is characterised by limited space for opposition representation, resulting in a lack of a counterbalancing force in politics, which is nearly non-existent.[352] The media's agenda often reflects this political bias.[353]

Since 1986, Chinese investors have played a significant role in shaping ownership patterns. Despite the existence of laws such as The Broadcasting Bill No. 32/2002, designed to regulate ownership systems and restrict the concentration of media ownership, the issue of media concentration and its political implications is often disregarded.[354] The observed trend highlights how "large media corporations are progressively exerting control over the media, leading to a perceived erosion of societal roles and rights".[355] Additionally, these corporations wield the capacity to shape the political agenda of the nation.

Prior studies indicate that in post-authoritarian Indonesia, the configuration of media ownership exhibits limited alteration. However, local media corporations and their corresponding roles in the political and economic spheres have transcended the local level, extending their influence nationally and even establishing a presence in other regions. This hegemonic condition of cross-media ownership and conglomerates is exploited as a means for "the proliferation of money politics at the national, regional, and local levels". A pertinent illustration of this phenomenon is discernible in the 2004 and 2009 national presidential campaigns, where Surya Paloh[356] and Aburizal Bakrie[357] utilised their media outlets to further their political interests.

Media in Malaysia

In Malaysia, the television and video market currently constitutes the largest segment, accounting for over 42 per cent of total revenue.[358] The television segment comprises state-owned and private networks and pay TV platforms as well. However, there is a noteworthy shift anticipated in the near future, with the digital media sector poised for rapid growth in the coming years. It is projected that this sector may substantially increase its market share, potentially reaching around 17.92 per cent of the total revenue by the year 2028.[359] The revelation of this data comes as no surprise when considering the statistics on internet penetration, encompassing an impressive 96.8 per cent[360] of the entire population. The state-owned "Radio Television Malaysia (RTM) operates two main TV networks".[361] Private radio stations broadcast in various languages like Malay, Tamil, Chinese and English. [362]

In Malaysia, there is a diverse array of print publications, encompassing a variety of newspapers and magazines. The present condition of the print media industry appears to be on a downward trajectory, particularly following the advent of digital media, which has precipitated a shift in media consumption habits.[363] According to a survey, approximately 19 per cent of individuals derive their news from print media sources.[364] This specific sector, comprising print newspapers and magazines, accounts for approximately 8 per cent of the total revenue within the broader media market.[365]

When examining media ownership in Malaysia, it becomes evident that it is notably concentrated within the control of a limited number of conglomerates. For several years, Media Prima has held the position as the predominant conglomerate, overseeing the largest terrestrial broadcasting network in the country.[366] This conglomerate wields substantial influence over the media landscape of the country. An important consideration lies in the absence of anti-monopoly laws regulating media ownership concentration, thereby permitting conglomerates such as Media Prima to procure controlling stakes in diverse media outlets.[367] Despite this, the "government uses its control over the licensing system to ensure pro-government editorial policies, though establishing online media outlet is much easier as long as it does not cross the implicit red lines dictated by the government".[368]

Malaysia adheres to a system of parliamentary democracy with constitutional monarchy. This political framework facilitates the operation of a democratic system, wherein the federal structure can effectively operate.[369] "The right to freedom of expression in Malaysia is guaranteed under Article 10 Federal Constitution.... Although the enjoyment of one's freedom of expression may be restricted, such restrictions must always be grounded in law, and necessary and proportionately enforced to achieve legitimate aims".[370]

In the realm of media, this nation boasts of a historical backdrop marked by media regulation via legislation and consolidated ownership, affording the government the capacity to regulate information disseminated through mass media.[371] The government has historically employed a range of legislative measures to impede the unrestricted flow of information and opinions. Instruments such as the Printing Press Act and the Broadcasting Act serve to curtail political discourse by proscribing critical content directed at the government.[372] Moreover, laws pertaining to sedition and defamation equip authorities with the means to shield political figures from unfettered and critical public discourse. In addition to this, "The Internal Security Act and Official Secrets Act enable authorities to detain individuals accused of disrupting national harmony without trial".[373] It has come to light many times that mainstream media in Malaysia lacks space for citizens to engage in political discourse, pushing opposition and dissenting voices to create an alternative media.[374]

The media ecosystem in Malaysia has been shaped significantly by political and economic interests. This makes it an ideal subject for researchers aiming to analyse media narratives from the perspective of political economy. The impact of these political and economic influences on the media is notably reflected in both the quality of media content and the degree of diversity within it.[375] Mass media has solidified its presence in Malaysia, acting as a catalyst for the processes of modernisation and socioeconomic development. Additionally, the media's influence has played a pivotal role in prompting changes to economic policies within the political sphere.[376]

The political sphere has consistently emphasized the imperative for the media to operate within the framework of national development, underscoring the necessity of directing media practices toward the fulfillment of their social responsibilities.[377,378] Several studies have attempted to explore the connection between the concept of 'guiding the media' and the promotion of positive coverage of government initiatives.[379] This is attributed to the inclination of the political class, as their desire to guide media has, over time, evolved into fostering a compliant media that serves their interests. In limiting the role of media in disseminating information about the opposing political narrative, the struggles of political opposition, citizens and civil society are exacerbated.[380] This restriction, aimed at moulding the media into a compliant entity, results in a populace that lacks pertinent information crucial for active participation in democratic processes such as elections. Political processes have been trying to ensure for a submissive media against political interests through stringent laws,[381] which is further reflected in the pattern of media ownership.[382] The concentration of media ownership seems to have a close association with the ruling class or individuals sympathetic to those in power[383] and especially to the largest conglomerate.[384]

Media in Thailand

In Thailand, despite stringent regulations governing the media landscape, numerous news outlets operate within the country.[385] These encompass traditional print publications, such as newspapers, and conventional electronic news channels, like television and radio. Notably, the contemporary landscape is marked by an increasing prominence of digital media, which appears to be more prevalent and omnipresent in Thailand.

In Thailand, a total of at least 45 television channels operate, encompassing both terrestrial and digital platforms.[386] Notably, approximately six of these channels are directly affiliated with either the military or the government, classifying them as public broadcasters.[387] Additionally, about seven channels are specifically dedicated to news broadcasting, functioning as news channels. In addition to these aforementioned channels, Thailand boasts of a multitude of cable and satellite channels, particularly dedicated to sports, entertainment, movies, lifestyle and other genres. Studies shows that television penetration rate in Thailand is more than 75 per cent right now and the expected revenue generation was around US$2.36bn in 2024.[388]

Radio stands out as a prominent mass media platform in Thailand, primarily focussing on lifestyle matters and entertainment. The country boasts of a diverse array of both private and public radio stations. For instance, Radio Thailand, as the public radio representative, operates six FM national radio stations and 65 FM provincial radio stations.[389] An alternative source suggests the presence of approximately 11 online-listed news radio stations originating from Thailand,[390] although these figures may exhibit variations due to the absence of official data on specific dates.[391]

In terms of newspapers, Thailand boasts of approximately 20 daily publications in diverse languages such as Thai and English.[392] The historical roots of newspapers in Thailand trace back to the 19th century, with the initiation of print media dating back to 1844.[393] Despite the evolution of media landscapes, newspapers continue to play a pivotal role in shaping public discourse and disseminating information among the populace. Data on readership patterns indicate that roughly 17 per cent of the population opts for traditional print newspapers and magazines as their primary source of information.[394] Notably, 75 per cent of individuals belonging to the older demographic, aged 76 years and above, prefer consuming information through printed newspapers. In stark contrast, only 16.7 per cent of the younger Generation Z, aged 23 years and below, engage with printed newspapers in Thailand.[395]

Digital platforms are evidently supplanting traditional counterparts. A recent survey reveals a substantial shift, indicating that "36.6% of individuals in Bangkok and its surrounding areas who traditionally consumed newspapers now engage with online newspaper content".[396] This trend aligns with broader developments, exemplified by the fact that, as of the beginning of 2023, Thailand boasts of a noteworthy 61.21 million internet users, constituting an impressive 85.3 per cent penetration rate.[397] It is noteworthy, however, that this landscape is dynamic and subject to change with the emergence of new technologies and platforms.

Thailand identifies itself as a nation adhering to a parliamentary democracy framework coupled with a constitutional monarchy, wherein the king assumes the role of the head of state.[398] Throughout its democratic evolution, Thailand has experienced a history marked by numerous coups, comprising 12 successful instances and numerous attempted ones.[399] This has led to the notable prominence and ubiquity of the military's role in the nation's affairs. The military perceives itself as "organizations in security with capabilities in defending and protecting the monarchy with modern and effective organization deserved of the people and friendly countries confidence".[400] It is readily apparent that the military maintains a robust alignment with the monarchy and its vested interests.

In the recent parliamentary election in May 2023, the Move Forward Party and its alliance came out on top in terms of the popular vote.[401] They promised to bring in democratic changes in response to the influence of the monarch–military partnership. Even though they won in the polls, the leader of the victorious alliance, Pita Limjaroenrat, faced challenges in gathering enough support for a majority vote during the joint session of the House of Representatives and the Upper House (Senate). In the Upper House, which mainly consisted of conservative senators appointed by the military, there was a noticeable hesitation to back Pita, leading to the inability to reach a majority consensus.[402] Many have viewed this as a setback for the growing democratic movement in Thailand. After several twists and turns in the political landscape, a government was eventually established.[403] However, it heavily relied on the support of political factions aligned with the military. As a result, the Move Forward Party found itself playing a more passive role, highlighting a compromise compelled by the backing of military-affiliated groups.[404]

The government and the military exert control over the entire national terrestrial television network, as well as numerous radio networks. The ownership pattern for the print media is largely privately-run, with a handful of Thai-language dailies accounting for most newspaper sales.[405] Today, "almost all the newspapers are owned by private companies, some of which listed in the stock market. Broadcast media, on the other hand, is entirely owned by the state in accordance with the Radio and Television Act of 1955 although most of them were leased to private operators on short-term contractual basis or in the form of long-term concession".[406] The 1997 constitution facilitated the transformation of Thai media from a government-oriented entity to a market-oriented private enterprise. This transition was realised through shifts in media ownership patterns and the dynamic interplay between media owners and political leaders. Central to this framework is the influence of the monarch–military hegemony, which has championed nationalism.[407] Consequently, the media has evolved into a promoter of official nationalism, serving as a novel avenue for endorsing political agendas and shaping public perception.

Thailand stands out as a prominent illustration of the intricate interplay among politics, economics and power dynamics, wherein the media and communication systems have undergone sustained influence over an extended period. Following the constitutional reforms implemented in 1997, a process was initiated to establish a new regulatory regime. This initiative aimed to ensure greater "public oversight of telecoms and broadcasting".[408] Over time, however, concerns have surfaced regarding the repercussions of these reforms, posing challenges to various state agencies, including the military. This is because "new private monopolies"[409] are progressively supplanting established entities, especially in terms of 'propagation of desired narrative'. Despite periods of direct monarchy and military junta rule, Thailand has experienced intermittent episodes of elected democratic governance and influential leadership. Even during these democratic phases, the elected government succumbed to the temptation of suppressing free media, as exemplified during the prime ministership of Thaksin Shinawatra (2001–2006). The media was "pushed to support the government in return for economic rewards.... They were targeted for intimidation, harassment, closure and censorship".[410] Following the Thaksin government, the subsequent military regime imposed unreasonable demands concerning media coverage and introduced punitive measures, leading to the closure of several media outlets. Thaksin Shinawatra initially possessed the cable television and satellite channels during his time. Subsequently, he leveraged the state apparatus to enforce the Anti-Money

Laundering Office, intimidating reporters and imposing restrictions on foreign journalists.[411] Aven till date, an examination of the ownership structure of public broadcasters reveals a notable trend, with several government ministries, including the military, holding ownership stakes in TV channels.

Thai media landscape is quite polarised, where the mainstream media or most popular media "toe the government line".[412] Media outlets with the ambition of propagating an alternative point of view may face "harassment by the authorities".[413] Although "the media are free to criticize government policies and cover instances of corruption and human rights abuses"[414] beyond these controlled networks, there is a discernible tendency towards self-censorship in the creation of media content, particularly concerning matters related to the royal family, the military, the judiciary and other sensitive issues. This self-censorship is partly attributed to the existence of a "strict 'lese majeste' law, which prohibits media from reporting anything that could be deemed critical of the royal family".[415] This law has a provision for a 15-year sentence if any journalist goes against it.[416] "According to Reporters without Borders (RSF), defamation and cybercrime laws are systematically used in Thailand to harass journalists, and the government also has the power to suspend the licences of media outlets that threaten 'public decency'".[417]

Media in Singapore

Recent trends in Singapore suggest a shift in the political landscape, exerting control over opposition activities and media outlets. This development has led opposition politicians to exercise caution in their expressions. Another noteworthy concern pertains to the mainstream media, which appears to lean favourably towards the ruling powers. This inclination raises queries regarding regulatory measures directed at alternative media, "limiting their independence and financial viability, with the government justifying restrictions".[418]

Singapore boasts of a rich and illustrious history in the realm of press, exemplified by the enduring legacy of the prominent newspaper, *The Straits Times*, which was established during the early colonial era around 1824. "Originally named *The Straits Times and Journal of Commerce* (ST), the publication was directed towards a relatively modest yet expanding European community in Singapore, eager for updates pertaining to their home countries".[419] As of today, approximately 842,000 copies of newspapers[420] are circulated daily in Singapore through more than 16 active newspaper publications, [421] primarily in four languages: English, Mandarin Chinese, Malay and Tamil.

Television broadcasting in Singapore commenced in 1963.[422] Presently, the public broadcaster Mediacorp is the sole entity that owns and operates all six free-to-air terrestrial local television channels.[423] These channels predominantly broadcast content in the four official languages: Malay, Chinese, Tamil and English.[424,425] Despite restrictions on private television channels within the country, several are permitted to broadcast, and individuals have the liberty to access content from foreign television channels.[426]

Radio broadcasting commenced in Singapore in 1924 through amateur radio stations, subsequently evolving with the involvement of commercial entities.[427] Recognising the potential of this mass media, colonial rulers assumed control and nationalised radio broadcasts.[428] Today, public broadcaster (Mediacorp) radio stations attract 3.7 million people weekly, representing 88 per cent of total adults. The average engagement per week is close to 13 hours per listener.[429] Digital Radio is another added trend, which has become a popular streak, especially among the youth[430] because Singapore ranks among the leading nations globally in terms of internet usage, boasting a penetration percentage of nearly 97 per cent.[431] "Singaporeans' top three internet uses are all connected to keeping up with current events and learning new things, whether local or global news or researching a subject of personal interest. Singaporeans use the internet for various purposes, with 64.8% utilizing it to seek information, 57.2% to stay updated on local news, and 54.8% for researching how to perform various tasks".[432]

The Constitution of the Republic of Singapore, as stipulated in Article 14(1), affirms the entitlement of Singaporean citizens to "the rights to freedom of speech and expression, peaceful assembly without arms, and association".[433] However, a point of contention arises due to the constraints imposed, rendering this 'right to freedom' considerably circumscribed and subject to the discretion of the government or ruling class. Another sub section of Article 14 describes the restriction of these rights, which is 'necessary or expedient in the interest' of the grounds. The rational of this is the security of the nation, maintenance of public order, morality (freedom of speech and freedom of association) and friendly relations with other countries (freedom of speech only). Even the judiciary has decided that the Parliament has "an extremely wide discretionary power and remit that permits a multifarious and multifaceted approach towards achieving any of the purposes specified in Art 14(2) of the Constitution".[434] In recent times, efforts to combat the proliferation of fake news have resulted in the enactment of new laws, exacerbating the decline of press freedom. These laws, which were implemented in October 2019, empower authorities to suppress press freedom and impose restrictions on social media.[435]

In addition to this, various laws and provisions have been instituted, both directly and indirectly, to exert control over journalistic practices. An example is the 'sedition law', which bears remnants of the colonial era.[436] This legislation revolves around the concept of 'ill-will and hostility' towards the government, rendering such sentiments punishable by imprisonment. Despite the amendments introduced through the Sedition (Repeal) Act of 2021, it still contains provisions that target the "publication or circulation of material with the intent to incite any class of persons to commit an offense against another class of persons".[437] In simpler terms, this grants the government discretionary power to enforce the law. Since the adoption of this law, the government can also "correct" online content if it deems it to be "false" or decides that it must "prevent a diminution of public confidence in (...) the government".[438,439]

In the context of this constrained media landscape, two prominent entities emerge as major players. The first is the Singapore Press Holdings, intricately associated with the ruling party and exercising a near-monopoly over the press.[440,441] The second is Mediacorp, a media group essentially under the ownership of a state investment agency. These influential media conglomerates exert a pervasive influence across all forms of mass media, extending to online platforms.[442]

The established framework governing the operation of media has existed within a notably constrained constitutional structure. The stance taken by the political class reflects a preference for a 'guided press',[443] one that conforms to the government's interpretation of pertinent issues. This approach has been accompanied by official measures and penalties, ranging from the withholding of advertising to the prolonged incarceration of certain defiant newspaper professionals in instances perceived as hostile. Some Western observers identify a "regulatory arsenal that empowers the government to intervene directly in the selection of board members and editors for prominent media establishments, mandating alignment with the government's stance".[444]

It is abundantly clear that Singapore maintains a comprehensive regulatory framework that extends to both offline and online news platforms. This regulation is primarily facilitated through The Newspaper and Printing Presses Act, which employs a licensing system for newspaper companies.[445] In the realm of television and radio, the Broadcasting Act (1979) oversees the licensing of broadcasting services and extends its regulatory scope to internet content providers, encompassing online news sites. Moreover, the domination of one-party (People's Action Party) rule in Singapore has given rise to a distinctive ecosystem within the realm of the political economy of media. Previous studies and surveys suggest a prevalence of a dearth of critical content, indicating a tendency towards self-censorship in both private and public media spheres.[446] Even the ownership pattern of mass media is largely linked with government companies.[447] Digital media platforms have made their space during last few years, but the litigations and closure/blocking of a few prominent private media outlets (States Times Review,[448] The Online Citizen,[449] etc.) have given rise to apprehensions. The ownership structure of mass media is predominantly associated with government entities. Although digital media platforms have gained prominence in recent years, legal disputes and the closure or blocking of certain prominent private media outlets, such as States Times Review[450] and The Online Citizen,[451] have fuelled concerns.

In Singapore, the normative structure of governance and its institutional power play a pivotal role in shaping the media system and guiding the activities of media practitioners. The established political structure in this nation has created an environment that suppressesthe unfettered functioning of media content production.[452] Moreover, it significantly influences the professional values imposed by the political–economic framework, [453] thereby leading to the legitimisation of self-censorship in media content and the endorsement of the ruling dispensation. Since gaining independence, Singapore, under the leadership of the People's Action Party (PAP) and its enduring super-majority, has possessed the authority to shape and reshape the political–economic landscape through executive decisions and the ability to amend the constitution at its discretion.[454] This authority has inevitably manifested in the ownership patterns of the media and the factors influencing them.

Media in the Philippines

The Philippines experienced a significant period in the first half of 2020 amidst the challenges posed by the Covid-19 pandemic. During this time, the president made concerted efforts to stifle the media through various means, including threats, insults and legal actions targeting journalists and media organisations.[455] Notably, *ABS-CBN*, a major media outlet, was compelled to cease its operations. The suppression of media was exacerbated under the guise of the 'new anti-terror law', anti-fake news initiatives/guidelines and measures taken to curb the spread of the pandemic.[456] During an era marked by pronounced media suppression, the consequences have manifested in the form of a compromised media landscape. Consequently, mainstream news outlets have experienced a notable erosion of trust among the masses.[457] This decline in trustworthiness has been consistently observed in various international surveys, such as the Digital News Report.[458] "Radio and TV are the most popular media and, of these, the gigantic GMA-7 television network has an audience share of nearly 50%. Its main competitor, the *ABS-CBN* network, was stripped of its franchise in 2020 but continues to broadcast online, where its presence is growing".[459]

The waning influence of traditional print media is evident when juxtaposed with the burgeoning prominence of electronic and digital platforms, wherein television stands as the predominant source of information at a global scale.[460] Particularly in rural locales, the regional press and radio persist as the favoured means of communication, steadfastly maintaining their pre-eminence despite the pervasive impact of the digital revolution.[461] According to the available data, approximately 22 per cent of Filipinos rely on newspapers as their primary source of news, while the majority (55 per cent) prefer online platforms for news consumption.[462] "*The Philippine Daily Inquirer* remains the preeminent newspaper, now propelled by its digital iteration. In contrast, formerly dominant regional newspapers like the *Sunstar Baguio* and the *Visayan Daily Star* find themselves grappling for survival in the absence of a robust online presence".[463] The pervasive influence of commercialisation and political motivations casts a looming shadow upon the pristine principles of journalistic ethics and public service.[464] Despite these challenges, a noteworthy trend of growth has emerged within community newspapering, marked by the emergence of new publications and the expansion of existing ones.

In the context of the Philippines, television stands out as the preeminent and highly relied-upon conduit for political information, garnering a substantial 58 per cent trust rating.[465] In 2016, the Philippines boasted of a diverse landscape of more than 400 television stations, predominantly controlled by three major media conglomerates.[466] Following the cessation of operations at *ABS-CBN*, concerns arose regarding the vulnerability of the media sector to potential attacks. This perception was fuelled by allegations of political vendetta against *ABS-CBN*, which had faced verbal assaults and accusations of during the 2016 campaign, giving rise to concerns regarding bias within the media. As stipulated by regulations, all television franchises necessitate government approval, chiefly from the House of Representatives, and oversight by the National Telecommunications

Commission.[467] Furthermore, certain religious entities, such as religious organisations, have procured or established their own television stations.[468]

The 1987 Constitution of the Philippines guarantees freedom of expression and aims to establish a seamless working environment for the press.[469] However, since the implementation of this constitution, there has been increasing apprehension about the political and economic structure of the media system. Issues such as state apparatus involvement, litigation and defamation cases against media practitioners and media houses have become significant points of concern.[470] Recent political changes have offered a glimmer of hope, yet challenges persist. Critically, "the government employs laws related to media ownership and taxation to intimidate critical media outlets, such as the Rappler site".[471]

Since the introduction of presidential democracy in 1987, the Philippines has experienced a notable surge in the influence wielded by economic elites, business entities, media proprietors and politically influential figures on the functioning of the state.[472] This transformation has shaped the Philippines into a 'business-friendly' ecosystem, affording considerable leverage to these influential entities for fostering economic growth within the private sector. In the post-authoritarian era that began in 1987, a policymaking framework gradually emerged, pledging to usher in economic prosperity. However, this prosperity seems to have been confined predominantly to urban-centred growth, with a distinct emphasis on the sustained dominance of economic elites in the realm of governance through policymaking.[473] This political economic ecosystem constructed a media landscape, which has been the enduring 'cozy relationship' between media owners and political elites. As the political structure in the Philippines transitioned from martial law to democracy, new economic players emerged in the media market. This evolving political landscape served as the foundation for what is described as a 'cozy relationship'.[474] Despite the overthrow of the dictatorship, the transition to a democratic system and the advent of new media did not "ensure journalistic professionalism; instead, economic constraints replaced previous political censorship".[475] Another influential factor has been the impact of economic considerations on Philippine media outlets. The aforementioned event represents a noteworthy shift in the media landscape of the country, giving rise to an increased prevalence of "sensationalism and provocation"[476] within media content. The issue is also connected to disparities in revenue distribution from advertisers, especially in the case of political advertisement.[477]

Chapter Six

India in ASEAN Media: Study of Indonesia, Malaysia, Thailand, Singapore and the Philippines

India in ASEAN Media: Study of Indonesia

The production of news about foreign nations operates as an exercise in strategic narrative formation, where media outlets function as key actors in shaping discursive realities that influence both public perception and geopolitical positioning. This study examines how three prominent Indonesian English-language publications, *The Jakarta Post*, *Tempo* and *Indonesia expat*, construct narratives about India through selective prioritisation, sourcing and affective framing of news items in their online editions between May and October 2023. Analysing 81 news articles, the research investigates the mechanisms through which these newspapers deploy strategic communication to reinforce, contest or negotiate India's image within Indonesia's mediascape. Central to this enquiry is the interplay between headlines and lead paragraphs, a critical site where the narrative intentionality becomes most visible. Headlines, as compressed discursive acts, establish initial cognitive frames, while introductory segments either amplify or recalibrate their implied meanings. By assessing their congruence in tone and messaging, this study reveals how narrative coherence (or its deliberate disruption) serves strategic ends, whether in cultivating particular audience attitudes or aligning with broader editorial stances. Furthermore, the analysis traces the provenance of information sources, probing how reliance on certain actors, governmental, institutional or independent, shapes narrative authority and legitimacy.

Table 3: Indonesia's Top News Categories Related to India

Category of News Topic Wise	*Number of News Items*	*Percentage*
Domestic Politics	3	03.70%
Terrorism/Law & Order	2	02.46%
Global Economy and India	9	11.11%
India's Economy	15	18.51%
Bilateral Relations	20	24.69%
Geopolitics and India	15	18.51%
Climate Disaster	4	04.93%
Governance/Accident	5	06.17%
Science and Technology	6	07.40%
Cultural/Miscellaneous	2	02.46%
Total	81	100%

Table 4: Indonesia's Top Five News Categories Related to India

Bilateral Relations	20	24.69%
India's Economy	15	18.51%
Geopolitics and India	15	18.51%
Global Economy and India	9	11.11%
Science And Technology	6	07.40%
Governance/Accident	5	06.17%

A comprehensive analysis of news coverage across three major Indonesian newspapers from May 1 to October 31, 2023, reveals significant editorial patterns in the portrayal of India. These patterns suggest that Indonesian media prioritise international relations, economic developments and geopolitical considerations over India's domestic socio-political and cultural aspects. Out of the 81 news items analysed, only 3.70 per cent focussed on India's domestic politics, while terrorism, law enforcement and cultural or miscellaneous news received even lower coverage at 2.46 per cent each. This limited attention to internal political affairs indicates that Indonesian media does not see India's internal dynamics as immediately relevant to their readership. Instead, bilateral relations dominated the coverage with 24.69 per cent , highlighting diplomatic interactions, trade agreements and strategic partnerships, topics that have direct implications for Indonesia's own economic and geopolitical interests. News about India's economy and its role in geopolitics each constituted 18.51 per cent of the total coverage, reflecting an acknowledgment of India's growing influence as a global economic and strategic power. An additional 11.11 per cent of news reports connected India's economy to global trends, illustrating how India's financial policies, industrial growth and market behaviours contribute to global economic shifts. Science and technology in India accounted for 7.40 per cent of the news, signalling moderate interest in India's innovations and technological advancements, while governance and accidents formed 6.17 per cent of the coverage, demonstrating some level of attention to India's public administration and crisis management but not as a major focus area (Table 3).

A deeper analysis reveals that this editorial strategy is not merely a reflection of neutral journalistic priorities but is embedded within a larger political and economic media structure. The prioritisation of bilateral relations (24.69 per cent) over domestic politics (3.70 per cent) suggests that Indonesian media's coverage is driven by national interest considerations rather than purely objective assessments of newsworthiness. The relatively high emphasis on India's economy and geopolitics (both at 18.51 per cent) supports the idea that Indonesian media recognises India's growing influence and views it through the lens of regional cooperation and strategic partnerships. News items on India's integration into the global economy (11.11 per cent) further emphasise this perception, highlighting India's role in shaping worldwide financial trends and supply chain dynamics. Meanwhile, the moderate focus on science and technology (7.40 per cent) reflects an interest in India's digital transformation, technological advancements and innovation-driven economy, elements that could serve as models or points of cooperation for Indonesia's own development (Table 4).

Analysing the Source of India-Related News in Indonesian Media

Table 5: News Source Analysis (Indonesia)

Total news items	81	100%
News coverage by in-house reporters/news desk/editorial/op-eds	30	37.03%
News coverage by international agencies/national agencies/freelancers/contributors	51	62.96%

The data in Table 5 suggests that out of a total of 81 news items, 30 articles (37.03 per cent) were produced by in-house journalists, including newsroom staff, editorial pieces and opinion columns. Whereas 51 news items (62.96 per cent) were sourced from international agencies, national agencies, freelancers or external contributors. This breakdown highlights a critical reliance on external sources for India-related news, leading to multiple implications concerning editorial control, framing and public perception of India in Indonesia.

One of the key findings from the data is the relatively low proportion of in-house reporting on India (37.03 per cent). Indonesian newsrooms appear to produce limited first-hand coverage of India, relying instead on reports from international or national agencies. This raises concerns about the depth and contextual understanding of India-related issues, as reports produced externally may not align with Indonesian perspectives, priorities or regional interests.

An analysis of the 81 news items from three Indonesian newspapers reveals that 31 articles (38.27 per cent) express positive sentiments about India, highlighting its strengths in economic growth, bilateral relations and global influence. The positive coverage suggests that India's strategic partnerships and economic engagements are being noticed favourably in Indonesian media.

Table 6: Sentiment Analysis of Positive News (Indonesia)

Positive news articles out of a total of 81 news articles	31	38.27%
Positive stories by in-house reporters/news desk/opinion	18	58.06%
Positive stories by international agencies/national agencies/freelancers/contributors	13	41.93%

Table 7: Sentiment Analysis of Negative News (Indonesia)

Negative news articles out of a total of 81 news articles	22	27.16%
Negative stories by in-house reporters/news desk/opinion	6	27.27%
Negative stories by international agencies/national agencies/freelancers/contributors	16	72.72%

Analysis of the 81 news items in this study reveals that 31 articles, accounting for 38.27 per cent of the total, portray India in a positive light (Table 6). A significant portion of this favourable representation, 18 articles, or 58.06 per cent, originates from Indonesian media organisations, indicating an editorial preference within these outlets to highlight positive aspects of India. This suggests a possible strategic approach in media framing, potentially influenced by factors such as strengthening India–Indonesia bilateral relations, fostering economic and cultural cooperation or aligning with broader regional geopolitical considerations. However, the data itself does not explicitly confirm such motivations, necessitating further qualitative exploration of editorial policies and decision-making processes.

Conversely, 13 of the positive articles, comprising 41.93 per cent of the total favourable coverage, are sourced from external entities, predominantly Western-based news agencies. This suggests that global media narratives, largely shaped by Western journalistic perspectives, also play a substantial role in constructing India's image in Indonesia. The reliance on international sources for a considerable portion of the positive coverage reflects the transnational nature of media influence, where external factors contribute significantly to shaping public perceptions within local media ecosystems.

The division between domestically produced and externally sourced content highlights a dual dynamic in media representation. On one hand, Indonesian media outlets actively generate positive narratives about India, potentially as part of a localised editorial agenda that reflects domestic interests or regional diplomatic alignments. On the other hand, nearly half of the positive portrayal is shaped by global narratives, primarily Western-centric, which permeate Indonesian media discourse through syndicated reports and international collaborations. This interplay between localised editorial agency and transnational media flows underscores the complex and multifaceted nature of India's representation in Indonesian media. It also raises critical questions about the broader implications of media ownership, agenda-setting and geopolitical influences in shaping public discourse on international relations.

A comprehensive analysis of the 81 news articles reveals that 22 of them, or 27.16 per cent, portray India in a critical or negative light (Table 7). These narratives originate from two principal sources: internal contributors within media organisations and external entities such as international news agencies, national agencies, freelancers and independent journalists. Among the 22 critical articles, only 6 (27.16 per cent) were generated by internal media professionals, including staff journalists, newsroom personnel, desk editors and editorial staff. These individuals engage in original reporting and analysis, crafting narratives based on their own research and editorial oversight. In contrast, the majority, 16 articles (72.72 per cent), were produced by external sources, emphasising the dominant role of internationally sourced perspectives in shaping India's media portrayal.

This distribution underscores a critical aspect of media representation, highlighting the disproportionate influence of external actors in framing India's global image. The critical coverage largely focusses on economic performance, bilateral relations and India's international standing. Economic narratives often juxtapose India's rapid ascent, such as its emergence as the world's fifth-largest economy (now fourth largest) after surpassing the United Kingdom in 2022, with concerns about macroeconomic vulnerabilities, including inflation and fiscal challenges.[478] Similarly, bilateral relations are frequently analysed through the lens of regional power dynamics and global diplomatic engagements. One example is India's strategic partnership with Indonesia, a relationship built on shared interests in trade, maritime security and regional stability within the Indo–Pacific framework. While the data does not explicitly specify this bilateral equation, it remains relevant within the broader context of geopolitical discourse. The pre-eminence of external sources in shaping critical perspectives on India raises pertinent questions about the objectivity and balance of international media narratives. It suggests that global discourse surrounding India may not solely reflect neutral journalistic assessments but could also be influenced by broader geopolitical interests and power structures. The extent to which external media actors contribute to shaping perceptions of India underscores the complexities of international news dissemination, where narratives are often filtered through external lenses.

Table 8: Sentiment Analysis of Apprehensive and Neutral News (Indonesia)

Number of apprehensive news items of a total of 81 news items	13	16.04%
Number of neutral news items of a total of 81 news items	15	18.51%

The reviewed news items state that approximately 16 per cent (16.04 per cent) of the collected news items exhibit an apprehensive nature (Table 8). This means that these headlines are crafted in a way that stir feelings of uncertainty or anxiety among readers, a tactic often employed to capture attention in a crowded media landscape. This apprehensive quality is typically achieved through two main strategies: sensationalism and ambiguity. Sensationalism involves the use of exaggerated, dramatic or alarming language to create a sense of urgency, compelling the audience to engage with the story out of concern or shock. Ambiguity, on the other hand, relies on withholding critical details, leaving readers curious or uneasy and prompting them to delve deeper into the article for clarity. Among the 81 news articles, more than 18 per cent (18.51 per cent) of news headlines are neutral in tone (Table 8). These neutral headlines stand apart from those that are positive, negative or apprehensive as they focus solely on delivering information without leaning toward any particular emotional appeal. They are straightforward and factual, designed to inform rather than to provoke a strong emotional response or sway the reader's sentiment in any direction. This comparison suggests a deliberate variation in journalistic approaches, where some news items prioritise emotional engagement to hook the audience, while others adopt a more detached, informative stance, possibly to maintain credibility or cater to an audience seeking unembellished facts. Together these statistics and explanations shed light on the diverse strategies news outlets use to communicate with their readership, balancing emotional impact with neutrality depending on their goals.

Decoding India–Indonesia News Coverage: Priorities and Reasons

Empirical data from the study highlights a significant prominence in news coverage of bilateral engagements between India and Indonesia (24.69 per cent), closely followed by Indian economy and India's foreign policy and geopolitical news (both at 18.15 per cent) and India's integration with the global economy (11.11 per cent). This pattern of news prioritisation can be theoretically decoded through several lenses within international relations and communication studies. Firstly, the prominence of bilateral relations aligns with realist perspectives in international relations, which emphasise the state as the primary actor and bilateral interactions as crucial for pursuing national interests. News outlets, often reflecting the dominant foreign policy narratives of their respective nations, would naturally highlight diplomatic activities, agreements and potential areas of cooperation or contention between two significant regional powers like India and Indonesia. This focus is further amplified by the 'gatekeeping' theory in media studies, suggesting that news editor's prioritise stories that are deemed relevant to their national audience, and stories about bilateral relations that directly impact their state's national interests, security and economic well-being.

The substantial coverage of the Indian economy and India's integration with the global economy resonates with the increasing interconnectedness highlighted by globalisation theories. News concerning India's economic performance, trade relations, investment flows and participation in the global economic system are vital for both domestic and international audiences interested in economic opportunities and risks. This aligns with the market-driven approach to news, where economic news is considered high-value due to its direct impact on businesses, consumers and national development. Furthermore, from a neoliberal institutionalist perspective, the focus on economic integration reflects the importance of international institutions and agreements in fostering cooperation and interdependence, making news related to these aspects inherently significant.

Additionally, the equal weight given to India's foreign policy and geopolitical news underscores the strategic importance of both nations in the Indo–Pacific region. This can be explained through the lens of geopolitical theories, which emphasise the influence of geography and power dynamics on international relations.

The interconnectedness of these news categories is evident. Bilateral engagements often have direct implications on economic relations, foreign policy alignments and the degree of integration with the global economy. For instance, agreements on trade and investment directly link bilateral relations with economic news.

India and Indonesia in the News: Bilateralism, Economy, Geopolitics and Global Integration

The observed pattern in news coverage concerning India and Indonesia, with bilateral engagements leading at 24.69 per cent, followed by Indian economy and India's foreign policy and geopolitics (both at 18.15 per cent) and India's integration with the global economy (11.11 per cent), offers a rich ground for theoretical analysis within the fields of international relations, political economy and communication studies (Table 9). This prioritisation is not arbitrary but rather a reflection of the intricate and increasingly significant relationship between these two major players in the Global South and the Indo–Pacific region.

Table 9: India's News in Indonesia: Key Focus Areas and Drivers

Category	*Percentage*	*Potential Drivers*
Bilateral relations between India–Indonesia	24.69%	Historical ties, strategic partnerships, trade, security cooperation, public diplomacy
Indian economy	18.15%	Economic impact, trade opportunities, investment, business interests
India's foreign policy & geopolitical news	18.15%	Regional dynamics, Indo–Pacific strategy, geopolitical implications for Indonesia
India's relation with the global economy	11.11%	Broader global role, less immediate relevance, abstract nature

From an international relations (IR) perspective, the dominance of bilateral news strongly supports the enduring relevance of state-centric realism.[479]. Realism posits that states are the primary actors in the international system, driven by national interests, primarily survival and power maximisation. Bilateral relations, therefore, become the fundamental arena for pursuing these interests through diplomacy, negotiation and the formation of alliances or strategic partnerships. The high news coverage of India–Indonesia bilateral engagements signifies the perceived importance of direct state-to-state interactions in addressing mutual concerns, fostering cooperation in areas like defence (e.g., joint exercises like Garuda Shakti and Samudra Shakti, and the potential BrahMos missile deal), maritime security (especially in the strategically vital Indo–Pacific) and cultural exchange (as seen in the Cultural Exchange Programme 2025–2028). This emphasis on bilateralism can also be viewed through the lens of neorealism, which highlights the structural constraints of the international system that compel states to prioritise their relative power and security, often achieved through bilateral arrangements.

However, a purely realist interpretation is insufficient. The substantial coverage of the Indian economy and its integration with the global economy necessitates incorporating international political economy (IPE) theories. The focus on the Indian economy (18.15 per cent) reflects a growing understanding of economic power as a crucial component of national strength and influence in the contemporary international system (Gilpin, 2001). News regarding economic growth, trade (Indonesia being India's second-largest ASEAN trading partner), investment (Indian investments in Indonesian infrastructure, power, etc.) and financial cooperation (like the Memorandum of Understanding on Local Currency Settlement Systems) underscore the increasing interdependence between nations. This aligns with liberal IPE perspectives (Keohane & Nye, 1977), which emphasise the role of economic ties in fostering cooperation and mutual benefit. The coverage of India's integration with the global economy (11.11 per cent) further supports this, highlighting the importance of participation in global value chains, adherence to international economic norms and engagement with multilateral economic institutions (e.g., World Trade Organization, discussions on ASEAN–India Trade in Goods Agreement (AITIGA)). This also resonates with constructivist IPE, which examines how shared ideas and norms shape economic interactions and the perceived importance of global economic integration for national development and status.

The significant attention given to India's foreign policy and geopolitical news (18.15 per cent) can be best understood through the framework of geopolitical realism (Gray, 2005) and strategic studies. In an era of shifting global power dynamics, particularly the rise of China and the increasing strategic importance of the Indo–Pacific, the foreign policy choices and geopolitical positioning of major regional actors like India are inherently newsworthy. Coverage of India's Act East Policy, its engagement in forums like the Quadrilateral Security Dialogue (Quad), its stance on maritime disputes (including the South China Sea) and its balancing act in relations with major powers (e.g., the U.S. and Russia) reflects the strategic calculations aimed at securing national interests and maintaining regional stability. This also connects with securitisation theory (Buzan et al., 1998), where foreign policy and geopolitical issues are often framed as matters of national security, thus warranting significant public and media attention. Indonesia's growing role in the region and its recent BRICS membership further amplify the importance of understanding the geopolitical alignment and potential cooperation between these two nations.

Finally, the role of communication and media studies is crucial for understanding why these particular categories receive such prominence. The consistent coverage of bilateral relations, economic matters and foreign policy/geopolitics likely reflects a conscious or unconscious agenda-setting by news organisations, influenced by national priorities, government narratives and audience interest. This proposition further explains how these issues are presented to the public, often highlighting specific aspects (e.g., economic opportunities in bilateral trade, security implications of geopolitical developments) to shape understanding and interpretation. Moreover, the concept of news values (Galtung & Ruge, 1965) plays a role, as events related to high-level diplomatic engagements, economic performance and geopolitical shifts often possess characteristics like elite actor involvement, impact on a large number of people and relevance to national interests, making them inherently more newsworthy.

Analysing News Sentiment (Headlines) toward India in Indonesian Media

An examination of 81 news items pertaining to India, sourced from leading Indonesian print media (online version), unveils a multifaceted sentiment profile. In these sourced articles, 38.27 per cent exhibit a positive connotation, 27.16 per cent a negative connotation, 16.04 per cent an apprehensive tone and 18.51 per cent a neutral tone.

This distribution suggests a predominantly favourable depiction of India, tempered by notable currents of criticism and caution. To decode these findings, this analysis employs two theoretical frameworks: media ecology and political economy, which offer a rigorous exploration of how media structures, cultural dynamics and power relations shape the representation of India in Indonesia's media.

In Indonesia, several structural and sociocultural elements define the media ecosystem, providing insight into the observed sentiment distribution. The Indonesian media landscape features a blend of private conglomerates and state-influenced outlets, operating under regulatory oversight that varies in stringency. This structure shapes editorial priorities and the diversity of perspectives available to audiences.

The sentiment breakdown, 38.27 per cent positive, 27.16 per cent negative,

16.04 per cent apprehensive and 18.51 per cent neutral, mirrors distinct editorial priorities within this ecology. Positive sentiment laden (38.27 per cent) news items likely underscore efforts to promote bilateral goodwill, spotlighting India's economic strides and shared developmental goals. Such coverage aligns with Indonesia's interest in deepening ties with India, a fellow emerging economy. The news items carrying negative connotation, which focusses on India's domestic challenges, economic challenges, governance issues, climate disaster, news related to geopolitics and India's setbacks or its assertive regional posture, reflect a journalistic impulse to interrogate power and highlight flaws. At the same time, news with an apprehensive tone (16.04 per cent) is another intriguing factor. This cautious framing could signal uncertainty about India's economic stability, governance and climate disaster or its geopolitical ambitions, particularly in the Indo–Pacific, where Indonesia has its own strategic stakes. Of these 81 sourced articles, 18.51 per cent news items carry neutral sentiments. Objective reporting, emphasising trade figures or diplomatic updates, suggests a commitment to factual integrity, possibly serving as a counterweight to more interpretive narratives. In these articles positive framing dominates, likely driven by diplomatic and economic imperatives, yet the substantial presence of negative and apprehensive tones reflects a critical engagement with India's complexities, shaped by Indonesia's own regional and domestic priorities.

Structural imperatives of Indonesian Media and Representation

The Indonesian media landscape is dominated by a small cluster of conglomerates, often intertwined with political elites or business magnates, forming an oligopolistic structure that curtails editorial independence and aligns content with vested interests. In a crowded digital market, outlets compete for audience attention and advertising revenue, frequently favouring sensationalism or emotionally charged narratives over depth or impartiality. Though press freedoms expanded after the 1998 reforms, state influence, via licensing, regulations or state-owned media, subtly shapes discourse, especially on foreign affairs. This reflects a nuanced interplay of power, where media operates within a political–economic framework that prioritises elite agendas over unfettered expression.

In this study of the Indonesian media, the pervasive tendency toward favourable coverage in media narratives may be intricately linked to the vested economic and political interests of media proprietors, who derive substantial material benefits from the fortification of Indonesia–India bilateral relations. These benefits are particularly pronounced in key sectors such as coal, palm oil and technological exchange, which constitute critical nodes in the transnational economic networks binding the two nations. The consistent deployment of positive framing within these media discourses can be theorised as a strategic instrument of soft power, operating in alignment with state-driven diplomatic agendas. Such framing not only amplifies the perceived mutual advantages of enhanced cooperation but also functions as a performative mechanism to bolster the legitimacy and efficacy of formal geopolitical frameworks, such as the Indo–Pacific partnership. This partnership, emblematic of broader regional aspirations, exemplifies a concerted effort to consolidate strategic alliances amid shifting global power dynamics. Consequently, the media's role transcends mere reportage, emerging as an active agent in the co-construction of a narrative that reinforces the ideological underpinnings of state-led initiatives, while simultaneously reflecting the interplay between economic imperatives and diplomatic objectives in shaping public perception.

The prevalence of favourable and positive coverage within print media regarding Indonesia–India relations can be rigorously interrogated through various lenses of the news making within media organisations, wherein editorial policies and the structural dynamics of newsrooms play pivotal roles in shaping news production. Such coverage may reflect the vested interests of media proprietors, whose financial stakes, often tied to lucrative bilateral trade in commodities such as coal, palm oil or burgeoning technology sectors, benefit from robust diplomatic and economic ties between the two nations. This alignment is not merely incidental but is embedded within the broader framework of media ownership, where profit motives intersect with geopolitical strategies, such as the Indo–Pacific partnership, which both Indonesia and India leverage as a state-led mechanism to enhance regional influence. Drawing from the sociology of news-making, this phenomenon exemplifies how knowledge production in newsrooms is less an autonomous pursuit of truth and more a negotiated outcome of power relations between media elites, state actors and corporate interests.

Conversely, the emergence of critical or negative narratives within certain print media outlets warrants a deeper exploration of editorial autonomy and audience dynamics, rooted in the structural tensions of news production. Such coverage might stem from outlets striving to assert their independence from hegemonic state or corporate influences, a stance often cultivated to enhance legitimacy in the eyes of readerships sceptical of mainstream alignments. Alternatively, the appeal to audiences drawn to controversy, where reports of India's social unrest, governance failures or regional tensions with neighbours like China or Pakistan are foregrounded, may reflect a deliberate editorial inclination to exploit sensationalism as a market differentiator. Yet, these critical narratives are rarely unmoored from the broader journalistic norms of accountability, which compel newsrooms to balance adversarial reporting with structural biases inherent in their reliance on Western news agencies (e.g., Reuters, AP) as primary news feed providers. These agencies, headquartered in the Global North, often frame developing nations like India through a lens of liberal democratic critique, subtly shaping the tone and selection of stories available to local editors. This dependency underscores an asymmetry in the global flow of information, where editorial choices in Indonesian newsrooms are partially predetermined by the epistemological frameworks of external gatekeepers.

The apprehensive tone or cautious connotation in certain news items about India, whether addressing its domestic policies or its geopolitical rivalries, introduces a further layer of theoretical complexity, interpretable as a strategic manoeuvre within the news production process. This hedging can be understood as a pragmatic editorial approach, enabling media outlets to gesture towards contentious issues without fully committing to a polemical stance. From a political economy perspective, such restraint may originate in the newsroom's awareness of its precarious position within a media ecosystem where state subsidies, advertising revenue from multinational firms and diplomatic sensitivities exert overlapping pressures. The sociology of news-making further illuminates this dynamic, revealing how journalists and editors, as social actors, internalise these constraints, producing knowledge that is tentatively critical yet strategically restrained. This ambivalence is not merely a stylistic quirk but a structural artefact of the newsroom's negotiation between its public watchdog role and its embeddedness in systems of power.

Finally, the presence of fact-based or neutral reporting on India-related matters invites scrutiny of the operational logics underpinning news production, particularly the interplay between resource constraints and credibility imperatives. Such neutrality may signal a form of resource-driven minimalism, where overstretched newsrooms, lacking the capacity for in-depth investigative journalism, rely heavily on wire services for pre-packaged, ostensibly objective content. This reliance, however, is not ideologically neutral; the editorial inclination of Western news agencies often privileges a technocratic, depoliticised style that flattens complex socio-political realities into digestible data points, a process critiqued by scholars like Herman and Chomsky in their propaganda model as serving elite interests under the guise of objectivity. Alternatively, neutral reporting may reflect a deliberate editorial choice to cultivate credibility amid the competing pressures of partisan readerships and sensationalist rivals, appealing to an imagined audience segment that valorises unvarnished information. In this sense, the sociology of knowledge production reveals a dual tension: newsrooms as sites of both mechanical reproduction (via wire feeds) and active meaning-making, where editorial policy mediates between external inputs and internal priorities.

News Sourcing, Impact on Sentiments and India's Representation

The internal production of news within Indonesian print media, accounting for 37 per cent (Table 3) of total headlines and skewing toward positive portrayals of India (58.06 per cent) (Table 4), suggests a deliberate editorial policy shaped by organisational priorities and newsroom structures. Newsrooms, as sites of content creation, operationalise these policies through gatekeeping processes, wherein editors and journalists select and frame stories to align with institutional goals. The sociology of news production, as articulated by scholars like Michael Schudson, underscores how routines, hierarchies and professional norms within newsrooms influence output. In this case, the preference for positive internal coverage may indicate a strategic allocation of limited resources toward stories that reinforce national interests or audience expectations, leaving negative coverage to external providers to maintain a balanced narrative without expending additional editorial capital.

The pronounced role of international news agencies, supplying 62.96 per cent (Table 3) of total headlines and a striking 72.72 per cent (Table 5) of negative news about India, points to their editorial inclinations as a critical determinant of content. Predominantly Western agencies, such as Reuters, AP and AFP, operate within a global news ecosystem historically dominated by Euro–American perspectives. This dominance can be traced to the political economy of media, where resource-rich Western agencies maintain extensive networks of correspondents and infrastructure, enabling them to cover distant regions like India with greater immediacy and scale than Indonesian newspapers can afford. However, their editorial output is not neutral; it is shaped by news values, criteria like conflict, negativity and drama that elevate the newsworthiness of negative events. Galtung and Ruge's seminal work on news values posits that negative news inherently garners higher priority due to its capacity to disrupt expectations and captivate audiences, a tendency amplified in Western agencies serving competitive, attention-driven markets.[480]

Moreover, the editorial inclination of these agencies may reflect a latent bias toward highlighting governance failures, climate disaster, accidents or economic setbacks in developing nations like India. This framing aligns with a liberal democratic ethos emphasising accountability journalism, yet it may also perpetuate stereotypical narratives about the Global South, catering to Western audiences and reinforcing hegemonic discourses. Stuart Hall's encoding/decoding model is instructive here:[481] Western agencies encode news with meanings reflective of their cultural and market contexts, which Indonesian newspapers then decode and republish, often with limited capacity to reframe due to resource constraints or deference to the agencies' perceived credibility.

Media organisations, as profit-oriented entities, navigate the tension between cost-efficiency and content control. Subscribing to Western news agencies is a pragmatic choice for Indonesian newspapers, offering timely, cost-effective access to international news compared to maintaining foreign bureaus, a resource-intensive endeavour constrained by budgets and personnel. This dependency, however, cedes significant influence to external providers, embedding Indonesian media within an asymmetrical news flow where Western agencies act as epistemic gatekeepers. Reliance on institutional sources like news agencies shapes content to reflect the interests and biases of those sources' primary markets, here, Western audiences and advertisers, rather than the local Indonesian context.

The economic incentives of agencies exacerbate this skew toward negativity. Negative news, with its high audience appeal, drives circulation and engagement, aligning with the commercial logic of both the agencies and the subscribing newspapers. Yet, the internal production of positive news suggests a countervailing economic and political logic within Indonesian media: by investing in proprietary content, newspapers can assert editorial autonomy, cater to local audience preferences for positive Indo–Indian narratives and align with state or corporate interests seeking to bolster regional ties.

Integrating these insights, the production of news texts in Indonesian print media emerges as a contested field, per Pierre Bourdieu's concept of the journalistic field. Western news agencies wield symbolic capital, credibility, reach and immediacy that Indonesian newspapers leverage to compensate for their structural limitations. This reliance, however, imports external editorial inclinations, skewing coverage toward negativity (72.72 per cent of negative headlines) (Table 5) and reflecting the agencies' news values and market-driven priorities. Internally, the field's rules shift: newspapers deploy their limited capital (staff, budget) to produce positive content (58.06 per cent of positive headlines), aligning with editorial policies that serve national or economic agendas. The result is a bifurcated news landscape where internal and external forces compete to define the representation of India.

This bifurcation also underscores a global hierarchy in news production. The 63 per cent dominance of external sources, primarily Western, reflects a historical asymmetry in media power, where the Global South remains a consumer of Northern narratives. The high proportion of negative news from agencies (72.72 per cent) versus the internal focus on positivity (58.06 per cent) suggests not only differing editorial priorities but also a division of labour: agencies supply the 'hard', often negative, news, while newspapers craft 'soft', positive stories to maintain local relevance and legitimacy.

Sentiment Dynamics between News Headlines and Introductions of the News

In the realm of media studies, the interplay between news headlines and their introductory paragraphs (introductions) has garnered significant scholarly attention due to its profound impact on audience perception and comprehension. Headlines serve as the initial point of engagement, often crafted to capture attention through emotive or sensational language, thereby setting the preliminary tone for the news piece. However, this initial sentiment can sometimes be misleading or overly simplistic. Introductions provide the necessary context and elaboration that can either reinforce or recalibrate the sentiment conveyed by the headline. This dynamic underscores the necessity of a dual-faceted analysis as discrepancies between headline and introduction sentiments can lead to varied interpretations and emotional responses from readers. Studies have demonstrated that while headlines may exhibit a trend toward negativity to enhance virility, the accompanying introductions often present a more balanced perspective, mitigating potential biases introduced by the headline. Therefore, a comprehensive examination of both components is imperative for an accurate assessment of the news content's overall sentiment and its potential influence on public perception.

Table 10: Overview of Sentiment Alignment between News Headlines and Introductions (Indonesia)

Category	*Number of News Items*	*Percentage of Total*
Total news items	81	100%
Headlines and introductions with different sentiments	20	24.70%

The study examines sentiment alignment between headlines and introductions across 81 news items, revealing key insights into their consistency and implications. Of the total, 20 news items (about 24.7 per cent) show a mismatch between headline and introduction sentiments, indicating that in roughly a quarter of cases, the headline's initial tone doesn't fully reflect the introduction (Table 10).

Table 11: Breakdown of News Items with Positive Headlines (Indonesia)

Category	*Number of News Items*	*Percentage of Total (31)*
Total with positive headlines	31	100%
Introductions with different sentiments	6	19.4%
• Introductions with apprehensive sentiments	2	6.5%
• Introductions with negative sentiments	0	0
• Introductions with neutral sentiments	4	12.9%

Specifically, 31 news items (38.3 per cent) feature positive headlines, and within this group, six (19.4 per cent) have introductions that diverge from positivity, two (6.5 per cent) shift to an apprehensive tone, suggesting caution or worry, while four (12.9 per cent) adopt a neutral tone, diluting the headline's optimism (Table 11). This leaves 25 of the 31 positive-headline items with introductions likely aligning with their upbeat headlines. The prevalence of positive headlines is notable, yet the 19.4 per cent shift in the introductions' tone could influence reader perception, with apprehensive introductions signalling concern and neutral ones reducing emotional impact. Overall, the data suggests a pattern where some news items use positive headlines to grab attention but temper them with cautious or neutral introductions, seen in 20 of 81 cases, including six of the 31 positive-headline items, possibly reflecting editorial tactics like clickbait or nuanced storytelling. This inconsistency might affect how readers interpret or trust the news, highlighting a tension between engagement and accuracy in sentiment presentation.

The study looks at 22 news items with negative headlines. It shows how headlines and introductions communicate with different sentiments. According to the framing theory media shapes how we see things.

Table 12: Breakdown of News Items with Negative Headlines (Indonesia)

Category	*Number of News Items*	*Percentage of Negative Headlines (22)*
Total with negative headlines	22	100%
Introductions with different sentiments	3	13.6%
• Introductions with positive connotation	1	4.5%
• Introductions with neutral sentiments	1	4.5%
• Introductions with apprehensive sentiments	1	4.5%

Table 13: Breakdown of Introduction Sentiments for Apprehensive Headlines (Indonesia)

Category	*Items*	*Percentage of Apprehensive Headlines*
Total with apprehensive headlines	13	100%
Introductions with different sentiments	7	53.80%
• Introductions with positive sentiments	2	15.4%
• Introductions with negative sentiments	3	23.10%
• Introductions with neutral sentiments	2	15.40%

Here, 22 headlines are negative. But three introductions (13.6 per cent) don't match them. Among these three introductions, one introduction is positive (4.5 per cent), one is neutral (4.5 per cent) and one is with an apprehensive connotation (Table 12). Negative headlines grab attention. A positive introduction softens the story. A neutral introduction lowers the urgency. An apprehensive introduction adds caution. Usually, media picks what we focus on. Negative headlines push worry or crisis. The three different introductions shift that focus. Most of the time gatekeeping means editors choose the tone. Negative headlines hook readers whereas positive introductions balance sensationalism. Audience reception matters too. A negative headline with a positive introduction can confuse people. A neutral introduction weakens the headline's pull. This feels like clickbait in print. Negative headlines draw eyes. The three odd introductions add nuance. Headlines set the mood. Introductions tweak it. This shows how print media plays with perception. It balances grabbing readers and keeping trust.

This enquiry probes the ontological dissonance between apprehensive headlines and their introspective counterparts across 13 news items, unveiling a profound rupture in the epistemic flow of print media discourse. The communication process in print media relies on a clear, cohesive flow from headline to introduction to convey a message effectively. Headlines act as the initial signal, setting the tone and expectation, while introductions provide context and elaboration. When sentiments differ between them, as seen in the studyed 13 news items with apprehensive headlines. The empirical data reveals that out of 13 apprehensive headlines (suggesting caution, unease or tension), seven introductions (53.8 per cent) diverge: two are positive (15.4 per cent), three are negative (23.1 per cent) and two are neutral (15.4 per cent) (Table 13). This misalignment creates several disruptions.

An apprehensive headline primes readers for uncertainty or concern. A positive introduction (two cases) contradicts this, jarring the audience with an unexpected shift to optimism. The three negative introductions against apprehensive headlines amplify negativity beyond the initial caution, potentially overwhelming readers because this phenomenon shifts from measured worry to outright alarm, breaking the emotional buildup and risking desensitisation or distrust if the tone feels inconsistent. The two neutral introductions flatten the apprehensive headline's urgency. Moreover, this shift of sentiment strips the story of its emotional weight, disrupting the communication flow. Readers may feel misled or disengaged when the introduction fails to match the headline's intensity.

In communication theory, 'noise' is anything that distorts the sender's message. Here, seven out of the 13 introductions (53.8 per cent) introduce noise by clashing with the headline's apprehensive sentiment. This high rate of disruption, over half of the sample, suggests a breakdown in encoding (editorial intent) and decoding (reader interpretation), as the mixed signals obscure the story's core message. Consistent sentiment reinforces reliability in print media. When two introductions turn positive, three go negative and two become neutral against apprehensive headlines, readers might question the outlet's authority or suspect sensationalism (e.g., exaggerated headlines softened or intensified in introductions). This erodes trust, a critical element of the communication process. Readers process headlines quickly, forming instant impressions. The seven divergent introductions force a mental recalibration, positive ones defy caution, negative ones escalate it and neutral ones mute it, adding cognitive load. This can lead to misinterpretation (e.g., missing the nuance) or abandonment of the article if the disruption feels manipulative.

In this study of 15 news items with neutral headlines, the introductions display varying sentiments. The communication process involves a sender (news outlet) encoding a message (headline and introduction) for a receiver (reader) to decode. Fifteen news items feature neutral headlines, implying an objective, unemotional tone, but four introductions (26.7 per cent) diverge: three are positive (20 per cent), one is apprehensive (6.7 per cent) and none are negative. This misalignment disrupts the process of communication (Table 14).

Neutral headlines signal impartiality, setting a baseline expectation. A positive introduction (three cases) shifts to optimism, while an apprehensive introduction (one case) injects unease. This creates 'noise', a distortion between the sender's intent and the receiver's interpretation, breaking the seamless transmission of meaning. Readers rely on headlines for quick understanding. The four divergent introductions force a reinterpretation, potentially confusing or engaging readers differently. Positive introductions may uplift, while apprehensive ones risk undermining the neutral frame, affecting trust or attention. Inconsistent sentiments could alter reader feedback (e.g., scepticism or curiosity), influencing how newsrooms adjust future messaging.

Table 14: Breakdown of Introduction Sentiments for Neutral Headlines (Indonesia)

Category	*Items*	*Percentage of Neutral Headlines*
Total with neutral headlines	15	100%
Introductions with different sentiments	4	26.70%
• Introductions with positive sentiments	3	20.00%
• Introductions with apprehensive sentiments	1	06.70%
• Introductions with negative sentiments	0	00.00%

Headlines are often written last or by sub-editors, aiming for brevity and impact (here, neutrality). Introductions, penned earlier by reporters, carry more narrative weight. The four mismatches (26.7 per cent) suggest adisconnect between these stages, reporters adding sentiment (positive or apprehensive) which sub-editors strip from headlines, disrupting the unified story arc. Editors act as gatekeepers, balancing raw reporting with publication goals. The shift to positive introductions (three cases) might reflect a push for reader appeal, while the apprehensive introduction (one case) could signal caution amid uncertainty, showing how gatekeeping tweaks the process (Table 14).

The mismatch between the sentiments expressed in news headlines and those conveyed in the introductory paragraphs of the news articles presents a significant challenge to effective communication. Headlines are designed to encapsulate the essence of a news item in a succinct, attention-grabbing manner, often employing emotionally charged or sensational language to attract readers. However, when the first paragraph, the introduction, exhibits a sentiment that diverges from the headline, it creates a communicative dissonance that can lead to misinterpretation of the news content. This incongruence not only disrupts the clarity of the message but also undermines the credibility of the news organisation, suggesting an arbitrary and potentially strategic manipulation of the news narrative. This phenomenon invites scrutiny into the editorial practices and underlying motivations within newsrooms. It raises critical questions about the balance between attracting readership and maintaining journalistic integrity. When headlines and introductions are misaligned, they contribute to a distorted understanding of events, as the emotive appeal of the headline may override the nuanced context provided in the body of the text. It challenges readers to critically assess the information presented and underscores the importance of engaging with the full spectrum of the news article rather than relying solely on the initial impression offered by the headline. In essence, ensuring congruency between the headline and the introductory content is not merely a matter of stylistic coherence, it is crucial for the preservation of trust in the media, effective public communication and the overall transparency of the news production process.

Qualitative Analysis of News Headlines

The analysis of varied news headlines reveals how the choice of wording and framing sets distinct tones and sentiments, ranging from negative and apprehensive to positive and inviting. Each headline, published by different media outlets on specific dates, employs particular language constructs that influence how audiences perceive the news.

News Item: 1

At Least 261 Dead in India's Worst Train Accident in Over Two Decades

Editor
Laila Afifa

June 3, 2023 | 10:26 pm

A headline from *Tempo English* dated June 3, 2023, "At Least 261 Dead in India's Worst Train Accident in Over Two Decades" (News Item 1) , is a clear example of negative framing. Key phrases such as 'at least', 'worst' and 'over two decades' not only quantify the tragedy but also emphasise its historical severity. By invoking a long timeframe and underscoring the magnitude of the accident, the wording intensifies the sense of systemic failure and crisis, evoking strong feelings of alarm, outrage and national grief. This deliberate choice of language shifts the story from a neutral report to one that resonates deeply with the audience's sense of loss and urgency.

News Item: 2

India Launches Rocket to Study the Sun

Editor
Laila Afifa

September 3, 2023 | 01:13 am

In contrast, another *Tempo English* headline from September 3, 2023, "India Launches Rocket to Study the Sun" (News Item 2), presents the news with a distinctly positive tone. Here, the focus is on progress and achievement. The act of launching a rocket is associated with technological prowess and ambition, conveying a narrative of advancement and scientific curiosity. The news emphasises a peaceful mission aimed at expanding humanity's knowledge of the sun, fostering national pride and reinforcing a positive image of India's capabilities on the global stage.

News Item: 3

Why India Risks a Quantum Tech Brain Drain

Editor
Petir Garda Bhwana

July 30, 2023 | 09:22 am

A third example from *Tempo English*, published on July 30, 2023, with the headline "Why India Risks a Quantum Tech Brain Drain" (News Item 3), introduces an element of apprehension. The use of the word 'risks' signals a potential vulnerability, while the term 'brain drain' implies a concerning loss of skilled professionals in a critical technological field. This headline is laden with anxiety as it warns of future challenges in the domains of national security and economic competitiveness. The apprehensive tone here is a call for urgent strategic measures to prevent long-term adverse effects in a rapidly evolving area of technology.

News Item: 4

Featured | Food & Drink

Savour the Holistic Indian Culture at Kalture

by Razi Faruqi Pasha July 13, 2023

Indian cuisine is a vibrant tapestry of flavours, where every dish tells a story and every bite is a journey to the heart of culinary artistry.

I've finally got a chance to have a tasty experience at one of the well-known Indian restaurants in Jakarta, Kalture Resto & Club. This is the very first time I visit an Indian restaurant, in particular this one. The first thing that comes to my mind when I visit Kalture is the lavishness. This restaurant is located on the R floor of BTPN Tower in the Mega Kuningan area, which is one of the reputable business districts in Jakarta. The whole floor is specialised only for Kalture.

Moving to a different context, a news item from *Indonesia expat* on July 13, 2023, "Savour the Holistic Indian Culture at Kalture" (News Item 4), employs an entirely positive and promotional tone. The word 'savour' suggests a pleasurable, immersive experience, while 'holistic' conveys completeness and depth in cultural representation. The emphasis on celebrating Indian culture through appealing and emotionally rich language invites readers to appreciate and indulge in an experience that is both authentic and uplifting. The absence of negative language in this headline further reinforces its inviting and celebratory nature.

News Item: 5

WORLD • ASIA & PACIFIC

Maldives election may be key for China, India rivalry

Home to about 521,000 people, the Maldives is famous for its sun-kissed atolls and luxury tourist resorts but the rival Asian giants have both invested millions of dollars in infrastructure in the islands as they seek to build goodwill and influence.

Mohamed Junayd (Reuters)

Male • Wed, September 6, 2023

Lastly, two headlines from *The Jakarta Post* offer insights into geopolitical tensions with an apprehensive undertone. The headline dated September 6, 2023, "Maldives Election May Be Key for China, India Rivalry" (News Item 5), frames a democratic process within the context of strategic rivalry. The suggestion that the Maldives could be drawn into a tug-of-war between China and India introduces uncertainty and concern over the erosion of sovereignty and regional stability.

News Item: 6

TheJakartaPost

Xi, Modi hold rare sit-down for China-India border talks

Chinese President Xi Jinping and Indian Prime Minister Narendra Modi held "candid and in-depth" talks to ease tensions along their disputed frontier, Beijing said on Friday, after a rare face-to-face encounter between the two leaders.

Andre Arditya (The Jakarta Post)
Beijing • Sat, August 26, 2023

Similarly, the August 26, 2023, headline, "Xi, Modi Hold Rare Sit-Down for China–India Border Talks" (News Item 6), uses the adjective 'rare' to imply that such high-level engagements are exceptional, hinting at underlying tensions and historical mistrust. Both headlines underscore an atmosphere of caution and scepticism, reflecting a broader narrative of geopolitical instability and unresolved conflicts.

Overall, these examples illustrate that the sentiment behind a news headline is intricately linked to the specific language and framing adopted by the reporter. While some headlines stimulate confidence, pride and optimism through celebratory language and a focus on achievement, others invoke alarm and apprehension by emphasising tragedy, risk or geopolitical tension. This comprehensive analysis underscores the power of words in shaping public perception and highlights the nuanced interplay between language and sentiment in journalism.

Qualitative Analysis of Discrepancies and Contradictions between Headlines and Introductions in News Articles

The relationship between a news article's headline and its introductory paragraph (introduction) is critical in shaping readers' initial perceptions of a story. Headlines often aim to capture attention with concise, emotive or sensational language, while introductions provide context and detail, setting the tone for the article. However, discrepancies in tone, sentiment or emphasis between the two can lead to contradictions, potentially misleading readers or skewing their interpretation of the news. This analysis examines five news articles from *The Jakarta Post*, *Tempo English* and *Indonesia expat*, published between May and October 2023, to explore the qualitative differences and contradictions between their headlines and introductions. Each case highlights how the framing of the headline contrasts with the introductory paragraph, affecting the conveyed sentiment and reader perception.

News Item: 7

TheJakartaPost

NEWS • INDONESIA

Biden, Modi salute 'defining relationship' as US bets big on India

Shaun Tandon and Aurelia End (Agence France-Presse) (The Jakarta Post)
Washington • Sat, June 24, 2023

United States President Joe Biden and Indian Prime Minister Narendra Modi said on Thursday that the two democracies' partnership would define the next century, as Washington eyes a counterweight to China and brushes off allegations of growing authoritarianism in New Delhi.

The Jakarta Post, in its June 24, 2023, edition, published a positively toned article headlined: "Biden, Modi Salute 'Defining Relationship' As US Bets Big on India" (News Item 7). The headline conveys optimism, emphasising mutual respect and strong cooperation between the U.S. President Joe Biden and Indian Prime Minister Narendra Modi. The phrase 'defining relationship' underscores the strategic importance of U.S.–India ties, while 'bets big on India' suggests confidence in India's potential and America's commitment to the partnership. The tone is celebratory, framing the alliance as a forward-looking, mutually beneficial endeavour. The introduction of that news items is "United States President Joe Biden and Indian Prime Minister Narendra Modi said on Thursday that the two democracies' partnership would define the next century, as Washington eyes a counterweight to China and brushes off allegations of growing authoritarianism in New Delhi". The introduction, while echoing the headline's focus on a transformative partnership, introduces underlying tensions. The reference to countering China reveals geopolitical anxieties, framing the partnership as a strategic manoeuvre rather than purely cooperative. Furthermore, the phrase 'brushes off allegations of growing authoritarianism in New Delhi' injects unease, suggesting that the U.S. is compromising ethical concerns for geopolitical gains. This duality, hopeful rhetoric alongside strategic and moral ambiguities, creates an apprehensive tone. This creates a contradiction, as the headline projects unqualified optimism while the introduction reveals a more cautious, layered narrative, potentially leading readers to overestimate the harmony of the U.S.–India partnership.

The *Jakarta Post* reported on August 24, 2023, with a negative sentiment that "India Set to Ban Sugar Exports for First Time in 7 Years" (News Item 8).

News Item: 8

TheJakartaPost

India set to ban sugar exports for first time in 7 years

Rajendra Jadhav and Mayank Bhardwaj (Reuters)

Mumbai and New Delhi • Thu, August 24, 2023

India is expected to ban mills from exporting sugar in the next season beginning October, halting shipments for the first time in seven years, as a lack of rain has cut cane yields, three government sources said.

The headline carries a negative tone, signalling a disruption in India's sugar industry. The word 'ban' suggests a drastic measure, implying domestic shortages due to poor harvests or environmental pressures. It also hints at adverse impacts on farmers, exporters and global sugar markets, framing the decision as a crisis with far-reaching consequences. The introduction of this news items says that "India is expected to ban mills from exporting sugar in the next season beginning October, halting shipments for the first time in seven years, as a lack of rain has cut cane yields, three government sources said". The introduction reframes the ban as a pragmatic and responsible decision driven by environmental necessity, insufficient rainfall reducing cane yields, rather than protectionism or mismanagement. By emphasising the need to ensure domestic sugar availability and price stability, the introduction portrays the government's action as a measured response prioritising consumer welfare, thus casting it in a positive light.

The headline's alarmist tone contrasts sharply with the introduction's contextual justification. The headline's negative framing suggests a crisis without explaining the rationale, while the introduction highlights the ban's necessity and governance-driven intent. This contradiction risks misleading readers into viewing the policy as detrimental, whereas the introduction underscores its protective, strategic nature, reflecting disconnect in how the issue's severity is communicated.

The Jakarta Post's September 6, 2023, headline, *"Maldives Election May Be Key for China, India Rivalry"* (News Item 9), conveys an apprehensive sentiment, reflecting concern over escalating geopolitical tensions in the region.

News Item: 9

TheJakartaPost

WORLD • ASIA & PACIFIC

Maldives election may be key for China, India rivalry

Mohamed Junayd (Reuters)
Male • Wed, September 6, 2023

A presidential election in the Maldives on Saturday could be decisive in determining whether China or India win a competition for influence over the tiny Indian Ocean island chain.

The headline conveys apprehension by framing the Maldives election as a pivotal event in the China–India geopolitical rivalry. The word 'key' suggests high stakes and 'rivalry' evokes tension, implying that the election's outcome could disrupt regional stability or shift power dynamics in the Indian Ocean, fostering uncertainty about its implications. The introduction of this news items is "A presidential election in the Maldives on Saturday could be decisive in determining whether China or India win a competition for influence over the tiny Indian Ocean island chain". This introduction adopts a factual, balanced tone, objectively describing the election's potential to influence China–India competition. Phrases like 'could be decisive' and 'competition for influence' are descriptive rather than emotive, avoiding judgment about the outcome or its desirability. This neutrality contrasts with the headline's anxious undertone. This discrepancy may lead readers to anticipate greater tension than the introduction warrants, highlighting a contradiction in emotional framing.

News Item: 10

Why India Can Afford to Wait and Watch Before Regulating AI

Editor
Petir Garda Bhwana

July 31, 2023 | 06:15 am

India should not rush with a "comprehensive" law that might become outdated quickly.

India's position on regulating AI has swung between extremes – from no regulation to regulation based on a "risk-based, no-harm" approach.

In April this year, the Indian government said it would not regulate AI to help create an enabling, pro-innovation environment which could possibly catapult India to global leadership in AI-related tech.

The *Tempo English* article dated July 31, 2023, titled "Why India Can Afford to Wait and Watch Before Regulating AI" (News Item 10), conveys a positive sentiment toward India's measured approach to AI regulation. The headline conveys confidence in India's strategic patience regarding AI regulation. The phrase 'can afford' suggests a position of strength, framing India's cautious approach as a deliberate choice to learn from global experiences and avoid premature policies. The tone is optimistic, portraying India's strategy as thoughtful and advantageous. The introduction of this news items reads, "India should not rush with a 'comprehensive' law that might become outdated quickly. India's position on regulating AI has swung between extremes – from no regulation to regulation based on a 'risk-based, no-harm' approach". The introduction expresses caution about rushing into AI regulation, highlighting the risk of outdated laws due to rapid technological change. It also notes inconsistency in India's regulatory stance, suggesting uncertainty and a lack of clear direction. This apprehensive tone underscores potential pitfalls, contrasting with the headline's confidence. The headline implies a deliberate strategy, while the introduction reveals underlying uncertainties, creating a contradiction that may confuse readers about whether India's approach is proactive or reactive.

News Item: 11

Featured News

Two Indian Nationals Arrested at Bali Airport in Connection to Murder Case

by Indonesia Expat May 15, 2023

I Gusti Ngurah Rai Airport Police have arrested two Indian nationals, with the initials AS (21) and GS (24) under suspicion of murder.

A man with the initials FRF (39), from Jakarta, was found dead covered in blood in a house located in Sanur, South Denpasar, Bali, on Saturday, 13th May 2023 around 10.30am.

The two foreigners were arrested later that day, at around midnight at the departure terminal of I Gusti Ngurah Rai Airport, Bali.

The *Indonesia expat* article published on May 15, 2023, titled "Two Indian Nationals Arrested at Bali Airport in Connection to Murder Case" (News Item 11), conveys a negative sentiment. The headline carries a negative tone by linking Indian nationals to a serious crime, murder, evoking fear and suspicion. Words like 'arrested' and 'murder case' are alarming and by highlighting the suspects' nationality the headline risks casting a negative shadow on India's image, reinforcing stereotypes and public unease. The introduction of this news item says, "I Gusti Ngurah Rai Airport Police have arrested two Indian nationals, with the initials AS (21) and GS (24) under suspicion of murder. A man with the initials FRF (39), from Jakarta, was found dead covered in blood in a house located in Sanur, South Denpasar, Bali, on Saturday, 13th May 2023 around 10.30am. The two foreigners were arrested later that day, at around midnight at the departure terminal of I Gusti Ngurah Rai Airport, Bali". The introduction presents the incident factually, detailing the arrests, victim and circumstances without emotive language or assumptions of guilt. Its formal, objective tone avoids sensationalism, allowing readers to interpret the event based on verifiable details, contrasting with the headline's negative framing. The headline's negative sentiment, driven by its focus on crime and nationality, contrasts with the introduction's neutral, fact-based reporting. The headline's alarming tone risks prejudicing readers against the suspects and their nationality, while the introduction maintains impartiality, creating a contradiction that may skew initial perceptions of the incident's gravity.

Analytical Synthesis

Across these cases, the discrepancies between headlines and introductions reveal a pattern of tonal and thematic misalignment. Headlines, designed to attract attention, often amplify emotional resonance, whether positive or apprehensive. Introductions, tasked with providing context, tend to adopt more nuanced or neutral tones, unpacking complexities that the headlines omit or oversimplify. This misalignment can mislead readers, as headlines shape first impressions that the introductions may contradict or reframe.

India in ASEAN Media: Study of Malaysia

This empirical study examines the coverage of India-related news in three prominent Malaysian English-language newspapers, *The Star, New Straits Times* and *Malay Mail*, over a six-month period from May 1 to October 31, 2023. With a total of 804 news items analysed, this research seeks to explore several key dimensions of news reporting: the prioritisation of India-related content, the sourcing patterns of information and the sentiment conveyed in headlines and introductory segments (leads). Through systematic content analysis, we aim to uncover patterns that define India's representation in Malaysian English-language dailies, providing a foundation for further discourse on media objectivity and cross-border reportage.

Table 15: Malaysia's Top News Categories Related to India

Category of News Topic Wise	*Number of News Items*	*Percentage*
Domestic Politics	68	8.45%
Terrorism/Law & Order	49	6.09%
Global Economy and India	121	15.04%
India's Economy	148	18.40%
Bilateral Relations	69	8.58%
Geopolitics and India	167	20.77%
Climate Disaster	57	7.08%
Governance/Accident	74	9.20%
Science and Technology	40	4.97%
Cultural/ Miscellaneous	21	2.61%
TOTAL	804	100%

Table 16: Malaysia's Top Five News Categories Related to India

Category of News Topic Wise	*Number of News Items*	*Percentage*
Geopolitics and India	167	20.77%
India's Economy	148	18.40%
Global Economy and India	121	15.04%
Governance/Accident	74	9.20%
Bilateral Relations	69	8.58%

The data from the study offers in Table 15 a detailed quantitative breakdown of how India was represented in the online editions of three major Malaysian newspapers, *The Star*, *New Straits Times* and *Malay Mail* between May 1 and October 31, 2024. In the 804 news items analysed, the coverage was categorised into 10 distinct thematic areas, revealing clear patterns in the Malaysian media's portrayal of India. The most dominant category was Geopolitics and India, which accounted for 20.77 per cent (167 news items), indicating a strong emphasis on India's strategic positioning in regional and global affairs. This was closely followed by India's Economic at 18.40 per cent (148 items), reflecting significant interest in India's economic policies, growth trends and market dynamics. The third most-covered topic was Global Economy and India at 15.04 per cent (121 items), suggesting that Malaysian media frequently contextualised India within broader international economic discussions.

Other notable categories included Governance/Accident (9.20 per cent, 74 items), which likely covered domestic Indian governance issues, policy decisions or notable incidents, and Bilateral Relations (8.58 per cent, 69 items), highlighting diplomatic engagements between India and Malaysia or other nations. Domestic Politics (8.45 per cent, 68 items) also received moderate attention, pointing to coverage of India's internal political developments, elections or party dynamics. In contrast, topics such as Terrorism/Law & Order (6.09 per cent, 49 items) and Climate Disaster (7.08 per cent, 57 items) were less prominent, suggesting that while security and environmental issues were reported, they were not central to the narrative. The categories with the least coverage were Science and Technology (4.97 per cent, 40 items) and Cultural/Miscellaneous (2.61 per cent, 21 items), indicating that India's technological advancements, cultural exchanges or softer news stories received minimal attention compared to its political and economic dimensions.

This distribution underscores a clear editorial prioritisation in Malaysian newspapers, where India's geopolitical influence and economic activities dominated the news cycle, while other aspects remained peripheral. The data suggests that Malaysian media primarily framed India as a significant player in global and regional affairs, with its economic and political developments taking precedence over social, cultural or scientific narratives. Such a trend may reflect Malaysia's own strategic interests in India as an economic partner and geopolitical actor, as well as the broader newsworthiness of these themes in international reporting. The limited coverage of cultural or technological topics, however, indicates a potential gap in representing the multifaceted nature of India's global engagement. Overall, the findings provide a structured insight into how Indian-related content was curated and emphasised in Malaysian digital news platforms during the observed period.

The data from this study also reveals critical insights into the sourcing patterns and structural dynamics that shape the representation of India in the online editions of prominent Malaysian newspapers.

Table 17: News Source Analysis (Malaysia)

Total News Items	804	100%
News coverage by reporters/news desk/editorial/op-eds	153	19.02%
News coverage by international agencies/national agencies/freelancers/contributors	651	80.97%

Out of the total 804 news items related to India, a significant majority of 651 items (80.97 per cent) were produced by external contributors such as international agencies, national agencies, freelance journalists and other external sources (However, the study also reveals that international news agencies heavily dominate the coverage, with most being American or European, such as AP from the U.S., Reuters from the UK and AFP from France.), while only 153 items (19.02 per cent) originated from in-house staff including reporters, news desks, editorial teams and op-ed writers (Table 17). This distribution suggests a pronounced reliance on externally sourced content for news coverage about India, indicating that Malaysian media's portrayal of India is predominantly mediated through global or third-party narratives rather than through locally generated, independent journalistic enquiry. The dominance of external inputs may result in a framing of India's geopolitical, economic and sociocultural activities that mirrors broader international media trends or agency-driven agendas, potentially limiting the scope for context-specific and locally anchored interpretations. The relatively low proportion of in-house contributions may reflect practical constraints related to resource allocation and the globalised nature of news dissemination, yet it also risks homogenising the narrative by concentrating on high-impact, event-driven reporting at the expense of deeper, regionally nuanced analyses. This dual narrative framework, characterised by the efficiency and breadth of external sourcing and the limited presence of domestically produced, context-sensitive journalism, intersects with media dependency and agenda-setting theories, wherein the perceptions of India among Malaysian audiences are shaped more by transnational news flows than by locally contextualised insights. Consequently, the data underscores the need for further examination of how such sourcing structures influence the plurality, authenticity and depth of public discourse concerning India in Southeast Asian media ecosystems.

Table 18: Sentiment Analysis of Positive News (Malaysia)

Positive news articles out of a total of 804 news articles	276	34.32%
Positive stories by reporters/news desk/opinion	64	23.18%
Positive stories by international agencies/national agencies/freelancers/contributors	211	76.44%

Table 19: Sentiment Analysis of Negative News (Malaysia)

Negative news articles out of a total of 804 news articles	232	28.85%
Negative stories by reporters/news desk/opinion	37	15.94%
Negative stories by international agencies/national agencies/freelancers/contributors	195	84.05%

Table 20: Sentiment Analysis of Apprehensive and Neutral News (Malaysia)

Number of apprehensive news items out of a total of 804 news items	112	13.93%
Number of neutral news items out of a total of 804 news items	184	22.88%

The representation of India in Malaysian online version of three top newspapers, as reflected in the provided dataset, highlights significant trends in the intersection of communication, international news flow and diplomacy. A total of 804 news items about India appeared during the study period. Among these, 276 articles, accounting for 34.32 per cent, featured positive headlines, whereas 232 articles, or 28.85 per cent, had negative headlines (Tables 18 and 19). Additionally, 112 articles, representing 13.93 per cent, were categorised as apprehensive in tone and 184 articles, or 22.88 per cent, were classified as neutral in nature based on their headlines (Table 20). While positive news coverage slightly outweighs the negative, the presence of apprehensive headlines adds a critical dimension to understanding the nature of India's representation. Apprehensive headlines though not explicitly negative, tend to frame stories with uncertainty, speculation or concern, often raising questions or doubts. This framing can subtly influence public perception by creating a sense of unease or mistrust, thereby placing India in a potentially unfavourable or ambiguous light.

To further unpack the nature of these apprehensive headlines, it is important to consider their narrative tone. Unlike overtly negative headlines, which clearly criticise or condemn, apprehensive headlines often ask questions, suggest risks or imply potential controversy. This can leave the reader in a state of interpretive uncertainty, subtly leading to a negative or sceptical impression. Thus, even without taking a definitive stance, such headlines may contribute to the erosion of positive perception or confidence. In terms of communication impact, apprehensive news items function in the space between neutrality and negativity, and their psychological effect can lean more towards the latter.

A closer analysis of content sourcing further deepens our understanding of this representational dynamic. Of the 276 positive news articles, only 64 (23.18 per cent) were written by Malaysian reporters or produced by in-house editorial desks. A majority, 211 articles or 76.44 per cent, were sourced from international or national agencies, including freelancers and contributors, largely represented by global wire services such as AP, AFP and Reuters. Similarly, in the case of negative news coverage, only 37 items (15.94 per cent) were domestically produced, while 195 articles (84.05 per cent) were supplied by external news providers.

This heavy reliance on foreign wire services to construct the narrative about India reveals an asymmetrical international communication flow, wherein global media actors significantly shape public understanding of foreign states. For Malaysia, this dependence may reflect limited resources or editorial prioritisation for on ground reporting on Indian affairs. For India, however, the consequences are more profound. The portrayal of India in Malaysian media is being shaped largely by third-party sources that operate outside the bilateral sphere. As a result, India's image abroad, even in a regionally proximate and diplomatically significant country like Malaysia, becomes vulnerable to distortions, oversimplifications or misrepresentations that arise from external framing. In terms of diplomacy and strategic communication, this situation underscores the importance for India to not only engage directly with the host-country's media but also to understand and navigate the wider international media ecosystem that shapes perceptions.

It seems evident that while positive and negative headlines are straightforward in their messaging, apprehensive headlines occupy a complex and often under-examined space in the discourse of international communication. Their subtle framing of doubt and uncertainty has the potential to leave lasting impressions, particularly when repeated across multiple reports. We will try to understand and explain this issue qualitatively further. When coupled with the predominance of international news sourcing, this creates a representational environment where India's image is mediated not just through direct content, but through nuanced narratives of ambiguity and concern. Recognising and addressing the implications of such framing is essential for both host-country media systems seeking to assert editorial independence and foreign policy actors aiming to shape global perception through informed public diplomacy.

Decoding India–Malaysia News Coverage: Priorities and Reasons

The representation of India in Malaysian online newspapers, based on an analysis of 804 news items, highlights several critical conceptual and theoretical challenges for India's public diplomacy and strategic communication efforts in Southeast Asia, particularly in Malaysia. The distribution of headlines, 34.32 per cent positive, 28.85 per cent negative, 13.93 per cent apprehensive and 22.88 per cent neutral, reveals a nuanced media environment. Notably, the presence of apprehensive headlines, which suggest uncertainty, speculation or concern, adds a complex layer to India's image construction. Drawing on the media framing theory, it becomes evident that even without overt criticism, apprehensive tones can subtly undermine positive perceptions by fostering scepticism or unease among readers.

This framing challenge is compounded by the overwhelming reliance on international wire services such as AP, AFP and Reuters. This heavy dependence reveals a pronounced asymmetry in international communication flow, where narratives about India are shaped predominantly by external, often Western, sources rather than local or regional voices. Theories of global communication highlight how such asymmetrical flows distort the portrayal of foreign states, undermining India's efforts to project a consistent and favourable image abroad.

This external mediation of India's image creates significant vulnerability for India's soft power, as conceptualised by Joseph Nye. India's ability to influence perceptions is weakened not only by external distortions but also by Malaysian media's pursuit of editorial independence, which may resist foreign-influenced narratives to safeguard domestic credibility. Furthermore, the agenda-setting theory suggests that the psychological effect of apprehensive framing can prioritise concerns about India within the Malaysian public's consciousness, making anxiety or doubt about India more salient in public discourse. Over time, the cultivation theory warns that repeated exposure to such ambiguous narratives could reinforce and normalise sceptical attitudes toward India, potentially solidifying unfavourable perceptions that are difficult to reverse.

The situation is further exacerbated by structural constraints within the Malaysian media landscape. Media ownership is concentrated among a few conglomerates, leading to editorial prioritisation of domestic issues over sustained international reporting. This limited space for organic, in-depth coverage of India further reduces opportunities for balanced narrative-building. Consequently, Malaysia's understanding of India often remains shallow and externally framed, limiting the effectiveness of India's public diplomacy and cultural engagement efforts.

Given these challenges, India's strategic communication approach must become more multilayered and proactive. It is essential to engage not only with Malaysian journalists and media houses but also with the global wire services that dominate international news narratives. Monitoring media portrayals, providing timely clarifications and building long-term partnerships with Southeast Asian media actors will also be critical. Recognising the interconnectedness of global media ecosystems and the psychological dynamics of news framing is essential for India to navigate misrepresentations, strengthen its public diplomacy and enhance its regional influence in Southeast Asia. In essence, the intersection of asymmetrical information flows, subtle psychological framing effects and systemic media constraints calls for a strategic recalibration of India's public diplomacy to effectively manage and shape favourable public perceptions in a competitive international environment.

India in Malaysian News Ecosystem: Geopolitical Emphasis, Economic Narratives and the Underrepresentation of Bilateral Ties

The data related to representation of India in this study offers a valuable window into the evolving patterns of diplomatic perception, media framing and bilateral engagement between India and Malaysia. The overall trend suggests that India is predominantly portrayed through the prisms of geopolitics, economic growth and global economic participation, reflecting Malaysia's broader strategic interests and sensitivities to global power shifts. This framing is consistent with Malaysia's emphasis on regional stability, economic partnerships and active engagement with major actors in the Indo–Pacific region, as well as its positioning within ASEAN and other multilateral forums.

Notably, while India's growing prominence on the international stage is recognised, the relatively limited coverage of direct India–Malaysia bilateral relations signals a potential area of concern. The bilateral dimension, while present, is overshadowed by broader geopolitical narratives, suggesting that India's diplomatic efforts to highlight specific areas of cooperation, such as trade, technology partnerships, defence collaboration and cultural exchanges, may not be receiving proportional media attention. Similarly, coverage of India's cultural influence and technological advancements remains minimal, indicating an underutilisation of India's considerable soft power resources.

The thematic prioritisation observed in the dataset, where coverage overwhelmingly concentrates on India's geopolitical activities, economic reforms and position within the global economy, suggests a selective interest in aspects of India's rise that are most immediately relevant to Malaysia's own foreign policy and economic imperatives. The relatively moderate attention given to governance issues and domestic political developments further underscores that internal Indian affairs are considered less critical unless they bear significant regional or global consequences. The implications for India's public diplomacy in Malaysia are therefore profound. There is a pressing need to strengthen narratives around bilateral cooperation, making achievements in trade, education, tourism and defence more visible and relatable to Malaysian audiences. Soft power diplomacy must be reinvigorated by leveraging cultural heritage, cinema, cuisine and historical ties, thus making India's presence more tangible in Malaysian public life beyond the realm of strategic or economic analysis. In addition, addressing apprehensive or occasionally negative framings through timely clarifications, positive counter-narratives and targeted media campaigns would contribute significantly to safeguarding and enhancing India's image, and given Malaysia's strategic location within Southeast Asia and its importance as a partner in India's Act East Policy and Indo–Pacific initiatives, the ability to shape public perceptions in Malaysia acquires even greater significance. A more comprehensive and sustained media engagement strategy, combining traditional diplomacy, cultural outreach, economic messaging and local media empowerment, would not only serve to balance the current thematic skew but also reinforce the long-term foundations of India's bilateral relationship with Malaysia. Such an approach would ensure that India's evolving global role is perceived not merely through the lens of hard power and economic metrics but as a complex, dynamic and culturally resonant partner within Malaysia and the wider Southeast Asian region.

Analysing News Sentiment (Headlines) and Contextualisation of Sentiments of News toward India in Malaysian Media

The analysis of sentiments of Malaysian media coverage concerning India suggests that while Malaysia's communication environment is inclined towards fostering cooperative diplomatic ties with India, there remains a significant undercurrent of cautious or ambiguous framing that could potentially complicate the perception of India among Malaysian audiences. Positive headlines often emphasise India's economic reforms, technological achievements, international engagements and contributions to regional stability, aligning with the liberal international relations theory, which emphasises the importance of interdependence, diplomacy and institutional cooperation. However, negative and apprehensive headlines, focussing on domestic challenges, political controversies or regional tensions, reflect realist concerns within the international relations theory, where issues of security, power dynamics and strategic competition shape narratives and perceptions. Notably, the analysis indicates that a substantial majority of these news articles are sourced externally from international agencies such as AP, AFP and Reuters, demonstrating a heavy reliance on global news flows, a phenomenon that resonates strongly with the concerns articulated in the UNESCO MacBride Commission's report. The MacBride Commission, advocating for the democratisation of communication flows and warning against the dominance of a 'one-way flow' of information from the developed to the developing world, emphasised the need for strengthening national media systems to ensure pluralism, balance and equitable representation. The Malaysian reliance on externally sourced narratives about India, rather than locally produced or contextualised reporting, highlights the continuing relevance of the MacBride Commission's call for a New World Information and

Communication Order (NWICO) to counter the structural inequalities in global news dissemination.

Malaysian media headlines direct public interpretation by selectively highlighting certain aspects of India's actions while omitting others, thus constructing meaning and guiding audience perceptions towards particular narratives. The consistent focus on specific India-related topics (such as economic agreements, failed Foreign Direct Investment agreements or the issues of governance) amplifies these issues in the public consciousness, making them seem more significant than others and influencing the framework through which India is perceived. In addition to this, repeated exposure to apprehensive or cautious headlines can subtly influence the cognitive shortcuts that audiences use to interpret future news about India, leading to a predisposition towards scepticism or critical engagement. The cultivation theory suggests that long-term exposure to such media frames may cultivate a particular worldview among audiences, reinforcing perceptions of India as either a strategic opportunity or a potential source of regional instability, depending on the balance of coverage. The influence of international news agencies in setting the tone of coverage also aligns with the structures of international communication, where Western media narratives disproportionately influence the representation of developing countries, potentially perpetuating stereotypes, selective visibility and a narrow range of discourses about nations like India.

A realist lens interprets negative and apprehensive headlines as manifestations of Malaysia's underlying strategic calculations in an evolving Indo–Pacific landscape, where India's rise is both an opportunity and a source of strategic recalibration. A liberal interpretation would highlight the opportunities for enhancing economic and diplomatic ties, noting that positive media representations support greater interdependence and collaboration within regional frameworks such as ASEAN. On the other hand, these data underscore the role of shared identities, historical narratives and the significant Indian diaspora in Malaysia in shaping how India is framed, suggesting that the symbolic dimensions of India–Malaysia ties are just as influential as material factors in shaping media narratives.

For India's strategic communication and public diplomacy efforts, these findings present both opportunities and challenges. While the slightly positive overall sentiment in the media landscape provides a foundation for building goodwill and strengthening bilateral relations, the prevalence of apprehensive framing and the heavy reliance on international news feeds necessitate a more proactive and strategic approach. India must enhance its engagement with Malaysian media houses, encourage collaborative journalism initiatives, promote locally authored narratives about India and invest in long-term media partnerships that foster a deeper, more nuanced understanding of India's domestic developments, foreign policy objectives and cultural richness. Such efforts would align with the MacBride Commission's vision for a democratised, pluralistic international communication order and help balance the current dominance of externally sourced narratives. Public diplomacy strategies should also integrate cultural diplomacy tools, leveraging India's diverse cultural heritage, cinema, cuisine, academic exchanges and technological achievements to deepen India's presence in Malaysian public life and counterbalance any apprehensive or negative framings. The observed patterns of news sentiment in Malaysian media coverage of India emerge from a complex interplay of media dynamics, international news flows and strategic diplomatic considerations.

Structural imperatives of Malaysian Media and Representation

The structural imperatives of Malaysian media significantly influence its representation of other nations like India, creating a complex interplay shaped by media ownership patterns, regulatory frameworks, dependency on international news sources and the socio-cultural and bilateral dynamics that underpin Malaysia–India relations. Malaysia's media environment is dominated by a handful of powerful conglomerates, such as Media Prima and Astro, whose close affiliations with political and corporate elites consolidate their ability to shape narratives. Earlier studies have described Malaysian media as a 'tangled nexus of power dynamics', where concentrated ownership and strict legislative oversight, through instruments like the Printing Presses and Publications Act, Official Secrets Act and sedition laws exert tight control over editorial content. These regulatory measures give authorities sweeping powers to penalise outlets that deviate from the official narrative, encouraging widespread self-censorship and instilling editorial caution among journalists. Consequently, the media's portrayal of sensitive issues, including foreign countries like India, tends to mirror the government's strategic interests and preferred narratives as well rather than reflecting pure independent journalistic enquiry. Within this tightly controlled framework, Malaysian media's dependence on external news flows becomes a critical factor in the portrayal of international affairs. This empirical research demonstrates that local outlets rarely deploy foreign correspondents, instead republishing reports from global wire services such as Reuters, AFP and AP, or relying minimally on the state-owned Bernama agency. This reliance leads to an indirect but potent form of framing: the issues that the Malaysian public associates with India are often those selected and emphasised by Western news agencies, which, in accordance with established theories of global news flow and media dependency, tend to prioritise conflict, disaster, elite diplomacy and systemic challenges over cultural, developmental or nuanced stories.

Thus, Malaysia's portrayal of India frequently adopts a cautious and apprehensive tone, focussing on political disputes, security dilemmas and economic challenges rather than offering a locally situated, balanced view of India's multifaceted realities. Yet, this depiction is not uniformly negative. Where Malaysia's national interests align with positive narratives, such as those promoting trade relations, investment cooperation, cultural exchanges and highlighting the role of the vibrant Indian diaspora, Malaysian media selectively underscores positive aspects, portraying India as a strategic partner and an important cultural reference point. Official statements regularly emphasise 'deep-rooted ties of friendship' and the significance of the Indian diaspora, which comprises approximately seven per cent of Malaysia's population, providing a platform for positive media framing that reinforces the state's foreign policy goals. Nonetheless, despite these cultural and diplomatic affinities, global narratives continue to dominate the overall portrayal, reflecting broader structural dependencies. The pattern of India's representation suggests that the repetitive highlighting of India's governance issues or economic challenges subtly cultivates an audience perception of India as a nation characterised by complexity and instability, even when overtly positive developments, like technological achievements or economic growth, are also reported.

From a political economy perspective, the constraints imposed by concentrated media ownership and regulatory mechanisms exacerbate this phenomenon. The Malaysian media landscape has historically been intertwined with political interests, particularly under the long-dominant Barisan Nasional coalition, resulting in editorial lines that privilege governmental priorities, including maintaining inter-ethnic harmony and promoting stable foreign relations. The legal environment further curtails journalistic independence as laws such as the Communications and Multimedia Act and the Sedition Act create a climate of precaution, wherein media houses avoid controversial portrayals that could be construed as undermining national unity.

The socio-cultural proximity between Malaysia and India also plays a nuanced role. Studies comparing cultural traits highlight that both societies exhibit collectivist orientations and high power distance, fostering mutual cultural empathy that can, under certain conditions, lead to more nuanced or empathetic portrayals.

In Malaysia, It can be said tha India's image is not constructed purely through Malaysian lenses but is mediated by global narratives that prioritise certain frames, particularly conflict, governance issues and strategic rivalries, over others. Such coverage is further amplified by the digital ecosystem, where Malaysian social media users often consume international content directly, bypassing local gatekeeping mechanisms. Social media platforms, while offering opportunities for grassroots engagement and alternative narratives, also pose challenges in the form of misinformation and fragmented public spheres, making it harder for India to maintain a coherent and favourable image among Malaysian audiences.

From a realist perspective, negative portrayals could reflect latent regional competition, particularly in the context of India's Act East Policy and its increasing strategic engagement in Southeast Asia, which sometimes intersects with Malaysia's own regional ambitions. From a liberal viewpoint, the substantial bilateral trade, which reached a record high of US$19.5 billion by 2024,[482] should encourage positive portrayals, since economic interdependence generally promotes favourable media narratives. Constructivist theories highlight the role of shared cultural identities and diaspora networks in creating more positive framing opportunities, although these are often secondary to the structural dominance of external news agendas. Independent Malaysian outlets, such as Malaysiakini, offer somewhat more critical or diversified perspectives on India, occasionally highlighting human rights issues or democratic backsliding, but their reach remains limited compared to mainstream media conglomerates. Overall, the interplay of these factors results in a media environment where India's representation is shaped by a complex amalgamation of cautious optimism, selective positivity, globalised apprehension and structural dependencies.

News Sourcing, Impact on Sentiments and India's Representation

In the Malaysian media's portrayal of India, one discerns a methodical cadence of sentiment that does not merely report events but actively fashions collective understanding through a recurring four-stage production cycle: initial laudation, guarded speculation, pointed critique and formal neutral reflection. At the outset, headlines extol India's strategic partnerships, economic breakthroughs or cultural initiatives, deploying celebratory language that aligns with liberal ideals of interdependence and mutual advancement; this phase harnesses official statements and polished dispatches to construct a narrative of shared progress. As articles progress, however, a second phase of epistemic hesitation emerges, in which editors, responding to limited local expertise or seeking to pre-empt charges of bias, employ hedged phrasing, question marks and conditional verbs, thereby transmitting uncertainty and inviting readers to approach India's actions with caution. The third phase shifts decisively toward scrutiny: controversies over governance, security dilemmas or regional rivalries are magnified through emphatic verbs and selective sourcing, enacting a realist frame that underscores competition and risk. Finally, headlines retreat into the veneer of 'objective' neutrality, stripping away overt evaluative language even as they tacitly reinforce preceding frames by omitting context or avoiding deeper analysis. Far from incidental, each of these tonal pivots is choreographed by the newsroom's structural imperatives, wire-service dependency channels, externally authored copy into Malaysian pages; corporate ownership and commercial pressures reward attention-grabbing conflict frames; professional norms valorise cautious wording to preserve credibility; and editorial conventions mandate a semblance of balance that often defaults to linguistic restraint. Through these institutional routines, a particular 'way of knowing' India is legitimised: the public is habituated to welcome hope, brace for doubt, confront conflict and then reset into a posture of mediated calm, only for the cycle to recommence with the next incoming dispatch. Over time, this repetitive modulation does more than mirror audience sentiment, it conditions it, cultivating a collective cognitive schema in which India is alternately a partner to be celebrated, a subject of tentative enquiry, a source of contestation and an object of detached observation. In sociological terms, headlines become knowledge artifacts that embody and reproduce power relations, editorial hierarchies and epistemological conventions, rather than neutral mirrors of reality. The oscillation between positivity, apprehension, negativity and neutrality thus serves a dual function: it satisfies market demands for novelty and drama, while simultaneously embedding in readers' minds a rhythmic pattern of emotional engagement that both reflects and shapes Malaysia's collective perceptions of India. By acknowledging that sentiment is not a natural property of news events but a socially constructed effect of journalistic practices, we can see how the sociology of knowledge in news production reveals sentiment patterns as engineered rather than emergent, and how interventions aimed at diversifying sources, recalibrating editorial incentives and nurturing contextual expertise might disrupt this cycle to foster a more nuanced and balanced public discourse.

Qualitative Analysis of News Headlines

The qualitative analysis of news headlines is crucial for understanding the sentiment and portrayal of any foreign country in media coverage. Headlines serve as the primary framing device that shapes first impressions and heavily influence audience perceptions even before they engage with the full news content. By examining the tone, word choice, emotional connotation and thematic focus of headlines, researchers can identify patterns of positive, negative, neutral or apprehensive sentiment towards a foreign country.

The headline "India Launches Seven Singaporean Satellites" (News Item 12) from *The Star* (July 30, 2023) adopts a predominantly with subtle positive undertones of headline. Written in a straightforward, factual style, it objectively reports the event without embellishment or criticism.

News Item: 12

The Star

StarPlus News Asean+ ESG Business Sport Metro Lifestyle Food Tech Education Opinion

India launches seven Singaporean satellites

INDIA

Sunday, 30 Jul 2023

6:50 PM MYT

The use of technical language ('launches', 'satellites') maintains professional neutrality, while the mention of international collaboration ('Singaporean satellites') implicitly suggests a constructive bilateral relationship. Though devoid of overtly celebratory terms, the inherent significance of space missions lends the headline a mildly positive connotation by default. This balanced approach aligns with standard journalistic practice, informing readers without sensationalism while allowing the newsworthiness of the space achievement to speak for itself. The absence of negative qualifiers or contrasting contexts further reinforces its positive framing, presenting the launch as an uncontroversial milestone in space cooperation.

News Item: 13

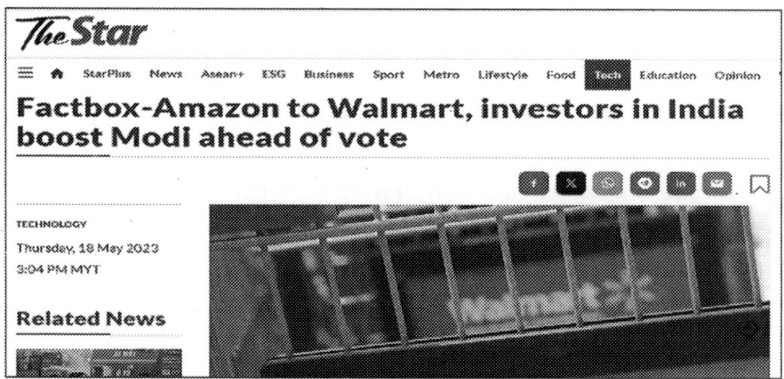

The Star

StarPlus News Asean+ ESG Business Sport Metro Lifestyle Food Tech Education Opinion

Factbox-Amazon to Walmart, investors in India boost Modi ahead of vote

TECHNOLOGY

Thursday, 18 May 2023

3:04 PM MYT

Related News

The headline "Factbox-Amazon to Walmart, Investors in India Boost Modi Ahead of Vote" (News Item 13) from *The Star* (May 18, 2023) carries a 'neutral to cautiously optimistic (positive) sentiment' with political undertones. This headline adopts a primarily positive, informational tone through its fact box-style presentation, focussing on corporate investments in India ahead of elections. The phrase 'investors in India boost Modi' suggests a mildly positive economic narrative, implying business confidence in the political leadership. However, the careful avoidance of overtly celebratory language ('boost' rather than 'strongly endorse') and the clinical 'factbox' prefix maintain journalistic objectivity. The mention of major multinational corporations (Amazon, Walmart) lends credibility to the economic angle while subtly framing Modi as business friendly. The temporal reference 'ahead of vote' introduces a political dimension without explicit partisan bias, though the implication that foreign investment could influence domestic politics might carry an undercurrent of strategic significance.

News Item: 14

The Star

StarPlus News Asean+ ESG Business Sport Metro Lifestyle Food Tech Education Opinion

India finds two more toxic syrups months after poisoning deaths

By KRISHNA N. DAS and SUMIT KHANNA

WORLD

Wednesday, 04 Oct 2023

8:45 PM MYT

The sentiment of the newspaper headline published in *The Star* on Wednesday, October 4, 2023, "India Finds Two More Toxic Syrups Months after Poisoning Deaths" (News Item 14). is negative, reflecting concern and alarm The headline highlights a serious public health issue in India, specifically the discovery of additional toxic syrups following previous poisoning incidents. The use of words like 'toxic' and 'poisoning deaths' contributes to the negative sentiment, indicating a severe threat to public safety. The phrase 'months after' suggests a recurring problem or a lack of resolution to the initial crisis, further amplifying the negative tone. Overall, the headline conveys a sense of urgency and emphasises the gravity of the situation, aiming to capture the reader's attention and inform them about the critical health issue.

News Item: 15

India train crash survivor recounts: 'We thought we were dead'

By JATINDRA DASH and KRISHN KAUSHIK

WORLD

Sunday, 04 Jun 2023

3:12 AM MYT

The sentiment of the headline, published in the Malaysian online version of *The Star* on June 4, 2023, "India Train Crash Survivor Recounts: 'We Thought We Were Dead'" (News Item 15) is one of fear, shock and trauma. The phrase 'we thought we were dead' clearly conveys the intense fear and the perceived life-threatening nature of the situation experienced by the train crash survivors. The headline aims to capture the immediate emotional impact of the event on those who lived through it. It reflects the survivors' belief that they were in imminent danger of losing their lives, highlighting the severity of the crash.

News Item: 16

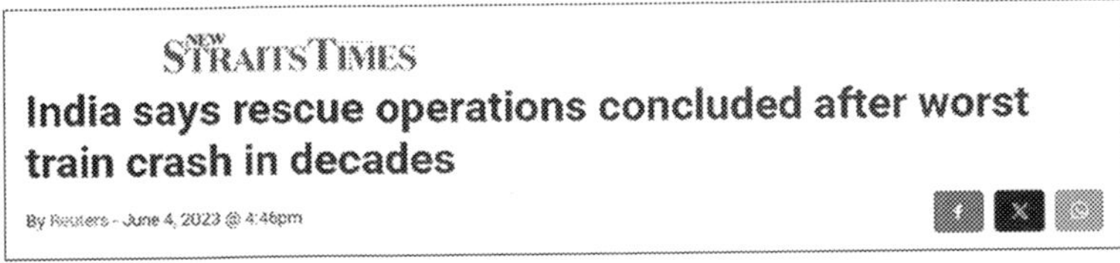

NEW STRAITS TIMES

India says rescue operations concluded after worst train crash in decades

By Reuters - June 4, 2023 @ 4:46pm

The headline from *New Straits Times* on June 4, 2023, "India Says Rescue Operations Concluded after Worst Train Crash in Decades" (News Item 16), conveys apprehension due to the phrase 'worst train crash in decades', indicating a significant loss of life and potential long-term consequences. While the conclusion of rescue operations suggests an end to the immediate crisis, it also implies that the focus will now shift to addressing the aftermath, including investigations, recovery efforts and support for the victims and their families. The use of the word 'worst' emphasises the severity of the incident, contributing to the apprehensive sentiment surrounding the news.

News Item: 17

The Star

StarPlus News Asean+ ESG Business Sport Metro Lifestyle Food Tech Education Opinion

Booker Prize winner Arundhati Roy facing prosecution in India

By AGENCY

ARTS

Wednesday, 11 Oct 2023

6:11 PM MYT

The headline "Booker Prize Winner Arundhati Roy Facing Prosecution in India" (News Item 17) from *The Star* newspaper, dated October 11, 2023, indicates that the acclaimed author Arundhati Roy is potentially facing legal action in India. The headline is apprehensive due to the use of the phrase 'facing prosecution', which suggests an ongoing legal process and uncertainty about the outcome. The article, published by an agency, highlights a serious situation for a well-known figure, raising concerns about freedom of expression and the potential implications for the literary and activist communities. The use of 'prosecution' implies formal legal proceedings, which could lead to significant consequences for Roy.

News Item: 18

malaymail

HOME MALAYSIA SINGAPORE MONEY WORLD LIFE EAT/DRINK SHOWBIZ OPINION

MONEY

India approves export of 170,000 tonnes of white rice to Malaysia, says High Commission

Thursday, 19 Oct 2023 5:19 PM MYT

KUALA LUMPUR, Oct 19 — The Indian government yesterday approved export of 170,000 metric tonnes of non-Basmati white rice to Malaysia as mark of special friendly gesture between the two countries.

"The decision by the Government of India is reflective of the close ties between India and Malaysia and in line with India's continued policy of supporting efforts of governments in the friendly countries towards safeguarding domestic food security," according to the Indian High Commission in Kuala Lumpur.

The newspaper headlines published in *Malay Mail* on October 19, 2023, (News Item 18) exhibits a positive sentiment due to its focus on the approval of the export of 170,000 metric tonnes of non-Basmati white rice from India to Malaysia. This positive tone stems from several factors: the article describes the export as a "mark of special friendly gesture between the two countries", highlighting the goodwill and strong diplomatic relations between India and Malaysia. It also quotes the Indian High Commission in Kuala Lumpur, emphasising that the decision reflects the "close ties between India and Malaysia", reinforcing the notion of robust bilateral relations. Additionally, the article notes that the export aligns with India's policy of supporting friendly countries in safeguarding domestic food security, suggesting a proactive and benevolent approach by India. The significant volume of the rice export further indicates economic cooperation and mutual trust between the two nations. The article conveys a positive sentiment by depicting international cooperation, diplomatic goodwill and mutual support in the spheres of trade and food security between India and Malaysia.

News Item: 19

NEW STRAITS TIMES

India imposes 40pc export duty on onions till Dec 31

By Bernama - August 20, 2023 @ 10:53am

NEW DELHI: India, the world's biggest exporter of onions, has imposed a 40 per cent export duty on onions with immediate effect.

The additional duty will be in force until Dec 31.

The UAE is among the biggest markets for Indian onions along with Bangladesh, Nepal, Malaysia and Sri Lanka, Emirates News Agency reported.

The curbs on export have been prompted by the scantiest rainfall in a century this month in onion-growing states in India, which are creating onion shortages in the domestic market.

The headline "India Imposes 40pc Export Duty on Onions till Dec 31" (News Item 19), published in *New Straits Times* on August 20, 2023, neutrally reports India's decision to impose a 40 per cent export duty on onions until December 31. This decision, as detailed in the article, is a response to scant rainfall affecting onion-growing states in India, leading to domestic shortages. The headline is neutral because it objectively states the action taken by the Indian government without expressing opinion or bias. *New Straits Times*, being a Malaysian newspaper, presents the information factually, focussing on the economic implications for its readers, particularly concerning the United Arab Emirates (UAE) and other countries that import Indian onions. The date is important as it provides context to the policy change, indicating its immediacy and duration.

Sentiment Dynamics between News Headlines and Introductions of the News

Headlines serve two key purposes, first to capture attention and the other to summarise an article's core message, while lead paragraphs (commonly referred to as 'intros') provide balanced, factual context to clarify the story. The content analysis of 804 online news articles from three leading Malaysian newspapers, *The Star*, *New Straits Times* and *Malay Mail*, reveals in Table 21 that approximately 27.61 per cent (222 articles) exhibited a mismatch in sentimental tone between headlines and their introductory lead paragraphs.

Table 21: Overview of Sentiment Alignment between News Headlines and Introductions (Malaysia)

Category	*Number of News Items*	*Percentage of Total*
Total News Items	804	100%
Headlines and introductions with different sentiments	222	27.61%

This discrepancy arises when the sentiment conveyed by a headline (positive, negative, apprehensive or neutral) diverges from the tone of the article's opening section, which is designed to provide immediate context and present key facts objectively. For instance, an optimistic headline might precede a neutral or pessimistic introduction, or vice versa. Such inconsistencies risk confusing readers.

The study's findings highlight a significant issue: nearly one in four articles present conflicting cues between headlines and introductions, which could erode reader trust, hinder comprehension and weaken the effectiveness of journalistic communication. When headlines prioritise emotional appeal over alignment with the article's substance, they risk distorting the narrative before readers even engage with the full text, a critical concern in an era where skimming headlines often replaces deep, thoughtful reading.

Table 22: Breakdown of News Items with Positive Headlines (Malaysia)

Category	*Number of News Items*	*Percentage of Total (31)*
Total with positive headlines	276	100%
Introductions with different sentiments	62	22.46%
• Introductions with apprehensive sentiments	11	3.98%
• Introductions with negative sentiments	1	0.36%
• Introductions with neutral sentiments	50	18.11%

In setting the initial frame, headlines prime readers to anticipate a particular narrative trajectory, often upbeat when the headline is positive. Yet, empirical analysis reveals in Table 22 a frequent disruption of this expectation: a study of 276 news articles with explicitly positive headlines found that in 22.46 per cent of cases (62 articles), the introduction adopted a different tone, 50 were neutral, 11 were apprehensive and one was negative. This tonal misalignment between the headline and the lead paragraph generates a tension between the story 'promised' and the story 'told', unsettling readers and complicating the communication of the intended message.

This disconnect has broader implications when viewed through classic models of communication. According to Shannon and Weaver's theory, any disturbance between the sender and the receiver constitutes 'noise',[483] which may distort the intended message as it travels through the channel. A mismatched headline acts as a form of semantic noise, warping the signal before the audience can fully interpret it. Readers primed by an optimistic headline but greeted by a neutral or cautious introduction may feel confused, misled or even cynical, leading to what can be termed a breakdown in communication fidelity. This study corroborates this phenomenon: approximately 24 per cent of readers express distrust toward headlines because they feel that the headline's emotional cues often do not align with the article's substantive message.

In this current empirical study, out of a total of 232 news items with negative headlines, there are variations in the sentiments of their introductions. Among these, 68 news items (29.31 per cent) have introductions with different sentiments than their negative headlines. Specifically, four news items (1.72 per cent) feature introductions with a positive connotation, while 29 (12.5 per cent) have a neutral sentiment. Additionally, 35 news items (15.08 per cent) contain introductions with an apprehensive sentiment (Table 23). This illustrates how different introduction sentiments are distributed within the set of negative news headlines.

Table 23: Breakdown of News Items with Negative Headlines (Malaysia)

Category	*Number of News Items*	*Percentage of Negative Headlines*
Total with negative headlines	232	100%
Introductions with different sentiments	68	29.31%
• Introductions with positive connotations	4	1.72%
• Introductions with neutral sentiments	29	12.5%
• Introductions with apprehensive sentiments	35	15.08%

The mismatch between headlines and the introductions reflects nuanced context, balance or even optimism, aligning with journalistic ideals of fairness or objectivity. When every headline of 232 news items convey negativity but only about 70.78 per cent of the corresponding introductions actually continue that tone, the balance 1.72 per cent are positive, 12.5 per cent neutral and 15 per cent merely apprehensive, readers experience a jarring disconnect between expectation and reality Table 23). A uniformly grim headline primes audiences for bad news, yet nearly one in three leads softens or even contradicts that framing, which can feel misleading and undermine the outlet's credibility. This mismatch not only risks being perceived as clickbait sensationalism but also creates cognitive dissonance, prompting readers to wonder whether they are being manipulated or simply encountering incoherent reporting. Moreover, the abrupt shift from strong negativity to neutrality or mild concern disrupts the emotional pacing of the story, diminishing engagement and encouraging skimming rather than thoughtful reading.

News headlines are intentionally crafted to capture attention, frequently employing emotionally charged or alarming language that evokes apprehension, using terms like 'crisis' or 'unfinished' to create a sense of urgency and compel readers to engage with the content. However, this approach often contrasts sharply with the tone of article introductions, which typically present a more balanced perspective by incorporating positive, negative and neutral elements.

Table 24: Breakdown of Introduction Sentiments for Apprehensive Headlines (Malaysia)

Category	*Items*	*Percentage of Apprehensive Headlines*
Total with apprehensive headlines	112	100%
Introductions with different sentiments	40	35.71%
• Introductions with positive sentiments	8	7.14%
• Introductions with negative sentiments	10	8.92%
• Introductions with neutral sentiments	22	19.64%

This study also offers a breakdown of introduction sentiments for apprehensive headlines, revealing that out of 112 apprehensive headlines, 35.71 per cent (40 headlines) feature introductions with different sentiments. Further analysis shows that within these 40 headlines, 7.14 per cent (8 headlines) have positive sentiment introductions, 8.92 per cent (10 headlines) have negative sentiment introductions and 19.64 per cent (22 headlines) have neutral sentiment introductions (Table 24).

This empirical data suggests that while a significant portion of apprehensive headlines maintains a consistent sentiment throughout, a notable percentage employ introductions with varying sentiments, potentially to create nuance or engage readers differently.

The prevalence of neutral introductions within this group could indicate an attempt to provide objective context before delving into the apprehensive core of the headline. This inconsistency creates a fault line in the communication process: readers, primed by headlines designed to evoke anxiety, encounter introductions that either soften, contradict or neutralise the expected mood.

The analysis of neutral headlines reveals an interesting divergence between headlines and introduction tones. While 184 of the 804 examined headlines maintained a strictly neutral classification, 28.26 per cent (52 headlines) featured introductions that departed from this neutral stance. Among these, positive sentiment introductions were most prevalent at 13.58 per cent (25 headlines), followed by apprehensive introductions at 8.69 per cent (16 headlines) and negative introductions at 5.97 per cent (11 headlines) (Table 25).

Table 25: Breakdown of Introduction Sentiments for Neutral Headlines (Malaysia)

Category	*Items*	*Percentage of Neutral Headlines*
Total with neutral headlines	184	100%
Introductions with different sentiments	52	28.26%
• Introductions with positive sentiments	25	13.58%
• Introductions with apprehensive sentiments	16	8.69%
• Introductions with negative sentiments	11	5.97%

This breakdown demonstrates that even when headlines adhere to complete neutrality, nearly a third of accompanying introductions introduce emotional valence—particularly leaning toward positive framing—suggesting a deliberate or systemic tendency to enhance neutral stories with more affectively charged opening paragraphs. The data highlights how journalistic practice often balances neutral headline framing with more sentiment-driven introductions, possibly to engage readers while maintaining an appearance of objectivity in the initial content encounter. This phenomenon indicates a notable mismatch between the initial framing and the story development. Readers expecting a straightforward, balanced report may encounter unexpected emotional cues, creating subtle cognitive dissonance. This divergence suggests either editorial strategy to balance credibility with engagement or reflects structural fragmentation in the news production process. Such inconsistencies can weaken narrative coherence, affect audience trust, and highlight growing tensions between traditional journalistic norms and digital era demands.

Qualitative Analysis of Discrepancies and Contradictions between Headlines and Introductions in News Articles

The present study underscores the critical necessity of examining the contradictions between headlines and introductions in news articles to fully comprehend the processes underlying the dissemination of information. The disjunction between headlines and introductions serves as a crucial site for uncovering the selective presentation, strategic framing and potential distortion of information as it transitions from occurrence to public consumption. Accordingly, the following section systematically examines the contradictions between headlines and introductions in the sampled Malaysian newspapers, elucidating their role in the construction and mediation of information flows.

The image depicts a news article titled *"Modi Inaugurates Grand New Indian Parliament"* (News Item 20), published by *New Straits Times* on May 28, 2023. The news is supplied by the news agency AFP, the article covers the inauguration of the new Indian parliament building in New Delhi.

News Item: 20

NEW STRAITS TIMES

Modi inaugurates grand new Indian parliament

By Afp - May 28, 2023 @ 4:48pm

NEW DELHI: Flanked by priests, Hindu nationalist Prime Minister Narendra Modi inaugurated a new Indian parliament on Sunday in a ceremony steeped in religious symbolism but boycotted by opposition parties.

The hexagonal new building – shaped like a coffin, one opposition party said – is the centrepiece of a remodelling of the heart of New Delhi by Modi aimed at ridding the Indian capital of the vestiges of British colonial rule.

While the headline projects a celebratory tone, emphasising the 'grand' nature of the structure and highlighting the significance of the event, the introductory paragraph offers a more nuanced and critical perspective. It notes that the ceremony was 'steeped in religious symbolism' and was boycotted by opposition parties, reflecting the underlying political tensions. Additionally, the article points out that one opposition party likened the hexagonal design of the building to a coffin, introducing a starkly negative connotation. This contrast between the upbeat headline and the more complex introduction creates a tension in the narrative, showcasing how news reporting often balances eye-catching headlines with deeper, more critical content in the article body.

News Item: 21

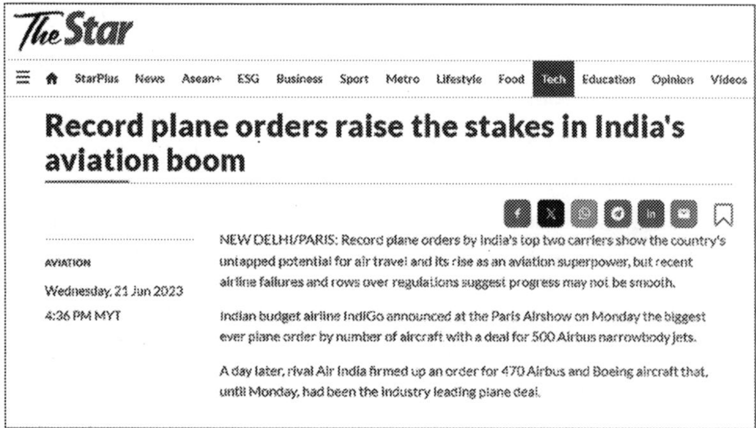

The Star

StarPlus News Asean+ ESG Business Sport Metro Lifestyle Food Tech Education Opinion Videos

Record plane orders raise the stakes in India's aviation boom

AVIATION

Wednesday, 21 Jun 2023

4:36 PM MYT

NEW DELHI/PARIS: Record plane orders by India's top two carriers show the country's untapped potential for air travel and its rise as an aviation superpower, but recent airline failures and rows over regulations suggest progress may not be smooth.

Indian budget airline IndiGo announced at the Paris Airshow on Monday the biggest ever plane order by number of aircraft with a deal for 500 Airbus narrowbody jets.

A day later, rival Air India firmed up an order for 470 Airbus and Boeing aircraft that, until Monday, had been the industry leading plane deal.

The article, published in *The Star* on June 21, 2023, discusses the significant aircraft orders placed by Indian airlines IndiGo and Air India. IndiGo ordered 500 Airbus aircraft, while Air India placed an order for 470 aircraft from both Airbus and Boeing. The article highlights India's potential for rapid air travel growth and its emergence as an aviation superpower. However, it also notes that recent airline failures and regulatory disputes could hinder this progress. A contradiction emerges between the headline and the introduction: the headline, "Record Plane Orders Raise the Stakes in India's Aviation Boom" (News Item 21), presents an optimistic view, suggesting that these large orders will directly boost the industry, whereas the introduction tempers this enthusiasm by warning that airline failures and regulatory issues could complicate the expected growth. This contrast underscores the complexity of India's aviation sector, balancing ambitious expansion with underlying structural challenges.

News Item: 22

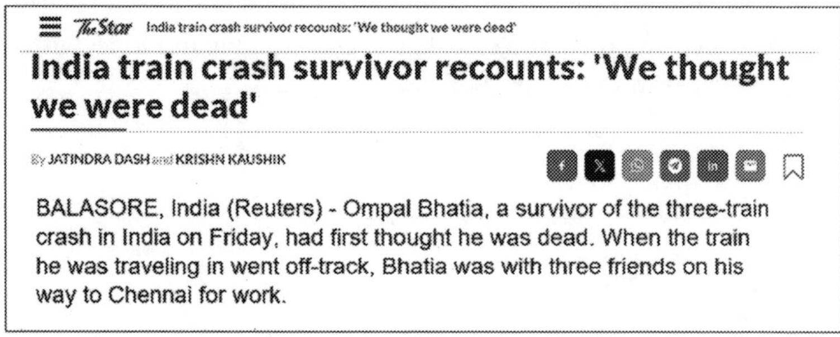

The Star India train crash survivor recounts: 'We thought we were dead'

India train crash survivor recounts: 'We thought we were dead'

By JATINDRA DASH and KRISHN KAUSHIK

BALASORE, India (Reuters) - Ompal Bhatia, a survivor of the three-train crash in India on Friday, had first thought he was dead. When the train he was traveling in went off-track, Bhatia was with three friends on his way to Chennai for work.

Another article under analysis, published in *The Star*, centres on the testimony of a survivor from the recent three-train collision in India, reportedly occurring on April 25, 2025. The headline, *"India Train Crash Survivor Recounts: 'We Thought We Were Dead'"* (News Item 22), foregrounds a sense of acute fear and trauma, employing emotionally charged language to immediately capture reader attention. In contrast, the introductory paragraph, which states, *"Ompal Bhatia, a survivor of the three-train crash in India on Friday, had first thought he was dead"*, while acknowledging the initial terror, subtly reorients the narrative toward resilience and survival. This divergence between the headline and the introductory paragraph illustrates a common journalistic practice wherein the headline serves a primarily attention-grabbing function, often at the expense of the more complex, nuanced depiction offered in the body of the article.

News Item: 23

The Star

StarPlus News Asean+ ESG Business Sport Metro Lifestyle Food Tech Education Opinion Videos Photos

Climate change: China, India to bear the brunt with half a million coal workers facing job cuts globally by 2035 due to mine closures and energy transition

By YUJIE XUE

ASEANPLUS NEWS

Thursday, 12 Oct 2023

1.23 PM MYT

Nearly half a million coal miners face unemployment globally by 2035 due to mine closures and a market shift towards cheaper wind and solar power generation, with China and India likely to be hit hardest, a new report said.

That equates to 100 workers being laid off every day for the next 12 years, according to a report released on Tuesday by San Francisco-based non-profit Global Energy Monitor (GEM). The report looks into the employment of nearly 2.7 million coal miners working at 4,300 active and proposed coal mines and projects around the world that are together responsible for more than 90 per cent of global coal production.

A news article from *The Star*, published on October 12, 2023, an article with the headline: *"Climate Change: China, India to Bear the Brunt with Half a Million Coal Workers Facing Job Cuts Globally by 2035 Due to Mine Closures and Energy Transition"* (News Item 23). The article elaborates on projections that approximately half a million coal miners worldwide may lose their jobs by 2035 as a consequence of mine closures and the broader transition toward renewable energy. The piece emphasises that China and India are expected to experience the most severe impacts. It further cites a report by the Global Energy Monitor (GEM), which forecasts that roughly 100 coal workers will be laid off daily over the next 12 years. From a media analysis perspective, a notable tension emerges between the headline and the article's introduction. The headline adopts a stark and regionally focussed framing, foregrounding job losses and explicitly identifying China and

India as principal victims of the energy transition. In contrast, the introductory paragraph, while acknowledging the same data, adopts a more measured and globally framed tone, presenting the phenomenon as part of a larger systemic shift with differential regional consequences. This divergence illustrates the discrepancy in emphasis and narrative scope, wherein the headline is crafted to evoke urgency and draw immediate attention through negative framing, while the introduction provides a more contextualised and analytical overview.

News Item: 24

NEW STRAITS TIMES

India imposes 40pc export duty on onions till Dec 31

By Bernama - August 20, 2023 @ 10:53am

NEW DELHI: India, the world's biggest exporter of onions, has imposed a 40 per cent export duty on onions with immediate effect.

The additional duty will be in force until Dec 31.

The UAE is among the biggest markets for Indian onions along with Bangladesh, Nepal, Malaysia and Sri Lanka, Emirates News Agency reported.

The curbs on export have been prompted by the scantiest rainfall in a century this month in onion-growing states in India, which are creating onion shortages in the domestic market.

A news article from *New Straits Times*, published on August 20, 2023, which reports that India, the world's largest exporter of onions, has imposed a 40 per cent export duty on onions, effective immediately and continuing until December 31. This policy decision was driven by a severe shortfall in rainfall (reported as the lowest in a century), in India's primary onion-growing regions, resulting in domestic supply concerns. Major importers affected by this measure include the UAE, Bangladesh, Nepal, Malaysia and Sri Lanka. An apparent contradiction between the headline and the introduction can be observed, rooted in the differing levels of detail and contextual framing. The headline, "India Imposes 40pc Export Duty on Onions till Dec 31" (News Item 24), is concise and ostensibly neutral, presenting the imposition of the duty as an isolated fact without reference to causative factors or potential repercussions. In contrast, the introduction, while similarly factual, stating that "India, the world's biggest exporter of onions, has imposed a 40 per cent export duty on onions with immediate effect", implicitly introduces a negative undertone by situating the development within the broader context of domestic agricultural distress. Subsequent elaboration within the article connects the policy action to environmental challenges and fears of domestic shortages, thus framing the duty as a response to an emergent crisis. Therefore, while no overt contradiction exists between the headline and the introduction, the divergence arises from the differential inclusion of contextual information, which shifts the reader's perception from neutral reportage to an interpretation laden with implicit concern.

India in ASEAN Media: Study of Thailand

This empirical study examines the coverage of news related to India in three prominent Thai newspapers: *Bangkok Post, The Nation and Thaiger*. The analysis covers the period from May to October 2024, during which a total of 166 news items were identified. By systematically evaluating the content from these sources, the study aims to understand how India is portrayed in the Thai media landscape. It explores patterns in framing, sentiment, sources of news, the focus of issues, the relationship between headlines and introductions and the broader implications for bilateral perceptions and public discourse. The data derived from this study presents a content analysis of India-related news coverage. The analysis categorises 166 news items into 10 thematic areas, providing both quantitative distribution and interpretive insight into prevailing media trends. The findings suggest a clear prioritisation of issues related to bilateral and geopolitical dimensions, which significantly shapes the portrayal of India in the Thai media landscape.

A substantial portion of the coverage is devoted to Bilateral Relations (27.10 per cent) and Geopolitics and India (24.69 per cent) (Table 26). This prominent focus indicates that Thai media largely frames India through the lens of diplomacy, strategic cooperation and regional power dynamics. Such framing underscores India's role as a significant political and strategic partner for Thailand within the broader Indo–Pacific context.

Table 26: Thailand's Top News Categories Related to India

Category of News, Topic Wise: Thailand	*Number of News Items*	*Percentage*
Domestic Politics	11	6.62%
Terrorism/Law & Order	11	6.62%
Global Economy and India	6	3.61%
India's Economy	20	12.04%
Bilateral Relations	45	27.10%
Geopolitics and India	41	24.69%
Climate Disaster	8	4.81%
Governance/Accident	14	8.43%
Science and Technology	4	2.40%
Cultural/Miscellaneous	6	3.61%
TOTAL	166	100%

Table 27: Thailand's Top Five News Categories Related to India

Top Five News Categories Topic Wise: Thailand	*Number of News Items*	*Percentage*
Bilateral Relations	45	27.10%
Geopolitics and India	41	24.69%
India's Economy	20	12.04%
Governance/Accident	14	8.43%
Domestic Politics	11	6.62%
Terrorism/Law & Order	11	6.62%

The coverage tends to emphasise formal engagements, high-level visits, bilateral trade and shared regional interests, reflecting a narrative of India as an emerging regional power and an essential actor in Thailand's foreign policy calculus. Economic narratives also figure prominently, with India's Economy comprising 12.04 per cent of the news content (Table 27). These articles often highlight India's growing market, trade opportunities and economic reforms, projecting India as a rising economic power with direct relevance to Thailand's own economic interests. However, the relatively low coverage of Global Economy and India (3.61 per cent) (Table 26) suggests that India's global economic influence is not as prominently featured in the Thai press, with greater emphasis placed on bilateral economic exchanges rather than India's position within the global financial architecture.

Coverage of India's domestic affairs, including Domestic Politics and Terrorism/Law and Order (each at 6.62 per cent), reflects a moderate degree of interest. These topics are typically portrayed through a lens of stability and security, often in relation to their implications for regional peace or bilateral cooperation. While the Thai media does not extensively engage with the nuances of India's internal political landscape, it selectively reports on events that have cross-border resonance or that relate to India's image as a democratic state navigating internal challenges. Other areas, such as Climate Disaster (4.81 per cent), Governance/Accident (8.43 per cent), Science and Technology (2.40 per cent) and Cultural/Miscellaneous (3.61 per cent), receive considerably less attention. This limited representation suggests that Thai media perceives these themes as peripheral to the core strategic and economic narrative that dominates India's portrayal (Table 27). Scientific achievements or cultural engagements, while occasionally acknowledged, are not central to how India is constructed in Thai media discourse.

The portrayal of India in Thai newspapers is selective and strategically framed, focussing heavily on political alignment, regional security and economic potential.

This reflects not only the priorities of Thai foreign policy but also the media's role in reinforcing a particular image of India, as a significant, pragmatic and increasingly influential partner. The relative marginalisation of softer themes such as culture, environment and innovation suggests that India's multifaceted identity is filtered through a utilitarian lens, where strategic relevance determines newsworthiness. These patterns of representation offer valuable insight into how media serves as a conduit for constructing and disseminating foreign policy narratives and public perceptions of international partners.

This study examines how news related to India shows that out of 166 news items, 88 (53.01 per cent) were produced by the newspapers' own resources (reporters, news desks or editorial teams), while 78 (46.98 per cent) were sourced from international news agencies, national agencies, freelancers or other outsider contributors (Table 28). This distribution reveals several important aspects of how India's news is presented to Thai audiences. The fact that more than half of the news items are generated in-house suggests that Thai media institutions consider India an important topic and allocate editorial resources to cover it actively.

Table 28: News Source Analysis (Thailand)

Total News Items	166	100%
News coverage by reporters/news desk/editorial/op-eds	88	53.01%
News coverage by international agencies/national agencies/freelancers/contributors	78	46.98%

This may reflect the growing strategic, economic and cultural ties between the two countries, especially in light of regional initiatives and Thailand's engagement in the Indo–Pacific policy framework. News produced by in-house reporters is likely to be shaped by Thai editorial perspectives, potentially framing India in ways that align with Thailand's foreign policy priorities or domestic interests, such as trade, tourism, regional cooperation or diplomatic relations. On the other hand, the nearly equal share of news sourced from external agencies points to a continued dependence on international news flows for foreign coverage. This means that a significant portion of the news about India in Thailand is filtered through international perspectives, which may not always reflect Thai-specific interests or understanding. News from international agencies may emphasise certain themes such as India's domestic politics, economic challenges or internal conflicts, depending on global news values and narratives. Consequently, this dual sourcing strategy, combining both local and external content, creates a mixed media portrayal of India, blending Thai-framed content with globally framed news stories. This pattern indicates that while Thai newspapers are increasingly engaging with India as a subject of importance, their reliance on international sources also shapes the way Indian developments are interpreted and presented to the Thai public.

A sentiment analysis of 166 news articles drawn from three Thai newspapers provides a quantitative assessment of how India is represented in Thai media during the specified period. The findings indicate that negative news coverage exceeds positive coverage, suggesting a discernible trend in the portrayal of India. Specifically, of the total 166 articles, 67 (40.36 per cent) were classified as negative in tone, while 50 (30.12 per cent) were positive, revealing a predominance of critical or pessimistic narratives (Tables 29 and 30). The remaining articles were presumably neutral or not easily classified within this binary. An analysis of the sources contributing to both positive and negative sentiment further refines this observation.

Table 29: Sentiment Analysis of Positive News (Thailand)

Positive news articles out of a total of 166 news articles	50	30.12%
Positive stories by reporters/news desk/opinion	25	50%
Positive stories by international agencies/national agencies/freelancers/contributors	25	50%

Table 30: Sentiment Analysis of Negative News (Thailand)

Negative news articles out of a total of 166 news articles	67	40.36%
Negative stories by reporters/news desk/opinion	34	50.74%
Negative stories by international agencies/national agencies/freelancers/contributors	33	49.25%

Positive news items were evenly divided between those generated by internal media resources like namely reporters, news desks and editorial teams (25 articles, constituting 50 per cent of the positive content) and those provided by external contributors, including international agencies, national wire services, freelancers and contributors (25 articles, or 50 per cent). Similarly, negative news coverage displayed an almost equal distribution: 34 articles (50.74 per cent of the negative content) originated from internal sources, while 33 articles (49.25 per cent) were derived from external contributors. This near-equal distribution across both sentiment categories and source types suggests that the tone of coverage is not strongly influenced by whether the article was internally produced or externally sourced.

The predominance of negative reporting likely reflects editorial prioritisation of conflict, crises or contentious issues, which are often perceived as more newsworthy according to conventional news values. At the same time, the balanced source attribution implies that both local editorial teams and global information providers are contributing similarly to the overall sentiment trends. In this context, 'sentiment' is defined as the evaluative orientation embedded within the article, broadly categorised as positive, indicating favourable, constructive or optimistic representations, and negative news, indicating unfavourable, critical or pessimistic depictions. This classification allows for an empirical measure of tone, offering insight into the narrative environment shaping public perceptions.

This analysis suggests that while there is a significant tendency towards negative coverage of India in Thai media, this tendency is not disproportionately driven by one particular group of news producers. Instead, it emerges as a consistent pattern across both domestic and international sources. These findings underscore the importance of examining not only the volume and themes of coverage but also the tone and sourcing dynamics that shape the mediated portrayal of foreign countries. Such insights contribute to a more nuanced understanding of international media representation and its implications for bilateral perceptions and public discourse.

Table 31: Sentiment Analysis of Apprehensive and Neutral News (Thailand)

Number of apprehensive news items of a total of 166 news items	21	12.65%
Number of neutral news items of a total of 166 news items	28	16.89%

The data in Table 31 also reveals that 21 articles (12.65 per cent) were identified as conveying an apprehensive tone, suggesting that a relatively small proportion of the news coverage expresses concern, unease or anxiety about India. Meanwhile, 28 articles (16.89 per cent) were classified as neutral, indicating that a slightly higher proportion of the content provided factual reporting devoid of overt emotional or evaluative language. These figures imply that a combined 70.46 per cent of the news items fall outside these two categories, encompassing positive and negative sentiment types. However, since those additional categories are not detailed in the present data, the complete sentiment landscape remains only partially visible. Sentiment, in this context, refers to the emotional tone or evaluative stance conveyed in news discourse. Apprehensive sentiment denotes the presence of caution or alarm, while neutral sentiment reflects an objective or un-opinionated reporting style. It is important to acknowledge several limitations in this analysis. First, the lack of explicit criteria for categorising articles as 'apprehensive' or 'neutral' may affect the validity and replicability of the findings. Second, the exclusion of other sentiment categories narrows the analytical scope, reducing the potential to fully interpret the nature and balance of sentiment in the news.

Decoding India–Thailand News Coverage: Priorities and Reasons

The study covers category priorities, sentiment, sources and issue focus, offering insights into how India is perceived in Thailand. The data shows a strong emphasis on bilateral relations and geopolitics, with economic aspects at 12.04 per cent. However, softer themes like science and technology and culture are underrepresented.

These data provide a detailed examination of the conceptual issues surrounding India's representation in Thai media, based on an empirical study conducted from May to October 2023. The findings reveal several interconnected challenges that shape how India is portrayed and perceived in Thailand, with implications for bilateral relations, strategic communication and public diplomacy. The analysis provides both quantitative distribution and interpretive insights into prevailing media trends, offering a robust basis for identifying conceptual issues.

The high focus on Bilateral Relations and Geopolitics and India (51.79 per cent combined) suggests that Thai media frames India primarily through the lens of diplomacy, strategic cooperation and regional power dynamics, where media shapes audience perceptions of issues of importance. However, this selective framing risks narrowing public understanding and marginalising softer dimensions like culture and science, which are crucial for a holistic view of bilateral relations.

The higher proportion of negative news (40.36 per cent) compared to positive (30.12 per cent), with an additional 12.65 per cent apprehensive, reflects news-value criteria favouring negativity and event salience. This creates a conceptual challenge, as it may undermine public diplomacy efforts to foster trust and favourable perceptions, potentially affecting bilateral relations. The balanced source attribution (50 per cent in-house, 50 per cent external for both positive and negative) suggests this bias is consistent across production types, highlighting a systemic issue in tone.

Additionally, the near-equal split between in-house (53.01 per cent) and external (46.98 per cent) sources indicates a reliance on international news agencies, and shows a potential dilution of Thai-specific perspectives, emphasising the need for robust information subsidies and localised media engagement to assert greater narrative control.

These conceptual issues collectively underscore the need for a theoretically informed approach to public diplomacy in Thailand's media coverage of India. Effective strategies must integrate insights from communication frameworks, fostering reciprocal, multi-dimensional communicative channels beyond traditional state-to-state narratives. The selective and strategically framed portrayal reflects Thai foreign policy priorities and media's role in reinforcing a particular image of India as a significant, pragmatic partner. However, the relative marginalisation of softer themes suggests that India's multifaceted identity is filtered through a utilitarian lens, where strategic relevance determines newsworthiness.

Analysing News Sentiment (Headlines) and Contextualisation of Sentiments of News toward India in Thailand Media

The analysis of India-related news coverage in Thai media reveals a strategic emphasis on themes that align with pragmatic diplomatic and economic priorities, reflecting broader state interests rather than a holistic representation of India's societal or cultural dimensions. By disproportionately focussing on geopolitical alliances, bilateral engagements and trade dynamics, the media constructs a narrative that positions India as a critical actor in Thailand's regional calculus, particularly within the Indo–Pacific framework. This prioritisation mirrors the selective amplification of issues that serve national agendas, where media functions as an intermediary to reinforce state-aligned narratives, emphasising stability, mutual benefit and shared security concerns. Such framing aligns with the idea that media institutions act as gatekeepers, filtering international realities through a lens that privileges strategic utility over comprehensive storytelling, thereby shaping public perceptions to align with foreign policy objectives.

The sourcing dynamics, nearly equal reliance on in-house reporting and external agencies, highlight a tension between editorial autonomy and globalised information flows. While the significant share of internally generated content signals a deliberate effort to craft India's image as a partner of relevance to Thailand's economic and diplomatic goals, the dependence on external sources introduces competing narratives shaped by global news values. These external contributions often foreground crises, political volatility or economic challenges, which may not inherently align with Thailand's localised priorities but still permeate coverage due to the structural reliance on international wire services. This duality creates a hybridised discourse where India is simultaneously framed as a collaborator and a site of complexity, reflecting the interplay between local editorial agency and the homogenising tendencies of global news ecosystems. The balanced attribution of both positive and negative sentiments across sources further underscores that critical narratives are not merely imported but are systemically normalised, suggesting that adversarial or cautionary tones are embedded in both domestic and international journalistic practices.

The predominance of negative sentiment in coverage underscores a broader media inclination toward conflict-driven storytelling, where issues like failure on the part of governance, rollback of foreign investment decisions, diplomatic setbacks and management of natural disasters are deemed inherently newsworthy. This trend transcends sourcing origins, indicating a universal journalistic bias toward dramatisation and risk amplification. Such patterns may cultivate public perceptions of India as a nation grappling with instability, despite its simultaneous portrayal as an economic and strategic ally. The marginalisation of softer themes, cultural exchanges, environmental cooperation, or scientific innovation, reveals a narrowed narrative scope that sidelines opportunities to humanise India or present it as a multifaceted society. Instead, its identity is reduced to transactional value, undermining the potential for deeper relational diplomacy that could foster mutual understanding beyond utilitarian interests.

The limited presence of apprehensive and neutral tones further illustrates a polarised media landscape, where coverage oscillates between strategic optimism and critical scrutiny. Neutral reporting, though present, is overshadowed by evaluative narratives, suggesting that even ostensibly factual content is often contextualised within frameworks of opportunity or risk. This polarisation reflects a media environment where complexity is sacrificed for clarity, and ambivalence is subsumed by dominant binaries of partnership versus peril. Such dynamics highlight the role of media in constructing symbolic architectures of international relations, where nations are discursively positioned not merely as geopolitical entities but as sites of projected aspirations, anxieties and interests. These patterns collectively demonstrate how media serves as both a mirror and a mould, reflecting state priorities while actively shaping the discursive terrain through which bilateral relationships are negotiated and understood in the public sphere.

Structural imperatives of Thailand Media and Representation

The analysis reveals that Thailand's media landscape operates within a set of institutionalised constraints and strategic priorities that systematically inform the production, circulation and reception of international news, particularly in the representation of India. The predominance of content focussing on bilateral diplomacy, regional geopolitics and economic engagements illustrates how news coverage is implicitly structured to reflect the imperatives of statecraft. Media narratives, in this context, do not merely mirror events but are embedded within broader national agendas, aligning reportage with Thailand's external policy orientations and regional positioning. The portrayal of India as a critical economic and strategic interlocutor serves not only informational but legitimising functions, projecting an image calibrated to domestic expectations of national interest, development and geopolitical coherence.

This alignment is further reinforced through editorial practices that privilege in-house reporting, enabling greater control over narrative framing and thematic emphasis. Nearly half of the coverage originates from internal journalistic resources, indicating a deliberate effort to curate India's image through a lens that foregrounds its relevance to Thailand's strategic calculus. The construction of India as a 'partner of consequence' reflects a form of editorial sovereignty exercised in tandem with state priorities, whereby the media functions less as an autonomous watchdog and more as a mediating apparatus that channels policy-driven representations into the public domain. This systemic arrangement facilitates a selective visibility of India, emphasising those attributes that resonate with national objectives, such as market potential and regional security contributions, while rendering peripheral its cultural plurality or environmental trajectories.

Conversely, the substantial dependence on transnational news syndicates introduces a secondary axis of influence, characterised by cost-driven outsourcing and the embedded logics of international news production. External content introduces frames shaped by the priorities of global media conglomerates, which tend to accentuate volatility, conflict and political risk. This reliance produces a representational tension: while domestic reporting constructs India as a stable, strategic collaborator, externally sourced material frequently situates it within narratives of disorder or democratic fragility. The resultant hybridity in India's media image reflects a structural disjuncture, one that arises from the simultaneous pursuit of strategic coherence and economic pragmatism in news production. The tendency across both domains toward negative affect, whether via the dramatisation of crises or the editorial filtering of contentious issues, further underscores the normative bias that privileges disruption over continuity, spectacle over substance.

This dual structure of content production, involving local curation intersecting with external dependency, reveals deeper contradictions within Thailand's media system. The marginal presence of themes unrelated to immediate political or economic utility, such as cultural heritage, scientific collaboration or environmental diplomacy, signals an epistemological narrowing of foreign representation. Such exclusions are not incidental but symptomatic of systemic hierarchies wherein informational relevance is defined by proximity to material returns or policy leverage. The resultant narrative economy thus distils foreign nations into instrumental categories, emphasising functionality over complexity, and positioning international actors according to their perceived strategic yield rather than their societal totality.

Taken together, these dynamics illustrate how Thailand's media apparatus negotiates the competing demands of national alignment and global integration. The selective construction of India's image exemplifies a broader pattern in which foreign realities are mediated through an institutional logic of pragmatism, constrained by editorial economics, audience calibration and policy proximity. Media here emerges not as a passive observer but as an active participant in the production of international visibility, shaping public understanding through narrative selections that echo, amplify or selectively obscure dimensions of geopolitical relevance. In doing so, it not only reflects but also reproduces the asymmetries of global engagement, offering a curated window into the world that privileges strategic affinity over pluralistic representation.

Qualitative Analysis of News Headlines

This study undertakes a qualitative analysis of headline sentiment across three leading English language news outlets in Thailand, *Bangkok Post, The Nation* and *Thaiger* over a six month period from May 1 to October 31, 2024. In all, 166 headlines were sampled and coded for affective tone (positive, negative, neutral and apprehensive), enabling a systematic examination of how each publication frames its coverage of India. By comparing sentiment distributions and identifying recurring linguistic patterns, this research seeks to uncover whether and to what extent these newspapers diverge in their editorial outlooks, and how such differences might shape reader perceptions of national and regional affairs.

News Item: 25

Bangkok Post

OPINION

China ministers' India trips show warming of relations

Diplomatic meetings set stage for possibility of President Xi Jinping to visit India for G20 Summit in September

RABI SANKAR BOSU

PUBLISHED : 12 MAY 2023 AT 09:50
NEWSPAPER SECTION: OPED WRITER: RABI SANKAR BOSU

Relations between two neighbouring countries and the world's first and second-most populous countries, China and India, have witnessed a downward spiral in recent years after the bloody clash between the two countries' border troops in the Galwan Valley in June 2020, along the Line of Actual Control (LAC) in the western section of the Sino-Indian border.

In its May 12, 2023, online edition, *Bangkok Post* published the headline "China Ministers' India Trips Show Warming of Relations" (News Item 25), a formulation that conveys optimism by framing high level diplomatic visits as evidence of a thaw in bilateral tensions. The choice of the metaphor 'warming' implies a conscious shift away from the 'frostiness' that followed the June/ 2020 Galwan Valley clashes, suggesting instead a trajectory toward cooperation and mutual goodwill. By highlighting the possibility of President Xi Jinping attending the forthcoming G20 Summit in India, the headline not only underscores the strategic importance Beijing attaches to its relationship with New Delhi but also elevates India's international stature. Understanding this positive framing is crucial for India's representation because it signals to regional audiences that India is regarded as a credible and desirable partner by one of the world's leading powers, thereby reinforcing New Delhi's image as an effective and respected actor on the global stage.

News Item: 26

THE nation

India's Ascension from Middle Power to Emerging Great Power: A Geopolitical Analysis

In its October/ 6, 2023, online edition, *The Nation* ran the headline "India's Ascension from Middle Power to Emerging Great Power: A Geopolitical Analysis" (News Item 26), a formulation that radiates optimism by framing India's international trajectory as not merely progressive but transformative. The choice of the word 'ascension' conveys upward mobility and strategic momentum, while 'emerging great power' elevates India's status from a regional actor to a contender on the global stage. Such positive framing is significant for India's representation because headlines serve as the gateway to public perception: by foregrounding India's rise, this headline not only bolsters national prestige but also shapes external audiences' expectations of India's capabilities and influence, reinforcing a narrative of India as an increasingly consequential force in world affairs.

News Item: 27

Bangkok Post

'Like hell': India's burning coalfields

PUBLISHED : 14 JUL 2023 AT 12:51
WRITER: AFP

In its July/ 14, 2023, online edition, ***Bangkok Post*** ran the striking headline "'Like Hell': India's Burning Coalfields" (News Item 27), which immediately conveys a negative tone by equating the country's coal regions with an inferno. The colloquial simile 'like hell' magnifies the environmental and public health crisis, invoking graphic imagery of uncontrolled fires and smog choked skies. Such dramatic wording not only underscores the severity of India's coal mining impacts but also frames the nation as struggling with ecological mismanagement. For international audiences, this kind of headline is particularly influential: it can cement perceptions of India as an environmental laggard and overshadow its efforts to diversify its energy mix, thereby affecting India's broader reputation in foreign media as it seeks to balance economic growth with sustainable development.

News Item: 28

Thaiger

Indian man steals money from Thai vendors near Bangkok

Petch Petpailin · Thursday, August 3, 2023 Last Updated: Thursday, August 3, 2023 · 1 minute read

Share this article

The headline "Indian Man Steals Money from Thai Vendors Near Bangkok" (News Item 28) from an online newspaper presents a negative narrative due to its focus on a criminal act tied to a specific nationality, potentially fostering stereotypes about Indians. Published on August 3, 2023, by *Thaiger*, the story highlights an Indian man committing theft in Thailand, which can harm India's global image by associating the country with illegal behaviour abroad. This type of reporting is significant for understanding India's representation in foreign lands, as it risks straining diplomatic relations with Thailand, increasing scrutiny on Indian travellers and overshadowing their positive contributions in areas like business and culture. Recognising the impact of such headlines is crucial for promoting cultural sensitivity, encouraging responsible behaviour among Indian citizens abroad and mitigating negative stereotypes to maintain a positive international reputation.

News Item: 29

Thaiger

Cyclone Biparjoy threatens India's Gujarat, Pakistan's southern coast

Sara · Monday, June 12, 2023 Last Updated: Thursday, December 21, 2023 · 2 minutes read

Share this article · Facebook · X · LinkedIn · Messenger · Share via Email · Print

The headline "Cyclone Biparjoy Threatens India's Gujarat, Pakistan's Southern Coast" (News Item 29), published by *Thaiger* on June 12, 2023, carries an apprehensive tone due to its focus on an impending natural disaster with the potential for widespread destruction, loss of life and disruption across two countries. The use of 'threatens' highlights the urgency and uncertainty surrounding the cyclone, fostering anxiety about its impact on India's Gujarat and Pakistan's southern coast. Understanding this news is vital for India's representation in foreign lands, as it can generate global awareness and empathy, portraying India as a resilient nation facing a challenge beyond its control, rather than perpetuating negative stereotypes. Additionally, the shared threat with Pakistan emphasises the need for regional cooperation, potentially showcasing India's role in international disaster response efforts, while the effective management of the crisis can enhance its global image as a capable and prepared nation, fostering a positive perception abroad.

News Item: 30

THE nation

Asean, India hold joint exercises in disputed sea for first time

MONDAY, MAY 08, 2023

The headline "Asean, India Hold Joint Exercises in Disputed Sea for First Time" (News Item 30) from *The Nation*, published on Monday, May 8, 2023, is written in a neutral tone, primarily conveying factual information without any explicit bias, emotional charge or sensationalism. It states a significant development, with India and ASEAN nations conducting their first joint exercises in a disputed maritime region, without framing it in a confrontational, provocative or overly celebratory manner. This neutrality is evident in the absence of judgmental language or suggestive phrasing that might indicate either criticism or endorsement. Understanding this headline is important in the context of India's foreign policy and regional representation because it reflects India's increasing strategic engagement with Southeast Asia, especially in sensitive maritime zones like the South China Sea.

Sentiment Dynamics between News Headlines and Introductions of the News

The data offered in Table 32 illustrate that out of 166 news items, 54 (32.53 per cent) exhibit divergent sentiment between the headline and the introduction.

Table 32: Overview of Sentiment Alignment between News Headlines and Introductions (Thailand)

Category	*Number of News Items*	*Percentage of Total*
Total news items	166	100%
Headlines and introductions with different sentiments	54	32.53%

The data offered in Table 33 highlight a critical disjuncture between the sentiment of news headlines and the sentiment of their introductions, revealing deeper implications for media framing and strategic communication. Although all 60 news items analysed feature positive headlines, a significant portion, 25 per cent, exhibits introductions that diverge from this positivity.

Table 33: Breakdown of News Items with Positive Headlines (Thailand)

Category	*Number of News Items*	*Percentage*
Total with positive headlines	60	100%
Introductions with different sentiments	15	25%
• Introductions with apprehensive sentiments	3	5%
• Introductions with negative sentiments	0	0%
• Introductions with neutral sentiments	12	20%

Specifically, 20 per cent of the introductions are neutral in tone, and 5 per cent are apprehensive, while none are overtly negative. This discrepancy suggests that while headlines are carefully crafted to project optimism or reassurance, the accompanying introductions may carry a more cautious or neutral tone, indicating a layered approach to messaging. Positive headlines serve to attract or pacify readers, particularly those who engage only superficially with the content, while the introductions introduce more nuanced or restrained narratives.

Table 34 presents a breakdown of introduction sentiments accompanying news items with negative headlines, highlighting a notable disjuncture between headline framing and the tone of the article's introductory content. While all 67 news items in the dataset feature explicitly negative headlines, 26 of these, amounting to 38.80 per cent, exhibit introductions that do not align with the same degree of negativity.

Table 34: Breakdown of Introduction Sentiments for Negative Headlines (Thailand)

Category	*Number of News Items*	*Percentage of Negative Headlines*
Total with negative headlines	67	100%
Introductions with different sentiments	26	38.80
• Introductions with positive connotation	0	0%
• Introductions with neutral sentiments	13	19.40%
• Introductions with apprehensive sentiments	13	19.40%

Specifically, 19.4 per cent of the introductions are neutral in tone, and another 19.4 per cent express an apprehensive sentiment, suggesting a more cautious or uncertain framing rather than outright negativity. Notably, no introductions reflect a positive sentiment, indicating that while the editorial framing avoids direct contradiction, it often moderates the emotional impact implied by the headline. This divergence suggests an editorial strategy in which negativity is amplified at the headline level, possibly to attract reader attention or emphasise crisis, while the introduction adopts a more tempered or ambiguous stance. Such a pattern reflects a layered approach to news framing, where emotional intensity is heightened superficially but diluted in content, ultimately shaping reader perception in subtle yet strategic ways.

Another set of data in Table 35 brings a breakdown of intro sentiments for news items with apprehensive headlines, revealing a notable inconsistency in the alignment between headline tone and the opening narrative. Out of 21 news items that feature apprehensive headlines (100 per cent), 11 items, amounting to 52.38 per cent,have introductions that do not reflect the same tone of apprehension. Among these, 38.09 per cent of the introductions are neutral, and 9.52 per cent adopt a negative sentiment, while none exhibit a positive tone.

Table 35: Breakdown of Introduction Sentiments for Apprehensive Headlines (Thailand)

Category	*Items*	*Percentage of Apprehensive Headlines*
Total with apprehensive headlines	21	100%
Introductions with different sentiments	11	52.38%
• Introductions with positive sentiments	0	0%
• Introductions with negative sentiments	2	9.52%
• Introductions with neutral sentiments	8	38.09%

This data points to a significant editorial divergence, wherein the headlines signal uncertainty or cautious concern, but the introductions often adopt a more restrained or emotionally detached stance. The use of neutral introductions, in particular, suggests an effort to temper the emotional intensity introduced by the headline, possibly reflecting a strategy of editorial hedging. Such a pattern indicates that apprehension in headlines may function more as a rhetorical device to attract attention than as an accurate preview of the narrative tone. The absence of positive sentiment reinforces the general mood of caution, yet the moderation seen in many introductions reveals a subtle recalibration of emotional framing.

Table 36 provides a breakdown of introduction sentiments accompanying neutral headlines, revealing a nuanced yet important editorial pattern. Of the 28 news items featuring neutral headlines (100 per cent), three items, amounting to 10.71 per cent, exhibit introductions that depart from the ostensibly neutral framing of the headline. These include one introduction each with positive, negative and apprehensive sentiment, representing 3.57 per cent respectively.

Table 36: Breakdown of Introduction Sentiments for Neutral Headlines (Thailand)

Category	*Items*	*Percentage of Neutral Headlines*
Total with neutral headlines	28	100%
Introductions with different sentiments	3	10.71%
• Introductions with positive sentiments	1	3.57%
• Introductions with apprehensive sentiments	1	3.57%
• Introductions with negative sentiments	1	3.57%

While the majority of neutral headlines maintain tonal consistency with their introductions, the presence of sentimentally divergent introductions suggests that neutrality at the headline level does not uniformly extend into the narrative. This subtle disjuncture highlights the layered nature of journalistic framing, where the headline projects objectivity but the introduction may contain implicit emotional or evaluative cues. Such editorial choices point toward a strategic use of the introduction as a site for shaping reader perception without undermining the appearance of balance or neutrality.

Qualitative Analysis of Discrepancies and Contradictions between Headlines and Introductions in News Articles

Discrepancies and contradictions between headlines and their corresponding introductions have emerged as key indicators of editorial framing and implicit bias. This study employs qualitative methods to examine such inconsistencies in prominent Thai news outlets, with the aim of uncovering the editorial motivations that drive these narrative divergences and assessing their implications for the construction of public discourse, national image and policy perception.

News Item: 31

Bangkok Post

OPINION

China ministers' India trips show warming of relations

Diplomatic meetings set stage for possibility of President Xi Jinping to visit India for G20 Summit in September

RABI SANKAR BOSU | PUBLISHED : 12 MAY 2023 AT 05:00
NEWSPAPER SECTION: OPED WRITER: RABI SANKAR BOSU

Relations between two neighbouring countries and the world's first and second-most populous countries, China and India, have witnessed a downward spiral in recent years after the bloody clash between the two countries' border troops in the Galwan Valley in June 2020, along the Line of Actual Control (LAC) in the western section of the Sino-Indian border.

The news article from *Bangkok Post* (May 12, 2023), titled "China Ministers' India Trips Show Warming of Relations" (News Item 31), presents a positive sentiment in its headline, suggesting an improvement in diplomatic ties. However, its introduction adopts a more neutral tone while recounting negative historical context, stating that "Relations between two neighbouring countries... have witnessed a downward spiral in recent years after the bloody clash... in the Galwan Valley...". This apparent contradiction serves a specific journalistic purpose: the headline aims to capture attention and convey the article's main thesis, the positive development of warming relations. In contrast, the introduction provides essential background, establishing the challenging recent history. By detailing the prior 'downward spiral', the subsequent 'warming' highlighted in the headline gains greater significance and impact, a common technique in news analysis and opinion pieces to frame an argument effectively by contrasting new developments with past realities.

News Item: 32

THE nation

India's Odisha state takes centre stage in a tourism roadshow in Bangkok

THURSDAY, JULY 27, 2023

The roadshow, organised in association with the Federation of Indian Chambers of Commerce & Industry (FICCI), saw more than 130 tour and travel operators from Thailand networking with stakeholders from Odisha.

The ambassador of India to Thailand, Nagesh Singh, delivered the keynote address by lauding the strategic steps taken by the government of Odisha in promoting tourism.

"This networking event will open more avenues for bilateral trade relations between the two regions," he said.

News Item: 33

Bangkok Post

THAILAND › GENERAL

Russian, Indian nationals detained in Phuket villa raid

PUBLISHED : 27 OCT 2023 AT 10.58
WRITER: ACHADTHAYA CHUENNIRAN

PHUKET - A Russian and two Indian nationals were arrested and charged for overstaying their visas during a police raid on a villa in Bang Thao beach area of Thalang district on Thursday.

At about 1.15pm, a team of immigration and tourist police went to the villa, with a warrant issued by Phuket Provincial Court, for the arrest of an Indian man on charges of threatening and intimidating other people.

An article in *The Nation* published on July 27, 2023, demonstrates a common journalistic approach where the headline, "India's Odisha State Takes Centre Stage in a Tourism Roadshow in Bangkok" (News Item 32), conveys a distinctly positive sentiment by emphasising prominence and success. In contrast, the introduction, stating that "The roadshow, organised in association with the Federation of Indian Chambers of Commerce & Industry (FICCI), saw more than 130 tour and travel operators from Thailand networking with stakeholders from Odisha", maintains a neutral connotation by focussing on the factual details of the event.

The headline from *Bangkok Post*, published on October 27, 2023 reads: "Russian, Indian Nationals Detained in Phuket Villa Raid" (News Item 33). This headline carries a negative sentiment, largely due to the use of terms like 'detained' and 'villa raid', which evoke criminality, legal trouble and an image of disruptive or illicit behaviour. For Indian readers or international observers, the association of 'Indian nationals' with such language in a headline contributes to a portrayal of India or its citizens in a questionable or problematic light. However, the introduction of the article takes on a 'more neutral tone'. It simply reports that a Russian and two Indian nationals were arrested for overstaying their visas during a police operation, and it factually adds that a warrant was issued for one Indian individual for threatening and intimidating behaviour. The tone is descriptive and devoid of sensationalism; it frames the individuals' actions within legal and procedural terms rather than moral judgment or scandal.

News Item: 34

THE nation

Canada investigates India's possible link to Sikh activist's slaying

TUESDAY, SEPTEMBER 19, 2023

Canada expelled a top Indian diplomat Monday as it investigates what Prime Minister Justin Trudeau called credible allegations that India's government may have had links to the assassination in Canada of a Sikh activist.

Trudeau said in **Parliament** that Canadian intelligence agencies have been looking into the allegations after Sikh leader **Hardeep Singh Nijjar**, a strong supporter of an independent Sikh homeland known as **Khalistan**, was gunned down on June 18 outside a Sikh cultural centre in **Surrey, British Columbia**.

The news article from *The Nation* (September 19, 2023) presents a clear contradiction between the sentiment conveyed in its headline and the tone of its introductory paragraph. The headline, "Canada Investigates India's Possible Link to Sikh Activist's Slaying" (News Item 34), adopts an apprehensive sentiment, marked by cautious phrasing such as 'investigates' and 'possible link', which implies uncertainty and avoids making direct accusations. This choice reflects a moderated editorial tone, likely intended to maintain diplomatic neutrality and adhere to legal norms when addressing sensitive international allegations. In contrast, the lead paragraph shifts sharply to a negative connotation by stating that Canada expelled a top Indian diplomat and citing Prime Minister Justin Trudeau's assertion of 'credible allegations' against the Indian government regarding the assassination. The use of the word 'assassination' and the emphasis on diplomatic action project a tone of blame and confrontation. This discrepancy highlights a strategic editorial approach where headlines are crafted to appear neutral, while the article's body communicates a more accusatory narrative. Such framing suggests a deliberate attempt to balance the optics of impartial reporting with the need to convey the gravity of geopolitical tensions, ultimately shaping public perception through nuanced narrative layering.

News Item: 35

Phuket: Russian and Indians overstay visa leading to police raid

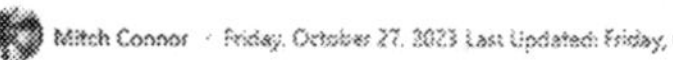

Mitch Connor · Friday, October 27, 2023 Last Updated: Friday, October 27, 2023 1 minute read

A **Russian** national and two **Indian** men were **apprehended** during a police raid in **Phuket's** Bang Thao beach district, charged with overstaying their **visas**. The **operation** was conducted by a joint team of **immigration and tourist police** yesterday afternoon around 1.15pm at a villa where they expected to arrest another **Indian** man under charges of **threats** and **intimidation**.

The **Phuket Provincial Court** had issued the warrant but the intended individual was not present during the raid. Instead, they encountered Georgi Shkodo, a Russian who was in the country despite an expired visa. The 33 year old was immediately taken to Cherng Talay Police Station for further inquiry while four law enforcement officers stayed behind at the villa for continued surveillance.

The news article from *Thaiger* (October 27, 2023) titled "Phuket: Russian and Indians Overstay Visa Leading to Police Raid" (News Item 35) exhibits a notable discrepancy between the sentiment expressed in the headline and the tone of the lead paragraph. The headline maintains a neutral sentiment, presenting the incident in a factual and procedural manner. It simply states the nationalities involved, the issue of visa overstays and the resulting police action, without employing emotionally charged language or implying guilt beyond the stated facts. However, the introductory paragraph conveys a distinctly negative connotation. It uses terms like 'apprehended', 'charged', 'intimidation' and 'threats', which suggest criminal behaviour and elevate the seriousness of the incident beyond administrative visa violations. The tone intensifies with the mention of a coordinated police operation, a court-issued warrant and continued surveillance, all of which frame the incident as part of a broader law enforcement crackdown. The focus on the individuals' national identities, particularly 'Indian men' and a 'Russian national', further adds an undertone of profiling and public alarm.

India in ASEAN Media: Study of Singapore

The study examines the media representation and coverage of India over a six-month period from May 1 to October 31, 2023. A total of 1,092 news items were systematically collected and analysed. The research aims to investigate editorial priorities, sourcing patterns and narrative construction, with particular attention to headlines and introductory paragraphs. Additionally, the study explores the thematic focus of India-related reporting within Singapore's mainstream media landscape. The analysis of 1,092 India focussed news items published by *The Straits Times*, *Today* and *The Business Times* reveals a highly selective representational regime in which India is predominantly cast as both a geostrategic actor and an emergent economic powerhouse.

Table 37: Singapore's Top News Categories Related to India

Category of News, Topic Wise: Singapore	*Number of News Items*	*Percentage*
Domestic Politics	76	6.95%
Terrorism/Law & Order	48	4.39%
Global Economy and India	218	19.96%
India's Economy	262	23.99%
Bilateral Relations	13	1.19%
Geopolitics and India	302	27.65%
Climate Disaster	34	3.11%
Governance/Accident	92	8.42%
Science and Technology	33	3.02%
Cultural/Miscellaneous	15	1.37%
TOTAL	1,092	100%

Fully 71.6 per cent of all items foreground India's geopolitical positioning (27.65 per cent), domestic economic performance (23.99 per cent) and integration into the global economy (19.96 per cent), thereby privileging narratives of strategic agency and market potential over other dimensions of India's national experience. Secondary attention is accorded to governance and accident reporting (8.42 per cent) and domestic political developments (6.95 per cent), which serve principally to contextualise India's institutional stability and policy trajectory (Table 37). Reports of major accidents, infrastructure failures and anti corruption drives function as barometers of administrative efficacy, implicitly signalling to Singaporean stakeholders the relative reliability of India's governance environment. Similarly, coverage of electoral contests, high level visits and other dynamics like cultural linkages offers a proximate lens through which readers may anticipate the continuity or transformation of macro economic and regulatory regimes, factors of considerable import to analysts of regional risk and opportunity.

Table 38: Singapore's Top Five News Categories Related to India

Category of News, Topic Wise: Singapore	*Number of News Items*	*Percentage*
Geopolitics and India	302	27.65%
India's Economy	262	23.99%
Global Economy and India	218	19.96%
Governance/Accident	92	8.42%
Domestic Politics	76	6.95%

By contrast, issues of internal security and law enforcement (4.39 per cent), environmental crises (3.11 per cent), scientific and technological innovation (3.02 per cent) and cultural or miscellaneous topics (1.37 per cent) are rendered peripheral (Table 37). This marginalisation suggests that, despite India's burgeoning role in global climate negotiations, frontier research and soft power diplomacy, such domains fail to satisfy the dominant news values of 'impact' and 'proximity' as defined by Singaporean editors. Standalone coverage of bilateral diplomacy, treaties, state visits and institutional dialogues, accounts for barely 1.19 per cent of the total corpus (Table 37), indicating that formal India–Singapore relations are rarely decoupled from broader strategic economic narratives. Instead, bilateral engagements are subsumed within discussions of multilateral security architectures or investment flows, reinforcing a transactional framing of India as a partner of convenience rather than as a subject of intrinsic bilateral interest.

Taken together, this pattern of coverage constructs a discursive frame in which India's primary relevance to Singapore lies in its capacity to buttress regional security and to generate commercial opportunities. Such framing not only shapes public perceptions by valorising India's strategic–economic attributes but also occludes the socio cultural, environmental and human rights dimensions of India's domestic landscape. From a theoretical standpoint, these findings align with both agenda setting and framing theories in international communication, demonstrating how media gatekeepers prioritise narratives that intersect with national interests and market considerations.

Table 39: News Source Analysis (Singapore)

Total News Items	1,092	100%
News coverage by reporters/news desk/editorial/op-eds	389	35.62%
News coverage by international agencies/national agencies/freelancers/contributors	703	64.37%

The data derived from the study provides a detailed quantitative breakdown of news sourcing in the coverage of India. Of the 1,092 news items, 389 (35.62 per cent) were attributed to local sources such as reporters, news desks, editorial teams and op-ed contributors. In contrast, a significantly larger proportion, amounting to 703 items (64.37 per cent), were sourced from international and national news agencies, freelancers or external contributors (Table 39). This distribution not only reveals the structural dynamics of news production within Singapore's mainstream media but also offers insights into the mechanisms that shape India's media representation in the country.

Locally produced news, attributed to in-house reporters and editorial teams, is likely to reflect the editorial priorities, institutional perspectives and cultural framing practices of Singaporean media organisations. Such content may incorporate domestically relevant narratives that align with Singapore's national interests, including trade relations with India, strategic convergence within ASEAN and issues concerning the sizable Indian diaspora residing in the city-state. Editorials and opinion pieces, in particular, offer a space for critical commentary on India's domestic and foreign policies, contextualised within Singapore's geopolitical outlook and socio-economic priorities.

Conversely, externally sourced content, comprising reports from global wire services such as Reuters and AFP, as well as international and national agencies and independent contributors, is often syndicated or aggregated with limited editorial intervention from the host media outlet. These items typically represent secondary content, meaning they were not originally produced by the Singaporean newspapers themselves. As a result, the framing of India within such articles may be shaped more by global geopolitical discourses and Western media narratives than by Singaporean editorial sensibilities.

The overwhelming reliance on external sources (64.37 per cent) aligns with the broader concept of global news flow, in which media systems in smaller states or those with limited international bureaus depend heavily on transnational wire services for foreign news. This reliance has significant implications for the portrayal of India in Singaporean media. It raises the possibility that India's image is often mediated through the lens of non-Singaporean perspectives, which may not prioritise issues of bilateral relevance or capture nuances specific to India–Singapore relations. Consequently, coverage risks reinforcing homogenised or Western-dominated narratives, potentially marginalising locally relevant themes such as the Comprehensive Economic Cooperation Agreement (CECA), diaspora contributions or collaborative regional efforts within ASEAN frameworks.

Furthermore, the limited proportion of locally produced content (35.62 per cent) suggests that Singaporean journalists and editorial teams may exert only partial influence over the construction of India's media image. This structural dependency on external content producers may curtail opportunities for nuanced, context-rich reporting that reflects Singapore's distinctive socio-political engagement with India. Such an imbalance underscores the importance of interrogating not just the content of India-related coverage but also its provenance, as the origin of news stories plays a critical role in framing how foreign nations are perceived in domestic public spheres.

The sourcing data reveals a deeper structural condition within Singapore's news production ecosystem, one that privileges external narratives over locally grounded perspectives. Recognising this dynamic is essential to understanding the mediated construction of India's image in Singaporean media. Without such analysis, there is a risk of assuming that media portrayals are wholly reflective of Singaporean perspectives, when in fact they may be reproductions of dominant global frames. The findings invite further enquiry into how source provenance interacts with editorial framing and how Singaporean media might expand its agency in shaping foreign representations that resonate with its national interests and cultural sensibilities.

Table 40: Sentiment Analysis of Positive News (Singapore)

Positive news articles out of a total of 1,092 news articles	366	33.51%
Positive stories by reporters/news desk/opinion	112	30.60%
Positive stories by international agencies/national agencies/ freelancers/contributors	254	69.39%

Table 41: Sentiment Analysis of Negative News (Singapore)

Negative news articles out of a total of 1,092 news articles	259	23.71%
Negative stories by reporters/news desk/opinion	87	33.59%
Negative stories by international agencies/national agencies/ freelancers/contributors	171	66.02%

Table 42: Sentiment Analysis of Apprehensive and Neutral News (Singapore)

Number of apprehensive news items of a total of 1,092 news items	150	13.73%
Number of neutral news items of a total of 1,092 news items	318	29.12%

The sentiment analysis of 1,092 news items about India in Singaporean newspapers reveals a nuanced portrayal, with 33.51 per cent (366 items) (Table

40) classified as positive, 23.71 per cent (259 items) (Table 41) as negative, 29.12 per cent (318 items) as neutral and 13.73 per cent (150 items) (Table 42) as apprehensive, indicating a generally balanced yet favourable coverage that likely emphasises India's economic growth, technological advancements, position as a leading global power, cultural contributions and bilateral ties with Singapore. External sources, including international and national agencies, freelancers and contributors, play a dominant role in setting the sentiment, contributing 69.39 per cent (254 items) positive stories and 66.02 per cent (171 items) negative ones (Tables 40 and 41), suggesting that global media narratives, often shaped by Western agencies like Reuters, AP, AFP, etc., prioritise topics such as India's economic potential, geopolitical tensions or governance challenges, which may overshadow more localised perspectives. In contrast, local reporters, news desks and opinion writers in Singapore contribute 30.60 per cent (112 items) positive and 33.59 per cent (87 items) negative stories (Tables 40 and 41), reflecting a smaller but significant role that might focus on Singapore-specific interests, such as trade partnerships, investment, geopolitical dynamics related to India and Singapore or regional security concerns, though their influence is constrained by the heavy reliance on external sources. This dynamic highlights a potential risk of homogenised global narratives marginalising Singaporean viewpoints, which is particularly significant given Singapore's media landscape, where outlets like *The Straits Times* often align with government priorities. Understanding these sentiment dynamics is crucial for decoding how India is perceived in Singaporean media, as it affects public opinion, strengthens or strains bilateral relations and shapes the cultural identity of the diaspora.

Decoding India–Singapore News Coverage: Priorities and Reasons

India's portrayal in Singaporean media reflects a narrowly focussed narrative that privileges strategic and economic dimensions while marginalising cultural, environmental and scientific facets. By spotlighting strategic partnerships, investment flows and macroeconomic performance, together accounting for 71.6 per cent of coverage, it casts India chiefly as a transactional actor whose value lies in bolstering regional security and generating economic opportunities. In this framing, headlines and leads routinely emphasise multilateral security architectures and market indicators.

This selective approach reflects the operation of strategic communication processes including editorial gatekeeping, sourcing choices, framing devices and sentiment management that collectively shape image of any country. Climate disasters (3.11 per cent), science and technology breakthroughs (3.02 per cent) and societal cultural narratives (1.37 per cent) fall outside the 'impact' and 'proximity' criteria prized by editors, rendering them news-value poor. Even reporting on governance issues (8.42 per cent), such as major accidents or anti-corruption drives, is treated less as human-interest storytelling than as a barometer of administrative efficacy, signalling 'reliability' or 'risk' to corporate and governmental stakeholders.

The sourcing patterns reinforce this narrow lens. Only 35.6 per cent of India-related items originate from locally produced reportage including reporters, news desks or op-eds, while 64.4 per cent are syndicated from international and national wire services, agencies or freelancers. This reliance on external copy imports frames leaving Singaporean newsrooms limited scope to develop context-rich, home-grown analyses of bilateral news (just 1.19 per cent of items). Sentiment analysis further reveals the affective contours of this framing. Positive stories (33.5 per cent) predominantly highlight India's successful journey in geopolitics, economic dynamics and partnership, while negative (23.7 per cent) and apprehensive (13.7 per cent) items serve as cautionary tales about governance or environmental vulnerabilities. External sources disproportionately drive both ends of this spectrum, contributing nearly 70 per cent of positive and two-thirds of negative coverage, underscoring how narrative control and emotional tone often rest with transnational entities rather than local editorial teams.

Only through systematic, quantitative disaggregation of topic frequencies, sourcing provenance and sentiment proportions can these latent biases and strategic imperatives be exposed. Such data-driven analysis challenges any assumption of balanced bilateral reporting and instead reveals a media environment tightly circumscribed by Singapore's security and economic priorities and the structural dependency on wire service copy. For India's public diplomacy, the findings point to the need for outreach that breaks free of these constraints by cultivating locally rooted storytelling, foregrounding diaspora voices and creating channels for genuine two-way engagement.

Analysing News Sentiment (Headlines) and Contextualisation of Sentiments of News toward India in Singapore Media

The contemporary portrayal of India in Singaporean media emerges as a carefully orchestrated narrative that privileges strategic and economic imperatives while systematically marginalising the rich and diverse dimensions of India's cultural heritage, environmental leadership and scientific innovation. This editorial prioritisation, manifested through repetitive framing around security cooperation, economic partnerships and transactional diplomacy, presents India as a utilitarian actor, one whose relevance is narrowly construed through the prisms of geopolitical alignment and market viability. Such a reductive portrayal not only simplifies a complex bilateral relationship but also undermines the capacity of media to act as a site of intercultural understanding and diplomatic nuance.

This phenomenon is embedded within broader structures of strategic communication, where editorial gatekeeping, sourcing decisions and framing devices coalesce to reinforce dominant narratives aligned with Singapore's perceived national interests. The privileging of governance stories through metrics of institutional risk or reliability, rather than through the lenses of social welfare, civic agency or lived experience, further consolidates a technocratic and risk-calibrated image of India, suited more to boardrooms than to broader public imagination.

The systemic reliance on syndicated wire content, predominantly sourced from global news agencies, exacerbates this narrative imbalance. Externalised reporting frameworks often lack the contextual sensitivity or local granularity required to capture the subtleties of India–Singapore interactions. This dependency not only constrains the editorial autonomy of Singaporean newsrooms but also perpetuates an asymmetrical information environment, wherein transnational media entities exert outsized influence over how foreign nations are represented. The result is a media discourse oscillating between celebration and caution, celebrating India's rising stature in global affairs or markets, while cautioning against its governance lapses or environmental vulnerabilities, yet rarely venturing into the everyday cultural, intellectual or ethical contributions that might deepen mutual understanding.

From a theoretical perspective, this dynamic can be interpreted through the interconnected lenses of agenda-setting, framing and gatekeeping theories. Together, they explain how certain themes acquire salience while others are omitted, based not merely on newsworthiness, but on ideological fit, audience alignment and institutional constraints. Furthermore, the narrative paradigm theory reveals how dominant media frames lack narrative fidelity and emotional coherence; the rational and strategic tone of coverage, while functional, fails to engage with audiences at the level of identity, meaning or affect.

Simultaneously, Singaporean media institutions must critically reflect on the epistemological implications of their sourcing practices and editorial logics. As a hub of cosmopolitan connectivity and cultural hybridity, Singapore is uniquely positioned to foster a more balanced and inclusive narrative ecosystem, one that not only serves state interests but also cultivates empathy, mutual recognition and regional solidarity.

Structural Imperatives of Singaporean Media and Representation

The structural imperatives that shape the representation of foreign countries in Singaporean media are deeply embedded in the city-state's broader political economy, which blends centralised governance, market-driven logic, cultural cohesion and strategic global positioning. Its media operates within a regulated framework that emphasises national stability, economic growth and social order over journalism. Major media outlets are either state-owned or closely aligned with national authorities, functioning under stringent laws that constrain external influence and promote values of self-censorship. These conditions foster a media environment where foreign nations are represented in ways that align with Singapore's diplomatic and economic interests. Coverage of major global powers is carefully calibrated to maintain diplomatic neutrality, while critical reporting is often avoided if it risks disrupting bilateral relations or economic partnerships.

Commercial interests further reinforce these tendencies, as the media prioritises content that supports Singapore's image as a competitive and reliable financial hub. Countries with strong trade or investment ties are often portrayed positively, with emphasis on economic opportunities and technological partnerships, while less economically relevant or politically sensitive nations receive minimal or highly curated attention. Cultural and ideological frameworks also shape how foreign nations are represented. Media narratives often reinforce values such as pragmatism, meritocracy and multiracial harmony, which results in sceptical portrayals of liberal democracies and more culturally resonant, though cautiously presented, narratives about countries with shared regional or ethnic affinities.

This landscape is further shaped by self-censorship among journalists, who internalise expectations of deference and caution, limiting the scope of critical or alternative perspectives. Sensitive issues, such as regional disputes or human rights violations, are downplayed unless they align with broader strategic objectives. The media also plays a crucial role in supporting Singapore's global identity, portraying the country as a neutral, dependable actor in regional and international affairs. In doing so, representations of foreign countries are tailored to reinforce Singapore's position as a stable node in the global economy.

Altogether, the structural imperatives of state oversight, economic alignment, cultural framing and global strategy converge to produce highly curated and selective portrayals of foreign nations. From a political economy perspective, this system ensures that the media functions not primarily as a space for critical discourse, but as an instrument that sustains national narratives and developmental goals, limiting pluralism while reinforcing dominant strategic priorities.

Qualitative Analysis of News Headlines

This section undertakes a qualitative examination of a few examples from 1,092 India-centric news items published across three leading English-language newspapers in Singapore, *The Straits Times*, *Today* and *The Business Times*. The representational patterns emerging from this corpus suggest a pronounced editorial selectivity, wherein India is predominantly framed through two principal lenses: as a pivotal geostrategic actor within the regional and global order and as a rapidly ascending economic entity. The following section presents a curated set of exemplar news items to facilitate a closer interrogation of how such representations are discursively constructed. Through a detailed qualitative engagement with these headlines and their corresponding introductory paragraphs, the section aims to foreground the underlying sentiment, structural tendencies and rhetorical divergences that characterise Singaporean media narratives on India. This analytical encounter not only illuminates the semiotic textures of headline framing but also reveals the disjuncture that may exist between the headline cues and the elaborative body of the news reports.

News Item: 36

THE BUSINESS TIMES

India seen as bright spot as China gloom weighs on steel demand

BT Published Tue, Aug 8, 2023 · 03:43 PM

The headline from *The Business Times*, published on August 8, 2023, reads: "India Seen as Bright Spot as China Gloom Weighs on Steel Demand" (News Item 36), exemplifying a positively framed representation of India within the global economic discourse. The use of the phrase 'bright spot' carries strong affirmative connotations, highlighting India as a symbol of resilience and opportunity amidst a regional downturn. By juxtaposing India's economic performance with China's 'gloom', the headline constructs a contrastive narrative that elevates India's status as a relatively buoyant and reliable economic actor. Such framing not only amplifies

India's visibility but also reinforces its identity as an emergent and attractive hub in global trade and supply chains, particularly in sectors, like steel, that are indicative of broader industrial vitality. Headlines of this nature play a vital role in shaping international perceptions, especially when published in business-focussed outlets targeting policy makers, investors and economic elites. They contribute to a strategic narrative wherein India is seen not just as a developing economy, but as a stabilising and promising force in the global order. In doing so, this type of media representation participates in reconfiguring India's image, moving it away from traditional frames of instability or underdevelopment and positioning it as a key actor in regional and global economic transformations. As such, this headline is not merely informative but functions as a discursive tool within the larger regime of representational politics concerning India.

News Item: 37

THE STRAITS TIMES

India approves Bill to reserve a third of Parliament Lower House seats for women

14 Nov 2023

NEW DELHI - Indian Prime Minister Narendra Modi said on Tuesday the Cabinet had approved a Bill to reserve one-third of seats in the Lower House of Parliament and state assemblies for women, reviving a proposal that has been hanging for decades.

The announcement by Mr Modi during a special session of Parliament comes eight months before general elections are due by May 2024.

On November 14, 2023, *The Straits Times* reported a pivotal legislative development in India through the headline, *"India Approves Bill to Reserve a Third of Parliament Lower House Seats for Women"* (News Item 37), signalling a transformative moment in the pursuit of gender parity within the country's political architecture. The report foregrounds the passage of the long-deliberated Women's Reservation Bill, approved under the leadership of Prime Minister Narendra Modi, which mandates the allocation of one-third of the seats in the Lok Sabha and state legislative assemblies to women, a provision scheduled for implementation ahead of the May 2024 general elections. This legislative enactment constitutes a structurally progressive intervention into India's historically male-dominated representative institutions, seeking to rectify entrenched patterns of gender-based exclusion in democratic participation. Moreover, the reform is discursively positioned as a challenge to patriarchal political norms, while simultaneously aligning India's democratic praxis with global benchmarks of inclusive governance. In this context, the bill's approval emerges not only as a domestic political milestone but also as a symbolic assertion of India's normative commitment to equitable representation, with implications for the reconfiguration of legislative priorities in favour of more diverse and representative policy agendas.

News Item: 38

THE STRAITS TIMES

India's biofuel targets at risk as government cuts rice supply to distilleries

UPDATED AUG 05, 2023, 12:00 AM

NEW DELHI – India could fall short of its biofuel production targets in 2023 because of a rice supply crunch, dealing a potential blow to its ambitious plans to use ethanol to cut fossil fuel imports and reduce vehicular emissions.

The government aims to blend petrol sold in the country with 12 per cent ethanol, produced domestically mostly from sugar cane and rice, by end-October. However, the government-run Food Corporation of India (FCI) stopped supplying surplus rice in early July to distilleries that produce this biofuel.

The headline from *The Straits Times*, dated August 5, 2023, *"India's Biofuel Targets at Risk as Government Cuts Rice Supply to Distilleries"* (News Item 38) presents a negative framing of India's energy policy and developmental coherence, foregrounding a potential shortfall in the country's biofuel production due to a government-imposed cut in rice supply to distilleries. The headline employs a crisis-oriented narrative, with phrases such as 'at risk' suggesting policy failure or vulnerability, while the attribution of causality to the government's decision signals internal mismanagement or competing priorities between food security and energy needs. This depiction implicitly questions the coherence of India's developmental planning, especially in balancing ambitious sustainability targets with domestic resource constraints. For international audiences, particularly in foreign policy and investment circles, such representation risks undermining India's image as a reliable actor in the global energy transition discourse. Moreover, this instance reflects a broader pattern in foreign reportage, where India's systemic or logistical shortcomings are often highlighted more prominently than its institutional innovations. Understanding such negative headlines is critical for assessing how international media construct narratives around India's development, governance and global credibility, revealing the representational tensions that accompany its dual identity as both an aspirational power and a developing economy navigating structural limitations.

News Item: 39

THE BUSINESS TIMES

India set to ban sugar exports for first time in 7 years

BT Published Wed, Aug 23, 2023 · 07:51 PM

On August 23, 2023, *The Business Times* published a headline, "India Set to Ban Sugar Exports for First Time in 7 Years" (News Item 39), signalling a concerning shift in the country's trade policy with potentially negative implications for its global economic standing. As one of the world's largest sugar producers, India's decision to halt exports after seven years suggests domestic challenges, such as poor harvests or rising internal demand, which could disrupt the global sugar market and drive-up prices for countries reliant on its supply. This move may negatively impact India's agricultural export economy, affecting farmers and traders, while also risking its reputation as a reliable trade partner in foreign markets. Understanding this development is important, as it highlights India's influence on global commodity markets and raises questions about its agricultural stability, potentially shaping foreign perceptions of its economic reliability and priorities on the international stage.

News Item: 40

THE STRAITS TIMES

Ambitious plans for US-India technology sharing face hurdles

UPDATED JUN 23, 2023, 11:13 PM

WASHINGTON - The United States unveiled agreements this week to sell weapons to India and share sensitive military technology with it, a clear sign of the Biden administration's desire to deepen ties with New Delhi to counter China's ambitions in Asia.

But those plans, announced on Thursday during a state visit by Indian Prime Minister Narendra Modi, and future defence cooperation face significant challenges from the US government's own weapons export rules.

The headline from *The Straits Times*, dated June 23, 2023, *"Ambitious Plans for US–India Technology Sharing Face Hurdles"* (News Item 40) encapsulates an apprehensive tone in its portrayal of bilateral strategic cooperation between India and the U.S. The headline, while acknowledging the forward-looking and expansive nature of the defence and technology agreements, simultaneously introduces a sense of uncertainty and potential stagnation by foregrounding the 'hurdles' these plans face. The juxtaposition of the word 'ambitious' with 'hurdles' signals a classic media framing device wherein optimism is immediately tempered by structural or procedural limitations, in this case, attributed to restrictive U.S. weapons export regulations.

This apprehensive framing is significant for India's representation in foreign media for several reasons. Firstly, it subtly casts doubt on India's capacity to fully capitalise on strategic opportunities, implying that despite New Delhi's rising geopolitical profile and closer alignment with Washington, bureaucratic and legal obstacles may undermine or delay tangible outcomes. Secondly, such representation projects India as a partner with potential, but still embedded in a matrix of dependency on both U.S. domestic legal processes and shifting diplomatic calculations. Therefore, this apprehensive headline reflects a cautious tone that tempers enthusiasm with realism, shaping a perception of India as a state caught between ambition and the constraints of international strategic systems.

News Item: 41

THE STRAITS TIMES

India PM urges UN to rethink priorities for the 21st century

14 Oct. 2023

NEW DELHI - Indian Prime Minister Narendra Modi called on the United Nations to reform in line with 21st century realities to ensure the representation of voices that matter, according to an interview published on Sunday.

A "mid-20th century approach cannot serve the world in the 21st century", Modi, who will host a summit of the Group of 20 big economies from next weekend, told the Press Trust of India news agency.

The headline from *The Straits Times,* dated November 14, 2024, *"India PM Urges UN to Rethink Priorities for the 21st Century"* (News Item 41) exhibits a neutral tone in its construction, marking the absence of overtly evaluative language or emotionally charged framing. The choice of the verb 'urges' reflects a diplomatic and procedural initiative rather than confrontation or acclaim, while the reference to the '21st century' situates the statement within a normative and forward-looking discourse. The headline neither critiques nor glorifies India's stance; instead, it presents Prime Minister Narendra Modi's call for institutional reform at the United Nations as a matter-of-fact proposition aligned with broader global governance debates. Understanding such neutral headlines is vital because they reveal how India is being portrayed not just through moments of crisis or triumph, but through institutional engagements and policy positions. This contributes to a more balanced international perception, where India's diplomatic voice is acknowledged without distortion.

Sentiment Dynamics between News Headlines and Introductions of the News

Another set of data related to the sentiment of headlines and introductions of news items encapsulates findings from an analysis of 1,092 India-focussed news articles. Table 43 reveals that in 408 of these instances, representing 37.36 per cent of the total sample, there was a discernible discrepancy between the sentiment expressed in the headline and that conveyed in the introductory paragraph.

Table 43: Overview of Sentiment Alignment between News Headlines and Introductions (Singapore)

Category	*Number of News Items*	*Percentage of Total*
Total news items	1,092	100%
Headlines and introductions with different sentiments	408	37.36%

This divergence is significant, as it points to a notable pattern wherein more than one-third of the news stories exhibit inconsistency in tone or evaluative framing between their most visible element (the headline) and the accompanying narrative. Such sentiment misalignment has critical implications for how India is represented in foreign media, particularly in the context of Singaporean news outlets examined in the study. This finding underscores the necessity of qualitative scrutiny in media analysis, especially when assessing how strategic actors like India are framed in the international information ecosystem.

Another set of data (Table 44) reveals a compelling discrepancy between the sentiment of headlines and the introductions of news items, suggesting while all 366 headlines maintain a distinctly positive sentiment, 110 of them (30.05 per cent) have introductions that diverge from this tone. This contrast indicates that while headlines set an optimistic frame to capture attention, the introductions shift toward more neutral or apprehensive sentiment, potentially altering how readers interpret the content.

Table 44: Breakdown of Introduction Sentiments for Positive Headlines (Singapore)

Category	*Number of News Items*	*Percentage of Total (31)*
Total with positive headlines	366	100%
Introductions with different sentiments	110	30.05%
• Introductions with apprehensive sentiments	14	3.82%
• Introductions with negative sentiments	0	0%
• Introductions with neutral sentiments	96	26.22%

A key irregularity is the prevalence of neutral introductions, which appear in 96 news items (26.22 per cent). Despite headlines signalling a clear positive outlook, these neutral introductions introduce a more measured or balanced perspective, neither reinforcing nor contradicting the optimistic stance. This suggests that news outlets may use positive headlines as a tool to engage readers while tempering expectations within the content itself. Additionally, 14 articles (3.82 per cent) contain introductions with an apprehensive sentiment, subtly hinting at underlying concerns or uncertainties that contrast with the upbeat framing of the headline. While these apprehensive introductions are a minority, their presence reflects the complexities of news reporting, where cautious language may be employed to prepare the audience for deeper contextual nuances. Interestingly, no introductions carry explicitly negative sentiments, reinforcing the pattern that news outlets may actively avoid stark contradictions between headlines and introductions. Instead, they appear to favour a mix of positivity, neutrality and mild apprehension, shaping an information landscape where sentiment is carefully modulated rather than drastically opposed. This selective use of sentiment suggests a strategic editorial approach, one that leverages engaging headlines to draw readers in while maintaining a more tempered narrative within the body of the article.

Table 45: Breakdown of Introduction Sentiments for Negative Headlines (Singapore)

Category	*Number of News Items*	*Percentage of Negative Headlines*
Total with negative headlines	259	100%
Introductions with different sentiments	88	33.97%
• Introductions with positive connotation	4	1.54%
• Introductions with neutral sentiments	53	20.46%
• Introductions with apprehensive sentiments	31	11.96%

Among the 259 India-focussed news items distinguished by overtly negative headlines, a striking 33.97 per cent (n = 88) manifest a disjunction between the affective valence of the headline and that of the introductory paragraph, revealing a nontrivial pattern of editorial inconsistency (Table 45). Within this cohort of divergent cases, a scant 1.54 per cent (n = 4) of introductions unexpectedly project a positive connotation, effectively inverting the adverse framing signalled by the headline and creating a jarring semantic reversal that can leave readers questioning the veracity or intent of the reportage. A more substantial segment, 20.46 per cent (n = 53), adopts a neutral tone in its lead, thereby attenuating the alarm or critique implicit in the headline and recasting what might initially read as a crisis narrative into a matter-of-fact exposition. The remaining 11.96 per cent (n = 31) of introductions register an apprehensive sentiment, introducing a note of caution or uncertainty that while consonant with the headline's negativity nuances it with hedging language rather than outright condemnation. Moreover, in the crucible of international opinion formation, where first impressions are often predicated on headline cues, such sentiment discrepancies risk distorting global perceptions of India's political, economic or social trajectory. Consequently, this phenomenon warrants rigorous qualitative scrutiny, both to unpack the editorial logics that produce headline–introduction sentiment gaps and to assess their broader implications for India's image in the transnational media ecosystem.

Table 46: Breakdown of Introduction Sentiments for Apprehensive Headlines (Singapore)

Category	*Items*	*Percentage of Apprehensive Headlines*
Total with apprehensive headlines	150	100%
Introductions with different sentiments	68	45.33%
• Introductions with positive sentiments	11	7.33%
• Introductions with negative sentiments	22	14.66%
• Introductions with neutral sentiments	35	23.33%

The data in this study provide a detailed breakdown of sentiment irregularities between apprehensive headlines and their corresponding introductions, revealing notable contradictions in tone (Table 46). Of the 150 news items with apprehensive headlines, a significant portion, 68 items (45.33 per cent), present introductions with a different sentiment, demonstrating a meaningful shift in how the story is framed.

Table 47: Breakdown of Introduction Sentiments for Neutral Headlines (Singapore)

Category	*Items*	*Percentage of Neutral Headlines*
Total with neutral headlines	318	100%
Introductions with different sentiments	83	26.10%
• Introductions with positive sentiments	34	10.69%
• Introductions with apprehensive sentiments	27	8.49%
• Introductions with negative sentiments	19	5.97%

A closer look at these differences shows that 35 introductions (23.33 per cent) adopt a neutral sentiment, indicating that while the headline sets a tone of caution or concern, the opening text of the article tempers this emotion by neither reinforcing nor directly contradicting the apprehensive stance. Similarly, 22 introductions (14.66 per cent) introduce a negative sentiment, deepening the apprehensive nature of the headline and reinforcing a sense of unease or criticism. However, an intriguing finding is that 11 introductions (7.33 per cent) shift to a positive sentiment, contradicting the initial tone set by the headline. This suggests that certain articles may use apprehensive headlines to attract attention while transitioning to a more reassuring or optimistic narrative within the content itself.

Within the subset of 318 news items carrying ostensibly neutral headlines,

83 cases (26.10 per cent) exhibit a clear sentiment misalignment between headline and introduction (Table 47). Notably, while 34 introductions (10.69 per cent) infuse an unexpectedly positive tenor into an otherwise neutral framing, introducing an optimistic valence absent from the headline's literal phrasing, 27 introductions (8.49 per cent) adopt an apprehensive tone, injecting caution or uncertainty that contrasts with the headline's balanced register. Meanwhile, 19 introductions (5.97 per cent) convey a distinctly negative sentiment, directly contradicting the headline's neutral stance. These irregularities suggest that over a quarter of 'neutral' items conceal underlying affective biases in their opening paragraphs, revealing editorial strategies that leverage a neutral headline as a façade for more emotionally charged narrative shifts. From a discourse-analytic viewpoint, such headline–introduction divergences can recalibrate reader expectations: positive introductions can lend undue buoyancy, while negative or apprehensive leads may impart unwarranted gravity, thus undermining the coherence and credibility of media representations.

Qualitative Analysis of Discrepancies and Contradictions between Headlines and Introductions in News Articles

This study also explores the qualitative discrepancies and contradictions between headlines and introductory paragraphs in Singaporean online newspaper articles. It aims to understand how headline framing may diverge from or distort the main thrust of the article's introduction.

News Item: 42

THE STRAITS TIMES

PM Modi may give farm handouts as food export bans hit rural India

AUG 8, 2023

NEW DELHI – Prime Minister Narendra Modi may offer handouts to Indian farmers ahead of the elections as food commodity export bans to control inflation begin to hurt incomes and could cost him some votes.

There is already a ban on the export on wheat, and in July, the Modi administration halted the overseas sale of some rice varieties as well. Curbs on stockpiling some food staples were also imposed with an eye to keeping inflation in check.

The article from *The Straits Times,* dated August 8, 2023, presents a clear example of the contrast that can often exist between the tone of a headline and the actual content of a news story. The headline, "PM Modi May Give Farm Handouts as

Food Export Bans Hit Rural India" (News Item 42), conveys a largely positive or constructive sentiment. It suggests that the Indian prime minister is taking decisive action to support farmers who are suffering due to recent policy decisions, namely export bans on key food commodities. The use of the word 'handouts' in this context implies financial relief or aid, casting the government's move in a favourable light and framing it as a timely intervention to help rural communities.

However, a closer look at the opening paragraph of the article reveals a more nuanced and somewhat apprehensive undertone. It indicates that the potential handouts are not merely about supporting farmers but are also tied closely to electoral considerations. The paragraph notes that the export bans, implemented to control inflation, are beginning to hurt rural incomes, and could cost Prime Minister Modi some votes. This positions the handouts less as a proactive welfare initiative and more as a reactive political strategy aimed at minimising electoral damage. In doing so, the introduction introduces an element of scepticism about the government's motivations, suggesting that the policy may be driven more by political expediency than by genuine concern for farmers' welfare. This discrepancy between the headline and the introduction reflects a broader trend in digital journalism, where headlines are often crafted to draw clicks and create immediate interest, sometimes at the expense of fully conveying the complexity or critical tone of the article itself. While the headline creates an impression of government responsiveness and benevolence, the body of the article adds depth by highlighting the underlying political calculations and the unintended consequences of earlier policy decisions.

News Item: 43

THE BUSINESS TIMES

India announces car safety rating to cut accident rate

BT Published Tue, Aug 22, 2023 · 11:10 PM

INDIA will have a new safety rating system for passenger cars from October based on tests, including crashes from the front and side, to make its cars and roads safer, the country's Ministry of Road Transport and Highways said on Tuesday (Aug 22).

India, the world's third largest car market, has some of the deadliest roads where about 150,000 people died in accidents last year, according to government data.

The article from *The Business Times,* dated August 22, 2023, reveals a subtle contrast between the tone of the headline and the introductory paragraph. The headline, "India Announces Car Safety Rating to Cut Accident Rate" (News Item 43), carries a clearly positive and forward-looking sentiment. It highlights a government initiative aimed at improving road safety and reducing traffic fatalities, framing the move as a proactive and progressive step. However, the tone of the introductory paragraph is noticeably neutral. It simply states the factual details of the announcement that India will introduce a new safety rating system for passenger cars from October, based on crash tests, and attributes the information to the Ministry of Road Transport and Highways. The paragraph lacks any emotive or evaluative language, focussing instead on procedural details without interpreting the policy's broader impact. This creates a subtle contradiction: while the headline emphasises intent and impact, suggesting a meaningful stride toward public safety, the introduction adopts a more reserved, administrative tone. This contrast illustrates how headlines often aim to capture attention and shape perception through positive framing, while the body of the article may begin with more neutral, fact-based exposition.

News Item: 44

THE BUSINESS TIMES

India set to ban sugar exports for first time in 7 years

BT Published Wed, Aug 23, 2023 · 07:51 PM

INDIA is expected to ban mills from exporting sugar in the next season beginning October, halting shipments for the first time in seven years, as a lack of rain has cut cane yields, three government sources said.

India's absence from the world market would be likely to increase benchmark prices in New York and London that are

The article from *The Business Times,* dated August 23, 2023, displays a contrast between the sentiment of the headline and the tone of the introductory paragraph. The headline, "India Set to Ban Sugar Exports for First Time in 7 Years" (News Item 44), carries a distinctly negative sentiment. It emphasises disruption by highlighting a significant policy shift after a long period, using words like 'ban' and 'first time in 7 years' that suggest market disturbance and economic consequence, particularly for global stakeholders reliant on Indian sugar exports. This framing naturally evokes concern or alarm among readers, especially those in the international trade and commodity sectors.

However, the introductory paragraph adopts a neutral tone, offering a straightforward explanation for the decision without emotional language or bias. It simply reports that India is expected to halt sugar exports in the upcoming season starting in October, attributing the move to a shortfall in sugarcane yield caused by insufficient rainfall. The language is factual and devoid of judgment, focussing on the causality and quoting unnamed government sources. The second paragraph continues in the same vein, explaining the likely market impact without dramatisation.

This contrast arises because headlines are crafted to catch attention and often highlight conflict or disruption, whereas introductory paragraphs typically provide context or cause in an objective manner. In this case, the headline uses a negatively charged frame to underscore the seriousness of the export ban, while the introduction grounds the issue in natural factors and policy response, maintaining a neutral, explanatory tone. This difference in tone between headline and body is a common editorial technique to balance reader engagement with journalistic clarity.

News Item: 45

today

China think tank says India is 'sabotaging' G20 for its own agenda

Published September 9, 2023
Updated September 9, 2023

The harsh criticism by the China Institute of Contemporary International Relations, which is under the Ministry of State Security, comes as G20 leaders began their annual two-day summit, in India's capital New Delhi, with Chinese President Xi Jinping not attending.

The think tank accused India of bringing geopolitical "private goods" onto the global stage, which it said would not only help the country to fulfill its responsibility as the host of G20 but also create further problems.

The article from *Today*, published on September 9, 2023, presents a notable difference in sentiment between the headline and the introductory paragraph. The headline, "China Think Tank Says India is 'Sabotaging' G20 For Its Own Agenda" (News Item 45), conveys a strongly negative sentiment. It uses the word 'sabotaging', a highly charged and accusatory term that implies intentional disruption and malign intent. The headline frames India as acting in bad faith during a major international event, instantly setting a confrontational and critical tone.

In contrast, the introductory paragraph adopts a more apprehensive tone rather than directly negative. It notes that the criticism originates from the China Institute of Contemporary International Relations, which operates under China's Ministry of State Security, and it links the timing of the statement to the G20 summit in New Delhi, which Chinese President Xi Jinping did not attend. While the paragraph conveys tension and the gravity of the accusations, it maintains a cautious, descriptive tone without endorsing or amplifying the allegation. It implies geopolitical sensitivity and strategic undertones rather than outright condemnation.

This difference arises because headlines are crafted to grab immediate attention, often using provocative or emotionally loaded language, especially when quoting contentious views. The body or introductory paragraph, however, tends to provide context and attribution, often softening the impact of strong claims by identifying the source and its possible motives. In this case, the headline spotlights a direct accusation using a stark term ('sabotaging'), whereas the introduction takes a measured approach, highlighting the timing, origin and implications of the criticism, giving it an apprehensive, cautious feel rather than overt hostility.

News Item: 46

THE STRAITS TIMES

Why India is a 'good choice but not the first choice' for Taiwan companies

UPDATED MAY 14, 2023, 11:06 PM

BENGALURU - The Indian government has rolled out the red carpet for investors from Taiwan in its bid to become a global manufacturing hub that rivals China, offering subsidies, cheap land and incentives to attract semiconductor and electronics manufacturers to the South Asian nation.

However, India's efforts to woo Taiwanese firms that are looking to diversify their operations outside the Chinese mainland have run into hurdles such as infrastructure gaps, bureaucratic delays and competition from Vietnam and Thailand.

The article from *The Straits Times*, updated on May 14, 2023, displays an interesting contrast between the tone of the headline and the sentiment in the introductory paragraph. The headline, *"Why India is a 'Good Choice but Not the First Choice' for Taiwan Companies"* (News Item 46), carries an apprehensive sentiment. It subtly questions India's positioning as a top destination for Taiwanese investors by suggesting that while India is favourable, it is still not the preferred option. The phrase 'not the first choice' implies a lack of full confidence or lingering limitations that prevent India from leading the race in attracting Taiwanese firms.

In contrast, the introduction of the article conveys a positive connotation. It highlights India's proactive and welcoming approach toward Taiwancsc investment. The text emphasises how the Indian government has 'rolled out the red carpet' for Taiwanese companies, showcasing efforts to rival China by offering subsidies, cheap land and incentives to semiconductor and electronics manufacturers. This signals optimism and ambition in India's industrial policy and its strategic outreach to Taiwan.

This contradiction exists because headlines are crafted to balance intrigue with realism, especially when dealing with complex economic dynamics. In this case, the headline introduces a cautious outlook, suggesting that India's potential is promising but not fully realised, which grabs attention and invites further reading. The introductory paragraph, however, begins with the bright side of India's pitch to investors, reflecting government initiative and industrial progress. The overall effect highlights the gap between intent and perception, or ambition and reality, where India is working hard to become a global manufacturing hub, yet still faces challenges in surpassing regional competitors in investor preference.

News Item: 47

today

Anti-Muslim hate speech in India concentrated around elections, report finds

Published September 26, 2023
Updated September 26, 2023

There were 255 documented incidents of hate speech gatherings targeting Muslims in the first half of 2023, the report found. There was no comparative data for prior years.

It used the United Nations' definition of hate speech as "any form of communication... that employs prejudiced or discriminatory language towards an individual or group based on attributes such as religion, ethnicity, nationality, race, color, descent, gender, or other identity factors."

The news article from *Today*, published on September 26, 2023, presents a clear contrast between the tone of its headline and the sentiment found in the introductory paragraph. The headline, *"Anti-Muslim Hate Speech in India Concentrated Around Elections, Report Finds"* (News Item 47), carries a neutral sentiment. It is fact-based, stating the findings of a report without any emotional or judgmental language. The structure is clinical and investigative, simply relaying that hate speech incidents were concentrated around election periods, which gives it an informational tone.

In contrast, the introductory paragraph has a negative connotation. It reveals a disturbing reality: 255 documented incidents of hate speech targeting Muslims were recorded in just the first half of 2023. The paragraph also mentions the lack of comparative data, subtly hinting at potential underreporting or absence of systematic monitoring in earlier years. The reference to the United Nations' definition of hate speech, emphasising "prejudiced or discriminatory language", amplifies the seriousness of the issue, highlighting its deeply harmful and divisive nature.

The contradiction here lies in the presentation strategy. The neutral headline may aim to maintain journalistic objectivity and attract broader readership, especially when dealing with sensitive issues involving religion and politics. However, the introduction quickly pulls readers into the gravity of the situation, offering data and definitions that paint a stark and troubling picture of communal tensions during electoral periods. This approach reflects a deliberate editorial choice to balance neutrality in framing with the severity of the content to follow.

India in ASEAN Media: Study of the Philippines

This study undertakes a systematic content analysis of news reporting practices across three prominent Philippine media outlets, *Philstar Global, Inquirer* and *ABS-CBN*, over a six-month period from May 1 to October 31, 2024, encompassing a corpus of 158 news items. The research specifically interrogates the sentiment orientation of headlines, the attribution and credibility of news sources and the discursive tone employed in the introductory sections or leads of the articles. By conducting a comparative sentiment analysis between headlines and introductions, the study aims to uncover potential intra-textual dissonance, editorial framing strategies and their implications for reader perception, agenda-setting and media influence within the context of Philippines' political economy of media.

Table 48: Philippines' Top News Categories Related to India

Category of News, Topic Wise: Philippines	*Number of News Items*	*Percentage*
Domestic Politics	5	3.16%
Terrorism/Law & Order	5	3.16%
Global Economy, Investment, Investment and India	10	6.32%
India's Economy	17	10.75%
Bilateral Relations	18	11.39%
Geopolitics, External Affairs, Foreign Affairs and Defence	31	19.62%
Climate Disaster	22	13.92%
Governance/Accident	31	19.62%
Science & Technology	13	8.22%
Cultural/Society	6	3.79%
	158	100%

The content analysis of 158 India-related news items published across *Philstar Global*, *Inquirer* and *ABS-CBN* between May and October 2024 reveals a distinct editorial prioritisation within Philippine media, reflecting both regional strategic interests and normative framing practices. The data indicates a disproportionate focus on five key categories: Geopolitics, External Affairs, Foreign Affairs and Defence (19.62 per cent), Governance/Accident (19.62 per cent), Climate Disaster (13.92 per cent), Bilateral Relations (11.39 per cent) and India's Economic (10.75 per cent), which together constitute over 75 per cent of total coverage (Table 49).

Table 49: Philippines's Top Five News Categories Related to India

Category of News, Topic Wise: Philippines	*Number of News Items*	*Percentage*
Geopolitics, External Affairs, Foreign Affairs and Defence	31	19.62%
Governance/Accident	31	19.62%
Climate Disaster	22	13.92%
Bilateral Relations	18	11.39%
India's Economy	17	10.75%

This distribution underscores how India is predominantly constructed as a geopolitical actor, a governance model and a regional partner in crisis management and economic collaboration. The emphasis on external affairs and bilateral diplomacy suggests a media framing aligned with state-centric narratives and strategic regionalism, while the salience of governance and climate issues reflects an implicit valuation of institutional competence and resilience. Such patterns highlight agenda-setting imperatives that reinforce India's representation, mediated through selective editorial framing and thematic clustering that foregrounds strategic interdependence, regional security and technocratic governance, hallmarks of both media influence and the underlying political economy shaping transnational news flows.

The source analysis data underscores a critical dimension in understanding the media representation of India within the Philippine media ecosystem. Out of 158 India-related news items (used as a proxy to assess regional framing, including India's visibility), a striking 89.24 per cent (141 items) were sourced from international or national agencies, while only 10.75% per cent (17 items) originated from in-house reporters, editorial teams or op-eds (Table 50).

Table 50: News Source Analysis (Philippines)

Total News Items	158	100%
News coverage by reporters/news desk/editorial/op-eds	17	10.75%
News coverage by international agencies/national agencies/freelancers/contributors	141	89.24%

This overwhelming reliance on external content producers not only reflects structural dependencies in Philippine newsrooms but also signals a constrained discursive sovereignty when it comes to representing India and regional affairs. Such sourcing patterns diminish the possibility of localised, interpretive journalism that could contextualise India's role in ASEAN dynamics through culturally and politically nuanced lenses. Instead, the dominant use of syndicated or agency material tends to reproduce pre-framed narratives, often shaped by global or regional hegemonic information flows, which may dilute India's complex engagements with the Philippines and Southeast Asia.

From the perspective of the media representation theory and the political economy of communication, this sourcing imbalance limits agenda-setting power within domestic media, delegating interpretive authority to transnational content producers. It also reduces the potential for alternative framings, editorial critiques or public diplomacy efforts from a uniquely Filipino standpoint. Understanding this data is essential for decoding how India is positioned in the mediated consciousness of Philippine audiences, not as an object of direct reportage or public discourse, but often as a secondary actor filtered through broader narratives of geopolitical alignments, investment patterns or multilateral diplomacy. This, in turn, raises concern about epistemic autonomy and the selective visibility of India in the Philippine media sphere, where representation is not merely about presence, but about the modes, sources and intentions of narrative construction.

The sentiment analysis data of India-related news coverage in the Philippine media reveals critical insights into how narratives around India are constructed, circulated and potentially perceived by domestic audiences. Of the 158 news articles studied, only 22.78 per cent were coded as positive and 19.62 per cent as negative, while the remaining proportion (implicitly over 57 per cent) presumably falls under neutral or mixed sentiments (Tables 51, 52 and 53).

Table 51: Sentiment Analysis of Positive News (Philippines)

Positive news articles out of a total of 158 news articles	36	22.78%
Positive stories by reporters/news desk/opinion	7	19.44%
Positive stories by international agencies/national agencies/freelancers/contributors	29	80.55%

Table 52: Sentiment Analysis of Negative News (Philippines)

Negative news articles out of a total of 158 news articles	31	19.62%
Negative stories by reporters/news desk/opinion	5	16.12%
Negative stories by international agencies/national agencies/freelancers/contributors	26	83.87%

Table 53: Sentiment Analysis of Apprehensive and Neutral News (Philippines)

Number of apprehensive news items of a total of 158 news items	28	17.72%
Number of neutral news items of a total of 158 news items	63	39.87%

Crucially, within the positive news cluster, a dominant 80.55 per cent were produced by international or national agencies, freelancers or contributors, while only 19.44 per cent originated from local reporters or editorial desks. A similar trend is evident in negative news, with 83.87 per cent of items produced by external sources and just 16.12 per cent by domestic newsroom actors. This asymmetry is indicative of a structural and editorial dependency, where Philippine media outlets rely heavily on wire services or syndicated sources for constructing narratives around India.

Understanding the sentiment data is not merely a statistical exercise but a foundational approach in decoding the ideological and representational position India occupies in the Philippine media realm. Sentiment is not a neutral descriptor; it reflects the evaluative stance taken by the media, which in turn influences public perception, agenda-setting and political imagination. The production source of sentiment-laden stories plays a key role here. External contributors, particularly international agencies, often package content through globally resonant but potentially detached frameworks, which may emphasise India's geopolitical tensions, economic reforms or crises without contextualising them for a Filipino audience. Conversely, when domestic reporters engage directly with India-related stories, they can bring in localised angles or comparative insights that better situate India within ASEAN or Philippines–India bilateral dynamics.

Moreover, the marginal presence of apprehensive news in the Philippines data set (17.72 per cent out of 158 items) compared to the relatively higher proportion of negative India-related stories (19.62 per cent of 158) suggests a differentiated representational logic that privileges Singapore as a stable partner while portraying India through more episodic or issue-specific lenses. This difference further emphasises how sentiment analysis, when coupled with source tracing, uncovers latent editorial hierarchies, geopolitical affinities and media economies of trust. In sum, recognising the interplay between sentiment and news sourcing is essential to deconstruct how India is selectively made visible, legible and meaningful within Philippine media narratives. It also foregrounds the urgent need for more direct, locally anchored journalism that can recalibrate these representations through critical engagement rather than mediated repetition.

Decoding India–Philippines News Coverage: Priorities and Reasons

Discursive prioritisation in news coverage operates through selective emphasis on particular issues, narratives and actors, thereby guiding how audiences perceive and engage with mediated realities. News outlets do not merely report events but actively shape interpretive frameworks by highlighting specific dimensions of a story, identifying causes, assigning responsibility and suggesting consequences. Through patterns of visibility and omission, media institutions establish hierarchies of relevance that structure public attention. Representational practices often draw from culturally embedded schemas and institutional power relations, privileging dominant perspectives while rendering alternative or subnational viewpoints peripheral. Strategic editorial techniques, such as clustering related stories and curating the prominence of sources within introductory passages, consolidate these dynamics and reinforce prevailing geopolitical and economic orientations. These discursive mechanisms are rarely neutral; they are embedded in broader media ecologies that are characterised by commercial compressions, content syndication and asymmetrical information flows. As a result, news representation becomes a curated terrain where meaning is produced through deliberate choices about inclusion, tone and emphasis. The mediated portrayal of international actors therefore reflects not only journalistic intent but also the structural conditions of media production and the ideological undercurrents that influence narrative construction. Recognising these embedded patterns is crucial for understanding how media contributes to the shaping of public consciousness and the symbolic ordering of global affairs.

Analysing News Sentiment (Headlines) and Contextualisation of Sentiments of News towards India in Philippine Media

The predominance of neutral and moderately valence headlines in Philippines–India reportage reflects a calibrated strategy of mediated engagement that aligns closely with the objectives of strategic communication and public diplomacy. By distributing positive and negative evaluative cues sparingly, and concentrating most items in a neutral register, Philippine outlets sustain relatively an image of editorial impartiality (in comparison with other studied media outlets in this study) that, paradoxically, advances diplomatic signalling more effectively than overt advocacy. This 'soft positioning' mirrors Joseph Nye's concept of soft power, in which reputational capital is accrued not through coercive messaging but via subtle alignment with shared norms and interests. At the same time, occasional insertions of critical headlines by syndicated agencies function as a credibility anchor: criticism signals independence, making subsequent favourable coverage more persuasive.

Viewed through the lens of two-step and networked agenda dynamics, these headline sentiment patterns perform a dual relay. First, they shape elite perceptions, which include policymakers, opinion leaders, and diplomats, by presenting India's actions in terms of reliability, partnership, or challenge. Second, through syndication networks, these distilled impressions cascade into wider public discourse, reproducing a meta-narrative in which India is alternately collaborator, reformer or foil. This interlocking sequence echoes the narrative paradigm, which posits that audiences make sense of events through coherent storylines structured around values and character roles; here, headline sentiment acts as the 'plot cue' that primes interpretive horizons. Moreover, the overwhelming dependence on external wire services underscores a propaganda model critique, wherein structural media imperatives and syndication economies subtly channel international information flows and privilege hegemonic frames over localised nuance. The sentiment architecture of headlines not only reflects but also constitutes a strategic communicative choreography, one that leverages narrative theory, network influence and the political economy of news to shape India's mediated image in the Philippines and beyond.

Structural imperatives of Philippine Media and Representation

Philippine media operate within an interconnection of commercial imperatives, political affiliations and syndication dependencies that together constitute their structural imperatives. Ownership concentration, where a handful of conglomerates control multiple platforms, inevitably steers editorial priorities toward content that safeguards advertising revenues and political patronage. Reliance on wire services and international agencies further entrenches a double bind: domestic outlets are pressed to fill space with cost-effective, pre-packaged stories even as those same stories perpetuate externally framed narratives. Regulatory frameworks and self-censorship add another layer, incentivising outlets to avoid material that might jeopardise lucrative business relationships or challenge entrenched power structures. In this environment, the representation of any foreign country becomes a function not solely of journalistic judgment but of newsroom economics, ownership interests and the transnational circulation of ready-made copy.

Interpreting the current study through the lens of the political economy of media is indispensable because it situates sentiment orientation, source attribution and discursive tone within these larger power relations. Without attending to how profit motives, syndication agreements and elite alliances shape news supply, one risks treating coverage patterns as purely editorial choices rather than outcomes of structural constraints. A political–economic perspective reveals why certain countries are rendered primarily as strategic partners or crisis actors, why outsourced content predominates and why nuanced, locally rooted analyses remain the exception. In doing so, it underscores that media representation is not an index of objective reality but a constructed reflection of the economic and political forces that govern news production.

Qualitative Analysis of News Headlines

This section presents a qualitative study analysing the sentiment expressed in selected news headlines from three prominent Philippines media outlets: *Philstar Global, Inquirer* and *ABS-CBN.* The study covers a six-month period from May 1 to October 31, 2024, drawing from a corpus of 158 news items. By examining a curated selection of headlines, the study aims to explore the variations in sentiments and identify patterns or differences in how these outlets frame their coverage.

News Item: 48

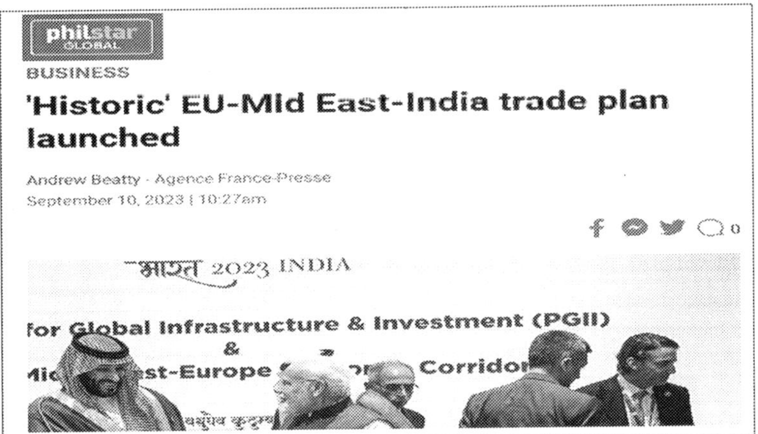
philstar GLOBAL

BUSINESS

'Historic' EU-Mid East-India trade plan launched

Andrew Beatty - Agence France-Presse
September 10, 2023 | 10:27am

The headline from *Philstar Global*, "'Historic' EU-Mid East-India Trade Plan Launched" (News Item 48), published on September 10, 2023, by Andrew Beatty from AFP carries a distinctly positive sentiment that underscores a significant milestone in international collaboration. The use of the word 'historic' emphasises the ground-breaking nature of the trade plan, suggesting a transformative moment in global economic relations, while 'launched' conveys the successful initiation of this initiative, fostering a sense of optimism and progress. This positivity is further reinforced by the focus on cooperation among the European Union, the Middle East and India, which highlights the potential for mutual economic benefits and strengthened diplomatic ties under the Partnership for Global Infrastructure and Investment (PGII). Such portrayal not only reflects India's growing diplomatic clout but also its strategic importance in international trade frameworks, which can shape perceptions among global audiences and investors. Additionally, the positive framing by a reputable outlet like *Philstar Global*, known for its international reach, can influence how India is perceived in Southeast Asia and beyond, potentially attracting economic opportunities while reinforcing India's narrative as a rising global leader in an increasingly interconnected world.

News Item: 49

INQUIRER.NET

BUT RISKS TO DOWNSIDE REMAIN

India to hold top spot for economic growth, survey shows

Reuters / 11:31 AM September 27, 2023

Share:

The headline from *Inquirer*, "India to Hold Top Spot for Economic Growth, Survey Shows" (News Item 49), published on September 27, 2023, and sourced from Reuters, conveys a positive sentiment by highlighting India's leading position in global economic performance. The phrase 'top spot for economic growth' emphasises India's success and prominence, fostering a sense of optimism and pride, while the reference to a survey adds credibility, grounding the positive outlook in data and enhancing reader confidence. Despite the subheading's mention of 'risks to downside', the main headline prioritises India's achievement, maintaining an overall positive tone that celebrates its economic progress. Understanding this headline is essential for assessing India's global representation as it positions India as a dynamic economic powerhouse, which can attract foreign investment and strengthen trade partnerships, particularly in the Global South.

News Item: 50

philstar GLOBAL

WORLD

India flood toll hits 56, army warns on stray munitions

Sailendra Sil - Agence France-Presse

October 8, 2023 | 12:08pm

0

The headline from *Philstar Global*, “India Flood Toll Hits 56, Army Warns on Stray Munitions” (News Item 50), published on October 8, 2023, and sourced from AFP, carries a distinctly negative sentiment by focussing on a tragic natural disaster and its dangerous aftermath. The phrase ‘flood toll hits 56’ immediately highlights the severity of the crisis, with the specific death toll evoking sadness and concern, while ‘army warns on stray munitions’ adds a layer of ongoing risk, suggesting potential for further harm and creating a sense of urgency and alarm. This focus on loss and unresolved danger, rather than recovery, crafts a grim tone that underscores the crisis in India. Understanding this headline is vital for assessing India’s representation in foreign lands, as it highlights the country’s vulnerability to natural disasters, potentially shaping international perceptions of India as a nation grappling with environmental and safety challenges. Published by a prominent Philippine outlet and sourced from AFP, this negative framing may elicit sympathy and humanitarian concern but could also reinforce stereotypes of India as a developing nation struggling with infrastructure, overshadowing its modern achievements, and affecting its global image in regions like Southeast Asia where *Philstar* holds influence.

News Item: 51

ABS-CBN

Overseas

Canada withdraws 41 diplomats from India over separatist killing

Agence France-Presse

Published Oct 20, 2023 05:46 PM PHT

The headline from *ABS-CBN*, “Canada Withdraws 41 Diplomats from India over Separatist Killing” (News Item 51), published on October 20, 2023, sourced from AFP, conveys an apprehensive sentiment through its focus on a deteriorating diplomatic relationship and underlying tensions. The phrase ‘withdraws 41 diplomats’ signals a significant and drastic action, reflecting strained bilateral ties, while the reference to a ‘separatist killing’ introduces a serious and contentious issue, likely tied to allegations of political violence, which fosters unease and concern about potential conflict or instability. This apprehensive tone is evident in the implication of escalating tensions between Canada and India, suggesting a diplomatic crisis that could have broader geopolitical repercussions. Understanding this headline is critical for evaluating India's representation in foreign lands, as it portrays India in a contentious light, potentially linked to controversial political actions, which may negatively impact its international image as a stable and cooperative global partner. Published by *ABS-CBN*, a leading Philippine media outlet, this headline reflects how India's diplomatic challenges are perceived in Southeast Asia and beyond, potentially influencing foreign perceptions of India's governance and its handling of separatist issues, which could affect its credibility and relationships with other nations in the global arena.

News Item: 52

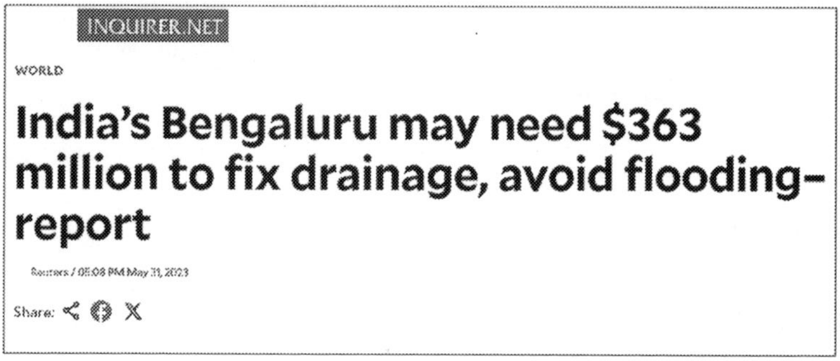

INQUIRER.NET

WORLD

India's Bengaluru may need $363 million to fix drainage, avoid flooding–report

Reuters / 05:08 PM May 31, 2023

Share:

The headline from *Inquirer*, "India's Bengaluru May Need $363 Million to Fix Drainage, Avoid Flooding - Report" (News Item 52), published on May 31, 2023, and sourced from Reuters, exhibits a neutral sentiment by presenting a factual and objective account of a potential infrastructural challenge in Bengaluru, a major Indian city. The phrase 'may need $363 million' uses speculative language to estimate the cost, avoiding emotional bias, while 'to fix drainage, avoid flooding' identifies both the problem and a solution in a balanced manner, focussing on practicality without evoking strong positive or negative emotions. The reference to a 'report' further enhances the headline's objectivity by grounding the information in data. Understanding this headline is significant for assessing India's representation in foreign lands, as it highlights urban challenges in a key tech hub, potentially shaping international perceptions of India's infrastructure and development trajectory, while its neutral tone ensures a balanced portrayal that neither glorifies nor criticises, fostering a realistic view of India as a developing nation addressing its needs.

Sentiment Dynamics between News Headlines and Introductions of the News

The data offered in Table 54 illustrate that out of 158 news items, 68 (43.03 per cent) exhibit divergent sentiments between the headline and the introduction (the lead paragraph).

Table 54: Overview of Sentiment Alignment between News Headlines and Introductions (Philippines)

Category	*Number of News Items*	*Percentage of Total*
Total News Items	158	100%
Headlines and introductions with different sentiments	68	43.03%

This suggests a significant prevalence of affective dissonance, which may reflect intentional discursive constructions aimed at maximising engagement or managing audience perception. Such sentiment shifts may also point to underlying tensions between the commercial imperatives of sensationalism and the normative ideals of balanced reporting. Understanding these dynamics is crucial for critically interrogating how affective framing influences public cognition and narrative construction in contemporary news media.

Table 55: Breakdown of Introduction Sentiments for Positive Headlines (Philippines)

Category	*Number of News Items*	*Percentage*
Total with positive headlines	36	100%
Introductions with different sentiments	11	30.55%
• Introductions with apprehensive sentiments	2	5.55%
• Introductions with negative sentiments	0	0%
• Introductions with neutral sentiments	9	25%

The data in Table 55 offers a granular view into the affective heterogeneity within news discourse, specifically among news items featuring ostensibly positive headlines. Out of 36 such items, 30.55 per cent reveal dissonance in sentiment between the headline and the introduction, a significant finding that complicates assumptions of sentiment consistency across journalistic structures. The predominance of neutral (25 per cent) and apprehensive (5.55 per cent) tonal shifts within these introductions indicates that even when initial cues suggest optimism or affirmation, the discursive body may reposition the narrative into a more ambivalent or cautious register. This discord underscores the layered construction of meaning in news texts, where different narrative components serve distinct affective and cognitive functions. Thus, the interplay between headline sentiment and introductory tone reveals a form of textual stratification, wherein affect is not uniformly distributed but selectively modulated across segments, shaping interpretive trajectories in subtle yet powerful ways.

Table 56: Breakdown of Introduction Sentiments for Negative Headlines (Philippines)

Category	*Number of News Items*	*Percentage of Negative Headlines*
Total with negative headlines	28	100%
Introductions with different sentiments	13	46.42%
• Introductions with positive connotation	0	0%
• Introductions with neutral sentiments	12	42.85%
• Introductions with apprehensive sentiments	1	3.57%

The data in Table 56 reveals that nearly half (46.42 per cent) of news items with negative headlines present a divergence in sentiment at the level of the introductory paragraph, with 42.85 per cent adopting a neutral tone and a marginal 3.57 per cent reflecting apprehension. This pattern of sentiment modulation suggests that while negative headlines function as strong initial affective cues, potentially oriented toward eliciting urgency, concern or moral judgment, the subsequent narrative often tempers this intensity, embedding the event within a more dispassionate or context-sensitive register. The complete absence of positive reframing at the introductory level points to a bounded spectrum of permissible sentiment shifts, wherein the reversal of negative affect is constrained by normative conventions of seriousness and credibility in journalistic practice. The prevalence of neutral introductions in this corpus signals a textual negotiation between affective provocation and informational stability, indicating that news production involves not only the representation of events but the careful calibration of emotional tone.

Table 57: Breakdown of Introduction Sentiments for Apprehensive Headlines (Philippines)

Category	*Items*	*Percentage of Apprehensive Headlines*
Total with apprehensive headlines	31	100%
Introductions with different sentiments	22	70.96%
• Introductions with positive sentiments	0	0%
• Introductions with negative sentiments	7	22.58%
• Introductions with neutral sentiments	15	48.38%

The data in Table 57 illustrate a pronounced sentiment divergence within news items that employ apprehensive headlines, with 70.96 per cent of the corresponding introductions deviating from the initial tonal register. Of these, nearly half (48.38 per cent) transition into neutral sentiment, while 22.58 per cent escalate the affective weight by adopting explicitly negative tones. The absence of positive sentiment in all introductions suggests a discursive boundary in how apprehension is narratively resolved or re-contextualised. Rather than offering a redemptive or reassuring counterpoint, these introductions predominantly re-anchor the affect within either a neutral explanatory framework or a more explicitly distressing register. This pattern underscores how apprehensive headlines function as precursors to more complex affective elaborations that resist simplification. The divergence may reflect an editorial imperative to move from emotional ambiguity to discursive clarity, positioning apprehension as a transitional affect rather than an endpoint. Thus, the high rate of sentiment shift not only reveals the stratified architecture of news composition but also the careful management of uncertainty in public discourse, where headlines evoke unease and introductions act as sites of epistemic containment or intensification, shaping how readers navigate the tension between emotional provocation and informational authority.

Table 58: Breakdown of Introduction Sentiments for Neutral Headlines (Philippines)

Category	*Items*	*Percentage of Neutral Headlines*
Total with neutral headlines	63	100%
Introductions with different sentiments	22	34.92%
• Introductions with positive sentiments	5	7.93%
• Introductions with apprehensive sentiments	12	19.04%
• Introductions with negative sentiments	5	7.93%

Table 58 reveals that approximately 34.92 per cent of news items with neutral headlines manifest a departure from neutrality in their introductory segments, with affective shifts dispersed across positive (7.93 per cent), apprehensive (19.04 per cent) and negative (7.93 per cent) tones. This distribution highlights the latent volatility embedded even in ostensibly impartial headline formulations. The prevalence of apprehensive sentiment among these shifts suggests that neutrality may function less as an affirmation of objectivity and more as a rhetorical veil under which affective complexity is deferred to subsequent textual layers. In this regard, the headline operates as a discursive threshold, muting emotional valence at the point of entry while leaving space for its later articulation within the introduction. Such stratification complicates conventional assumptions that neutrality in news texts ensures consistency in tone or intent. Instead, it foregrounds a layered architecture of meaning-making in which neutrality is not a stable descriptive category but a flexible rhetorical posture.

Qualitative Analysis of Discrepancies and Contradictions between Headlines and Introductions in News Articles

Within the media landscape, headlines function as pivotal instruments in shaping audience perception, often serving as the primary source of news content in digital formats. Discrepancies and contradictions between headlines and their corresponding leads have emerged as critical indicators of editorial manipulation. This study employs qualitative methods to scrutinise such inconsistencies in major Philippine news outlets, aiming to elucidate the editorial motivations behind these practices and to evaluate their implications for media narrative construction, public diplomacy and policymaking. Consequently, the analysis contributes to ongoing scholarly debates surrounding journalistic ethics and the distortion of information within market-driven and politically complex media environments.

News Item: 53

INQUIRER.NET

India's July wholesale price index falls less than expected on food prices

Reuters / 04:42 PM August 14, 2023

NEW DELHI -India's wholesale price index fell 1.36 percent year-on-year in July, but the decline was smaller than expected because of higher prices for food and some commodities.

Economists polled by Reuters had estimated the wholesale price index for July would fall 2.7 percent . It fell 4.12 percent in June.

The news article from *Inquirer,* dated August 14, 2023, presents a notable contrast between the sentiment conveyed in its headline and the tone of its lead paragraph. The headline, "India's July Wholesale Price Index Falls Less Than Expected on Food Prices" (News Item 53), adopts a positive framing by emphasising that the decline in the Wholesale Price Index (WPI) was milder than anticipated. This suggests a narrative of relative economic resilience, as a smaller-than-expected fall in prices may be perceived as indicative of stabilising market conditions. However, the introductory paragraph introduces an apprehensive undertone by revealing that the 1.36 per cent year-on-year decline was driven primarily by higher food and commodity prices. This detail introduces concerns about inflationary pressures in essential sectors, which can adversely affect consumer purchasing power and signal underlying structural issues within the economy. The body of the article introduces economic concerns that warrant caution. Such divergence underscores how editorial strategies may prioritise engagement in headlines while the article's content delivers a more nuanced economic analysis.

News Item: 54

WORLD

India visa processor in Canada says told to stop services

Agence France-Presse

September 21, 2023 | 5:56pm

NEW DELHI, India — India's official visa processor in Canada said Thursday it had been told to stop handling applications, before taking down the notice amid a diplomatic row sparked by Ottawa's accusation New Delhi was involved in the killing of a Sikh separatist.

Shortly after the announcement was splashed across Indian media, BLS removed the notice from their website. There was no immediate comment from India's foreign ministry.

An official at New Delhi-headquartered BLS said they did not want to be quoted and referred AFP to Indian authorities.

On September 21, 2023, *Philstar Global* published a front page headline that read, "India Visa Processor in Canada Says Told to Stop Services" (News Item 54). At first glance, this headline feels urgent and worrisome: it highlights a sudden interruption in visa processing and hints at a sharp disagreement between India and Canada. Such wording can make readers imagine long lines of frustrated applicants or a breakdown in diplomatic relations. Yet, when you read the very first paragraph of the same story, the tone shifts to something much more neutral. It simply reports that BLS International, the company India uses to handle visa applications in Canada, received instructions to pause its services. Soon afterward, the company removed its website notice, and the article briefly mentions that this action took place amid a diplomatic dispute over accusations related to a Sikh separatist's death. There are no charged words or dramatic details here, just the who, what and why in straightforward terms. In essence, the headline is designed to grab your attention by emphasising the most dramatic element, a forced service stoppage, while the opening paragraph focusses on relaying the basic facts without added emotional weight. This approach helps engage readers with a sense of urgency up front, then provides a calm, balanced account of the situation before diving into further explanation.

News Item: 55

philstar GLOBAL

NATION

2 Indians held for robbery

Emmanuel Tupas - The Philippine Star
September 10, 2023 | 12:00am

MANILA, Philippines — Police arrested two Indian men tagged in a robbery in Quezon City on Thursday.

The suspects are Dewinder Pal Singh Dhaliwal, 39, and Manjeet Singh Hansra, 41, who are residents of Caloocan City.

A manhunt is underway for the suspects' alleged accomplice, Randoj Singh Bhullar, Quezon City Police District director Brig. Gen. Redrico Maranan said.

The headline of *Philstar Global*, on September 10, 2023, "2 Indians Held for Robbery" (News Item 55), carries a noticeably negative tone. It frames the two men as suspected criminals by immediately referencing their arrest. However, the first paragraph adopts a more neutral tone, stating: "Police arrested two Indian men tagged in a robbery in Quezon City on Thursday". This opening is more factual and balanced, offering a restrained approach compared to the more provocative headline. This contrast reflects the distinct roles of headlines and lead paragraphs: editors use bold, attention grabbing phrasing in headlines to convey urgency or conflict, while the lead paragraph abides by journalistic objectivity, succinctly answering the basic questions before delving into further detail.

News Item: 56

ABS-CBN

News

India drops the periodic table, Pythagorean theorem and evolution from school textbooks

Deutsche Welle

Published Jun 05, 2023 08:04 AM PHT

On June 1, India cut a slew of foundational topics from tenth grade textbooks, including the periodic table of elements, Darwin's theory of evolution, the Pythagorean theorem, sources of energy, sustainable management of natural resources and contribution of agriculture to the national economy, among others.

In the *ABS CBN* report published on June 5, 2023, the headline "India Drops the Periodic Table, Pythagorean Theorem and Evolution from School Textbooks" (News Item 56) carries an apprehensive tone by spotlighting the removal of fundamental science and mathematics concepts, an implication that India's general curriculum is being stripped of essential knowledge. In contrast, the article's opening paragraph adopts a neutral stance, stating simply that "on June/ 1, India cut a slew of foundational topics from tenth grade textbooks, including the periodic table of elements, Darwin's theory of evolution, the Pythagorean theorem, sources of energy, sustainable management of natural resources and contribution of agriculture to the national economy, among others", without any emotive or judgmental language. This divergence reflects a common editorial approach: the headline is crafted to grab attention and signal potential risk, whereas the lead paragraph fulfils journalism's need for objectivity by calmly presenting the who, what and when before delving into any analysis or critique.

News Item: 57

INQUIRER.NET

WORLD

At least 207 dead, 900 injured in massive train crash in Odisha, India

Reuters / 07:00 AM June 03, 2023

BHUBANESWAR, India – At least 207 people were killed and 900 injured when two passenger trains collided in Odisha on Friday, according to government officials in the eastern Indian state, in India's deadliest rail accident in over a decade.

The death toll is expected to increase, state Chief Secretary Pradeep Jena said in a tweet.

In the *Inquirer* report of June 3, 2023, the headline, "At Least 207 Dead, 900 Injured in Massive Train Crash in Odisha, India" (News Item 57), uses neutral, fact driven language to relay casualty figures and location without embellishment. By contrast, the lead paragraph conveys a decidedly negative connotation, detailing that the collision of two passenger trains in Odisha killed at least 207 people and wounded 900 more, making it India's deadliest rail accident in over a decade. The headline of the article presents neutral information, simply stating the tragic event, the train crash, without strong emotional language. It's factual, focussed on the scale of the disaster. The lead paragraph, however, carries a negative connotation: the mentioning of casualties and injury count, as well as the anticipation of more deaths, creates a sombre tone. The contradiction arises because while the headline stays informational, the lead provides a grim emotional context to reinforce the severity of the situation.

Chapter Seven

Decoding India's News Coverage in ASEAN Media: Framing of the Narrative

The prioritisation of India-related news across select ASEAN media outlets reveals a systemic alignment with media framework, market-driven editorial logics, resource distribution, political economy, state-centric strategic narratives and geopolitical imperatives. This pattern underscores how media institutions function as intermediaries of strategic communication, where coverage is filtered through frameworks that prioritise India's instrumental value, as a geopolitical counterweight, economic partner or governance model, over its sociocultural or civilisational dimensions. Thematic emphasis on diplomatic engagements, economic integration and security alignments across Indonesia, Malaysia, Thailand, Singapore and the Philippines suggests that India's media representation is shaped by a 'hierarchy of strategic relevance', wherein editorial selectivity mirrors national foreign policy priorities and regional power dynamics. For instance, the recurrent focus on India's economic policies and bilateral trade agreements (as seen in Indonesian and Malaysian coverage) reflects a media narrative that positions India as a node within global supply chains and a participant in ASEAN-centric economic architectures, resonating with scholarship that frames media as a "discursive arena" for advancing state-commercial interests.[484]

The pronounced prominence of news pertaining to India's geopolitics, external affairs, and defense-related developments in the media ecosystems of major ASEAN countries, specifically Malaysia, Singapore, and the Philippines, reflects the growing regional attention to India's strategic role and policies. In these countries such topics consistently dominate coverage across nine prominent publications. In addition to this, in countries like Indonesia and Thailand, these topics in news media consistently rank among the top three news categories and it can be rigorously analysed through a multidimensional framework that integrates historical legacies, contemporary strategic imperatives and the shifting geopolitical architecture of the Indo–Pacific region.

This editorial hierarchy is reinforced by a 'structural dependency' on elite-driven narratives, where news outlets rely heavily on international wire services and major media organizations as the primary sources shaping India's image. Such dependency marginalises ground-level reporting, reducing India's multifaceted identity to a composite of policy announcements, summit diplomacy and crisis events. The underrepresentation of India's cultural innovations, grassroots governance experiments and societal transformations reflects what scholar's term "asymmetric epistemic visibility", where media systems reproduce the agendas of dominant political and economic stakeholders while neglecting subaltern narratives.[485] For example, the Philippine media's disproportionate focus on India's climate disasters and governance challenges, while overlooking its technological leapfrogging or social entrepreneurship echoes critiques of "disaster framing" in transnational reporting, which reduces Southern nations to sites of risk or resilience for Northern audiences.[486]

The prioritisation of India-related news coverage across five ASEAN countries, Indonesia, Malaysia, Thailand, Singapore and the Philippines, reveals a media logic that is deeply embedded within the broader architecture of regional strategic interests, national developmental imperatives and the political economy of media in Southeast Asia. In each of these countries, India is selectively constructed as a consequential actor primarily in three interrelated domains: as a geopolitical player in regional security configurations, as an emergent economic powerhouse relevant to trade and investment flows and as a governance model that signals institutional capacity and developmental reliability. This triadic framing, security, economy and governance, forms the conceptual bedrock of India's mediated image in the ASEAN context, reflecting the strategic calculus of the host countries rather than an even-handed journalistic engagement with India's multifaceted identity.

In the Indonesian case, for instance, the media's privileging of bilateral relations and India's geopolitical engagements over domestic political developments points to a representational economy shaped by Indonesia's own diplomatic aspirations and regional anxieties. Coverage of India is not simply a reflection of newsworthiness instead it operates as an extension of Indonesia's foreign policy grammar, wherein India is framed as a strategic partner in ASEAN multilateralism and Indo–Pacific security. Similarly, Malaysian media demonstrates a keen editorial interest in India's economic trajectory and global economic integration, which may be interpreted as an attempt to position Malaysia within larger circuits of regional trade and financial connectivity, where India represents both a comparative reference and a prospective collaborator. In these contexts, media coverage serves a dual function: it informs publics and it also legitimises policy alignments, thus acting as a soft instrument of statecraft. Thai media, while less explicit in its political leanings, nonetheless reflects a pragmatic editorial logic that places India within narratives of bilateral trade, regional peace and democratic stability. The foregrounding of formal state visits, strategic dialogues and economic cooperation underscores the Thai media's role in constructing a symbolic convergence between domestic priorities and India's perceived value as a partner in Southeast Asia's geopolitical ecosystem.

Singapore's media ecology, shaped by its hyper-rationalised and technocratic governance culture, offers a particularly illustrative case of how editorial prioritisation aligns with elite strategic thinking. The disproportionate emphasis on India's macroeconomic indicators, regulatory governance and foreign policy behaviour reflects an institutionalised effort to assess and anticipate India's role as a node in regional risk management, financial governance and innovation ecosystems. News stories about infrastructure failures, anti-corruption drives or electoral transitions are not random inclusions; rather, they function as discursive signifiers that help Singaporean audiences, especially investors, analysts and bureaucrats, evaluate India's policy stability, investment climate and governance credibility. These media practices thus reflect a highly instrumental use of international news to mediate perceptions of strategic coherence and institutional maturity, traits that Singapore privileges in its external engagements.

The Philippine media, while more varied in tone and less centralised in structure, nonetheless converges with this broader regional pattern by prioritising coverage of India's geopolitical alignments, disaster management frameworks and bilateral relations. What is particularly notable in the Philippine case is the inclusion of climate and environmental crises within the hierarchy of India-related coverage, a theme that connects strategic cooperation with existential risk management. Here, India is not only a partner in trade or diplomacy but also a co-actor in transnational regimes of resilience, especially in the face of climate-related vulnerabilities. This representational pattern foregrounds a deeper epistemic convergence between India and the Philippines, wherein state capacity and regional solidarity become intertwined in media narratives aimed at reinforcing intergovernmental legitimacy and collective preparedness.

Across all five countries, what emerges is a structurally consistent media strategy that foregrounds narratives of strategic interdependence, while marginalising cultural, social and non-strategic representations of India. This selective emphasis reflects the operational logic of what may be termed a 'strategic media regionalism', wherein national media systems participate in constructing and reproducing hierarchies of relevance based on perceived utility, alignment and policy significance. Media scholars such as Daya Thussu,[487] Philip Seib,[488] and Michael Curtin[489] have argued that international news flows are increasingly shaped by a convergence of state power, market imperatives and ideological positioning, resulting in representations that are less about foreign realities and more about domestic strategic priorities. The data from these five ASEAN countries appears to substantiate this proposition. India is not covered comprehensively or holistically but rather is filtered through a lens of instrumental relevance that privileges narratives of power, performance and partnership.

Moreover, this form of editorial prioritisation reflects the entanglement of media institutions with broader political economies, both national and regional. Many Southeast Asian media organisations operate under varying degrees of state influence, regulatory control or market pressure, which constrains the scope of editorial autonomy and renders international reporting a carefully managed domain. As such, the representation of India is not an autonomous editorial choice but the outcome of intersecting pressures from foreign ministries, economic lobbies, strategic think tanks and journalistic norms. In this framework, media does not merely reflect public interest but actively participates in the construction of it, mediating between foreign policy imperatives and audience perceptions. The consequence is a regional information order in which India's image is not passively observed but strategically curated, projecting India as a partner of consequence, a competitor of merit or a model of relevance depending on the narrative requirements of each country's foreign policy agenda.

This analytical synthesis suggests that the editorial prioritisation of India in ASEAN media is less about India per se, and more about how India serves the strategic imagination of these countries. In privileging certain themes, geopolitics, economics, governance, over others, these media systems effectively delineate the contours of India's relevance to Southeast Asia, thereby constructing a discursive geography of partnership, influence and alignment. This media logic mirrors the region's broader strategic orientation, where information flows are mobilised not only for consumption but for positioning, signalling to domestic and international audiences the terms on which regional actors engage with the global order, and the role India is expected to play within it.

India's Portrayal, News Sentiment and the Manufacturing of Narrative

In an age where narratives shape diplomacy as much as doctrines do, the representation of India in ASEAN media holds consequences far beyond visibility alone. It influences regional perceptions of India's intentions, capacities and relevance. Within Southeast Asia, a region marked by pluralism, strategic hedging and rising digital interconnectedness, India's presence in public discourse is curiously uneven. While it is widely acknowledged as a key strategic actor, economic partner and democratic counterweight to China, its cultural and civic presence remains faint, fragmented and often filtered through reductive or external lenses.

India is seen, but not always understood; acknowledged, but seldom emotionally engaged with. Its image is largely mediated through the prisms of strategic summits, defence dialogues and foreign policy engagements, but lacks the deeper narrative texture that builds long-term regional familiarity. The dominant themes in which India appears across ASEAN media revolve around its role in maritime security, economic connectivity, digital infrastructure and as a member of multilateral formations like the ASEAN–India Dialogue, Quad, Bay of Bengal Initiative for Multi-Sectoral Technical and Economic Cooperation and the Indo–Pacific Economic Framework. These stories portray India as a rational, pragmatic actor, one that balances its interests with caution and assertiveness, particularly in response to China's growing assertiveness and the geopolitical recalibrations triggered by US–China competition. However, this framing is mostly elite-centric, emerging during ministerial visits or headline-making events, and fails to filter down into the wider public imagination. Moreover, these narratives often cast India in a derivative light, important primarily in relation to other powers, rather than as an agent with its own regional vision. While this visibility benefits India diplomatically, it remains a visibility without intimacy or recognition without depth.

Table 59: Media Representation Patterns of India in Foreign Coverage

Aspect	*Pattern*	*Implication*
Thematic Focus	Emphasis on diplomacy, security and economics, marginalising culture/science	Reduces India to strategic-economic actor
Sentiment	Mix of positive, negative and cautious tones, often ambivalent	Cultivates risk-reward lens, limits trust
Sourcing	Heavy reliance on international wire services, limited local reporting	Introduces global biases, lacks local nuance

The representation of India in ASEAN media is shaped by a series of recurring editorial and structural patterns that collectively create a fragmented, externally driven and often superficial image of the country. Thematic focus across most coverage emphasises India's role in diplomacy, regional security and economic strategy, effectively narrowing the country's portrayal to that of a strategic actor. This lens sidelines India's vibrant cultural, scientific and civilisational narratives, thus limiting its visibility beyond official corridors and disengaging wider audiences. Sentiment within this coverage tends to be mixed and ambivalent, oscillating between cautious admiration and sceptical detachment. This reflects a 'risk-reward' perception of India, where it is seen as a counterbalance in regional geopolitics but not necessarily as a trusted or emotionally resonant partner.

Interpreting Projected Sentiment

In Indonesia and Malaysia, where media coverage skews predominantly positive, the narratives likely reflect deeper synergies with India's maritime diplomacy, cultural linkages and economic outreach, particularly under initiatives like the Act East Policy, which resonate with these nations' efforts to diversify partnerships. Conversely, Thailand's disproportionately negative media portrayal of India fosters scepticism toward India's capacity to deliver substantive alternatives. Singapore's relatively balanced coverage, marked by cautious optimism, mirrors its pragmatic statecraft: it acknowledges India's role as a stabiliser in maritime security and as a node in supply chain resilience, yet tempers enthusiasm with realist neutrality, wary of alienating Beijing or overcommitting to New Delhi's still-nascent Indo–Pacific institutionalism. The Philippines' muted polarity in media sentiment, with neither pronounced positivity nor overt criticism, epitomises its fragmented geopolitical identity. Interpreting these disparities through the prism of Indo–Pacific geopolitics, the data signals India's uneven penetration into ASEAN's collective consciousness. Positive sentiment in Indonesia and Malaysia highlights India's soft power successes and diplomatic agility in cultivating middle-power coalitions, positioning itself as a benign alternative to China's coercive economic statecraft. Singapore's measured tone reflects the city-state's calibration of India's potential: a useful but incomplete partner in balancing hegemony, constrained by bureaucratic inertia and infrastructural deficits. The Philippines' ambiguity, meanwhile, underscores the limits of India's influence in states where U.S. and Chinese dominance precludes third-party ascendancy. Collectively, these media narratives reveal ASEAN's fragmented consensus on India's role. The region's media sentiment acts as both a mirror and a mould, reflecting extant power asymmetries while shaping domestic public opinion that, in turn, influences state policies.

Table 60: Overall Sentiment Data

Total News Articles from All Studied Countries: 2,301		
Positive News	759	32.98%
Negative News	611	26.55%
Apprehensive News	324	14.08%
Neutral News	608	26.42%

One of the key conceptual premises embedded within the study is sentiment, categorised into four distinct types, with positive and negative sentiments being the most analytically significant, particularly as they are prominently manifested in news headlines (Table 60). The distribution of these sentiments provides a crucial empirical foundation for interrogating the processes through which national images are constructed and mediated within regional news ecosystems. The relative prevalence of positive and negative headlines across the surveyed ASEAN countries not only illuminates the degree of India's media visibility, but also exposes the editorial logics and framing practices through which India's diplomatic postures, policy orientations and regional engagements are interpreted, filtered and disseminated to domestic audiences. In Indonesia and Malaysia, the relatively balanced occurrence of positive and negative headlines suggests that India occupies a discernible and contested space in the media narrative, neither uniformly welcomed nor categorically resisted. This balance indicates that India's diplomatic overtures, economic engagements and cultural initiatives are being covered with both interest and scrutiny. The fact that a substantial share of headlines reflects positive sentiment in these two countries suggests a partial alignment with India's strategic communication goals; however, the coexisting presence of negative sentiment equally highlights the necessity for India to refine its messaging and adapt its outreach to local sensibilities and media dynamics. Such coverage reflects the operation of news media as an active agent in the making of strategic narratives, not merely as a conduit of diplomatic information.

In Thailand, a markedly higher prevalence of negative headlines signals a significantly more critical media stance toward India. This lopsided distribution points to a communicative environment where Indian initiatives may be perceived less through their intended message and more through localised lenses of scepticism or competing geopolitical interests. It suggests that in Thailand, India's narrative is either being overshadowed by competing actors or is encountering editorial filters that amplify dissonance over resonance. In strategic communication terms, this underscores a gap between India's intended messaging and its actual reception in Thai media discourses, implying the need for a recalibration of public diplomacy tools and narrative framing mechanisms that can better accommodate local editorial norms and policy priorities. However, this study also examines the source of news information; we have seen in Chapter Eight that various Western news agencies dominate the supply of news, which impacts the sentiments. We will discuss this issue in Chapter Nine. Singapore, with its near parity between positive and negative headline sentiments, presents a more calibrated reception of India's presence in the Indo–Pacific narrative. Here, India is recognised as a relevant strategic actor, but this recognition is mediated through Singapore's characteristic policy of balance and its editorial preference for analytical and multi-perspective reporting. The relatively favourable tilt in headline sentiment suggests that Indian narratives may find resonance when articulated in terms of shared regional stability, rule-based order and economic complementarities. In contrast, the Philippines show the least polarised sentiment distribution, marked by low overall percentages for both positive and negative headlines. This suggests a media environment where India is either underrepresented or not deemed a central geopolitical actor in the domestic news agenda. Rather than signalling indifference, this could point to a structural marginality in India's strategic communication efforts vis-à-vis the Philippines, demanding greater engagement and visibility-building activities to reposition India as a relevant actor in the Filipino strategic imagination.

The overall sentiment analysis unveils a dual narrative in how India's role is depicted in ASEAN news outlets. A clear predominance of affirmatively toned articles suggests that the media largely perceives India as a proactive and dynamic stakeholder in the region. This positive messaging emphasises narratives of progress, constructive diplomacy and shared regional aspirations that align with broader Indo–Pacific strategic initiatives. However, the existence of a considerable volume of negatively framed articles introduces a counterpoint, reflecting caution and underlying critiques regarding certain aspects of India's engagement. This critical perspective, infused with scepticism, signals that while India's potential as a strategic partner is widely acknowledged, there remains a healthy degree of scrutiny concerning its policy measures and broader geopolitical ambitions. The overall messaging projected by the data paints a picture of a complex interplay between celebration and critique, a narrative that both lauds India's transformative diplomatic efforts and invites continuous, informed debate about the implications of its rising influence in ASEAN countries.

Deconstructing Sentiment Polarity

The preceding discussion initially suggests an analysis of media narratives through a binary lens of positive and negative framing. However, such an approach overlooks the inherent complexity of textual production in news discourse. Media texts rarely conform to rigid dichotomies; rather, they often employ layered narratives that reflect shifting or ambivalent sentiments. By broadening the analytical framework of this study beyond sentiment polarity, a more nuanced understanding emerges regarding India's representation in ASEAN media, one that acknowledges the interplay of geopolitical, economic and cultural factors shaping these mediated portrayals.

Positive sentiment in headlines suggests the successful penetration of favourable messaging aligned with India's diplomatic, economic or strategic objectives. However, negative sentiment, within this framework, not only challenges India's positioning but also actively reshapes its perception through editorially embedded critique and scepticism. What intensifies this narrative complexity is the presence of apprehensive headlines, those not overtly negative, but marked by caution, doubt or latent pessimism. These articles, often constructed through speculative framing or anticipatory language, occupy a critical discursive space in the media ecosystem. While they do not categorically delegitimise India's actions or role, they problematise it in subtle ways, generating interpretive friction that may foster public uncertainty rather than consensus. In the Indonesian and Philippine contexts, the presence of apprehensive headlines is notably high, indicating a communicative environment where India's actions are often read through a lens of conditionality or possible adverse outcomes. When apprehensive headlines are analytically grouped with explicitly negative ones, a broader phenomenon emerges: a significant proportion of the overall news discourse surrounding India becomes tinted with scepticism or caution, which cumulatively acts as a drag on the potential affirmative reception of India's public diplomacy efforts.

Neutral headlines, on the other hand, offer a distinct but equally significant interpretive function. Far from being merely passive or irrelevant, neutral coverage signifies editorial restraint, objectivity or prioritisation of descriptive reporting over evaluative framing. In countries like Singapore and the Philippines, where the share of neutral news is relatively higher, it suggests a media environment where India's representation is less editorially predetermined and more contingent upon the event itself, providing a discursive middle ground that neither amplifies nor undermines India's standing. However, the strategic impact of neutral reporting in shaping public perceptions is ambivalent. On one hand, it mitigates polarisation by offering unembellished narratives; on the other, its lack of persuasive framing may fail to galvanise public support or emotional engagement, thereby weakening the affective dimension of India's strategic communication.

When aggregating the effects of positive, negative, apprehensive and neutral headlines, a composite picture emerges: India's media portrayal in ASEAN is defined less by consistency and more by fragmentation and editorial variation. Such a fragmented narrative landscape implies that India's strategic communication must not only contend with explicit opposition but also engage with the subtler forces of narrative hesitation and neutrality, which shape public opinion in less predictable but no less impactful ways. For a country seeking to consolidate its regional image in the Indo–Pacific, this underscores the imperative of deepening media engagement strategies that go beyond event-based outreach and embrace narrative stewardship across diverse editorial cultures. Moreover, the insights derived from this dataset are instructive not only for India but for any developed nation aiming to enhance its soft power and influence through public diplomacy in Southeast Asia. In conclusion, the sentiment structure of news articles related to India in these ASEAN countries reveals an uneven communicative terrain shaped not merely by content, but by the editorial disposition and sentiment framing of the media. Apprehensive articles, though less forceful than outright negative ones, play a decisive role in creating doubt, thereby diluting the clarity of India's strategic narratives. Neutral articles, while potentially reinforcing factual awareness, may lack persuasive power. The interplay between these sentiment categories suggests that India's standing in the Indo–Pacific is mediated not simply by geopolitical alignments but by the everyday discursive practices of news production, interpretation and dissemination. Strategic communication in such a milieu requires not only the articulation of national interests but also the cultivation of narrative environments where these interests can be interpreted as legitimate, credible and mutually beneficial by diverse Southeast Asian publics.

Structural Mediation and Semantic Encoding in News Discourse

The sentiment profile derived from the studied corpus of news articles about India in ASEAN's online print media provides a valuable entry point into understanding the deep structure of news discourse, especially when approached through the headlines and the process of making of narratives through strategic communication. Within the communicative architecture of news, headlines are not merely summarising devices but are ideologically charged signifiers. They encapsulate the epistemic stance of the news institution and operate as affective triggers that shape audience reception before the full narrative unfolds. In media studies, headlines function as what Gérard Genette conceptualised as "paratexts", liminal elements that mediate between the text and its readers, serving not only to attract attention but to position the story within a broader discursive frame.

Table 61-A: Overall Sentiment Data of Headlines

Total News Articles from All Studied Countries: 2,301		
Positive	759	32.98%
Negative	611	26.55%
Apprehensive	325	14.08%
Neutral	608	26.42%

Table 61-B: Overall Sentiment Data of Headlines

Total News Articles from All Studied Countries: 2,301		
Positive + Neutral	1,367	59.40
Negative + Apprehensive	936	40.67

When coverage of a foreign state like India leans predominantly toward positive and neutral tones, as is evident in the dataset under review, it signals a strategic orientation of media framing. According to Entman's theory of framing, news selection and presentation do not merely reflect reality but actively construct it through processes of inclusion, exclusion and emphasis. The preference for positivity and neutrality in the reporting of India suggests that media institutions in ASEAN may be subscribing to a functionalist logic of regional harmony and constructive engagement, potentially influenced by state-level diplomatic priorities or cultural proximities that discourage overtly adversarial reporting. This trend aligns with the broader functioning of newsrooms in Southeast Asia, where editorial decisions often blend journalistic autonomy with tacit policy alignments, shaped by both market incentives and geopolitical interests.

The presence of apprehensive or negative sentiment, though less dominant, should not be dismissed as marginal. Rather, it reflects the selective activation of frames of insecurity, competition or ideological divergence, which are periodically mobilised in response to specific events or policy postures. These sentiments are embedded within a larger schema of agenda-setting, whereby the media does not tell the audience what to think, but what to think about. The affective and interpretive weight of such framing is often frontloaded into the headline, the first textual contact point for readers and arguably the most cognitively influential. Once the headline establishes a narrative anchor, the subsequent introduction or lead paragraph either deepens the resonance or undermines it, depending on the coherence of tone and thematic continuity.

In this light, the function of headlines in the communication realm must be understood not just as textual artifacts but as operational nodes within the production of ideology. According to Van Dijk's critical discourse theory, headlines are implicated in the reproduction of social cognition: they activate scripts and mental models that shape how audiences process and recall news events. A headline that projects optimism about India's technological or economic trajectory, for instance, sets into motion an interpretive schema that frames India as a rising, benign actor. This interpretive schema is then either reinforced or dissonantly contradicted by the introduction paragraph, which should ideally elaborate the claim, provide context and align the affective tone with the headline's narrative cues. However, when there is misalignment between the headline and the introductory paragraph, when, for instance, a positive headline is followed by an introduction that introduces scepticism or veiled critique, the narrative coherence is fractured. This disjunction not only confuses the reader but also dilutes the ideological effect of the piece. In communication theory, such fragmentation impairs the encoding–decoding process theorised by Stuart Hall. In Hall's framework, news producers encode meaning within a preferred reading that audiences may accept, negotiate or oppose. For the preferred reading to succeed, the structural elements of the text, chief among them the headline and the introduction, must work in tandem to project a unified ideological message.

This necessity of alignment brings us to a central theoretical proposition: that of narrative synchronisation within news discourse. Drawing from Goffman's frame analysis, every news item can be seen as a structured performance wherein the headline and the introduction act as sequential framing devices. If these elements are misaligned, the frame becomes unstable and the communicative efficacy of the piece is compromised. Therefore, the synthesis of the headline and the introduction is not a stylistic luxury but a communicative imperative, particularly in international reporting where affective and interpretive signals are crucial in shaping geopolitical perceptions.

In sum, the study of India-related news coverage in Indonesian media reveals not only the distribution of sentiment but also the structural logic of mediated representation. The dominance of positive and neutral frames points to a calculated discursive strategy, while the occasional activation of apprehensive tones suggests a responsive rather than adversarial press orientation. Within this configuration, headlines emerge as powerful semiotic instruments, anchoring the affective tone and interpretive direction of the news item. Their efficacy, however, is contingent on a coherent alignment with the introductory paragraph, which must function not as a narrative detour but as an extension and deepening of the headline's discursive promise. This insight underscores the broader communicative principle that the persuasive and ideological potency of news depends not on the headline alone but on the seamless integration of all textual components into a singular narrative frame.

Dissecting Headline–Introduction Discrepancies

Communication scholars warn that media often *frame* events by "select[ing] some aspects of a perceived reality and make[ing] them more salient in a communicating text". Entman (1993) argues that framing defines problems and assigns moral judgment and remedies within a news story. By contrast, in this study of 2,301 news articles about India, roughly one-third (772 items, or 33.55 per cent) exhibit *sentiment misalignment* between the headline and the introductory paragraph (introduction). Such discrepancies can distort framing: a negative or sensationalist headline primes readers to see an issue one way, even if the article's body presents a more nuanced or opposite tone.

Table 62: Overview of Sentiment Alignment between News Headlines and Introductions

Category	*Number of News Items*	*Percentage of Total*
Total news items	2,301	100%
Headlines and introductions with different sentiments	772	33.55%

In effect, the headline sets one interpretive *frame* while the introduction offers another, undermining coherence. This is especially important because 'headlines act as the agenda' for readers. Media 'shapes the political debate by choosing which topics and issues should feature in the news broadcasts', and an issue's prominence in the headline leads audiences to view it as important. If headlines carry a different sentiment (e.g., positive or apprehensive) than the subtler content of the articles, the public's perceptions may be guided by the initial, possibly misleading cue.

Moreover, recent research shows that headlines with more *negative* wording significantly boost readership. Robertson et al. (2023) demonstrate that each additional negative word in a headline increases click-through rates by about 2.3 per cent. In short, 'it bleeds, it leads': sensational or frightening headlines draw readers, whereas positive wording dampen engagement. Thus, commercial logic pressures editors to accentuate emotion. A headline–introduction misalignment can thus be strategic: a stingy, provocative headline grabs attention, while the body text delivers a more balanced account. This dynamic amplifies framing effects — the initial frame (anger, fear, optimism) is broadcast by the headline, setting the agenda, regardless of later nuance. As Yoon et al. note, detecting incongruence between headlines and bodies is "timely and important…for minimizing the negative consequences of potential misinformation". Inconsistent sentiments in headlines risk misleading readers or causing misinformation by prejudicing interpretation before any detail is read.

Roselle, Miskimmon and O'Loughlin (2014) argue that strategic narratives give states and actors "purchase on the complexities of international politics", showing how influence operates in modern media environments. In this view, news is not neutral fact-recounting but a medium for projecting national and ideological stories. A strategic narrative blends facts into a coherent plot that advances policy or identity goals. As Roselle et al. emphasise, "the ability to develop strategic narratives are especially important in determining foreign policy success and failure". If media outlets — consciously or under pressure — inject dissonant sentiments between headlines and introductions, they may be fragmenting or amplifying a narrative with purpose. For example, a rowdy or alarmist headline about India's actions could serve a narrative of India as a regional provocateur, even if the article's introduction tempers that by citing context or official statements. Such editorial decisions can thus forward a subtle propaganda aim: to draw on audience biases or fears via the headline's frame, then issue a kinder introduction that ostensibly balances the story without undoing the initial impact.

In sum, the communication theory predicts that misaligned sentiments between headlines and introductions can amplify framing distortions and steer public attention on partial cues. The agenda-setting function of the headline is potentiated when its emotional tone diverges from the article's content. The strategic-narrative perspective adds that headlines may be tailored to broader foreign-policy messages: as Monroe Price observes, governments and media regimes often control information to influence both domestic and foreign audiences. A headline–introduction gap could thus serve political ends (by evoking the desired reaction in readers) while preserving journalistic deniability in the body.

These theoretical insights take on specific significance in the context of ASEAN press coverage of India. Recent analysis[490] finds that leading Southeast Asian newspapers rely heavily on international wire services and external sources when reporting on India. This dependency tends to produce 'superficial narratives' in which India is often cast unfavourably; the study notes a 'skewed representation, with a majority of headlines presenting India in a negative or apprehensive light'. If ASEAN outlets frequently echo external reports, a misalignment of sentiments may arise simply because editors copy sensational headlines from agencies but write more cautious introductions. But more deeply, it reflects strategic communication choices. ASEAN nations have diverse relations with India — some see India as an emerging partner (economic and strategic), others as a competitor or outsider in Asian diplomacy. Headlines that highlight India's challenges or controversies can serve domestic or allied narratives (e.g., aligning with U.S.-led 'Indo–Pacific' rhetoric that is wary of India's regional role), while the introductions can present the official, factual angle (for instance, quoting Indian diplomats or domestic context).

Importantly, about 33.6 per cent of the 2,301 sampled articles from ASEAN media exhibit divergent sentiments between the headlines and the introductions (our analysis). This high rate indicates that such misalignment is systemic, not sporadic. It suggests that for one in three stories on India, the initial emotional framing conflicts with the main thrust of the narrative. The implications are grave for India's image in the region. While on one hand aggressive, emotionally charged headlines can cement negative stereotypes of India (as a troublemaker or unstable emerging power), on the other, the corresponding introductions can attempt to smooth over these notions with balanced reporting or with India's perspective. The net effect may leave readers with mixed signals: a salient negative impression (from skimming the headline) that is moderated by the text upon closer reading. But research suggests that many readers don't get to the nuance. Allen et al. (2024) find that "more than 90% of people read nothing beyond [the headline] when browsing social media"; so headlines essentially shape public perception. Accordingly, even if the introduction is benign, the initial negative narrative often 'sticks' with audiences.

This study examining 2,301 news items also reveals that 769 articles feature headlines with positive sentiment. However, upon further analysis, it was discovered that 204 of these articles have introductions that diverge from the positive tone set by the headline (Table 63).

Table 63: Breakdown of News Items with Positive Headlines Overall

Category	*News Items*	*Percentage*
Total with positive headlines	769	100%
Introductions with different sentiments	204	26.52%
• Introductions with apprehensive sentiments	32	4.16%
• Introductions with negative sentiments	1	0.13%
• Introductions with neutral sentiments	171	22.23%

This misalignment, where a headline promises optimism while the introduction shifts to a different emotional register, illustrates a critical lapse in the communication. The discrepancy disrupts the narrative flow, leaving readers feeling misled and questioning the underlying intent of the content. Delving into the specific breakdown of these inconsistencies, the data indicates that among the 204 mismatched cases, 32 news stories have introductions that adopt an apprehensive tone, despite the cheerful promise of the headline. In one instance, the introduction even takes on a negative sentiment, starkly contrasting with the positive opening. The majority, 171 articles, showcase introductions that adopt a neutral tone rather than matching the upbeat headline. Such variations not only diminish the persuasive power of the communication but also contribute to a fragmented narrative, which can ultimately erode audience engagement.

The observation that 171 news articles feature neutral introductions paired with positive headlines speaks volumes about the multi-layered process of encoding messages in media production. Media institutions, in their drive to capture attention in a competitive digital environment, often craft headlines with an overtly positive spin. This technique is designed to attract clicks and signal an upbeat narrative at first glance. However, the subsequent shift to a neutral tone in the introduction suggests that behind the market-driven, attention-grabbing headline lies a more cautious and measured approach to storytelling. This divergence reflects an internal balancing act: while the headline is tailored to garner immediate interest, the introduction is more aligned with traditional journalistic responsibilities of objectivity and factual reporting. For the common reader, this discrepancy introduces a subtle yet significant gap in meaning-making. When readers encounter a positive headline, they form an initial expectation of optimism or uplifting content. A neutral introduction, however, does not fully confirm this expectation, requiring readers to re-adjust their interpretation of the story. Such a gap can lead to cognitive dissonance, prompting readers to seek a more nuanced understanding or to question the underlying realities that have been subtly downplayed. In this way, the reader is impelled to engage in a higher level of scrutiny, weighing the emotional lure of the headline against the more restrained narrative that follows. Adding another layer to this analysis is the contrasting instance of 32 articles that employ an apprehensive tone in their introductions despite sporting positive headlines, a juxtaposition that borders on the ironic. In these cases, the headline likely serves to capture attention, but the introduction immediately reorients the reader towards caution or concern. This ironic twist could be interpreted as a deliberate strategy: an attempt to leverage the emotional appeal of positivity to draw the reader in while simultaneously ensuring that the more critical or sobering details of the story are not ignored. Such a move exemplifies the dual imperatives that media institutions navigate, balancing the need for engagement with the ethical responsibility of conveying more measured and accurate information.

For statecraft and policy makers, the encoded message in the media becomes a complex signal. On one side, a positive headline can project an image of public optimism and stability, potentially influencing political narratives or policy agendas. On the other, the neutrality of the introduction serves as a corrective, hinting at a more balanced reality that might temper overly rosy interpretations of the situation. This discrepancy might alert policy makers to the risk of over-relying on superficial media signals and underscore the necessity of engaging with the substance of the news. It also emphasises the need for a discerning approach when parsing media messages, particularly in contexts where public sentiment and policy decisions are interdependent.

Table 64: Breakdown of Introduction Sentiments for Negative Headlines

Category	*News Items*	*Percentage*
Total with negative headlines	599	100%
Introductions with different sentiments	198	33.05%
• Introductions with positive connotation	9	1.50%
• Introductions with neutral sentiments	108	18.03%
• Introductions with apprehensive sentiments	81	13.52%

This study also reveals significant sentiment misalignment in news articles featuring negative headlines (Table 64). Of the 599 such articles, 198 exhibit divergent sentiments in their introductory paragraphs, 108 maintain a neutral orientation, 81 convey an apprehensive tone and nine adopt an unexpectedly positive stance. This mismatch suggests that the practice is not incidental but is embedded within editorial and making of media making frameworks aimed at controlling narrative perception. The incongruity between the headline and the introduction serves multiple communicative objectives. It is important here to underscore a particularly ironic observation: among the 599 news articles with negative headlines, nine articles surprisingly convey a positive sentiment in their introductory paragraphs. Additionally, 108 articles maintain a neutral tone despite beginning with negatively framed headlines. This notable misalignment between headline sentiment and introductory content reflects a broader communicative discrepancy that warrants deeper analysis through the lens of communication theory, particularly the processes involved in encoding and disseminating information during news production. Furthermore, the communicative process becomes more complex when readers approach the news article expecting a strongly negative narrative about India based solely on the headline, only to encounter a more nuanced or even positive tone in the article's content. Such divergence may induce cognitive dissonance, as the reader must reconcile an initial expectation with contradictory information, thereby disrupting the decoding of the message. This psychological dissonance can result in misinterpretation, confusion or even biased conclusions, especially if the reader lacks the time or inclination to engage with the full article. Negative or provocative headlines are known to attract more clicks, social media shares and overall reader interest, even if the actual article content is more balanced or subdued. This form of clickbait journalism reflects the commercial pressures of the digital news economy. Beyond economics, ideological framing also plays a central role in the portrayal of India. According to the framing theory, as advanced by scholars like Goffman (1974) and Entman (1993), journalists selectively emphasise certain aspects of reality to shape how audiences interpret events. In this context, media outlets may deploy negative headlines to signal critique or scepticism, potentially reflecting broader geopolitical concerns, regional anxieties about India's rising influence or to be in alignment with dominant international narratives, while the introductions temper that critique with more neutral or constructive details. Furthermore, from a strategic communication perspective, the discrepancy may be a part of a dual messaging tactic aimed at different audiences: a sensational headline captures casual readers and resonates with domestic political concerns, while a more nuanced introduction speaks to informed audiences or diplomatic stakeholders. This editorial balancing act reflects the inherent tension between journalism's roles as both a commercial enterprise and a public information service. The phenomena of 'irony' and 'deflation' further illustrate the depth of this editorial strategy, wherein a negative headline is undercut by a neutral or even positive introduction, leading to a weakening of the initial emotional charge.

Table 65: Breakdown of Introduction Sentiments for Apprehensive Headlines

Category	*News Items*	*Percentage*
Total with apprehensive headlines	327	100%
Introductions with different sentiments	148	45.25%
• Introductions with positive sentiments	21	6.42%
• Introductions with negative sentiments	44	13.45%
• Introductions with neutral sentiments	82	25.07%

Table 65 illustrates another breakdown of introduction sentiments for apprehensive headlines: out of a total of 2,301 news articles examined, 327 were identified with having apprehensive headlines, those that evoke unease or concern regarding the subject matter, in this case, India. However, within this group of apprehensive headlines, a significant portion,148 articles, or approximately 45 per cent, reveal a mismatch in sentiment when comparing the headline to the introductory paragraph of the same article. This means that nearly half of these articles set an apprehensive tone at the outset but proceed with introductions that do not maintain that tone. Delving deeper, of these 148 mismatched cases, 6.42 per cent (21 articles) introduce their stories with a positive sentiment despite having headlines that suggest apprehension, a contrast that creates a strong sense of irony. This kind of discrepancy can leave readers puzzled or misled, especially if they form an early judgment based solely on the headline. Another 44 articles have introductions that lean into a clearly negative sentiment, subtly shifting the tone from apprehension to outright criticism or disapproval, indicating a deepening of sentiment rather than a reversal. The most substantial portion of these discrepancies, however, involves 82 articles where the introductions are neutral, despite the apprehensive framing in the headlines. This constitutes about 25 per cent of the total 327 apprehensive-headline articles and highlights a deliberate or unintended softening of the emotional tone once readers move past the headline. The presence of such a large volume of neutral introductions under apprehensive headlines raises questions about the intention behind such framing, whether it is to initially capture attention through emotionally charged language or a reflection of editorial inconsistencies in the news-making process. These discrepancies have consequences for readers, who may begin reading with a mindset conditioned by an apprehensive headline, only to find a calmer or even optimistic account in the body of the article. This emotional disconnect may not only impede accurate interpretation but may also diminish the reader's capacity to assess the gravity or immediacy of the issue under discussion. Furthermore, this concern becomes particularly relevant in instances where readers do not engage beyond the headline, a phenomenon frequently documented in previous studies.

Table 66: Breakdown of Introduction Sentiments for Neutral Headlines

Category	*Items*	*Percentage*
Total with neutral headlines	608	100%
Introductions with different sentiments	164	26.70%
• Introductions with positive sentiments	68	20.00%
• Introductions with apprehensive sentiments	57	06.70%
• Introductions with negative sentiments	36	05.92%

Out of 2,301 news items, 608 articles feature neutral headlines, ostensibly suggesting an objective or balanced stance (Table 66). However, within this subset, 164 articles, approximately 27 per cent, contain introductions that diverge in sentiment from their headlines, revealing a deeper layer of communicative inconsistency. Among these 164 instances of misalignment, 68 articles (about 20 per cent) begin with positive introductions, suggesting an upbeat or constructive narrative that is not hinted at in the emotionally detached headline. Similarly, 57 articles (6.70 per cent) contain introductions with an apprehensive tone, one that signals unease, tension or concern, despite the neutral headline. Furthermore, 36 articles (approximately 5.92 per cent) present negative introductions, introducing critical or unfavourable perspectives that were not projected in the headline.

The discrepancies between neutral headlines and introductions imbued with divergent sentiments, positive, apprehensive or negative, trigger significant cognitive and psychological impacts on readers. When a neutral headline masks a positive introduction (e.g., 'India's GDP Growth Reviewed' paired with 'record-breaking expansion'), readers experience tension between the headline's impartiality and the introduction's optimism, often resolving it by either embracing the positivity as a 'soft-sell' tactic or distrusting the outlet for downplaying good news, as seen in studies where such mismatches are perceived as strategic moderation to appease polarised audiences. Conversely, neutral headlines with apprehensive introductions amplify anxiety through 'uncertainty bias', priming readers to overestimate risks despite the neutral framing, a dynamic linked to increase dwell time but reduced factual recall in research. The most destabilising mismatch arises with negative introductions, where 'negativity bias' dominates, overshadowing balanced analysis and fuelling cynicism as readers interpret the dissonance as covert criticism or institutional hedging. These patterns reveal broader harms: cognitive overload from reconciling conflicting signals, erosion of trust through perceived deception and policy missteps as time-strapped decision-makers skim headlines while missing critical introductions.

Structural Asymmetries in the Communication Ecosystem

The comprehensive analysis of sentiment discrepancies between news headlines and introductions reveals profound systemic issues in contemporary journalism that demand urgent attention. Our research identifies three distinct but interrelated patterns of misalignment that collectively undermine effective communication and erode public trust in media institutions. The 'soft-sell positive' approach, where neutral headlines conceal optimistic introductions, represents the mildest form of cognitive manipulation, yet still establishes problematic precedents for information processing. More concerning is the 'anxiety hook' technique that strategically deploys apprehensive introductions after neutral headlines, exploiting fundamental human threat detection mechanisms to boost engagement at the cost of rational discourse. Most damaging of all is the 'bait-and-alarm' strategy, where jarring negative introductions follow ostensibly neutral headlines, creating acute cognitive dissonance that disproportionately influences audience perception and recall.

These patterns collectively demonstrate how modern media institutions have developed sophisticated techniques for sentiment layering that prioritise metrics over truth, engagement over understanding. The psychological impacts follow a clear and concerning hierarchy of effects, with negative introductions triggering the strongest neural responses in conflict-monitoring systems, while positive introductions produce more subtle but still consequential alterations in information retention. What makes these practices particularly insidious is their systematic nature—these are not random errors but calculated institutional strategies that leverage our cognitive vulnerabilities while maintaining plausible deniability through headline neutrality. The persistence of these discrepancies across media outlets and topics reveals fundamental structural flaws in contemporary news production. At their core, they reflect the unsustainable tension between journalism's democratic function and the commercial realities of the attention economy. Neutral headlines serve as institutional fig leaves, allowing organisations to claim objectivity while directional framing in article bodies does the actual work of shaping perception. This two-tiered communication model constitutes a fundamental breach of the implicit contract between journalists and their audiences.

The path forward demands nothing less than a recommitment to journalism's foundational purpose—not merely to capture attention, but to facilitate understanding; not to manipulate perception, but to illuminate reality. Only by aligning presentation with content, form with substance, can news media hope to regain the trust it has systematically eroded through these practices of sentiment discrepancy. The stakes could not be higher, for in an era of rampant misinformation and declining institutional trust, the costs of continued cognitive manipulation may prove catastrophic for democratic discourse itself.

Strategic Divergences in Narrative Framing and News Dissemination

The recurring mismatch between the sentiments of headlines and introductions in ASEAN media coverage of India reveals a layered and deliberate editorial practice that intersects with media economics, geopolitical alignment and audience psychology. These discrepancies are not accidental or sporadic anomalies; rather, they reflect an entrenched system of strategic messaging that uses sentiment modulation to balance competing communicative objectives. Headlines, as the most visible component of news articles, function as powerful cognitive frames that shape how audiences interpret subsequent information. In the case of India, a significant portion of ASEAN headlines adopt a neutral or even an optimistic tone, highlighting themes such as economic collaboration, cultural diplomacy or shared regional goals. These headlines often emphasise India's contributions to ASEAN infrastructure projects, educational exchanges and broader initiatives like the Act East Policy. However, when readers proceed to the introductory paragraphs, they frequently encounter more complex narratives that introduce reservations, caveats or apprehensions, such as political delays, regional scepticism or unfulfilled commitments. This discord between the headlines and the opening of the articles constructs a dual-layered narrative that serves multiple audiences simultaneously: the headline appeals to casual or diplomatic readers, while the body content addresses more discerning or policy-aware publics.

This editorial duality aligns with theoretical insights from media framing, agenda-setting and strategic communication. From a framing perspective, the positive or neutral headline directs the reader's cognitive attention toward favourable aspects of India's engagement, even before deeper reading occurs. The agenda-setting theory further reinforces this by suggesting that such headlines disproportionately influence what topics or sentiments readers prioritise, especially in fast-paced digital environments where headlines often substitute for full reading. The implications of this become particularly salient when considering that most media consumers, especially those engaging via mobile devices or social media, rarely proceed beyond the headline. In such cases, the optimistic or diplomatic framing presented at the outset may shape public perceptions more strongly than any critical nuance buried within the article. The result is not just a misrepresentation of facts, but a skewed public understanding, where India is consistently perceived as a cooperative actor, regardless of emerging frictions or policy contradictions noted later in the article. This phenomenon becomes even more complex when viewed through the lens of strategic narrative theory. ASEAN countries may deliberately employ such sentiment mismatches to maintain diplomatic balance: signalling warmth and partnership in headlines to align with regional solidarity and India's soft power diplomacy, while embedding more cautious or critical tones in the text to reflect domestic concerns, policy complexities or geopolitical hedging strategies.

At the same time, the rise of the attention economy and the economics of digital journalism exacerbate these tendencies. Media outlets are incentivised to craft headlines that maximise clicks, shares and visibility, often at the expense of content congruence. A headline that promises cooperation or success invites broader readership, especially among international audiences or stakeholders. This commercial logic, while understandable, introduces ethical and cognitive tensions. As empirical studies show, misleading or sentimentally inconsistent headlines can lead to cognitive dissonance, mistrust and distorted memory recall among audiences. When the body of a story contradicts the headline, readers may experience confusion, feel manipulated or selectively internalise whichever message aligns with their pre-existing biases. Over time, such experiences can erode confidence in media credibility and reduce the perceived transparency of journalism itself. Furthermore, for countries like India that invest heavily in regional image-building and soft power strategies, this kind of sentiment mismatch can dilute narrative coherence. If headlines consistently promote an image of India as an engaged and benevolent actor, but introductions raise doubts or concerns, the net impact is a fragmented portrayal that undermines India's ability to maintain a consistent strategic narrative across the region.

Moreover, these discrepancies also pose significant risks to democratic information ecosystems. When headlines, which serve as cognitive anchors, do not align with the substance of reporting, they distort the public's ability to make informed judgments. This breach of narrative coherence becomes especially troubling in the context of international relations, where public sentiment can influence diplomatic engagement, foreign policy support and cross-border collaboration. For ASEAN media, allowing such discrepancies to persist may unintentionally contribute to regional ambiguity or misperception, not just about India, but also about the reliability of the media itself. Editorial decisions that appear to placate one audience while quietly informing another create a two-tiered communication structure that lacks transparency and accountability. From a communicative ethics perspective, this undermines the journalistic obligation to present information clearly, honestly and coherently. In effect, what emerges is a form of strategic ambiguity that leverages sentiment layering to meet multiple goals: engaging audiences, sustaining commercial viability and navigating diplomatic sensitivities.

The sentiment gap between headlines and introductions in ASEAN coverage of India is more than a stylistic quirk, it is a revealing symptom of the complex interplay between media framing, regional geopolitics and the economics of digital journalism. This practice allows news outlets to balance optimism and critique, diplomacy and realism, visibility and nuance. Yet, it also creates a fragmented media environment where headlines function as standalone narratives divorced from the deeper, often more balanced, substance of reporting. For India's strategic communication efforts, this poses challenges to the clarity and stability of its soft power narrative. For ASEAN media, it highlights the need for greater editorial alignment and communicative integrity. And for regional audiences, it underscores the importance of critical media literacy in navigating the increasingly layered and strategic world of international news.

Chapter Eight

Curated Narratives: External Dependency and the Strategic Framing of India's Image in Southeast Asia

An empirical analysis of 2,301 news items from the online editions of leading newspapers across the five most economically significant ASEAN countries, Indonesia, Malaysia, Thailand, Singapore and the Philippines, reveals a pronounced asymmetry in the sourcing of India-related news.

Table 67: Overall Source Data

Total News Items	*2,301*	*Percentage*
News coverage by reporters/news desk/editorial/op-eds	677	29.42%
News coverage by international agencies/national agencies/ freelancers/contributors	1,624	70.57%

Only 29.42 per cent of the content was produced through the internal journalistic mechanisms of these media organisations, encompassing contributions from staff reporters, news desks, editorial columns and opinion pieces (Table 67). In stark contrast, 70.57 per cent of the coverage was derived from external sources, overwhelmingly dominated by Western wire services such as Reuters, AFP and AP. This disproportionate reliance on international news agencies not only signals a dependency in journalistic practice but also foregrounds a deeper structural imbalance in the mediation and representation of India within the ASEAN media space. The data, drawn from 15 of the most influential publications in the region, underscore how Western-centric narratives continue to shape the contours of India's image in ASEAN countries. The heavy outsourcing of content generation to Western agencies entrenches epistemic hierarchies within the global flow of information, whereby the perspectives, priorities and frames of Euro–

American institutions are privileged over regional or indigenous understandings. As a result, the portrayal of India is frequently filtered through lenses that are often misaligned with the socio-political, cultural and strategic contexts of Southeast Asia, producing a mediated vision of India that is less reflective of India's story and desired narrative and more indicative of Western editorial understanding.

This pattern of news production reflects a deep-seated legacy of unequal information flows embedded within the global media architecture, wherein dominant Western news agencies, operating from historically privileged geopolitical centres, continue to exert a disproportionate influence over the production, dissemination and framing of news narratives in the Global South. These hegemonic information structures not only marginalise indigenous and regional voices but also standardise the contours of international news through ideologically charged lenses that mirror the strategic and normative priorities of Western powers. Consequently, even when the Western coverage of countries like India is factually accurate, the slanted priorities and the misalignment between headlines and introductions influence how readers determine the sentiment (as discussed in the Chapter Nine) It is rarely ideologically neutral; instead, it tends to privilege themes and tropes that align with broader geopolitical imaginaries and policy discourses emanating from the Global North. Such coverage frequently foregrounds India's domestic political tensions, perceived democratic regressions, governance inefficiencies, socio-economic disparities, law and order failures, climate vulnerabilities and institutional fault lines.

Table 68: Overall News Source Data with Sentiment Categorisation

Positive news articles out of a total of 2,301 news articles	759	32.98%
Positive stories by reporters/news desk/opinion out of the total positive news articles	226	29.77%
Positive stories by international agencies/national agencies/freelancers out of the total positive news articles	532	70.09%
Negative news articles out of a total of 2,301 news articles	611	26.55%
Negative stories by reporters/news desk/opinion out of the total negative news articles	169	27.65%
Negative stories by international agencies/national agencies/ freelancers/contributors out of the total negative news articles	442	72.34%
Number of apprehensive news items of a total of 2,301 news items	324	14.08%
Number of neutral news items of a total of 2,301 news items	608	26.42%

When we further breakdown the empirical date and analyse the overall news source data with sentiment categorisation, we see numerical snapshots of how positive news articles are distributed among various sources (Table 68). With 32.98 per cent news items, that is, 759 out of 2,301 total articles classified as positive, this data invites a deeper reflection on media operations. This study examines how the flow of information, from the origin of content to its dissemination, can inadvertently disrupt effective communication and lead to the imposition of a slanted narrative. By deconstructing the data into its constituent parts, we gain insights into the inherent biases and potential pitfalls in the structuring of media messages.

The data divides the positive news articles into two principal categories. First one is about the production of media text through their own resources. Among the 759 positive articles, 226 (29.77 per cent) are produced by internal sources such as reporters, news desks or through editorial opinions. This subset reflects a segment where the narrative can be more rigorously edited and shaped by the internal agenda of the organisation and moreover control by the organisation and editors/policy makers. Another category of those news articles consists of items that are essentially supplied by external and independent contributors. The remaining 70.09 per cent of news related to India (532 articles) comes from international agencies, national agencies, or freelance journalists. This larger percentage implies a heavy reliance on external content providers. The varied origins inherently introduce an element of heterogeneity in perspectives; however, when aggregated, these voices may smooth over significant local issues or alternative narratives due to standardised professional journalistic practices or broader geopolitical pressures.

This bifurcation is pivotal to understanding how the media's sentiment, when largely positive, might not offer a comprehensive picture of events. The origin of these articles, especially from external sources, amplifies certain viewpoints while potentially silencing dissenting or more nuanced stories. With over 70 per cent of the positive content deriving from external agencies and freelancers, there is a tendency toward homogenisation. These sources often operate under similar editorial frameworks and common geopolitical narratives. As a result, the diversity of perspectives is diminished, and the prevailing narrative may be perpetuated across multiple platforms. This echo chamber effect can disrupt communication by reducing the incident of opposition voices and critical viewpoints.

The predominance of positive coverage, representing approximately one-third of all news articles, when interpreted without context, might skew public perception. For instance, an overt focus on positive sentiments, especially from sources not firmly embedded within the local context, can mask critical issues and challenges. Such a bias may not only sanitise or oversimplify complex issues but also lead to an imbalanced understanding of events, thus affecting public trust and informed discourse. Moreover, the reliance on both internal and external contributors introduces variability in quality control. While established news desks may adhere strictly to journalistic integrity, freelancers and external agencies might not apply a uniform standard. This fragmentation can result in discrepancies in reporting, where the flow of information may be disrupted by inconsistencies, further impeding a coherent narrative. The resultant mixed quality of reporting may confuse audiences about the reliability of positive portrayals and even contribute to the circulation of incomplete or biased information.

Our quantitative analysis of sentiment-based content sourcing (Table: 68) reveals a profoundly asymmetrical dependence on syndicated wire services across both commendatory and critical coverage within our publications, thereby calling into question the robustness of our in-house journalistic infrastructure. Specifically, although approximately 29.77 per cent of positive news items are generated by reporters and editorial teams, an almost similar pattern emerges in the realm of adverse reporting: a mere 27.65 per cent of negative stories originate from internal sources, while an overwhelming 72.34 per cent of such content is furnished by external wire agencies. This near-perfect symmetry between positive and negative internal sourcing highlights a systematic tendency to outsource how both positive and negative narratives are selected and framed. In effect, it transfers the organization's editorial judgment to the priorities and biases of global news syndicates. The effects of this dependence are significant. First, it limits the organization's ability to provide investigative depth and contextual understanding. Wire-fed reports, though often accurate, are shaped to fit the geopolitical, ideological, and commercial interests of the wire services, rather than reflecting the organization's local perspectives or regional expertise. Second, the fact that the internal production of negative stories is even lower than the organization's own positive content suggests hesitation or lack of resources to pursue critical, accountability-focused journalism, areas essential for academic and civic self-reflection. Thirdly, this external sourcing dynamic risks homogenising editorial voice, thereby undermining our credibility among discerning readers who seek independent analysis rather than repackaged global narratives. From an academic standpoint, such outsourcing of critical discourse can attenuate the pedagogical function of our newsroom, which ideally should serve as a crucible for investigative scholarship, experiential learning and reflexive critique. In effect, by ceding editorial control over the majority of our negative coverage to wire services, we inadvertently position our institution as a passive conduit for externally defined agendas, rather than as an active producer of original, contextually rich journalism.

Internal journalistic mechanisms, comprising staff reporters, news desks and editorial opinions, contribute roughly 27–29 per cent of the content for both positive and negative news. These locally produced narratives have the potential to reflect nuanced, context-specific issues and counterbalance the standardised framing produced by external agencies. However, with local production representing a minority share, their ability to reframe or challenge the dominant narrative is diminished. Consequently, the strategic communication process is influenced more by external priorities than by locally attuned sensitivities. Although explicit breakdowns for the internal versus external sourcing of apprehensive and neutral news are not provided, the overall sentiment distribution, 14.08 per cent apprehensive and 26.42 per cent neutral, suggests these categories form a substantial portion of the media output. If these categories follow the sourcing patterns seen in the positive and negative news, it could imply that strategic messaging across the sentiment spectrum is subject to the same external editorial oversight despite the very different tones they project. The weight of external sources potentially ensures that even more subtle forms of sentiment, such as apprehension and neutrality, are embedded within an overarching framework influenced by Western journalistic standards.

The marked reliance on external sources enables international wire services to shape not only the substance of the news but also its framing and tone. Through a process of standardisation and repetition, wire agencies establish an 'echo chamber' effect where the narrative, be it positive, negative, apprehensive or neutral, unfolds in a consistent manner across different media outlets. This narratively uniform landscape can constrain the diversity of perspectives and limit the capacity of internal journalism to introduce context-specific narratives that might challenge prevailing ideologies.

Implications for Epistemic Sovereignty, Credibility and Strategy

ASEAN news outlets overwhelmingly depend on major wire agencies (Reuters, AFP, AP) for India coverage. This reflects entrenched structural factors: most leading media houses are parts of large conglomerates and operate under tight political constraints. For example, Indonesia's media is dominated by a few family-owned conglomerates aligned with elites, and even its Press Council notes that only a sliver of outlets meet professionalism standards. In Malaysia the market is similarly concentrated (e.g., Media Prima controls most TV) with no anti-monopoly laws and licenses tightly controlled to favour pro government content. Thailand's broadcast sector is state leaning (military/monarchy hold national TV licenses), while Singapore's press is almost entirely run by state linked groups (Mediacorp, SPH Media) under strict licensing laws. In the Philippines, a few conglomerates control TV and print, and hostile laws and interventions (e.g., taxation or licensing challenges against critical outlets) deter independent foreign reporting. Under these conditions, local newsrooms have limited resources or autonomy to generate original India news. Subscribing to wire services is cheaper and politically safer. As one study notes, "Southeast Asian newspapers heavily depend on external sources for their portrayal of India"[491], producing mainly agency copy. This explains why roughly 70.6 per cent of India-related stories in the dataset come from Reuters/AFP/AP rather than from local reporting.

This structural dependence has significant consequences. When foreign wires drive most coverage, ASEAN countries lose *epistemic sovereignty*—the capacity to independently interpret and frame international affairs. Instead, a Western centric perspective of India predominates. Media credibility can suffer as audiences notice the uniform, impersonal tone of syndicated content. Indeed, where domestic outlets lack original reporting, public trust can erode, for example, Philippine data show that mainstream news lost credibility amid political pressure. Earlier studies suggest that ASEAN populations receive a 'skewed' image of India that aligns with global information flows favouring the West. This undermines informed opinion in the region.[492] Strategically, it means that India's voice is faint in regional discourse: ASEAN publics mainly see India through outside eyes. For India's diplomacy and Act East Policy, this is costly — local nuances and positive developments in India may be underreported, while critical issues are magnified. This anaysis thus calls for more local reporting and diverse sourcing to build a balanced image.

News Sourcing and Prioritisation within Bilateral Frameworks

This empirical study reveals stark differences in how five Southeast Asian media ecosystems assign their own reporters to cover India (Table 69). Thailand leads by a wide margin—53.0 per cent of Thai India stories are produced by internal sources (staff or local sources in India)—compared to only 10.8 per cent in the

Philippines. Indonesia (37.0 per cent) and Singapore (35.6 per cent) occupy a middle ground, while Malaysia (19.0 per cent) also remains low on this metric.

Table 69: The Country That Reports Most Extensively on India Using Internal Sources

Country	*Total News Coverage on India*	*Internal Source Stories*	*Percentage (Internal)*
Thailand	166	88	53.01%
Indonesia	81	30	37.03%
Singapore	1,092	389	35.62%
Malaysia	804	153	19.02%
Philippines	158	17	10.75%

In absolute terms, Singapore produces by far the most India related content (1,092 stories) but still relies on agencies for roughly two thirds of it. These figures in Table 69 indicate that Thailand and Indonesia have made the greatest institutional commitment to independently covering India to an extent, whereas Singapore, Malaysia and especially the Philippines largely depend on international wire services for India news.

High internal commitment (> per cent of India stories): Thailand (53.0 per cent), Indonesia (37.0 per cent) – in these markets, over one third of India news is generated by domestic reporters.

Moderate internal commitment: Singapore (35.6per cent) – high volume of coverage, but only about one third internally sourced, implying reliance on agencies for most stories.

Low internal commitment: Malaysia (19.0 per cent), Philippines (10.8 per cent) – in each case fewer than one in five India stories is produced in house, signifying heavy dependence on external news agencies.

These patterns reflect editorial priorities and capacities. Thailand's extremely high internal sourcing suggests that Thai newsrooms consider India an important beat and allocate correspondents or stringers there. By contrast, Philippine media virtually ignores India unless an international story appears via wire services. Singaporean outlets publish many India stories (likely due to large business and diaspora interest), but still use outside agencies for most content, perhaps valuing the efficiency and global perspective of Reuters/AP feeds. In sum, the relative size of the internal sourced share can be read as a proxy for how high India figures in each country's foreign news agenda: high shares (Thailand, Indonesia) imply India is treated as a strategic or priority partner, while low shares (Malaysia, Philippines) indicate it is treated as a more peripheral or routine topic.

These internal sourcing patterns must be interpreted in the context of each country's media environment. Press freedom rankings and media structures provide clues about why outlets do or do not invest in foreign bureaus. Thailand and Indonesia—the two leaders in internal coverage—also have relatively more vibrant media landscapes in ASEAN terms. Thailand (ranked around 85th globally in Reporters Sans Frontieres' (RSF) 2025 index) and Indonesia (around 127th) allow more independent reporting (though still with significant constraints). In Thailand, RSF notes a "vibrant media with a crop of new publications", suggesting journalists can pursue foreign stories (subject to taboos such as lese-majeste). Indonesia's press is described as a "pioneer of press freedom in Southeast Asia" (despite some new legal threats), indicating a relatively strong tradition of investigative and foreign reporting. These freer contexts may embolden Thai and Indonesian news organisations to station correspondents or commission stringers in India, and to present India news with local perspective rather than merely relaying agency copy.

By contrast, Singapore and Malaysia—despite economic clout—have historically tighter media environments. Singapore's press is famously constrained: RSF reports that Singapore "boasts of being a model of economic development" but is "an example of what not to be" in terms of press freedom, which is "almost non-existent". In practice, Singaporean outlets (like *The Straits Times* or *CNA*) face strict regulations and self censorship. This likely discourages heavy investment in foreign bureaus; instead, newsrooms rely on international agencies for global reporting, including India news. Malaysia's media freedom improved sharply after 2022 (climbing dramatically in the RSF index under a new government), but the older restrictions still exist. The recent relaxation may not yet have translated into more India coverage. In Malaysia, mainstream outlets tend to focus on domestic politics and Malay–Chinese issues; coverage of India (or even of the Indian–Malaysian Tamil community) remains comparatively niche. The low 19 per cent internal sourcing suggests that Malaysian newsrooms either have few India correspondents or defer to wires.

The Philippines presents a mixed case. Its 2023 RSF rank (132) reflects an "extremely vibrant" press that is nevertheless under frequent pressure and often consumed with domestic and Western agendas. Philippine media traditionally prioritise ties with the U.S. and Southeast Asian regional affairs, with China looming as a major security issue. India is not a leading strategic partner, so few Filipino media dedicate their own staff to it. Indeed, only about one in 10 Philippines–India stories uses a local reporter. Many Philippine outlets (like *Philippine Star* or *ABS-CBN News*) simply pick up Reuters, AFP or wire photos when India matters. In this sense, press freedom is not the binding constraint in the Philippines; rather, it is editorial choice and interest. Even in a relatively free environment, coverage reflects perceived national priorities — and India appears low on that list for Filipino newsrooms.

The allocation of journalistic resources also mirrors each country's geopolitical orientation and bilateral relationship with India. Over the past two years, four of these five nations have significantly upgraded ties with India, yet media follow through varies. For example, India elevated relations to a Comprehensive Strategic Partnership with both Singapore and Malaysia in 2024. In Singapore (one of India's closest economic and security partners in ASEAN), this formal deepening of relations coincided with massive trade and investment links. Nevertheless, Singaporean media — despite their volume of India stories — still relies largely on global agencies for content. This may reflect both Singapore's media practice of outsourcing international coverage and a cautious approach: the government likely prefers to project stable, positive ties rather than ground up analysis. In Malaysia, Prime Minister Anwar Ibrahim's August 2024 visit to Delhi culminated in a new strategic partnership, but Malaysian newsrooms have shown little sign of a media 'pivot' to India. Apart from a few high profile visits, India news in Malaysia often comes via international feeds or occasional commentary. Domestic concerns (political reform, Malay-majority economics and China policy) tend to dominate coverage, leaving India relatively under covered despite the official partnership.

Thailand officially upgraded its relationship with India to a Strategic Partnership in April 2025. Interestingly, Thai media had already been producing over half of its India news through internal sources well before this formal announcement. This suggests that Bangkok (both government and press) has long viewed India as an important ally. Geographically, Thailand shares land and maritime links with India (via the Bay of Bengal); culturally, both are Asian powers with Buddhist heritage. Strategically, Thailand may see India as a counterbalance to China's regional dominance. Thus, Thai newsrooms arguably devote more reporter time to India–Thailand defence cooperation, investment deals and cultural exchanges. The Thai example shows that when a government prioritises engagement with India, domestic media tend to follow suit in allocating correspondents.

Indonesia has no recent 'new' partnership announcement (it maintains its long standing ties), but as ASEAN's largest member it plays a central role in regional diplomacy. Indonesia and India cooperate in forums like the East Asia Summit and Indian Ocean Rim Association. Indonesian journalists have sometimes covered India's economic rise, elections and disasters with their own staff (e.g., *Jakarta Post* correspondents in Delhi). The 37 per cent internal sourcing suggests a moderately strong commitment: not as extreme as Thailand's, but well above Malaysia or the Philippines. Indonesia's robust Non-Governmental Organisation and media sector (and a tradition of covering fellow democracies) likely contributes to this. Moreover, the Indonesian public has shown interest in India's democracy and technology, which can motivate newsrooms to report independently. Geopolitically, Indonesia and India both champion a 'Free and Open Indo–Pacific', and this conceptual alignment probably justifies editorial attention.

In contrast, the Philippines maintains only a basic partnership with India (e.g., Jaishankar's 2024 Manila visit), reflecting growing but still secondary bilateral ties. Economic links are modest (trade and investment figures between Manila and Delhi are much smaller). Security cooperation is limited. As a result, Philippine media appear to regard India as a low salience story. The data (10.8 per cent internal) imply that no Philippine newsroom considers India a top foreign beat. India appears in Filipino newspapers mostly when there are big global events (elections, Bollywood stars) picked up from AP or CNN; local journalists are rarely sent to India. This likely mirrors Manila's own foreign policy: despite interest in diversifying partnerships, the Philippines still focusses more on Japan, Australia, the U.S. and China.

Taken together, the internal sourcing decisions suggest how each country positions India in its foreign news strategy. Thailand's very high internal coverage implies that Indian affairs are a priority story category; Thai editors presumably view Indian developments as having direct relevance. In practice, Thai outlets may contextualise Indian news through a Thai lens (e.g., reporting on India's Look East/Act East Policy because it impacts Thailand). Indonesia's moderate commitment indicates that India is treated as an important but not dominant foreign affairs topic. Singapore's approach — high volume but low internal share — suggests that while India matters (especially economically), Singaporean newsrooms prefer to repackage already vetted content rather than invest heavily in original reporting. Malaysia and the Philippines clearly rank India lower: by providing few staff generated pieces, their media effectively relegate India to 'outsourced' coverage. In editorial terms, this means Indian affairs may not receive in-depth analysis or local angles in those markets.

In media studies terms, this pattern reflects agenda-setting and resource allocation. Countries that see India as strategically or economically central (Thailand, and to a lesser extent Indonesia) have placed more journalistic 'weight' on it, signalling to their public that India is a significant partner. By contrast, the Philippines' reliance on wires for India news suggests a lack of agenda priority — India's profile is set by global narratives rather than local interpretation. This can shape public perception: if domestic reporters do not frame India stories, the country is less likely to be viewed as intimately relevant.

Finally, broader economic and geopolitical dynamics underpin these media choices. ASEAN as a whole is India's fourth largest trading partner, so one might expect robust coverage everywhere; the uneven data show that bilateral nuances matter more. Diaspora communities also play a role: Singapore and Malaysia have substantial Indian-origin populations, but only Singaporean media (mostly English-language) tap them heavily — yet still through wire services. The relatively small Indian diaspora in Thailand and the Philippines suggests that their high/low coverage is driven more by state policy than community demand. It is important to highlight that the allocation of internal journalistic resources reflects each country's perceived stakes in India. Thailand and Indonesia clearly signal that India is a priority of interest; Malaysia and the Philippines do so far less; Singapore occupies an intermediate position, valuing information on India but preferring syndicated supply over its own reporting.

Statecraft and Media Governance: Ownership, Regulation and Strategic Communication

The role of media in policymaking, especially concerning strategic communication, belongs to a system that includes various elements like normative structure of the state, economic structure, geo-political equations, etc. It is obvious that this conveys certain messages or propagates specific ideas because a selective approach is embedded in the process of media text production. Moreover, the media itself develops a system for this propagation. "The mass media serve as a system for communicating messages and symbols to the general populace... To fulfill this role requires systematic propaganda".[493] In the midst of this deliberation one significant issue has been whether the given media system is instrumental in endorsing or undermining a free and independent structure of communication and democratic institution and practices. "Are media a force for social justice or oligarchy?"[494] As we discussed earlier in this sub-section that media text is essentially a content that conveys some idea through information. As John Pilger[495] says that the entire media content is not only about dissemination of information, it is also about power, which it generates through the propagation of ideas. In addition to this, "The people who are able to engineer consent are the ones who have the resources and the power to do it, the business community, and that's who you work for".[496] At the granular level, while media narratives or the state cannot directly control a society, but through frequent and consistent opinionated information infusion, it may influence what you think. [497] Schiller highlights how powerful nations or groups use public media,[498] which includes mass media, for example, television, radio and newspapers. Mass media as a tool to spread their influence in other societies. Obviously, as the purpose is to spread this influence to make it widespread and effective, these dominant powers need to take control of the media systems themselves. This domination may help in shaping the messages and information that reach the public, aligning them with their own interests and values. Making of this dominated ecosystem, is part of what Schiller refers to as "cultural imperialism",[499] where a dominant culture imposes its beliefs and practices on another, often through subtle means through media and communication, rather than through direct force. Subtle control over media content promotes its own way of life and perspectives, potentially overshadowing or replacing local cultures and viewpoints. In other words, Schiller is warning about the power of media as a tool for cultural domination,[500] where control over information can lead to control over how people think and perceive the world.

In the given political–economic normative ecosystem, there are various tools that have been instrumental in controlling the media functioning, and according to cultural theorist Raymond Williams, 'advertisement' has been like "the official art of modern capitalist society".[501] It is obvious that there are various tools and according to Noam Chomsky and Edward S. Herman, the state influences media through structural biases rooted in ownership, advertising, sourcing, flak and shared norms. This outlines how these five filters create a systemic distortion of news coverage, shaping public opinion.[502] Moreover, the initial content of news must go through multiple layers of screening, leaving only the refined remains suitable for publication.[503] It seems very evident that media industries operate in a system, and this is true for other businesses, but businesses deal with some sort of products in one way or another.[504] In the case of the media industry, it deals with the structuring and shaping of information into a media product. In the agreed system, each and every element tends to alter itself to operate; and in a given political–economic ecosystem, "Media themselves undergo transformations in the course of political transitions".[505] In the case of Southeast Asia, there are many practices as far as the media system is concerned and it has been in flux as per political transitions in the region. "The media's contributions to political transitions in Indonesia, Myanmar, and Malaysia are not easy to pin down. For the most part, the pre-transition media were highly restricted, limiting their capacity to communicate dissent and turning them into ready vehicles for their respective regimes' favored narratives, whether on economic policies, political debates, or social relations. State control, however, was never total. The market orientation of commercial media and a democratic ethos among media professionals meant that there was always some resistance within news organizations to the state's preference for media that served a purely propaganda function".[506]

In Indonesia, the media backdrop is subjugated by conglomerates with direct links to political entities that have been influencing media content. Earlier studies suggest that media dynasts have been instrument in using media outlets for supporting of political campaigns, for example we can name the chairman of Nasdem Party (who owned Metro TV) was supporting Joko Widodo in his 2014 presidential election. It is quite an overt preposition that "Media moguls use their outlets to serve their personal interests, not to form cartels".[507] Another factor has been the concentration of ownership among elites, and this further complicates the media landscape. This concern comprises increasing dominance, which may push a domination that bounds public discourse.[508] In the case of Malaysia, the media ecosystem has been inclined towards the ruling architecture. The evidence leans toward significant government control, with outlets like Bernama owned by the state and Media Prima by UMNO, a Barisan Nasional (BN) component. "Many media outlets in Malaysia are owned by the government or by component parties of the Barisan Nasional (BN) coalition, which was in power until May 2018. For example, Bernama, the national news agency, is owned by the government, while Media Prima, the largest media group in Malaysia, is owned by the United Malays National Organisation (UMNO), a component party of BN".[509] Another studied country in this study is Thailand, where the media ecosystem is represented by ownership by oligarchs with links to the royal family and armed forces. It is important to highlight that this structure of media ecosystem shapes content. "Leading media outlets are owned by oligarchs with links to the royal family and the armed forces. Public and semi-public media groups, such as MCOT, are accused of avoiding any criticism of the government."[510] Another normative structure is the legal preposition, like the lèse-majesté law (Article 112), punishable by up to 15 years in prison, which further influences media content, with recent arrests of journalists for reporting on anti-royalist graffiti in August

2024.[511] This recent example can be explained through the incident of the suspension of the Move Forward Party in August 2024, when the Constitutional Court intervened over proposed amendments to Article 112, which has further entrenched suppression.[512]

If we try to assess Singapore's scenario, the statecraft operates through specific ownership rules (such as powerful 'management shares'), which efficiently sanction dominating political entities associates in media organisations. In other words, a regulatory rule "enables the ruling coalition to co-opt establishment and market forces, nurturing a vested interest among these stakeholders in maintaining a stable political climate".[513] Normative practices and the political economic structure suggest that Singapore's conventional media steadily resonates with government priorities.[514] In the Philippines, research suggests that media concentration influences content, and this domination was demonstrated a few years ago when the Duterte government's actions, such as the closure of *ABS-CBN* in 2020, underscored the political influence on media,[515] where a strong tradition of watchdog journalism struggling under increasing authoritarianism. In addition to this, the socio-economic disparities, largely due to urban–rural gaps, uphold legacy media hegemony, and this state of affairs projects an ecosystem that shapes media content embedded with elements that limit critical discourse.[516]

There is ample evidence that illustrates the interconnected relationship between the media and the dominant normative structure. We can generalise the phenomenon in these ASEAN countries, about the pattern of concentrated media ownership besides the political and economic elites, apart from this government regulations influence the freedom, and economic tools like advertising revenue further put filters over the content. Indonesia and the Philippines show significant elite capture, Malaysia and Singapore exhibit strong government control and Thailand combines oligarchic and royal influence with legal threats. There are high possibilities that, in this given media and normative ecosystem, media content has been subject to alteration, aligning with political and economic comforts, thus impacting public discourse and democratic processes. Therefore, media content represents the overall deliberations on issues, including the sensitive issue of policymaking.

Structural Constraints and India's Framing in Southeast Asian Media

The media landscape of Southeast Asia is marked by concentrated ownership, tight state influence and deep integration with global news networks. A handful of conglomerates or government-linked entities control much of the press in countries like Indonesia, Malaysia and Thailand, often aligning editorial agendas with prevailing political interests. At the same time, most newsrooms lack the resources to send reporters abroad; foreign news budgets have shrunk and coverage is heavily syndicated from international wire agencies. UNESCO and media scholars have long warned that such imbalances skew global information flows. In practice, Southeast Asian outlets tend to rely on Western and regional wire services for international reporting, reinforcing a 'North-to-South' dependency in news content. For example, one study found that Indonesia's leading newspaper relied on foreign agencies for 74 per cent of its India stories, with only ~26 per cent produced by its own reporters.[517] Similarly, a major Malaysian daily sourced 67 per cent of its India-related content from external agencies.[518] These structural factors, media concentration, the economic imperatives of market-driven news and transnational news flows profoundly constrain what topics are covered and how. As McQuail[519] and McCombs & Shaw observe, the political–economic context of a media system shapes its 'agenda-setting': with limited local reporting, news agendas default to events deemed important by global wire editors rather than nuanced bilateral issues.

In normative terms, most Southeast Asian media operate under hybrid models that blend state control with market aims. In fully authoritarian or 'development' systems (e.g., Vietnam, Laos or historically Malaysia), the press is explicitly guided to support national development goals and avoid sensitive topics, curtailing critical or foreign policy coverage. Even in nominally liberal democracies, such as Indonesia, the Philippines and Thailand, political or legal pressures induce pervasive self-censorship. In Singapore and Brunei, 'public service' or nationalist media models prevail: major outlets are state-owned or tightly regulated, broadcasting a pro-government narrative. By contrast, only a minority of Southeast Asian countries exhibit a truly 'liberal' press free from state interference (and often even these, like the Philippines, are now backsliding under populist populism). In sum, the dominant normative ethos in the region treats media as subordinate to elite and state interests. This means foreign issues — especially those not directly affecting domestic elites — receive perfunctory coverage or are framed through a domestic lens. As Siebert et al. note, non-democratic regimes "impose strict controls over mass communication"[520], whereas democracies allow free media. In practice, Southeast Asia's press often reflects this tension: it is freer than in North Korea or China, but far from the robust pluralism of the West.

These political–economic and normative constraints jointly shape 'how India is framed' in the Southeast Asia media. Because local newsrooms seldom dispatch correspondents to South Asia, India stories tend to be episodic and shallow. Coverage often derives from press releases, official visits or wire reports on crises – for example, reportage of disaster, economic setbacks, negative geopolitical dynamics and religious tensions. The focus is typically on sensational or stereotype confirming angles (terrorism, poverty or disaster) rather than deep political or social analysis. Scholars have observed that Southeast Asian audiences "view India with mixed feelings: both with a sense of deep-rooted cultural connections, but also with a lack of understanding of India and Indians beyond what the media makes superficially visible".[521] In other words, media frames reduce India to caricatures. At the same time, any positive or nuanced stories (India's IT boom, democratic debates or foreign policy vision) struggle to break through the noise.

A study on ASEAN–India Media portrayal confirms this: "newspapers heavily depend on external sources for their portrayal of India, often resulting in superficial narratives" [522], with a majority of headlines casting India in a negative or apprehensive light. Indeed, much of the (often negative) India coverage in Malaysia, Indonesia and elsewhere comes straight from international news agencies. The net effect is a skewed, episodic image of India that aligns with Western news agendas more than with India's self-image or bilateral priorities.

The implications for India's strategic communication and soft power are significant. Media agendas help determine foreign policy salience: as Cohen notes, "the media may not tell people what to think, but it is remarkably successful in determining what issues they think about". If India rarely appears as an issue except in fleeting headlines, publics in ASEAN states remain unaware of India's perspectives, policies or partnerships. Survey data bear this out: a 2024 ISEAS survey found only \~14 per cent of ASEAN respondents felt confident India would "do the right thing" on global issues, and merely 0.4 per cent of respondents viewed India as the region's most influential power. In other words, India's visibility and credibility in the region are low, making it hard to translate cultural ties or economic initiatives into tangible influence. From the standpoint of the 'dependency theory', this dynamic is unsurprising: news flows remain heavily North-to-South, so a rising power like India is still peripheral in Asia's media landscape.

Normative Logics of ASEAN News Frameworks

The representational patterns emerging from media coverage of India in five ASEAN countries, Indonesia, Malaysia, Thailand, Singapore and the Philippines, reflect a deeply structured and ideologically saturated process that is less about journalistic neutrality and more about systemic alignment with national and regional strategic imperatives. Across these contexts, the prioritisation of specific news categories, such as geopolitics, bilateral diplomacy, economic trends, governance and regional cooperation, indicates a media logic shaped by the political economy of news production and the normative functions that media is expected to perform in each country. This logic privileges news items that serve as extensions of state narratives, facilitate foreign policy goals or resonate with elite concerns about regional stability, economic opportunity and governance credibility. Rather than engaging with India's complex internal realities in a comprehensive or nuanced manner, media in these ASEAN states constructs India primarily as a strategic referent, an actor whose relevance is determined by its capacity to reinforce the host country's diplomatic, economic or developmental orientations. The Indonesian case, for example, suggests a media apparatus that functions as a transmitter of national interest, selectively highlighting India's geopolitical alignment and market integration to mirror Indonesia's broader aspirations within the Indo–Pacific framework. Similarly, Malaysian media's heavy emphasis on India's economic and geopolitical roles reveals a selective affinity shaped by trade interests and shared participation in regional groupings like the East Asia Summit or ASEAN–India mechanisms. In both cases, coverage choices align closely with government discourses and business priorities, underscoring the entwinement of editorial judgment with institutional agendas.

In Thailand and the Philippines, where political contestations over media autonomy are more visible, the press nonetheless operates within a bounded space in which foreign policy narratives and strategic relevance override any broader cultural or human-interest engagement with India. Coverage of India's domestic politics or social issues is minimal and often instrumentalised to make inferences about stability, regulatory coherence or governance standards, all of which bear implications for regional partnerships or bilateral exchanges. The Thai media's emphasis on formal state engagements and bilateral economic interests exemplifies how the press functions as a legitimising mechanism for existing diplomatic alignments, echoing what scholars of media sociology describe as 'indexing' to elite sources (Bennett, 1990). Even in the Philippines, where climate and disaster coverage features more prominently, India is framed less as a society coping with environmental risk and more as a co-participant in global crisis management architectures, a framing that reflects international policy discourse rather than indigenous storytelling. Singapore's media system, the most technocratic and elite-oriented among the five, exemplifies how journalistic prioritisation is driven by a managerial rationality that centres economic performance indicators, macro-political trends and institutional efficiency. Here, news serves a diagnostic purpose, providing stakeholders with cues about India's risk environment, policy continuity and investment climate, mirroring the city-state's strategic calculus as a global financial hub. This technocratic filtering of news content reveals how media systems in high-capacity states prioritise informational capital over civic engagement, treating international reporting as a site of strategic knowledge production rather than democratic deliberation (Chua, 2012; George, 2006).

What unites these diverse cases is a normative model of journalism that functions less as a check on power or a vehicle for cosmopolitan exchange, and more as a mechanism for strategic signalling, elite consensus-building and regional agenda-setting. This is especially pronounced in Southeast Asia, where many media systems are marked by varying degrees of state control, market dependency and editorial discipline, conditions that constrain the scope of foreign reporting and shape the editorial framing of international actors like India (Rodan, 2004). Within such systems, newsworthiness is not a neutral metric, but a strategic decision governed by what Hallin and Mancini (2004) describe as the media's embeddedness within political and economic institutions. The consistent foregrounding of India's geopolitical positioning, bilateral relations and economic performance across these countries points to a shared editorial logic that aligns with broader regional priorities, such as hedging strategies in the Indo–Pacific, economic diversification or the search for governance models that balance openness with institutional control. The marginalisation of cultural, social or grassroots-level themes reflects a deeper structural tendency within ASEAN media to filter international actors through a framework of functional utility and strategic relevance. In this sense, the media act as a curator of regional consciousness, shaping how publics and policymakers alike perceive external powers not in their full complexity, but through a prism of selective relevance and instrumental association.

This convergence between editorial priorities and regional strategic thinking underscores the need to analyse media representations as a part of a larger ideological apparatus that mediates global relations through domesticated frames. India's portrayal in Southeast Asian media is thus less an account of its own agency and more a mirror of the receiving country's foreign policy posture, economic strategy and normative expectations about regional order. As such, the study of media prioritisation in these contexts cannot be decoupled from the broader political economy that governs news production, nor from the discursive regimes that define what counts as relevant, credible or strategically significant. In privileging certain narratives while omitting others, ASEAN media does not merely report on India, it participates in constructing a vision of India that aligns with local priorities, institutional logics and regional imaginaries of partnership and progress (Thussu, 2006; Seib, 2010). This mediated vision, while functional for policy communication and elite discourse, remains partial and ideologically coded, reinforcing a strategic vocabulary that both reflects and shapes the contours of contemporary Asian geopolitics.

The assertion that media coverage of India in ASEAN countries is systematically shaped by state-centric agendas and transnational diplomatic priorities, rather than emerging from independent journalistic practices, finds robust support across multiple theoretical frameworks and empirical studies in media analysis, political science and international relations. At its core, this phenomenon reflects the broader interplay between media institutions and political power structures, wherein news narratives function not merely as informational outputs but as strategic instruments of statecraft. In the ASEAN–India context, this means that governments can indirectly, or in some cases, directly, steer media focus towards topics that reinforce their policy objectives, such as economic collaboration, security alliances or cultural diplomacy, while marginalising coverage that might complicate these narratives. For example, during periods of intensified trade negotiations, ASEAN media might disproportionately highlight India's economic potential, while underreporting domestic challenges within India that could undermine its image as a reliable partner.

Selective emphasis, lexical choices and contextual cues in the media text emphasise predispose audiences toward specific interpretations. When ASEAN media frames India as a 'democratic counterweight' to China or a 'growth engine' for regional trade, it is not merely describing reality but advancing a diplomatic narrative that aligns with state interests. Such framing is particularly evident in the coverage of multilateral forums like the ASEAN–India Summit, where media outlets often echo their governments' official stances, presenting India's role in terms that harmonise with broader regional strategies. States cultivate favourable international perceptions to advance foreign policy goals. ASEAN countries, for instance, may leverage media to amplify narratives of India as a stabilising force in the Indo–Pacific, thereby reinforcing bilateral and multilateral partnerships.

This is especially salient in light of initiatives like the Indo–Pacific Economic Framework (IPEF), where media portrayal of India's participation can sway public and elite opinion in ways that facilitate policy implementation.

Underpinning these dynamics is the 'political economy of media' (Murdock & Golding, 1977), which highlights how ownership models, regulatory environments and economic dependencies constrain journalistic autonomy. In many ASEAN states, where media outlets operate under varying degrees of state influence or corporate oligarchy, coverage of India is often filtered through the prism of national interest. For example, in Vietnam, where state-aligned media dominates, reporting on India's defence collaborations may emphasise mutual strategic benefits, while downplaying any friction that could arise from competing interests. Similarly, in Singapore, where media is corporatized but retains close ties with state priorities, coverage of India's digital economy might foreground opportunities for Singaporean investors, reflecting the city-state's economic diplomacy.

Empirical evidence substantiates these theoretical claims. A 2023 study by the Institute of Southeast Asian Studies (ISEAS) found that ASEAN media's portrayal of India shifted markedly during the negotiation of the Regional Comprehensive Economic Partnership (RCEP), with outlets in pro-trade states like Thailand and Singapore emphasising India's potential contributions, while those in more protectionist economies like Indonesia framed its eventual withdrawal as a setback. Similarly, an analysis of *The Straits Times* (Singapore) and *The Bangkok Post* (Thailand) revealed that coverage of India's Act East Policy consistently aligned with their respective governments' enthusiasm for deeper regional integration, while outlets in more sceptical ASEAN nations offered muted or critical perspectives. Historical precedents also illustrate this trend. During the 2018 ASEAN–India Commemorative Summit, media in the Philippines and Malaysia, both of which were seeking stronger defence ties with India, gave prominence to stories highlighting India's maritime security role, whereas Cambodian and Laotian media, whose governments maintain closer ties with China, offered minimal coverage. Such variations underscore how media narratives are tailored to local political exigencies.

It is significant to underline that the interplay of agenda-setting, framing, media diplomacy and political–economic structures demonstrates that ASEAN media coverage of India is far from a dispassionate reflection of events. Instead, it is a curated output, meticulously aligned with the strategic imperatives of states and the fluid terrain of transnational diplomacy. This alignment not only shapes public perception but also serves as a mechanism for reinforcing state power and advancing regional geopolitical objectives. Future research could further dissect the granular mechanisms of this process, such as the role of state-funded think tanks in shaping media discourse or the impact of digital platforms in challenging or reinforcing these curated narratives.

Chapter Nine

India's Media Portrayal through Strategic Communication Framework

Contextualising India's Media Portrayal in ASEAN

Within the complex structure of modern geopolitics, narrative power has come to be as determinative in shaping foreign policy as classic doctrines. This represents a new departure in the exercise and perception of power at the global level. States now increasingly find that in addition to economic or military power, the capacity to shape, spread and configure one's narrative worldwide is an essential element of foreign policy. This brings public diplomacy into a prime strategic role and highlights the absolute significance of a state's image.

For an emerging global power like India, particularly in the strategically critical and culturally pluralistic region of Southeast Asia, the articulation and dissemination of its image in news media take on central significance.[523] This research enquires into what ways India's image is being manufactured in ASEAN media as a part of strategic communication and how narrative practices shape public perception and diplomacy.[524] The emphasis on managing India's image highlights a proactive approach to foreign policy.[525] It is not solely about what India *does*, but critically, how its actions and identity are *perceived* by external audiences.[526] This generates a built-in tension: a country's strategic value may be understood at an elite level but if its media image and characterisation are disconnected or ruptured from its larger identity, its ability to convert hard power into soft power, and elite interaction into popular legitimation, is substantially eroded.[527] This opens up the central concern of this study, the disconnect between India's strategic recognition and its complex media presence in ASEAN.

Strategic Narratives and Media's Discursive Role

Scholars like Alister Miskimmon, Ben O'Loughlin and Laura Roselle argue that strategic narratives are key to pursuing foreign policy goals.[528] Under this approach, media outlets aren't regarded as neutral vessels for facts-reporting. Rather, they're understood to actively project national and ideological stories that determine international perception.[529] These stories serve as essential diplomatic tools for embedding symbols, rhetoric and strategically selected imagery into the larger narrative of public diplomacy. This argument goes as far as to say that media constitutes international reality in an active sense rather than simply reflecting an already constitutive power. To India, this means that its public diplomacy cannot simply be a case of 'getting the facts out'.[530] Rather, it must actively participate in narrative construction and contestation and recognise its image as an achieved outcome of media discourse rather than a *fait accompli*. The task here, then, isn't so much what is said but how it will be interpreted.

The media as a 'discursive arena' for promoting state–political–economic agendas also serves to further illuminate this dynamic.[531] This comes accompanied by the development of 'asymmetric epistemic visibility',[532] where the agendas of the elite commonly take precedence over 'subaltern narratives'.[533] This model explains why the media lens tends to fall back on what suits geopolitical and economic interests and why there is rarely a representative representation of India's holistic image.[534] This uneven level play in information dissemination means that state and political–economic agendas and interests tend to wield media to project narratives in support of them. This isn't a question of reported content per se but of what takes precedence and what happens to be omitted. The marginalized narratives, particularly the societal, cultural, and grassroots narratives of India, are structurally at a disadvantage in this system.[535] This bias in system architecture explains why India suffers from a form of 'visibility without intimacy',[536] in that the active projection by the media, with its bias in favour of agendas of influence, tends to filter out India's multifaceted and complex nature and reduce India's reality into a utility-driven triadic framing. This then represents a deep-structure obstacle to inclusive representation.

News media outlets, either consciously or unconsciously influenced by media logics as a result of the competition and pressures of the globalised media industry, have a tendency of injecting dissonance into strategic communication.[537] This either takes the form of intentional or unconscious fragmentation or the amplification of narrative production in the service of various objectives such as attracting an audience with sensationalism, signalling complex diplomatic postures to targeted audiences and projecting an exterior image of objectivity.[538] The interplay of these mechanisms demonstrates a sophisticated understanding of media's persuasive potential in shaping complex international relations.[539] Fragmentation frequently arises when initial, often sensationalised headlines, imprint a particular sentiment that is only superficially mitigated by subsequent text.[540] Given that many media consumers engage briefly with content, often only absorbing the headline, the negative or oversimplified narrative tends to persist, with long term implications for India's soft power.[541] This indicates that there are inherent, sometimes conflicting, incentives at play within media organisations.[542] Commercial imperatives (like sensationalism for readership) and political objectives (signalling nuanced diplomatic stances) can lead to a fragmented, oversimplified or even contradictory portrayal.[543] India's efforts to project a holistic image are thus challenged not only by misinformation but by the very structure of news production and consumption, where superficial engagement and sensationalism often prevail.[544]

Structural Realities and Media Ecosystem

The Southeast Asia media landscape is not monolithic; far from it, it is a diverse mosaic composed of different national contexts, each with distinct political systems, civic engagement and changing societal norms.[545] This structural foundation has a profound impact on how external actors, including India, are represented.[546] Southeast Asia contains a wide political spectrum, from mature democracies to authoritarian regimes and those in the midst of democratic backsliding.[547] This directly influences the extent to which media freedom is practiced as well as the limits as to what can be enquired into.[548] For example, some countries may have relatively liberal media environments, some impose stringent curbs on freedom of the press, with results in highly controlled narratives.[549] This is such a wide variation that whatever is known about India is filtered through radically different lenses, from comparatively independent questioning to state curated narratives.[550] This differential permeability of ASEAN media to external narratives includes that India's narrative is going to be construed otherwise in different ASEAN nations. The media freedom directly relates to how open a media environment is in a nation to external narratives within the political–economy framework, specifically those that may be counter framing to state preferred ones.[551] In more liberal systems, India may gain wider scope for nuanced cultural narratives; in controlled ones, it will be framed through political–economic centric or geopolitical lenses.[552] Hence, this requires a highly variable and personalised strategic communication approach for India in ASEAN, with a "one-size-fits-all"[553] approach being ineffective.

One characteristic structural feature of media systems in many Southeast Asian nations is the politically entrenched concentration of ownership in oligarchic networks and politically entrenched groups of conglomerates.[554] This pervasiveness not only undermines normative notions of media autonomy, but also enables the instrumentalisation of media as a means for promoting proprietorial interests, personal as well as political.[555] Indonesia is a particularly informative example, as powerful media moguls use their vast media holdings to promote personal agenda, often in a 'tightly knit hegemony' with the power in office.[556] This concentrated ownership also shows a critical dynamic: in addition to overt censorship, economic fragility and concentrated media ownership in Southeast Asia operate as potent, less obvious, control mechanisms for narratives.[557] This is a systemic prejudice in which stakeholder power meets editorial agendas that truncate nuanced, exhaustive reporting to political–economic narrative, often at the expense of media objectivity. Economic fragility is also a 'silent killer' that ensures that even if reporters wish to report objectively on India's cultural contribution, monetary compulsion and ownership arrangements may discourage it in a manner that is explicit or implicit in favour of advertiser-friendly or media owners-friendly material.[558] India's strategic communication cannot therefore target just government officials or traditional media; it must also address how to approach or contend with the commercial interests and forms of ownership that necessitate implicit control over media narratives, perhaps involving cooperation with business elites or with less commercialised media sites less susceptible to such pressures.[559]

The domestic architectural arrangements as well as the transnational communicational infrastructures in Southeast Asia mediate in a critical manner the epistemic bases for media production, especially in international reporting, where the input information is multifariously derived and transversally distributed. The international news flow has traditionally been, and to a large extent continues to be, controlled by Western-based news agencies, commonly known as the 'Big Four': Associated Press (AP), Reuters, Agence France-Presse (AFP) and United Press International (UPI).[560] These agencies supply well over 90 per cent of the foreign news appearing in the world's newspapers during the last century,[561,562] and their coverage is often less expensive as well as fuller in content than having a spotty system of 'own correspondents'. Among these big four, three of them still dominate.

Reuters, AP and AFP supply over 90 per cent of the international newswire content used by media organisations across the world. Estimates suggest that AP contributes approximately 39–40 per cent of this content, AFP accounts for about 30–31 per cent and Reuters provides roughly 21–22 per cent. These agencies maintain extensive networks, with Reuters operating in over 200 locations, AP maintaining a presence in more than 100 countries with over 250 bureaus and AFP covering 151 countries through 201 bureaus. Their operational model is based on a tiered subscription system, offering text, image, video and multimedia content to clients such as newspapers, digital platforms and broadcasters.[563]

A marked quantitative imbalance defines this news flow, where Western agencies relay a great deal more news to Asia than they take in from it. For example, AP sends a daily average of 90,000 words from New York to Asia but takes in a mere 9,000 words from the continent in the last century.[564] This produces a 'one-way' or unidirectional movement of information, mostly from developed to developing countries, as well as from technologically advanced to less advanced countries. The exorbitance of foreign bureau upkeep forces most ASEAN media organisations to rely extensively on these wire services for international news, including information from India. This reliance results in the original framing, selection, as well as even the very wording adopted for narrating situations in India being often dictated by the interests and priorities of the Western news organisations.[565] This reliance can quietly affect the bigger story about India even before that reaches the local populace. This enforces a form of "information colonialism",[566] where the framing, selection and terminology in international news is represented largely by actors in another area.[567] This is not a matter of bias; it is a matter of the very epistemology by which international events make sense. It curtails the narrative sovereignty of countries like India, as stories from them get narrated through the interests and lenses of outside, historically powerful, media institutions.[568] India's strategic communication must not merely counter individual negative narratives, but also tackle the systemic disparity. This includes investing in substitute news dissemination channels, promoting South–South media partnerships or directly contesting the current form of the information order so that narratives in it may not be perpetually relayed by outside gatekeepers.[569]

ASEAN media organisations display unique editorial practices, where narratives get fragmented or reconstituted to serve multiple and sometimes contradictory purposes.[570] Earlier experiences and study suggest that editorial discretion is often exercised in the name of state imperatives, economic calculations or dependence on international wire services.[571] Such practices create a two-level system of communication: one that, at a surface level, manages to satisfy public demands, but in a subtle manner, promotes different political–economic agendas. This duality is indicative of a wider trend whereby "strategic ambiguity" is deployed to wink at multiple diplomatic positions at the same time.[572] A part of strategic communication also involves the subtle manipulation of biases in the intended audiences.[573] Media narratives capture the implicit predispositions and anxieties of diverse audiences by framing media text in a strategic manner. This differential focus not just reconfirms the original depiction of sentiment but also reduces the potential for nuanced understanding and fair reportage. As a result, readers get a form of informational anchoring that is unbalanced, where the essence of a multifaceted India gets reduced to a limited number of preformed images and associations.[574] This dynamic produces a reinforcing cycle. The structural reality in the media (ownership, economic compulsion, wire dependence) inclines it to adopt certain framings.[575] These, in turn, get amplified by editorial practices that take advantage of biases in the audience and sensationalised headlines, leading to "informational anchoring" in a reduced-proportioned image.[576] This, in itself, works inverse to the public's capacity for making a well informed judgment, and can lead to cognitive dissonance that may fray public trust in media institutions. For India, this translates into not just counter propagating against negative narratives but breaking this cycle of unbalanced perception. The solution lies in strategies that counteract informational anchoring directly, promote critical media literacy in audiences and offer different, trustworthy, nuanced versions of information that can cut through the "strategic ambiguity" and fractured ness.[577]

A Dichotomy of Perception

Empirical evidence from this research points towards a stark divergence from India's formal acknowledgment as a strategic actor, economic partner and geopolitical counterbalance factor and its relatively subdued cultural and civic presence in ASEAN media. High-level strategic engagements like bilateral political exchanges, people-to-people contact, negotiations over shared strategic interests, economic cooperation and bilateral relations enter the public realm wherever they occur, but the wider story falls short in reflecting the nuanced multiplicity of India's sociocultural self. This division gives rise to what may be termed as a 'surface-level scrutiny' whereby India is noticed but not represented inclusively. This is also described as a 'recognition without depth'.[578] The differential presence of India in ASEAN media is not just a happenstance journalistic failure but a deliberate narrative strategy aiming at ambiguity. Fragmentation occurs as one-time, usually sensationalised headlines leave a particular emotion that is tangibly assuaged by subsequent content. Since a large number of media consumers read content for minutes at a time, often taking in just the headline, the adverse or oversimplification narrative is one that endures, with long-term fallouts for India's soft power. This is a serious strategic casualty for India, as soft power, dependent on attraction and cultural resonance, is created through depth of understanding and emotional connection. If recognition is 'divorced from deep cultural engagement', India's potential to create profound, long-lasting connections with the wider public is curtailed. Its power is reduced to "elite, transactional relations".[579] This denies India a broad reservoir of popular support and goodwill in the neighbourhood, essential for long-haul leverage and resilience in the face of geopolitical changes. India must make a deliberate attempt at closing this gap between its hard power acknowledgment and strategic narrative deficit, going beyond merely highlighting high-level engagements and consciously advancing its cultural, civilisational and grass-roots narratives as a vital part of its strategic narrative.[580]

ASEAN media does not merely report India; it actively constructs its image in ways that serve specific media ecosystems. India is framed for the most part for its 'instrumental value'.[581] This selective modelling, known as "triadic framing"[582] (one of the geopolitical actors, emerging economic power, rhetorical narrative on bilateral cooperation), prioritises those attributes in India that benefit the strategic calculus of the host ASEAN country. Singapore media, for example, emphasises India's macroeconomic statistics and regulatory rule-building to gauge its utility in managing risk in the region, and Malaysian media emphasises India's economic path to place Malaysia in the circuits of global commerce. This thus illustrates how policy abstraction is rendered meaningful in relatable narratives that, in the eyes of ASEAN citizens, produce a specific perception of the utility and relevance of India. This 'utilitarian reading' reduces India's multiple facets to a list of functional characteristics. It is not a matter of what India is as a society or a civilization, but what India can be for ASEAN in the ways of security, economic progress or models for governance. This framing, even as a gesture toward India's significance, inadvertently constrains the space for a more profound, finer understanding of its cultural, social and civilisational value. India's strategic communications need to make a deliberate effort to overcome this utilitarian framing by proactively introducing narratives that feature its cultural richness, social variety and contributions as a civilisation, illustrating that the value that India represents goes beyond mere utilitarian utility.[583]

This framing has significant implications for India's soft power and influence management, highlighting a "deficit in India's soft power"[584] within the region. Despite India's recognition as a strategic and economic player, the marginalisation of its cultural innovations, grassroots initiatives and broader societal transformations leads to 'recognition without depth'. Soft power, which thrives on attraction and cultural resonance, is built through deeper understanding and emotional engagement. By consistently sidelining these narratives, ASEAN media, driven by its own national strategic interests, inadvertently limits India's capacity to forge profound, enduring connections with the broader public. This suggests that India's influence might largely remain confined to elite, transactional relationships, rather than being deeply embedded in the collective public consciousness of Southeast Asia, thus risking reducing India to a temporary, transactional partner. This perception overshadows India's long-term potential as a comprehensive partner built on shared values, cultural affinity and civilisational ties.[585] If India's appeal is primarily functional, its influence could wane if geopolitical dynamics shift or if another actor offers a more compelling functional alternative.

Table 70: Key Themes in India's ASEAN Media Portrayal

Category	*Theme*	*Description*
Dominant framing (visibility without intimacy)	Security/Geopolitical Counterweight	Portrayed primarily as a strategic partner, particularly against China.
	Economic partner	Highlighted for macroeconomic indicators, trade potential and role in regional risk management.
	Governance model	Viewed for regulatory governance and democratic counterbalance.
Muted/marginalised Presence ('recognition without depth)	Cultural innovations/ Sociocultural identity	Limited coverage of India's rich cultural heritage, arts, traditions and societal transformations.
	Grassroots initiatives/ People-to-people contact	Insufficient attention to India's civil society efforts, local developments and broader human connections.

India's Media Ecosystem and Institutional Limits

The Indian wire agency ecosystem is a multifaceted and critical environment, with the focus being on basic wire services such as the Press Trust of India (PTI) and United News of India (UNI), which provide the necessary news coverage, such as text, photographs and video, to media organisations in the entire nation, thereby shaping the basic narrative.[586]/ PTI is a non-profit cooperative owned by more than 450 Indian newspapers, as compared to UNI, which is a public limited company; both serve mostly in Indian affairs for domestic subscribers.[587]/ They are supplemented by powerful actors such as Asian News International (ANI), a large commercial video news agency with widespread reach, often seen as promoting the views of the government,[588] and public broadcasters Doordarshan News (DD News) and All India Radio News (AIR News), the broadcast arms of Prasar Bharati.[589,590] These organisations, especially ANI, collect foreign information and cooperate internationally (e.g., with Reuters), but with a basic mandate focussed on Indian affairs for domestic consumption. DD News and AIR News, in contrast, directly address vast audiences through television and radio with a focus on direct public relations over providing material to be syndicated by other wires. These strategic functions are multifaceted: agenda setting, determining coverage and its prominence; framing, shaping presentation, often with a focus on development, national security, and cultural heritage; and rapid response, circulating official viewpoints swiftly in times of crisis. They have been disseminating India's perspective in the international sphere through institutions such as ANI and DD India (the international TV news channel of Prasar Bharati),[591] and fostering unity by highlighting the nation's achievements and strengthening a sense of common citizenship.

ANI has established notable media penetration across Southeast Asia primarily through syndication partnerships and digital distribution channels, though exact subscription figures remain undisclosed. As one of India's largest video news agencies, ANI supplies content to international news agencies like Reuters.[592] That said, ANI faces stiff competition from global wire services like Reuters and AFP that have deeper penetration, as well as from dominant local agencies such as Vietnam News Agency (VNA),/ / which operates more than 30 foreign bureaus and 63 domestic bureaus, and Indonesia's Antara/ —/ the state authorised national news agency founded in 1937. While ANI may not match the subscription volumes of these established players, its niche focus on South Asian affairs and digital redistribution strategy enables it to reach millions of viewers and readers indirectly through republication by partner outlets.

Prasar/ Bharati's recent foray into digital media further continually endows it with power, particularly for domestic consumption.[593] Launched in 2019, the Prasar/ Bharati News Service (PBNS) is a digital video news wire that provides ready-cut video packages to TV channels, digital media.[594] PBNS relays content from DD/ News and AIR/ News, ensuring that Prasar Bharati's and often the government's narrative reaches scores of newsrooms directly. It also presents a low-cost option for smaller media organisations, allowing for rapid visual transmission of India's story.[595] This is backed by PBshabd, launched in 2024, which is Prasar Bharati's multilingual digital news aggregator (website and application).[596] PBshabd directly engages with citizens, cutting through traditional media to transmit news, features and analysis in several Indian languages. Although primarily aimed at domestic audiences and Indian media subscribers, Prasar Bharati also engages in international content exchange through Asiavision (AVN), a non profit video news exchange by the Asia Pacific Broadcasting Union (ABU).[597] AVN shares over 13,000 developmental news stories every year, mostly by way of official/public broadcasters, although it has negligible effect on popular media agendas.[598] Indo Asian News Service (IANS) and Hindustan Samachar are the other news agencies from India,[599] but they have an even more limited and less influential reach than PTI and UNI.

The above data and analysis regarding the reach of India's disseminators or distributors of information has a limited role to play in Southeast Asia's ecosystem. This points to a paradox: India has a strong internal communication setup, but this strength does not automatically translate into global reach. The focus on 'internal communicative cohesion' and doing business with domestic stakeholders indicates that international dissemination is typically an extension of domestic imperatives rather than as a central strategic goal.[600]

This positions India in a space where it has a strong domestic foundation but limited capability to purposively shape international narratives, particularly in a competitive space with international players with a core mission to disseminate international news. For a successful projection of self in ASEAN, India's news agencies need a fundamental strategic tilt in approach, from a largely domestic with limited international outreach to a deliberate and funded international public diplomacy mandate. Despite this outreach, international reach for the news agencies from India is curtailed by a variety of structural constraints. Key among them is the uneven power and reach advantage enjoyed by established Western news agencies like Reuters and AFP, whose greater resources and well-entrenched worldwide infrastructures give them a structural advantage. It is important to highlight that, in seeming appearance notwithstanding, Indian news agencies essentially operate in a nationally based media economy. Their operations depend mostly on the subscriptions, catering to domestic stakeholders like newspapers, television channels, ministries and localised media channels. Therefore, the organisational goals and editorial priorities remain inward-looking communicative demands. This lack of competitiveness with the bigger players, and unavailability in media space in ASEAN, again supports the media in ASEAN in continuing to be dependent on Western wires, and so sustains the information asymmetry, curbing India's capacity to present itself. To break through this, one does not need just marginal improvements, but perhaps decisive investment and a rethink of the business model for disseminating international news by Indian agencies. It could be in the form of government intervention, public–private partnerships or even novel funding models to create a competitive international footprint.

This current study offers limited explicit discussion regarding India's integrated multi-level coordination of its communication efforts. While high-level bilateral engagements are noted, the text does not detail how India synchronises its diplomatic messaging across various communication platforms, from traditional channels to social media, or how it leverages interdisciplinary insights in its own public diplomacy. If there is a lack of integrated multi-level coordination, it implies that India's various diplomatic, cultural and economic agencies might be operating in silos, potentially sending fragmented or even contradictory messages.[601] This internal fragmentation then exacerbates the external fragmentation observed in ASEAN media, making it harder for a coherent and consistent narrative about India to emerge. It also suggests a missed opportunity to leverage the full spectrum of communication tools and interdisciplinary expertise. Effective strategic communication requires a 'whole-of-government' approach,[602] where messaging is harmonised across all relevant ministries, departments and public/private entities involved in India's international engagement. This is a foundational requirement for overcoming external narrative challenges.

Chapter Ten

Conclusion and Recommendations

The intricate landscape of international relations is increasingly being shaped by the narratives that define nations on the global stage. Depiction of India in Southeast Asian media, whilst formally a strategic and economic partner and democratic counterbalance, languishes from an absence of cultural and civic nuance. This constrained representation, coined as 'visibility without intimacy' or 'recognition without depth', diminishes India's soft power and renders it incapable of fostering deep influence in Southeast Asia. The argument made in this study highlights the ways in which structural and editorial considerations within ASEAN media organisations, including the disparate nature of the political environment, centralised media ownership, economic constraints and dependency on Western wire agencies complicate this imbalance. Furthermore, India's foreign policy strategy itself, its Act East drive being a prime example, albeit of crucial importance for strategic coordination, inadvertently institutionalises a reductionist 'triadic framing' that focusses on security, economy and governance in regional media reporting.

The media lens of top ASEAN countries primarily focusses on India's 'utility' in the realms of geopolitics, economics and governance, often to the exclusion of its larger sociocultural, civilisational or grass-root dimensions. This selective framing may call the 'priorities framing' (security, economy and governance) is the conceptual grounding of the representation of India in the ASEAN media. This reflects less of an impartial media text exploration of the many-slanted account of India and rather more of a calculus of the host nations' interests and the power architecture in the regions. This repetitive focus also implies that the media representation of India is naturally determined by a 'hierarchy of strategic importance', such that selective reporting reflects the national foreign policy agenda and regional power structure of the given ASEAN states. This indicates that the selective reporting of the larger identity of India is not an incidental neglect but an intentional strategic move on the part of ASEAN media. Editorial filtering on their part selects the value of India on the basis of its functionality for the host country agenda and thereby instrumentalises the image of India.

Another crucial aspect of this instrumental framing is the broad under-coverage or exclusion of the soft-power innovations, grass-roots experiments or larger-scale social shifts of India. This narrow framing actively contributes to a significant imbalance of India's regional soft power. Soft power, based on attraction and cultural affinities, is built on greater appreciation and emotional bonding with the people, values and social progress of a nation.

Editorial Logics and Foreign Policy Alignment

This study shows that media in every ASEAN nation has individualised editorial discourses that conform to the nation's foreign policy priorities, producing a discursive geography of partnership, influence and alignment. Indonesian media presents bilateral relations and the economic course of India as privileged themes, positioning India as an ASEAN multilateral and Indo–Pacific security partner of strategic importance. This representation functions as an extension of the grammar of Indonesia's foreign policy, an expression of its own regional anxieties and diplomatic ambitions. The Malaysian media reflects an intense editorial concern with India's economic course and integration into the world economy. This may be seen as a part of an effort to locate the position of Malaysia in broader circuits of regional economic and financial ties. Here, media reporting fulfils a twin purpose: informing publics and legitimising policy alignment, thus performing the task of being a soft tool of statecraft.

Thai media, albeit less explicitly political in its inclinations, does share the practical reasoning of editorials. This locates India in discursive imaginaries of bilateral trade, regional peace and democratic stability. Official state visits, strategic debates and economic engagement revolve on the media's construction of symbolic overlap between domestic interest and the perceived 'utility' of India for Southeast Asian geopolitics. The media ecology of Singapore, a product of its hyper-rationalised and technocratic regime, presents a compelling example of the ways that elite strategic thought maps on to editorial priority. The disproportionate focus on the macroeconomic metrics of India, regulatory statecraft and behaviour in the realm of foreign affairs indicates an institutionalised desire to gauge and project India's positioning as an actor in regional risk management, finance governance and innovation networks. The Philippine media, although less centralised in form and varied in tone, meets this larger regional trend by focussing on the geopolitics of India's alliances, disaster management strategies and bilateral ties. What is most striking about the Philippine experience, however, is the integration of climate and ecological crises into the order of priority of stories about India, a theme that links strategic engagement with managing existential threats.

The extensive country-specific analysis emphasises that the representation of India falls short of being an expression of India's essential identity or behaviour and that it is actually a strategically created representation on the basis of the perceived utility of India in each country's unique geopolitics and economic agenda. This variety of national framings necessitates that the public diplomacy of India will have to be extremely customised and subtle.

Structural Determinants of Media Representation

Beyond country-specific editorial choices, broader structural factors profoundly shape India's media portrayal in ASEAN, influencing the very informational terrain upon which strategic communication operates.

The major influence here is the 'structural dependency' of ASEAN media on global wire networks and traditional media constructs as the main determiners of the image of India. This dependency has a far-reaching impact: ground reporting from India becomes marginalised, with the resultant mediated image being highly externally sourced and superficial. This process can be described as one of 'asymmetric epistemic visibility', in which the media systems mainly reproduce the agendas of the highest-ranking economic and political stakeholders. This structure of dependency creates a strong self-reifying cycle. Global media bias establishes the initial template for one-sided representations, which national strategic imperatives process and sharpen to meet national agendas. This forms an auto-reifying cycle that actively restricts a comprehensive and detailed representation of India.

In addition, the media's political economy is not a passive context but an active driver of the effectiveness of strategic communication. The pressure of the profit motive and advertising reliance directly compromises the editorial autonomy, with the media environment tending to be sensationalist and restricted in leaning. This weakens the common epistemic foundation important for the effectiveness of strategic communication. The intrinsic tension between media being a public good and media being a business makes it an ongoing predicament for strategic communication that seeks to serve public or national interests.

This situation introduces extra layers of complexity when analysing the epistemological basis of the information available. The interrelation of news content and its source of origin is undoubtedly vital in the construction of news stories from available information. News isn't a reflection of reality but a symbolic world, an ordered narrative with specific messages and themes embedded within. Translating the raw data into significant information and subsequently into an engaging narrative requires an active process, one that will always be influenced by the sources of the raw materials and the making of media text process that interprets them. The self-imposed interdependence of media on sources, together with an underlying struggle for control over the presentation of the information, makes that news narrative frequently the negotiated compromise of competing interests.

Sentiment, Misalignment and Discursive Fragmentation

The general sentiment analysis of the news depiction of India across ASEAN media indicates a 'dual narrative', with a complex interplay of celebration and critique. Although an evident dominancy of positively phrased articles infers that India is generally seen as an energetic and proactive regional stakeholder, a significant amount of negatively worded articles adds a counterpoint of wariness and underlying critique. This creates an overall sentiment that's mixed and ambivalent, swinging between cautious admiration and sceptical distance, capturing a 'risk-reward' understanding of India. Critically, a binary positive/negative framing of the news discursive structure fails to comprehend the representation of India. The analysis requires the extension of the frame to encompass 'apprehensive' and 'neutral' headlines for a richer understanding.

The meticulous categorisation of sentiment beyond the simple positive or negative polarity discloses a more subtle and complex kind of narrative dilution than explicit, straightforward negative reporting. Pure negativity is clearly recognisable and can be counteracted directly through strategic communication. Yet the ubiquitous existence of fear and neutrality, being less assertive and subtle, can undermine trust, develop scepticism or forestall the establishment of very strong, positive public attitudes without inducing instant alarm or necessitating a direct response. This underscores the deep complexity of 'narrative stewardship' in an atomised and intricate media environment.

The critical observation here is the spread of sentiment misalignment between introductory paragraphs and the headlines of news stories. Such mismatches are problematic because they interfere with framing: an attention-grabbing negative or sensationalist headline primes the reader to interpret an issue in a specific manner, even when the article's content delivers a more subtle or contrary tone. Essentially, the headline establishes one interpretive frame, and the introduction presents the reader with an alternative, thus compromising narrative coherence. This process typically draws on a given media system's manoeuvring with the pressures of the political–economic logic to heighten the emphasis on emotion. A sensational headline provokes attention, but the subsequent text delivers the more balanced reportage, reconciling the economic pressure to capture instant interest with the journalistic mandate of presenting measured and accurate information. This use of the 'anxiety hook' or 'bait-and-alarm' strategy plays on the primal human threat detection processes to increase engagement, attracting readers with sensationalist copy but keeping the lid on with plausible deniability coded in the headline's objectivity. When coupled with anxious introductions accompanying neutral headlines, this heightens anxiety through the operation of 'uncertainty bias', priming the reader to exaggerate threats despite the countervailing framing. This incompatibility may provoke dissonance, as the reader must come to grips with an expectation followed by contrary information, with a resultant likelihood of misreading, misunderstanding or even opinionated appraisal. 'Negativity bias' tends to prevail, dominating even-handed analysis and fuelling suspicion, thus undermining media credibility. The 'bait-and-alarm' model, with its displeasing sentiment misalignment, exemplifies the underlying tension between media's democratic mission and commodification within the attention economy. This is not an isolated technical defect but an exemplar of a systemic pathology where commercial imperatives take precedence over informational integrity, giving rise to the 're-feudalization of public space'. This qualitatively suggests a decline in the public's standards of debate where sensationalism prevails over hard facts, collapsing the very basis of informed citizenship.

Towards a More Nuanced and Reciprocal Engagement

This empirical study illuminates the fundamental paradox of India's visibility in ASEAN media: strategically recognised yet culturally excluded, increasingly prominent yet frequently subjected to structural neglect. The evidence implies that without the critical restructuring of information streams and representation practices, the region faces the danger of embedding a kind of 'discursive neo-colonialism', with Southern voices always mediated through Northern lenses, and with partnership potential always contained by narrative asymmetries of the past. As the India–ASEAN relationship evolves from transactional mutual support to the development of an authentic civilisational exchange on the basis of respect and shared values, the future holds the answer to the creation of an enriched and sustainable alliance. This change from strategic coordination to civilisational and cultural understanding reflects the importance of addressing issues of representation imbalances for achieving sustainable mutual growth.

India's Strategic Communication in ASEAN: Opportunities and Strategic Recommendations

India's strategic communication within the ASEAN domain plays out in a highly asymmetrical global media space, where deeply rooted structural imbalances continue to restrict non-Western voices from visibility and agency. In spite of the widespread articulation of initiatives such as digital diplomacy, cultural engagement and direct media outreach, India's communicative reach still suffers from a deficiency of global media infrastructure. These deficiencies are acutely felt in Southeast Asia, a key region for Indian strategic, economic and civilisational interests at a time when rapidly changing global geopolitics dominate. Current efforts, although valuable, function within a general narrative architecture dominated by Western and state-backed media outlets and actors who increasingly define and set agendas for India's image. Therefore, India's potential to present its own narrative, counter misinformation and promote its normative agenda continues to remain severely handicapped.

In order to surmount these difficulties, India needs to go beyond fragmented or ad hoc public diplomacy instruments towards achieving a sustained and coherent media presence. An internationally accepted, autonomous Indian news agency can act as a powerful instrument for projecting India's democratic values, developmental successes and multicultural diversity. It would improve India's credibility and make it possible for more balanced and multi-polar global flows of news. It would make it possible for greater engagement with ASEAN media environments while strengthening India's voice within multilateral and regional fora. In this regard, a planned institution of India's global media voice in a multipolar information order towards an independent Indian news agency for global impact would be a timely and urgent step towards consolidating India's soft power and securing enhanced narrative sovereignty at international levels.

Direct Media Engagement

India has a significant opportunity to bypass traditional gatekeepers by directly engaging with a broader spectrum of ASEAN media outlets, including independent and digital-native platforms. This approach can facilitate the co-creation of narratives that are more authentic and less susceptible to external biases. Building relationships with diverse media ecosystem requires a proactive public diplomacy campaign.

Proactive Digital Diplomacy

The rise of digital platforms offers India a chance to enhance its strategic communication through proactive digital diplomacy. By leveraging social media for rapid responses to disinformation and for fostering genuine online communities, India can amplify its voice and engage directly with ASEAN audiences. This requires a deep understanding of local digital cultures, preferred platforms and the nuances of online discourse in each ASEAN country.

Adopting International Best Practices

Learning from successful models like the US Department of State's Asia Pacific Media Hub can provide India with a framework for institutionalising effective media engagement. Establishing a dedicated media hub to connect Indian policymakers and experts with ASEAN journalists can streamline access to authoritative information, ensure consistency in messaging and build trust over time.

Advocacy for Balanced News Flow: Support initiatives for direct news exchange between Indian and ASEAN media to reduce reliance on external gatekeepers, fostering regionally centric narratives and mutual understanding.

Diversify Information Channels: Move beyond state-to-state communication to engage with a wide range of ASEAN media, including independent outlets and digital platforms. This involves proactive outreach and relationship building with journalistic communities.

Promote Cultural Narratives: Invest in cultural exchange programmes, digital content and people-to-people initiatives to highlight India's sociocultural identity and build emotional connections.

Establishing India's Global Media Voice in a Multipolar Information Order

India's burgeoning global stature, marked by its robust economic growth and increasing diplomatic engagement, necessitates a sophisticated and effective strategic communication architecture. The current landscape, however, reveals a significant gap in India's international media representation, particularly within the ASEAN media ecosystem. Existing Indian efforts by public organisations, such as Prasar/ Bharati News Service (PBNS) and PBshabd, are primarily focussed on domestic consumption, leaving India's narrative underrepresented and vulnerable to external framing. This contrasts sharply with the pervasive global reach and influence of established Western news agencies like Associated Press (AP), Agence France-Presse (AFP) and Reuters, and the rapidly expanding "go global"[603] strategy of China's state-backed Xinhua News Agency.[604]

Global news wires like AP, AFP and Reuters go beyond their historical function of being mere conduits of unprocessed facts. This can result in the oversimplification of intricate international developments or the swift dissemination of specific narratives, which may either disregard India's multifaceted interests and strategic goals or deal them potentially debilitating blows. For example, China's Xinhua News Agency is already actively pursuing its "go global" strategy with a view to "increasing China's global influence" and offering an "alternative to the hegemonic Western voice",[605] potentially picking up considerable ground in areas of Indian interest too.

This reliance on global news wires can seriously impact India's soft power projection, stifle its diplomacy and expose it to misrepresentation. The far-reaching implication is that India's strategic communication gap today is no longer an issue of lack of presence, but a seminal lack of control on its own narrative within the powerful global information discourse. This reliance can seriously impact its soft power projection, stifle its diplomacy and expose it to misrepresentation, particularly within strategically crucial groups like ASEAN where competing narratives, such as Xinhua's, are actively taking hold.

Key Learnings from Global Players

The analysis of leading global news agencies reveals several critical lessons for India's strategic communication ambitions:

Different Funding Structures: The study identifies a range of funding systems, from mainly commercial (Reuters) to hybrid public-private (AFP, AP's system) and fully state-sponsored (Xinhua) systems. Each type of structure offers a distinct set of trade-offs regarding financial sustainability, operational scope, editorial autonomy and perceived reputation.[606]

Global Reach and Local Depth: For genuine global impact, however, it is not enough to have a broad presence, it needs deep local immersion. This means large networks of correspondents, carefully situated bureau offices and a localised understanding of settings to guarantee wide and culturally relevant reporting.[607]

Credibility as Paramount: In all these models, trust, precision, impartiality and perceived independence stand out as most valued and irreplaceable assets for any international news agency. These are essential for securing and maintaining audiences' trust and influence.[608]

Strategic Use of Technology: Sustained and significant investment in leading technology, such as Artificial Intelligence (AI), advanced multi-platform distribution systems and contemporary content management systems, is imperative to remain competitive, maximise reach and amplify influence within the digital world.[609]

The Importance of Global Bureau Presence and Local Contextualisation

Successful international reporting demands not only large networks of stringers and correspondents located in various countries, but also a fine-grained equation of journalistic objectivity and sensitivity to local context, coupled with an understanding of possible diplomatic fallout. Reporters covering conflict zones and places with restricted press freedoms must resort to creative means, like reporting undercover and drawing on anonymous sources, backed by strict training and tight security. In these fast changing times, user-generated content and citizen journalism have become essential sources of instantaneous, on-the-ground views supplement and challenge orthodox reporting, particularly from places unapproachable for traditional reporters. Though quantitative reach is gauged by how many foreign bureaus, like the presence of AFP's bureau in 260 cities within 150 countries, an agency has, it becomes a reflection of media influence only when it is matched with qualitative engagement and penetration. For India, to intensify international media reach and presence, it (media text/information) needs to be coupled with culturally textured reporting, trust building among local populations and growing the capacity to engage various local publics. This calls for investment in highly trained, culturally attuned journalists and partnering with local media actors and citizen reporters in order to wean away from a state-centric, top-down model of reporting.

India's Current Strategic Communication Footprint

India has a rich domestic media scene comprised of various national press agencies like Asian News International (ANI), Hindusthan Samachar, Indo-Asian News Service (IANS), Press Trust of India (PTI) and United News of India (UNI).[610] Yet, when it comes to the user's question, it specifically points to some of India's current strategic communication efforts, such as PBNS and PB Shabd, and describes them as "concentrating basically on domestic consumption."[611] This suggests a basic restriction on their design and scope of operation, serving mostly internal information needs and less international projection. Although these agencies function importantly within India, their global reach is restricted or minimal when contrasted with the large international operations of others like AP, AFP, Reuters and Xinhua.[612]

Notes

1 Joan Pedro-Carañana, Rodrigo Gómez, Thomas F. Corrigan and Francisco Sierra Caballero, *Political Economy of Media and Communication: Methodological Approaches*, 1st ed., Taylor & Francis, Oxfordshire, 2024.

2 Janet Wasko and Eileen R. Meehan, 'Critical Crossroads or Parallel Routes? Political Economy and New Approaches to Studying Media Industries and Cultural Products,' *Cinema Journal*, 52 (3), 2013, pp. 150–57.

3 Vincent Mosco, *The Political Economy of Communication*, 2nd ed., SAGE, Thousand Oaks, 2009, p. 27.

4 Janet Wasko and Eileen R. Meehan, no. 2.

5 "ASEAN Countries GDP 2027" at https://www.statista.com/statistics/796245/gdp-of-the-asean-countries/imf (Accessed April 19, 2022).

6 Indonesia (1,289 Billion US Dollars), Thailand (522 Billion US Dollars), Malaysia (439 Billion US Dollars), Singapore (424 Billion US Dollars) and the Philippines (412 Billion US Dollars) in 2022. (According to an International Monetary Fund study at https://www.statista.com/statistics/796245/gdp-of-the-asean-countries/imf. (Accessed April 19, 2022).

7 Soonh Taj, Baby Bakhtawer Shaikh and Areej Fatemah Meghji, "Sentiment Analysis of News Articles: A Lexicon Based Approach", Paper presented at the 2nd International Conference on Computing, Mathematics and Engineering Technologies (iCoMET), IEEE, 2019, pp. 1–5.

8 Lei Zhang and Bing Liu, "Sentiment Analysis and Opinion Mining", in *Encyclopedia of Machine Learning And Data Mining*, Springer, Boston, MA, 2017, pp. 1152–1161.

9 Tin Cheuk Leung and Koleman S. Strumpf, "All the Headlines that Are Fit to Change" at *https://papers.ssrn.com/sol3/papers.cfm?abstract_id=4075398*.

10 John Seely, *Oxford Guide to Effective Writing and Speaking: How to Communicate Clearly*, OUP Oxford, UK, 2013.

11 Nathaniel Wang, 'Exploring Headlines Using Sentiment Analysis and Word Embedding,' Directed Research Report – Fall 2022, Department of Computer Science, Columbia University, 2023.

12 Ali Yadollahi, Ameneh Gholipour Shahraki and Osmar R. Zaiane, 'Current State of Text Sentiment Analysis from Opinion to Emotion Mining,' *ACM Computing Surveys (CSUR)*, 50 (2), 2017, pp. 1–33.

13 Lei Zhang and Bing Liu, no. 8.

14 Ali Yadollahi, Ameneh Gholipour Shahraki and Osmar R. Zaiane, no. 12.

15 Bei Zhang, "Asian Images in Advertising and the Crisis of Asian American Identities", in *NAAAS Conference Proceedings*, National Association of African American Studies, 2009, p. 1355.

16 Ali Yadollahi, Ameneh Gholipour Shahraki and Osmar R. Zaiane, no. 12.

17 *Ibid.*

18 Nicolas Blarel, 'India: The Next Superpower?: India's Soft Power: From Potential to Reality?,' London School of Economics and Political Science IDEAS Reports - Special Reports, SR010, 2012.

19 Kirk Hallahan, Derina Holtzhausen, Betteke van Ruler,Dejan Verèiè and Krishnamurthy Sriramesh, 'Defining Strategic Communication,' *International Journal of Strategic Communication,* 1 (1), 2007, pp. 3–35. doi:10.1080/15531180701285244.

20 *Ibid.*

21 Joseph S. Nye, Jr., 'Public Diplomacy and Soft Power,' *The Annals of the American Academy of Political and Social Science,* 616, March 2008, pp. 94–109.

22 Kamal Sheel, 'Hu Shih and 'The Indianisation of China': Some Comments on Modern Chinese Discourses on India,' *China Report,* 50 (3), pp. 177–188.

23 Joseph Nye, 'Soft Power: The Origins and Political Progress of a Concept,' *Nature,* February 21, 2017, at https://www.nature.com/articles/palcomms20178 (Accessed May 28, 2025).

24 Alexander Stafford, 'The Role of the Media During the Cold War,' E-International Relations, March 29, 2021, at https://www.e-ir.info/2013/10/26/the-role-of-the-media-during-the-cold-war/ (Accessed May 28, 2025).

25 Alex Inkeles, 'The Soviet Characterization of the Voice of America,' *Columbia Journal of International Affairs,* 1951, pp. 44–55.

26 Mina Mudric, 'Soft Power Diplomacy,' Diplo, at https://www.diplomacy.edu/topics/soft-power-diplomacy/#:~:text=What%20is%20soft%20power?,its%20interests%20and%20values%20globally (Accessed May 28, 2025).

27 Jan Melissen, "The New Public Diplomacy: Between Theory and Practice", in *The New Public Diplomacy: Soft Power in International Relations,* Palgrave Macmillan, London, 2005, pp. 3–27.

28 Tommy Kimani, 'The Impact of Cultural Diplomacy on Perceptions of Foreign Policy,' *Global Journal of International Relations,* 1 (1), 2023, pp. 1–12.

29 'What is PD?,' USC Center on Public Diplomacy, October 23, 2023 at https://uscpublicdiplomacy.org/page/what-is-pd (Accessed May 28, 2025).

30 Simon Anholt, "Nation-Brands and the Value of Provenance", in *Destination Branding,* Routledge, 2007, p. 15.

31 Simon Anholt, 'Beyond the Nation Brand: The Role of Image and Identity in International Relations,' *Exchange: The Journal of Public Diplomacy,* 2 (1), 2013 at https://surface.syr.edu/exchange/vol2/iss1/1/ (Accessed May 29, 2025).

32 Kirk Hallahan & D. Holtzhausen, B. Ruler, D. Verèiè, K. Sriramesh, Defining Strategic Communication. International Journal of Strategic Communication. Vol. 1. 2007, pp. 3-35. 10.1080/15531180701285244.

33 Joseph S. Nye, "Soft Power," Foreign Policy, no. 80, 1990, pp. 153–71. https://doi.org/10.2307/1148580.

34 Q&A With CPD: Joseph S. Nye, Jr., USC Center on Public Diplomacy, 18 April 2017, at https://uscpublicdiplomacy.org/story/qa-cpd-joseph-s-nye-jr (Accessed on 5 November 2025).

35 Preventive Diplomacy, Britannica, at https://www.britannica.com/topic/preventive-diplomacy (Accessed 5 November 2025)

36 Simon Anholt, *Competitive Identity: The New Brand Management for Nations, Cities and Regions,* Palgrave Macmillan, London, 2007, p. 15.

37 Christopher Paul, *Strategic Communication Origins, Concepts, and Current Debates,* Praeger, California, 2011, p. 17 at https://books.google.co.in/books?id=VIxuxcmt5qQC&printsec=frontcover&source=gbs_ge_summary_r&cad=0#v=onepage&q&f=false.

38 *Ibid.*

39 John A. Robinson, 'Communicating Airpower: Strategic Communication and the United States Air Force Since 9/11,' Defense Technical Information Center, 2008 at https://apps.dtic.mil/sti/citations/ADA494748 (Accessed August 1, 2008).

40 Christopher Paul, p. 16, no. 32.

41 Matusitz, J., *Fundamentals of Public Communication Campaigns,* John Wiley & Sons, New Jersey, U.S., 2022, p. 221 at https://www.wiley.com/en-us/Fundamentals+of+Public+Communication+Campaigns-p-9781119878094

42 Nirupama Rao, "The Pursuit of National Goals Needs Strategic Communication, Not Chaos and Noise" *Commentary, The Wire*, October 31, 2016 at https://thewire.in/external-affairs/india-must-consider-strategic-communication-to-achieve-national-goals.

43 Brig. Vivek Lall, SM (Retd), 'Revising India's 'Strategic Communication' Strategy to Deal with China,' Issue Brief, Defence Research and Studies, July 30, 2020 at https://dras.in/revising-indias-strategic-communication-strategy-to-deal-with-china/

44 *Ibid.*

45 Nirupama Rao, no. 37.

46 Yuvraj Mehta, "Policies That Build a Nation: How Can Strategic Communications Establish an Organisation's Equity?" *Report, Financial Express*, June 19, 2021 at https://www.financialexpress.com/brandwagon/writers-alley/policies-that-build-a-nation-how-can-strategic-communications-establish-an-organisations-equity/2274359/.

47 Quoted in Charles S. Gramaglia, "Strategic Communication: Distortion and White Noise" in Joint Information Operations Warfare Command, IOSphere, Winter 2008, p. 10.

48 Barbara Pfetsch, 'Government News Management - Strategic Communication in Comparative Perspective,' EconStor, No. FS III 99-101, 1999, p. 10 at https://www.econstor.eu/bitstream/10419/49821/1/30895761X.pdf,

49 *Ibid.*

50 Selective attention is simply the act of focussing on a particular object for a while, simultaneously ignoring irrelevant information that is also occurring.

51 Selective perception refers to the process by which we select, categorise and analyse stimuli from our environment to create meaningful experiences while blocking out stimuli that contradict our beliefs or expectations.

52 Ansgar Zerfass and Huck Simone, 'Innovation, Communication, and Leadership: New Developments in Strategic Communication,' *International Journal of Strategic Communication*, 1 (2), 2007, p. 107–122.

53 Haseeb Tariq, "Council Post: Five Components of a Successful Strategic Communications Plan" *Forbes*, November 9, 2022 at https://www.forbes.com/sites/forbescommunicationscouncil/2021/06/22/five-components-of-a-successful-strategic-communications-plan/.

54 J. Kurlantzick, "Beijing's Global Media Offensive: China's Uneven Campaign to Influence Asia and the World" *Report, Axios China*, December 13, 2022 at https://www.axios.com/2022/12/13/beijings-media-power-southeast-asia.

55 "Narrative" at https://www.vocabulary.com/dictionary/narrative (Accessed May 31, 2025).

56 "Narrative," in *The Random House Dictionary of the English Language*, Random House, New York, 1979.

57 Steven Livingston and Jack Nassetta, 'Framing and Strategic Narratives: Synthesis and Analytical Framework,' *The SAIS Review of International Affairs,* 38 (2), 2018, pp. 101–110.

58 J.K. Hanska, 'Storytelling or Non-Kinetic Weaponry? Strategic Communication from a Narratological Perspective,' *Journal of Information Warfare*, 14 (1), 2015, pp. 24–38.

59 *Ibid.*

60 Alister Miskimmon, Ben O'Loughlin and Laura Roselle, *Strategic Narratives: Communication Power and the New World Order*, Routledge, New York, 2013, p. 3.

61 *Ibid.*, p. 5.

62 Lucian-Stefan S. Dumitrescu, "The Role of Strategic Narratives in Information Warfare" at

https://www.academia.edu/36221948/THE_ROLE_OF_STRATEGIC_NARRATIVES_IN_INFORMATION_WARFARE (Accessed May 29, 2025).

63 Lawrence Freedman, *The Transformation of Strategic Affairs,* Routledge, London, 2006, p. 22.

64 Joseph Nye, quoted in "30 Best Joseph Nye Quotes With Image" at https://www.bookey.app/quote-author/joseph-nye.(Bookey) (Accessed May 29, 2025).

65 Craig Hayden, 'Logics of Narrative and Networks in US Public Diplomacy: Communication Power and US Strategic Engagement,' *The Journal of International Communication,* 19 (2), 2013, pp. 196–218.

66 *Ibid.*

67 *Ibid.*

68 Dal Yong Jin, 'The Rise of Digital Platforms as a Soft Power Apparatus in the New Korean Wave Era,' *Communication and the Public,* 9 (2), March 2024, pp. 161–177. doi:10.1177/20570473241234204.

69 Füsun Topsümer, Yasemin Durmuº and Ahmet Yýlmaz, *Media and Communication in the Digital Age: Changes and Dynamics,* Ozgur Yayin-Dagitim Co. Ltd. , October 2023 at https://www.researchgate.net/publication/375116310_Media_and_Communication_in_the_Digital_Age_Changes_and_Dynamics/citations.

70 Finn Frandsen and Winni Johansen, "The Role of Communication Executives in Strategy and Strategizing", in Derina Holtzhausen and Ansgar Zerfass (eds.), *The Routledge Handbook of Strategic Communication,* Routledge, New York, 2015, pp. 229–243.

71 *Ibid.*

72 *Ibid.*

73 G. Wolfsfeld, "Promoting Peace through the News Media: Some Initial Lessons from the Peace Process", *The International Journal of Press/Politics,* 2, 52–70, quoted in Marc Jungblut, *Strategic Communication and its Role in Conflict News: A Computational Analysis of the International News Coverage on Four Conflicts,* 1st ed., Springer Nature, Wiesbaden, Germany, 2020, pp. 11–18.

74 *Ibid.*, pp. 11–18.

75 *Ibid.*

76 *Ibid.*

77 Jay G. Blumler, "Core Theories of Political Communication: Foundational and Freshly Minted", *Communication Theory,* 25 (4), October 2015, quoted in Marc Jungblut, *Strategic Communication and its Role in Conflict News: A Computational Analysis of the International News Coverage on Four Conflicts,* 1st ed., Springer Nature, Wiesbaden, Germany, 2020, pp. 54–62.

78 Marc Jungblut, *Strategic Communication and its Role in Conflict News: A Computational Analysis of the International News Coverage on Four Conflicts,* 1st ed., Springer Nature, Wiesbaden, Germany, 2020, pp. 13–19.

79 *Ibid.*

80 *Ibid.*

81 *Ibid.*

82 *News Value and the Strategic Communication Professional – Writing for Strategic Communication Industries,* The Ohio State University, Pressbooks at https://ohiostate.pressbooks.pub/stratcommwriting/chapter/news-value-and-the-strategic-comm/ (Accessed June 1, 2025).

83 *Ibid.*

84 *Ibid.*

85 Ahmad Khan, 'Understanding the Dynamics of International Communication,' *Global Media Journal,* 22 (67), 2024.

86 *Ibid.*

87 Oliver Boyd-Barrett and Tanner Mirrlees (eds.), *Media Imperialism: Continuity and Change*, Rowman & Littlefield, Washington, DC, 2019.

88 S. Zielinski, *Deep Time of the Media: Toward an Archaeology of Hearing and Seeing by Technical Means*, MIT Press, U.S., 2008, p. 102 103.

89 Stephen W. Littlejohn and Karen A. Foss (eds.) *Encyclopaedia of Communication Theory*, 1, Sage, 2009, p. 408.

90 Andrea Prat and David Strömberg, "The Political Economy of Mass Media," CEPR Discussion Paper Series, 2011, p.135 at https://www.semanticscholar.org/paper/The-Political-Economy-of-Mass-Media-Prat-Str%C3%B6mberg/06cdb835cc00408a3b530fb5c224d1ea6cdac571.

91 Fredrik Engelstad, "Strategic Communication and Institutional Change", in Fredrik Engelstad, Håkon Larsen, Jon Rogstad, Kari Steen-Johnsen, Dominika Polkowska, Andrea S. Dauber-Griffin and Adam Leverton, De Gruyter (eds.), *Institutional Change in the Public Sphere: Views on the Nordic Model,* 1st ed., 2017, pp. 139–159 at http://www.jstor.org/stable/j.ctvbkk05k.10.

92 *Ibid.*

93 *Ibid.*

94 *Ibid.*

95 *Ibid.*

96 *Ibid.*

97 Paul Cornish, Julian Lindley-French and Claire Yorke, *Strategic Communications and National Strategy,* A. Chatham House Report, Chatham House, September 2011.

98 *Ibid.*

99 *Ibid.*

100 *Ibid.*

101 *Ibid.*

102 Corneliu Bjola, "Making sense of digital diplomacy", in Corneliu Bjola and Marcus Holmes (eds.), *Digital Diplomacy: Theory and Practice,* 1st ed., 1. Routledge, London, 2015, p.1.

103 *Ibid.*, p. 4.

104 *Ibid.*, p. 3.

105 *Ibid.*, p. 5.

106 *Ibid.*, p. 7.

107 Konrad Szpakowski and Matthew E. Brashears, 'Exposing the Obscured Influence of State-Controlled Media via Causal Inference of Quotation Propagation,' *Scientific Reports*, 15 (1), January 7, 2025, p. 376. https://doi.org/10.1038/s41598-024-51713-2.[](https://www.nature.com/articles/s41598-024-78586-x.

108 Samantha Bradshaw, "Influence Operations and Disinformation on Social Media," Centre for International Governance Innovation, November 23, 2020 at https://www.cigionline.org/articles/influence-operations-and-disinformation-social-media/ (Accessed May 31, 2025).

109 Erika Kinetz, 'How China is Using Social Media to Polish Its Image Globally,' *The Christian Science Monitor,* May 11, 2021 at https://www.csmonitor.com/World/Asia-Pacific/2021/0511/How-China-is-using-social-media-to-polish-its-image-globally (Accessed May 30, 2025).

110 S. Lee and S. Shahin, 'Tweeting Identity: Reciprocal National Identity Construction in Korea–US and Korea–Japan Diplomatic Tweets,' *International Communication Gazette*, 85 (1), 2023, pp. 1–20.

111 P. Surowiec and M. Kania-Lundholm, "Towards Soft Power 3.0: Digitalization and Soft Power", in *Soft Power and Public Diplomacy*, Palgrave Macmillan, 2018, p. 173.

112 David Ronfeldt and John Arquilla, "Whose story wins," RAND Corporation, 2020 at https://www.rand.org/pubs/perspectives/PEA237-1.html (Accessed May 31, 2025).

113 E. Hallams, 'Digital Diplomacy: The Internet, the Battle for Ideas & US Foreign Policy,' *CEU Political Science Journal*, 5 (4), 2010, pp. 538–574.
114 Christopher Paul, C. no. 32.
115 "3 Ways Technology is Improving Strategic Planning in the 2020s" *Commentary, Align*, November 10, 2022 at https://aligntoday.com/blog/3-ways-technology-will-improve-strategic-planning-in-the-2020s/.
116 Prabhjeet Bhatla, "How Social Media Is Changing Technology" *Entrepreneur*, December 17, 2020 at https://www.entrepreneur.com/en-in/technology/how-social-media-is-changing-technology/361871.
117 'Public Diplomacy Through Social Media: The Chinese Way,' China Research Center, August 25, 2024 at https://www.chinacenter.net/2024/china-currents/23-1/public-diplomacy-through-social-media-the-chinese-way/.
118 Alexander Chernev, *Strategic Marketing Management: Theory and Practice*, Cerebellum Press, Chicago, 2019.
119 Kristen Lovejoy and Gregory D. Saxton, 'Information, Community, and Action: How Non-Profit Organizations Use Social Media,' *Journal of Computer-Mediated Communication,* 17 (3), 2012, pp. 337–353.
120 Chahira Ben Abdallah, 'Media and Communication Geopolitics in the Context of International Information Disorder, Research Gate,' April 2025 at https://www.researchgate.net/publication/387857409_Media_and_Communication_Geopolitics_in_the_Context_of_International_Information_Disorder
121 *Ibid.*
122 *Ibid.*
123 'What is Strategic Communications?,' Strategic Communications Education and Research Unit at https://www.pp.u-tokyo.ac.jp/sceru/what-is/ (Accessed June 2, 2025).
124 'Global Strategic Communications, Diplomacy in the Digital Age,' at https://onlinemasters.jou.ufl.edu/global-strategic-communications-role-in-diplomacy/ (Accessed June 2, 2025).
125 Swaran Sandhu, 'Strategic Communication: An Institutional Perspective,' *International Journal of Strategic Communication*, 3 (2), 2009, pp. 72–92.
126 Muninggar Sri Saraswati and Namira Fathya Murti, "The Economy of Public Interest Journalism", Proceedings of the 5th International Conference on Global Innovation and Trends in Economy 2024 (INCOGITE 2024), Advances in Economics, Business and Management Research, 302, 2024. doi.org/10.2991/978-94-6463-585-0_5.
127 *Ibid.*
128 Dallas W. Smythe, "On the Audience Commodity and Its Work", in *Media and Cultural Studies: Keyworks,* John Wiley & Sons, Hoboken, 2009, p. 256.
129 Chahira Ben Abdallah, no.116.
130 *Ibid.*
131 Swaran Sandhu, no. 121.
132 Chahira Ben Abdallah, no. 116.
133 Dallas W. Smythe, no. 124.
134 Angelito Malicse, 'How the Profit Motive Influences Media's Role in Politics and Product Innovation,' PhilArchive, March 23, 2025, at https://philarchive.org/rec/MALHTP-2 (Accessed June 2, 2025).
135 Srinivasan Gopal Chari, 'Power, Pixels, and Politics: The Geopolitics of Emerging Technologies in the Digital Age,' *London Journal of Research In Humanities and Social Sciences*, 25 (2), 2025, pp. 1–99.
136 Dallas W. Smythe, no. 124.

137 Chahira Ben Abdallah, no. 116.
138 *Ibid.*
139 Doug Underwood, "Reporting and the Push For Market-Oriented Journalism: Media Organizations As Businesses", in L. W. L. Bennett and Robert Entman (eds.), *Mediated Politics: Communication in the Future of Democracy*, 1st ed., Cambridge University Press, Cambridge, 2001, pp. 99–116.
140 Swaran Sandhu, no. 121.
141 'What is Strategic Communications?,' no. 119.
142 Elisabeth Noelle-Neumann, 'The Spiral of Silence a Theory of Public Opinion,' *Journal of Communication,* 24 (2), 1974, pp. 43–51.
143 Leandro Pereira, Tomas Durao and José Santos, "Strategic Communication and Barriers to Strategy Implementation," Paper presented at the 2019 IEEE International Conference on Engineering, Technology and Innovation (ICE/ITMC), Valbonne Sophia-Antipolis, France, 2019, pp. 1–5. doi: 10.1109/ICE.2019.8792813.
144 Zoe Oxley, "Framing and Political Decision Making: An Overview", in *Oxford Research Encyclopedia of Politics*, 2020.
145 'Framing Theory,' Mass Communication Theory at https://masscommtheory.com/theory-overviews/framing-theory/ (Accessed June 2, 2025).
146 Zoe Oxley, no. 140.
147 *Ibid.*
148 Fazılat Abdulkhamidova, Agenda Setting Theory, ResearchGate, June 2021, at https://www.researchgate.net/publication/352465425_Agenda_Setting_Theory/citations (Accessed 6 November 2025)
149 Dr. Sarah Zaklama, "Exploring the Foundations of Media Framing Theory," *European Modern Studies Journal*, Vol. 9 (1), 2025. DOI: 10.59573/emsj.9(1).2025.7
150 Christopher Paul, pp. 175–178, no. 32.
151 Brent Kitchens, Steven L. Johnson and Peter Gray, 'Understanding Echo Chambers and Filter Bubbles: The Impact of Social Media on Diversification and Partisan Shifts in News Consumption,' *MIS Quarterly*, 44 (4), 2020.
152 Jane D. Brown, Carl R. Bybee, Stanley T. Wearden and Dulcie M. Straughan, 'Invisible Power: Newspaper News Sources and the Limits of Diversity,' *Journalism Quarterly*, 64 (1), 1987, pp. 45–54. doi:10.1177/107769908706400106.
153 Ziv Avtalion, Itzhak Aviv, Gil Luria and Oshri Bar-Gil, 'Digital Infrastructure as a New Organizational Digital Climate Dimension,' *Applied Sciences,* 14 (19), 2024, p. 8592. https://doi.org/10.3390/app14198592.
154 'Information Infrastructure: Everything You Need to Know When Assessing Information Infrastructure Skills,' Aloobo, at https://www.alooba.com/skills/concepts/data-management/information-infrastructure/ (Accessed June 4, 2025).
155 Srinivasan Gopal Chari, 'Power, Pixels and Politics: The Geopolitics of Emerging Technologies in the Digital Age,' *London Journal of Research in Humanities & Social Science*, Great Britain Journals Press, 25 (2), 2025.
156 Tanin Chakraborty, 'Is Data the New Oil?', Yubi, at https://www.go-yubi.com/blog/data-new-oil/#:~:text=In%20recent%20times%20numerous%20industry,predictive%20analytics%20and%20artificial%20intelligence (Accessed December 21, 2022).
157 Jan Nolin, 'Data As Oil, Infrastructure Or Asset? Three Metaphors of Data As Economic Value,' *Journal of Information, Communication and Ethics in Society*, November 2019. doi: 10.1108/JICES-04-2019-0044.
158 M.M. Kamruzzaman, 'Impact of Social Media on Geopolitics and Economic Growth: Mitigating

the Risks by Developing Artificial Intelligence and Cognitive Computing Tools,' *Computational Intelligence and Neuroscience,* May 11, 2022. doi: 10.1155/2022/7988894.

159 *Ibid.*

160 *Ibid.*

161 Darlington Nyambiya, "The Social Media Revolution and Political Activism. A Case Study of Zimbabwe," PhD dissertation, Bournemouth University, 2025.

162 Seth Flaxman, Sharad Goel and Justin M. Rao, 'Filter Bubbles, Echo Chambers, and Online News Consumption,' *Public Opinion Quarterly*, 80 (6), 2016. doi: 10.1093/poq/nfw006.

163 Sara K. Yeo, Michael A. Cacciatore and Dietram A. Scheufele, 'News Selectivity and Beyond: Motivated Reasoning in a Changing Media Environment,' *Publizistik und gesellschaftliche Verantwortung: Festschrift für Wolfgang Donsbach*, 2015, pp. 83–104.

164 Seth Flaxman, Sharad Goel and Justin M. Rao, no. 156.

165 Anne Damisa, "Fake News: Finding Truth in Strategic Communication," Doctoral Dissertations and Projects, 5201, *Liberty University*, 2024.

166 Andrew Kakabadse, Nada K. Kakabadse and Alexander Kouzmin, 'Reinventing the Democratic Governance Project through Information Technology? A Growing Agenda for Debate,' *Public Administration Review,* 63 (1), 2003, pp. 44–60.

167 Lydia Khalil, 'Digital Authoritarianism, China and C0VID,' Lowy Institute, November 2020.

168 M.M. Kamruzzaman, no. 152.

169 Ivana Z. Zirojević, 'Digital Transformation of Geopolitics: New Tools, Actors, and Power Dynamics,' *Kultura Polisa*, 21 (3), 2024, pp. 77–94.

170 Luyue Ma, 'Rethinking Democratizing Potential of Digital Technology: A Review of Technology and Communication Studies,' *Journal of Information, Communication and Ethics in Society*, 18 (1), 2020, pp. 140–156.

171 Shanta Barman, 'Digital Diplomacy: The Influence of Digital Platforms on Global Diplomacy and Foreign Policy,' *Vidya-A Journal of Gujarat University,* 3 (1), 2024, pp. 61–75.

172 Denton Forner, 'Contested Information Environment Framework for Assessing Networked Authoritarian Regimes,' *Journal of Information Policy,* 14, 2024.

173 Angela Ding, 'To What Extent Should the Government Censor Social Media?,' Adcox World History, January 27, 2025 at https://www.adcoxhistory.com/course-discussion-board/to-what-extent-should-the-government-censor-social-media (Accessed June 4, 2025).

174 Ronald Deibert, John Palfrey, Rafal Rohozinski and Jonathan Zittrain, *Access Denied: The Practice and Policy of Global Internet Filtering*, The MIT Press, 2008, p. 23.

175 Angela Ding, no. 167

176 Hilary Esivue Damissah, Adam Folorunsho Isiaka, Adenike Deborah Adejare and Ibrahim Oladayo Ogunlana, 'Media Independence and Democratic Accountability in Modern Governance Systems and Public Administration Frameworks,' *GSC Advanced Research and Reviews*, 23 (1), 2025, pp. 12–23. doi:10.30574/gscarr.2025.23.1.0102.

177 *Ibid.*

178 *Ibid.*

179 Anlan Zhang, 'MNEs' Media Strategies Under Geopolitical Tensions,' *AIB Insights,* 25 (2), 2025. https://doi.org/10.46697/001c.133574 (Accessed June 4, 2025).

180 *Ibid.*

181 *Ibid.*

182 *Ibid.*

183 *Ibid.*

184 *Ibid.*

185 Peter Lunt and Sonia Livingstone, *Media Regulation: Governance and the Interests of Citizens*

and Consumers, SAGE Publications, London, 2012, pp. 230–232.

186 Anlan Zhang, no. 173.

187 Peter Lunt and Sonia Livingstone, no. 179.

188 *Ibid.*

189 Peter Shields, 'Borders as Information Flows and Transnational Networks,' *Global Media and Communication,* 10 (1), 2014, pp. 3–33.

190 Elizabeth Magill, 'Agency Self-Regulation,' *The George Washington Law Review,* 77 (4), June 2009, p. 859 (Accessed June 5, 2025).

191 Everette E. Dennis, 'Internal Examination: Self-Regulation and the American Media,' *Cardozo Arts & Ent. LJ,* 13, 1994, p. 697.

192 Paul Manning, *News and News Sources: A Critical Introduction,* 1st ed., Sage, London, 2001, pp. 13–16.

193 *Ibid.*

194 *Ibid.*

195 Rasmus Kleis Nielsen and Richard Fletcher, 'Public Perspectives on Trust in News,' Reuters Institute for the Study of Journalism, June 17, 2024 at https://reutersinstitute.politics.ox.ac.uk/digital-news-report/2024/public-perspectives-trust-news (Accessed June 5, 2024).

196 Paul Manning, no. 186.

197 James Curran, and Jean Seaton, *Power Without Responsibility: Press, Broadcasting and the Internet in Britain,* 7th ed. Routledge, London, 2002, pp. 5–8.

198 Kusum Lata, "The Impact of Digital Media on the Decentralization of Power and the Erosion of Traditional Gatekeepers', *International Journal of Trend in Scientific Research and Development,* 8 (1), January–February 2024.

199 Bahiyah Omar, 'Online News Production, Consumption and Immediacy: The Remediation Perspective,' *Jurnal Komunikasi: Malaysian Journal of Communication,* 33 (3), 2017, pp. 250–266.

200 S. Steensen, 'Journalism's Epistemic Crisis and Its Solution: Disinformation, datafication and Source Criticism,' *Journalism,* 20 (1), 2018, pp. 185–189. https://doi.org/10.1177/1464884918809271.

201 *Ibid.*

202 Florian Primig, 'The Influence of Media Trust and Normative Role Expectations on the Credibility of Fact Checkers,' *Journalism Practice,* 18 (5), pp. 1137–1157. doi:10.1080/17512786.2022.2080102.

203 Carolyn M. Byerly, *Intersectionality, Political Economy, and Media*, Taylor & Francis, 2024.

204 Kenzo Tange, Gordon Bell, Hasan Ozbekhan and Daniel E. Noble, 'Movement of Ideas and Information,' *Ekistics,* 33 (197), 1972, pp. 339–345. http://www.jstor.org/stable/43621721.

205 Dilina Nawarathne, "The Mode of Journalistic Truth: An Ethnographic Inquiry into News-Making through Latour's Modes of Existence," PhD dissertation, University of Limerick, 2024.

206 Caroline Fisher, "News Sources and Journalist–Source Interaction", in *Oxford Research Encyclopedia of Communication,* 2018.

207 *Ibid.*

208 Herbert J. Gans, 'Deciding What's News: Story Suitability,' *Society*, 16, 1979, pp. 65–77. https://doi.org/10.1007/BF02701600.

209 Caroline Fisher, no. 200.

210 Herbert J. Gans, no. 202.

211 Stephen J. A. Ward, "Objectivity and Bias in Journalism", in *Oxford Research Encyclopedia of Communication*, March 26, 2019.

212 Stephen D. Reese and Jae Kook Lee, "Understanding the Content of News Media", in *The*

SAGE Handbook of Political Communication, 2012, pp. 253–263. doi:10.4135/9781446201015.n21.

213 'Upholding Journalistic Integrity: The Importance of Source Credibility,' Journalism University, November 9, 2023 at https://journalism.university/reporting-techniques/upholding-journalistic-integrity-source-credibility/ (Accessed June 5, 2025).

214 Caroline Fisher, no. 200.

215 *Ibid.*

216 Eduard-Claudiu Gross, "Pre-publication News Verification in Local Newsrooms: A Theoretical Approach", in Delia Cristina Balaban, Maria Mustatea and Andreea Voina (eds.), *Communication Approaches: Tools and Technologies across the Industry,* Accent, Cluj-Napoca, January 2023, pp. 36–44.

217 Process of News Selection - A Worldwide Based Informative and Educational, July 29, 2023 at https://e-articles.pk/Blog/BlogDetail/96?title=Process-of-News-Selection (Accessed June 5, 2025).

218 Naila Moreira and Benjamin Baumer, 'The Scoop on Data Journalism,' Stattr@k - American Statistical Association at https://stattrak.amstat.org/2024/02/01/the-scoop-on-data-journalism/ (Accessed June 5, 2024).

219 Caroline Fisher, no. 200.

220 *Ibid.*

221 *Ibid.*

222 *Ibid.*

223 *Ibid.*

224 Pamela J. Shoemaker, "Gatekeeping and Journalism", in *Oxford Research Encyclopedia of Communication*, January 30, 2020 at https://oxfordre.com/communication/view/10.1093/acrefore/9780190228613.001.0001/acrefore-9780190228613-e-819 (Accessed June 5, 2025).

225 Chris Peters and Tamara Witschge, 'From Grand Narratives of Democracy to Small Expectations of Participation: Audiences, Citizenship, and Interactive Tools in Digital Journalism,' *Journalism Practice*, 9 (1), 2015, pp. 19–34.

226 Caroline Fisher, no. 200.

227 Md Kutub Uddin, 'The Impact of Citizen Journalism on Campus Reporting,' Research Gate, September 2021 at https://www.researchgate.net/publication/354494532_The_Impact_of_Citizen_Journalism_on_Campus_Reporting.

228 'Upholding Journalistic Integrity: The Importance of Source Credibility,' no. 207.

229 *Ibid.*

230 *Ibid.*

231 'Source Credibility Assessment – Intro to Journalism,' Fiveable, 2024 at https://library.fiveable.me/introduction-journalism/unit-6/source-credibility-assessment/study-guide/6IahNXzPSOhJMw7B (Accessed June 5, 2025).

232 'Upholding Journalistic Integrity: The Importance of Source Credibility,' no. 207.

233 Sarah Lee, 'Transparency in Media Writing,' Number Analytics, May 25, 2025 at https://www.numberanalytics.com/blog/transparency-in-media-writing#google_vignette (Accessed June 5, 2025).

234 Anya Schiffrin, "Credibility and Trust in Journalism", in *Oxford Research Encyclopedia of Communication*, August 28, 2019 at https://oxfordre.com/communication/view/10.1093/acrefore/9780190228613.001.0001/acrefore-9780190228613-e-794 (Accessed June 5, 2025).

235 Jesper Strömbäck, Yariv Tsfati, Hajo Boomgaarden, Alyt Damstra, Elina Lindgren, Rens Vliegenthart and Torun Lindholm, 'News Media Trust and its Impact on Media Use: Toward a Framework for Future Research,' *Annals of the International Communication Association,* 44 (2), June 2020, pp. 139–156. https://doi.org/10.1080/23808985.2020.1755338.

236 'Attribution – Writing for Strategic Communication Industries,' The Ohio State University Pressbooks, Open Course Materials from Ohio State Instructors at https://ohiostate.pressbooks.pub/stratcommwriting/chapter/attribution/ (Accessed June 6, 2025).

237 Anya Schiffrin, no. 228.

238 *Ibid.*

239 Sarah Lee, 'Examining Media Bias: How News Shapes Public Perception Daily,' Number Analytics, March 11, 2025 at https://www.numberanalytics.com/blog/examining-media-bias-public-perception (Accessed June 5, 2025).

240 *Ibid.*

241 *Ibid.*

242 James N. Druckman, Jordan Fein and Thomas J. Leeper, 'A Source of Bias in Public Opinion Stability,' *The American Political Science Review*, 106 (2), 2012, pp. 430–454 at http://www.jstor.org/stable/41495086.

243 'Upholding Journalistic Integrity: The Importance of Source Credibility,' no. 207.

244 Yuni Wen, 'Public Interest vs Special Interest: The Strategic Framing Tactics of Technologies in the Political Arena,' *Research Policy*, 53 (8), 2024. https://doi.org/10.1016/j.respol.2024.105071.

245 'Upholding Journalistic Integrity: The Importance of Source Credibility,' no. 207.

246 James N. Druckman, Jordan Fein and Thomas J. Leeper, no. 236.

247 Joseph Dewey, 'Media Manipulation,' EBSCO Information Services, 2024 at https://www.ebsco.com/research-starters/social-sciences-and-humanities/media-manipulation (Accessed June 5, 2025).

248 'Upholding Journalistic Integrity: The Importance of Source Credibility,' no. 207.

249 Darren Kelsey, "News, Discourse, and Ideology", in Karin Wahl-Jorgensen, Thomas Hanitzsch (eds.), *The Handbook of Journalism Studies,* 2nd ed., Routledge, 2019, pp. 246–260.

250 Andreas Schwarz, 'The Theory of Newsworthiness Applied to Mexico's Press. How the News Factors Influence Foreign News Coverage in a Transitional Country,' *Communications: The European Journal of Communication,* 31 (1), 2006, pp. 45–64.

251 Errol Salamon, "The Political Economy of News Media and Journalism", in *Oxford Research Encyclopedia of Communication,* November 20, 2024.

252 Michael Palmer, *International News Agencies: A History*, 1st ed., Palgrave Macmillan, Switzerland, 2019, p. vii.

253 *Ibid.*, pp. v–vii.

254 Nour Dados and Raewyn Connell, 'The Global South,' *Contexts,* 11 (1), 2012, pp. 12–13.

255 *Ibid.*

256 *Ibid.*

257 'Non-Aligned Disruptions: Global Media Histories in the Wake of Decolonization,' *Annenberg* at https://www.asc.upenn.edu/news-events/events/non-aligned-disruptions-global-media-histories-wake-decolonization (Accessed June 7, 2025).

258 Matthew Crain, "Non-Aligned News Agencies Pool", in John DH Downing (ed.), *Encyclopedia of Social Movement Media,* Sage Publications, 2011, pp. 368–369. https://doi.org/10.4135/9781412979313.n161.

259 *Ibid.*

260 Boyd-Barrett and Joseph Oliver, *The World-Wide News Agencies: Development Organization, Competition, Markets and Product: A Study of Agence France Presse, Associated Press, Reuters and United Press, to 1975*, Open University, United Kingdom, 1978, pp. 3–5.

261 Peter Johan Lor and Johannes J. Britz, "Moral Problems in Information Flows from South to North", in *Information Ethics in the Electronic Age: Current Issues in Africa and the World,* p. 15, 2004.

262 'Reuters: About Us,' Reuters: The Trusted, International News Agency at https://reutersagency.com/about/. (Accessed June 7, 2025).

263 AFP, 'About Us,' Agence France-Presse at https://www.afp.com/en/agency/about/about-us?_gl=1*795c7k*_up*MQ..*_ga*MjA5MzU4NzgxNS4xNzI0MjUyNDA0*_ga_9NGK0BQW11*MTcyNDI1MjQwMy4xL jEuMTcyNDI1MjQxNy40Ni4wLjA (Accessed June 6, 2025).

264 Oliver Boyd-Barrett, 'National and International News Agencies: Issues of Crisis and Realignment,' *Gazette,* 62 (1), Leiden, Netherlands, 2000, pp. 5–18.

265 Xin Xu, 'A Policy Trajectory Analysis of the Internationalisation of Chinese Humanities and Social Sciences Research (1978–2020),' *International Journal of Educational Development,* 84, 2021 at https://www.sciencedirect.com/science/article/pii/S073805932100078X.

266 Victor Habib Lantyer, 'Data Colonialism: The Geopolitics of Information,' April 29, 2025. SSRN: https://ssrn.com/abstract=5236304 or http://dx.doi.org/10.2139/ssrn.5236304.

267 Claudia Padovani, 'New World Information and Communication Order (NWICO),' Wiley Online Library, July 23 2015. https://onlinelibrary.wiley.com/doi/abs/10.1002/9781405186407.wbiecn013.pub2 (Accessed June 7, 2025).

268 Kuldip R. Rampal, "Global News and Information Flow in the Digital Age", in *Global Communication: A Multicultural Perspective,* Rowman & Littlefield Publishers, 2019, pp. 149–178.

269 Rebekah J. Kowal, *Dancing the World Smaller: Staging Globalism in Mid-Century America,* Oxford University Press, 2020, p. 35.

270 *Ibid.*, p. 42.

271 Michelle Betz and Melissa Eveleigh, 'The Impact of COVID-19 on Communication, Community Engagement and Accountability,' CDAC Network, June 2022, p. 40.

272 Julien Nocetti, 'A Splintered Internet? Internet Fragmentation and the Strategies of China, Russia, India and the European Union,' The French Institute of International Relations, February 2024.

273 *Ibid.*

274 *Ibid.*

275 Kuldip R. Rampal, no. 262.

276 *Ibid.*

277 'Thomson Reuters Corporation (TRI): History, Ownership, Mission, How It Works & Makes Money,' DCF, SWOT, CANVAS, PESTEL, BCG Editable Templates, June 6, 2024 at https://dcfmodeling.com/blogs/history/tri-history-mission-ownership (Accessed June 5, 2025).

278 *Ibid.*

279 'Reuters: About Us,' no. 256.

280 *Ibid.*

281 'About Us,' Associated Press at https://www.ap.org/about/ (Accessed June 6, 2025).

282 "Down On the Wire" *Forbes,* February 13, 2008 at https://www.forbes.com/2008/02/13/media-newspapers-ap-biz-media-cx_lh_0214ap.html (Accessed June 6, 2025).

283 V. Kuitenbrouwer. "Neutral News. Forging a Small States' Transnational Media Network, 1914 40", in S. Kruizinga (ed.), *The Politics of Smallness in Modern Europe: Size, Identity and International Relations since 1800,* Bloomsbury Academic, London, 2022, pp. 115–132. https://doi.org/10.5040/9781350168916.ch-006

284 Clifford F. Weigle, 'The Rise and Fall of the Havas News Agency,' *Journalism Quarterly,* 19 (3), 1942, pp. 277–286.

285 Michael Palmer, 'European News-Agency Beginnings: The Role of S. Engländer,' *Media History,* 22 (1), 2016, pp. 27–39.

286 Peter Kenny, "News Agencies as Content Providers and Purveyors of News: A

Mediahistoriographical Study on the Development and Diversity of Wire Services," PhD dissertation, University of Stellenbosch, Stellenbosch, 2009.

287 Boyd-Barrett and Joseph Oliver, no.254.

288 Peter Kenny, no. 280.

289 *Ibid.*

290 Stijn Joye. *Raising Awareness, Challenging Establishment. The Surplus Value of a Global and Local Alternative News Agency*. Academia Press, 2006, pp. 10–13.

291 *Ibid.*

292 Vincent Obia, Ismail A. Ibraheem and Charles C. Onwunali, 'Borrowing Lenses from the West: Analysis of an African Media Representation of Western Nations,' White Rose Research Online, June 12, 2020 at https://eprints.whiterose.ac.uk/id/eprint/220544/1/Borrowing%20Lenses%20from%20the%20West.pdf.

293 Ta-Nehisi Coates, "The Myth of Western Civilization" *The Atlantic*, January 3, 2014 at https://www.theatlantic.com/international/archive/2013/12/the-myth-of-western-civilization/282704/ (Accessed June 7, 2025).

294 William McBagonluri Appiah and George Ayittey Baffour, 'Impact of Western Media Broadcasting on Culture Values and Democratization Process in Sub-Saharan Africa: Perspective from Ghana,' *African Journal of Emerging Issues,* 4 (4), April 2022, pp. 1–14.

295 *Ibid.*

296 Vincent Obia, Ismail A. Ibraheem and Charles C. Onwunali, no. 287.

297 An Nguyen and Minh Tran. 'Science Journalism for Development in the Global South: A Systematic Literature Review of Issues and Challenges,' *Public Understanding of Science,* 28 (8), 2019, pp. 973–990.

298 J. Dennison, 'Narratives: A Review of Concepts, Determinants, Effects, and Uses in Migration Research,' *Comparative Migration Studies,* 9 (50), 2021. https://doi.org/10.1186/s40878-021-00259-9.

299 Stijn Joye. no. 284.

300 Vincent Obia, Ismail A. Ibraheem and Charles C. Onwunali, no. 287.

301 Shiko Njoroge, 'Framing Africa's Ability to Self-Govern: An Analysis of Western Media's Representation of African Nations during the COVID-19 Pandemic,' *Njoroge*, May 2021 at https://scholarship.tricolib.brynmawr.edu/server/api/core/bitstreams/2f43bdc2-9eed-49ac-b912-5da163b299e1/content

302 *Ibid.*

303 *Ibid.*

304 William McBagonluri Appiah and George Ayittey Baffour, no. 288.

305 Shiko Njoroge, no. 295.

306 *Ibid.*

307 *Ibid.*

308 *Ibid.*

309 Janna Anderson and Lee Rainie, 'The Future of Truth and Misinformation Online,' Pew Research Center, October 19, 2017 at https://www.pewresearch.org/internet/2017/10/19/the-future-of-truth-and-misinformation-online/#:~:text='%E2%80%9D,the%20disinterestedness%2C%20of%20information.%E2%80%9D (Accessed June 7, 2025).

310 Anil Fernandes, 'MacBride Commission-One Voice Many Nations-NWICO,' Scribd, March 12, 2020 at https://www.slideshare.net/slideshow/macbride-commissionone-voice-many-nationsnwico/230156462 (Accessed June 7, 2025).

311 Eli Avraham, 'Changing the Conversation: How Developing Countries Handle the International Media during Disasters, Conflicts, and Tourism Crises,' *Journal of Information Policy*, 7, 2017,

pp. 275–296.

312 Chris Paterson, "Prospects for a Democratic Information Society: The News Agency Stranglehold on Global Political Discourse", Conference paper, London School of Economics and Political Science, London, April 23–26, 2003 at https://www.lse.ac.uk/media@lse/research/EMTEL/Conference/papers/Paterson.pdf.

313 Stijn Joye, no. 284.

314 Arif Md Tareque Habib, 'Influences of the Western Press on News Framing of Global Events in Developing Countries: Examining Covid-19 and Climate Coverage in a Bangladeshi News Organization,' UNM Digital Repository - University of New Mexico at https://digitalrepository.unm.edu/cj_etds/164/ (Accessed June 7, 2025).

315 *Ibid.*

316 William McBagonluri Appiah and George Ayittey Baffour, no. 288.

317 Stijn Joye, no. 284.

318 'The Role of Media in Public Policy: Influence, Impact, and Challenges,' Indian School of Public Policy, September 25, 2024 at https://www.ispp.org.in/the-role-of-media-in-public-policy-influence-impact-and-challenges/ (Accessed June 7, 2025).

319 Mathias Aboba, 'Media Influence, Reality or Perception: An Analysis of Pier Robinson Publication: "The CNN Effect: Can the News Media Drive Foreign Policy?"' JMU Scholarly Commons, 2019. https://commons.lib.jmu.edu/cgi/viewcontent.cgi?article=1009&context=scom542

320 P. Robinson, 'The CNN Effect: Can the News Media Drive Foreign policy?,' *Review of International Studies,* 25 (2), 1999, pp. 301–309.

321 Mathias Aboba, no. 313.

322 P. Robinson, no. 314.

323 Ratzinger E. E. Nwobodo, 'Western Media Representation of Africa: The Role of Bad Governance,' *Journal of Humanities and Social Policy*, 11 (3), 2025.

324 Gregory Gondwe. 'Framing the Schemata: Western Media Coverage of African Technological Innovations,' *Journalism and Media,* 5 (4), 2024, pp. 1901–1913.

325 Anya Schiffrin. 'Fighting for Survival: Media Startups in the Global South,' *Center for International Media Assistance,* 2019.

326 Rowan Philp. 'Donor Interest Vs. Editorial Independence: How to Defend Your News Integrity During a Global Funding Crisis,' Global Investigative Journalism Network. March 10, 2025 at https://gijn.org/stories/how-defend-news-integrity-during-global-funding-crisis/ (Accessed June 7, 2025).

327 Anya Schiffrin. no. 319.

328 K. C. Izuogu, O. Okpara and D. U. Omeonu, 'The Paradox of the Internet in Journalism in Nigeria: Between Flexibility and Accuracy Challenges,' *Baileo: Jurnal Sosial Humaniora,* 2 (2), 2025, pp. 256–267.

329 *Ibid.*

330 Vincent Mosco, 'Current Trends in the Global Political Economy,' *Global Political Economy,* 1 (1), 2008, pp. 45–63. doi:10.4324/9781315659695-16.

331 *Ibid.*

332 Luciana Retno Prastiwi, "Political Economy of Media in Indonesia with the Study of Law No. 32 of 2002 on Broadcasting", Proceedings of the 2nd Jogjakarta Communication Conference (JCC 2020), Surabaya, Indonesia, 2020.

333 International Monetary Fund Study, no. 6.

334 "ASEAN Countries GDP 2027", no. 5.

335 Luciana Retno Prastiwi, no. 326.

336 'Indonesian Media Landscape 2022 #1,' Imogen Public Relations Indonesia, March 13, 2022 at https://imogenpr.com/new-report-indonesian-media-landscape-2022/ (Accessed January 3, 2024).

337 'Indonesia,' Media Landscapes at https://medialandscapes.org/country/indonesia (Accessed January 3, 2024).

338 "Indonesia Media Guide" *BBC News*, "*Indonesia Profile - Media,*" February 24, 2023, sec. Asia–Pacific at https://www.bbc.com/news/world-asia-pacific-15105923 (Accessed December 3, 2023).

339 'Indonesia,' no. 331.

340 *Ibid.*

341 Krishna Sen, "Indonesia: Media and the End of Authoritarian Rule", in *Media Reform*, Routledge, 2003, pp. 81–100.

342 Krishna Sen and David Hill, *Politics and the Media in Twenty-First Century Indonesia: Decade of Democracy*, 1st ed., Routledge, London, 2010, p. 6.

343 Adam Fenton, 'Faith, Intolerance, Violence and Bigotry: Legal and Constitutional Issues of Freedom of Religion in Indonesia,' *Journal of Indonesian Islam,* 10 (2), 2016, pp. 181–212.

344 'Indonesia,' Reporters without Borders, 2023 at https://rsf.org/en/country/indonesia (Accessed January 3, 2024).

345 Sofie Syarief, 'The Media Landscape in Indonesia: The More Things Change, the More They Stay the Same,' *Perspective, Yusof Ishak Institute Analyse Current Events*, 77, August 2022.

346 Ignatius Haryanto, "Media Ownership and Its Implications for Journalists and Journalism in Indonesia", in David Hill and Krishna Sen (eds.) *Politics and the Media in Twenty-First Century Indonesia: Decade of Democracy*, Taylor & Francis, 2010, pp. 104–118.

347 Sofie Syarief, no. 339.

348 Masduki and Leen D'Haenens, 'Concentration of Media Ownership in Indonesia: A Setback for Viewpoint Diversity,' *International Journal of Communication,* 16, 2022, pp. 2239–2259 at https://ijoc.org/index.php/ijoc/article/download/17769/3759.

349 Yanuar Nugroho, Muhammad Siregar and Shita Laksmi, *Mapping Media Policy in Indonesia,* Centre for Innovation Policy and Governance, Indonesia, 2013.

350 *Ibid.*

351 Aep Wahyudin, "Supervision Polemics of Indonesian Broadcasting Commission (KPI) on Internet Content", Proceedings of the 2nd Social and Humaniora Research Symposium (SoRes 2019), 409, 2019, pp. 191–195. doi:10.2991/assehr.k.200225.039.

352 Randy Mulyanto, "Indonesians Head to the Polls in February. Here Are Key Issues Dominating the Elections" CNBC, January 3, 2023 at https://www.cnbc.com/2024/01/04/indonesia-2024-elections-economy-gaza-war-and-china-ties-dominate.html (Accessed January 4, 2023).

353 Robertus Robet, 'Who Are the Elites Who Control Indonesian Politics?,' Indonesia at Melbourne, April 11, 2023 at https://indonesiaatmelbourne.unimelb.edu.au/who-are-the-elites-who-control-indonesian-politics/ (Accessed January 4, 2023).

354 Krishna Sen and David Hill, p. 15, no. 336.

355 *Ibid.*, p. 16.

356 Surya Paloh is an Indonesian businessman and politician who owns Media Group, the Media Indonesia daily newspaper and MetroTV, a 24-hour news television channel.

357 Aburizal Bakrie is an Indonesian politician and a widely recognised successful businessman in Indonesia via his conglomerate Bakrie Group.

358 'Media – Malaysia, Statista Market Forecast,' Statista at https://www.statista.com/outlook/amo/media/malaysia. (Accessed January 12, 2024).

359 *Ibid.*

360 'Digital 2023: Malaysia – DataReportal – Global Digital Insights,' DataReportal – Global Digital Insights, February 13, 2023 at https://datareportal.com/reports/digital-2023-malaysia#:~:text=There%20were%2033.03%20million%20internet%20users%20in%20Malaysia%20in%20January,percent)%20between%202022%20and%202023 (Accessed January 12, 2024).

361 "Malaysia Media Guide" *BBC News*, May 19, 2023 at https://www.bbc.com/news/world-asia-pacific-15384221 (Accessed January 12, 2024).

362 *Ibid.*

363 'Whither the Print Media in Malaysia?,' National Press Club Malaysia, October 23, 2019 at https://nationalpressclub.org.my/whither-the-print-media-in-malaysia/ (Accessed January 12, 2024).

364 'Malaysia: Top Sources for News 2023,' Statista, June 14, 2023 at https://www.statista.com/statistics/982719/malaysia-top-news-sources/ (Accessed January 12, 2024).

365 'Print Newspapers & Magazines - Malaysia | Market Forecast,' Statista at https://www.statista.com/outlook/amo/media/newspapers-magazines/print-newspapers-magazines/malaysia (Accessed January 12, 2024).

366 "Malaysia Media Guide" no. 355.

367 Saodah Wok and Shafizan Mohamed, "Internet and Social Media in Malaysia: Development, Challenges and Potentials", in Beatriz Peña Acuña (ed.), *The Evolution of Media Communication*, Open Science Open Minds, May 31, 2017 at https://www.intechopen.com/chapters/55225 (Accessed January 13, 2024).

368 'Malaysia,' RSF at https://rsf.org/en/country/malaysia (Accessed January 12, 2024).

369 'Official Portal of the Parliament of Malaysia,' January 23, 2013 at https://www.parlimen.gov.my/pengenalan.html?&uweb=p&view=23&lang=en (Accessed January 12, 2024).

370 'Freedom of Expression,' Human Rights Commission of Malaysia at https://suhakam.org.my/portfolio/freedom-of-expression/#:~:text=The%20right%20to%20freedom%20of,development%20of%20every%20individual%20citizen (Accessed January 13, 2024).

371 Saodah Wok and Shafizan Mohamed, no. 361.

372 John A. Lent, 'Malaysia's Guided Media,' Sage Publication. https://journals.sagepub.com/doi/pdf/10.1080/03064227408532375 (Accessed January 13, 2024).

373 Emily Honstein, 'Malaysia,' International Centre for Not for Profit Law, November 30, 2023 at https://www.icnl.org/resources/civic-freedom-monitor/malaysia.(Accessed January 13, 2024).

374 Saodah Wok and Shafizan Mohamed, no. 361.

375 Azizul Halim Yahya, 'Political Economy of the Mass Media in Malaysia,' Pusat Penerbitan Universiti, UiTM, 2006.

376 Mustafa K. Anuar, 'Politics and the Media in Malaysia,' *Kasarinlan: Philippine Journal of Third World Studies 20*, 1, 2005, pp. 25–47.

377 Thomas B. Pepinsky, 'The New Media and Malaysian Politics in Historical Perspective,' *Contemporary Southeast Asia,* 35 (1), 2013, pp. 83–103. doi:10.1355/cs35-1d.

378 Mustafa K. Anuar, no. 370.

379 Pauline P. Leong, 'Political Communication in Malaysia: A Study on the Use of New Media in Politics,' *JeDEM - eJournal of eDemocracy and Open Government*, 7 (1), 2015, pp. 46–71. doi:10.29379/jedem.v7i1.372.

380 Mustafa K. Anuar, no. 370.

381 The Printing Presses and Publications Act (PPPA) Section 7(1) grants the minister authority to prohibit publication if it poses threats to morality, public order, security or national interest, creating legal obstacles for journalists. The Sedition Act remains highly problematic, prohibiting expression that has a tendency to cause ill will — regardless of the real risk of any harmful impact, or the intention of the speaker, or whether the statements are truthful.

382 Cherian George and Gayathry Venkiteswaran, *Media and Power in Southeast Asia,* Cambridge University Press, 2019, p. 60.
383 Zaharom Nain and Wang Lai Kim, "Ownership, Control and the Malaysian Media", in *Who Owns the Media,* Southbound, Penang, 2004, pp. 249–270.
384 "Malaysia Media Guide" *BBC News*, October 21, 2011 at https://www.bbc.com/news/world-asia-pacific-15384221 (Accessed December 30, 2023).
385 'The News Landscape in Thailand,' Statista, February 28, 2022 at https://www.statista.com/topics/9075/the-news-environment-in-thailand/#topicOverview (Accessed January 8, 2024).
386 'List of Television Stations in Thailand,' Academic Dictionaries and Encyclopaedias at https://en-academic.com/dic.nsf/enwiki/4365283#:~:text=List%20of%20television%20stations%20in%20Thailan d%20%C2%B7,Learning%20TV%20%C2%B7%20EDN%20Edutainment%20%C2%B7%20Faikham (Accessed January 10, 2024).
387 'List of Television Stations in Thailand,' Philippine Television Wiki at https://philippinetelevision.fandom.com/wiki/List_of_television_stations_in_Thailand (Accessed January 10, 2024).
388 'Traditional TV & Home Video - Thailand , Market Forecast,' Statista at https://www.statista.com/outlook/amo/media/tv-video/traditional-tv-home-video/thailand (Accessed January 10, 2024).
389 Radio Thailand at https://nbt1.prd.go.th/ (Accessed January 10, 2024).
390 'News Radio Stations from Thailand,' Free Internet Radio & Podcasts - Listen Online, MyTuner Radio at https://mytuner-radio.com/radio/country/thailand/genre/news-stations (Accessed January 10, 2024).
391 Sascha Funk, My-thai.org, 2021 at https://my-thai.org/the-most-famous-thai-media-channels/ (Accessed January 10, 2024).
392 'Thai Newspapers: List of All Thailand Newspapers,' Newspapers Land, October 12, 2023 at https://www.newspapersland.com/thailand/ (Accessed January 10, 2024).
393 Wanpen Pajai, 'The Profound Legacy of Thailand's First Newspaper, The Bangkok Recorder,' *Southeast Asia Globe*, May 27, 2021 at https://southeastasiaglobe.com/thailands-first-newspaper/ (Accessed January 10, 2024).
394 'Print Newspapers & Magazines - Thailand | Market Forecast,' Statista at https://www.statista.com/outlook/amo/media/newspapers-magazines/print-newspapers-magazines/thailand (Accessed January 10, 2024).
395 'Thailand: Share of Printed Newspaper Consumer by Generation 2019,' Statista, November 22, 2019 at https://www.statista.com/statistics/1181153/thailand-share-of-printed-newspaper-consumers-by-generation/ (Accessed January 10, 2024).
396 *Ibid.*
397 Simon Kemp, 'Digital 2023: Thailand,' DataReportal – Global Digital Insights, February 13, 2023 at https://datareportal.com/reports/digital-2023-thailand (Accessed January 10, 2024).
398 Thailand Center, 'Thailand's Politics and Governance,' SAWASDEE THAILAND at https://www.thailand.go.th/page/thai-politic (Accessed January 10, 2024).
399 Martin Russell, 'Thailand: From Coup to Crisis,' European Parliamentary Research Service, Brussels, 2020.
400 'Royal Thai Armed Forces Headquarters English Version,' Wayback Machine at https://web.archive.org/web/20090418003625/www.schq.mi.th/EN/vision_mission.htm (Accessed January 10, 2024).
401 "Progressive Leader Who Won Thai Election is Blocked from Power" NBC News, July 19, 2023 at https://www.nbcnews.com/news/world/thailand-parliament-vote-prime-minister-move-forward-rcna94535 (Accessed January 11, 2024).

402 Grant Peck and Jintamas Saksornchai, "Thailand's Move Forward Party Leader Pita Falls Short in Parliamentary Vote for Prime Minister" *The Diplomat – Asia-Pacific Current Affairs Magazine*, July 13, 2023 at https://thediplomat.com/2023/07/thailands-move-forward-party-leader-pita-falls-short-in-parliamentary-vote-for-prime-minister/ (Accessed January 11, 2024).

403 "Thai Parliament Blocks Pita from Being Renominated for Prime Minister" *The Diplomat – Asia-Pacific Current Affairs Magazine*, July 19, 2023 at https://thediplomat.com/2023/07/thai-parliament-blocks-pita-from-being-renominated-for-prime-minister/ (Accessed January 11, 2024).

404 Pavin Chachavalpongpun, 'Thai Election Politics and the Demise of the Monarchy,' Australian Institute of International Affairs, June 22, 2023 at https://www.internationalaffairs.org.au/australianoutlook/thai-election-politics-and-the-demise-of-the-monarchy/ (Accessed January 11, 2024).

405 "Thailand Media Guide" *BBC News*, May 26, 2023 at https://www.bbc.com/news/world-asia-15639421 (Accessed January 10, 2024).

406 Veera Prateepchaikul, "Media Ownership", in Chavarong Limpattamapanee and Arnaud Leveau (eds.), *State and Media in Thailand during Political Transition,* Institut de recherche sur l'Asie du Sud-Est, Bangkok, 2007.

407 Chakrit Tiebtienrat, 'Film Media and Nationalism in Thailand : Comparative Studies of Film Media Propaganda in Thailand and Its Influence on Thai Nationalism, Political Ideology, and Class Structure Since the Enactment of the Thai Constitution of 1997,' UC Research Repository at https://ir.canterbury.ac.nz/items/e1e6788f-655a-4af1-912c-561337033bc2 (Accessed December 29, 2023).

408 Glen Lewis and Peter Thompson, 'Communications Deregulation and Democratisation in Thailand,' *Media International Australia,* 96 (1), 2000, pp. 121–134. https://doi.org/10.1177/1329878X0009600115.

409 *Ibid.*

410 Jeffrey Hays, 'Media in Thailand: Censorship, Thaksin, Television, and Newspapers Full Of Gory Pictures,' Facts and Details at https://factsanddetails.com/southeast-asia/thailand/sub5_8e/entry-3267.html (Accessed January 11, 2024).

411 *Ibid.*

412 Reporters without Borders, Thailand page at https://rsf.org/en/country/thailand (Accessed January 10, 2024).

413 *Ibid.*

414 "Thailand Media Guide", no. 399.

415 *Ibid.*

416 Jeffrey Hays, "Thailand's Lese Majeste Laws," *Facts and Details.*

417 Reporters without Borders, no. 406.

418 BTI 2022 Country Report, Singapore Country Report 2022, Bertelsmann Transformation Index, 2022 at https://bti-project.org/en/reports/country-report/SGP (Accessed December 28, 2023).

419 Chantal Sajan, "The Straits Times Marks 178 Years as Region's Oldest Newspaper" *The Straits Times,* July 15, 2023 at https://www.straitstimes.com/life/home-design/the-straits-times-marks-178-years-as-region-s-oldest-newspaper (Accessed December 6, 2023).

420 'Singapore: Daily Newspaper Circulation 2021,' Statista, June 28, 2023 at https://www.statista.com/statistics/950259/singapore-daily-newspaper-circulation/ (Accessed January 6, 2024).

421 'Singapore Newspapers,' FamilySearch Wiki, December 4, 2019 at https://www.familysearch.org/en/wiki/Singapore_Newspapers#:~:text=Today%20 there%20are%20a %20total,distri

buted%20with%20The%20Straits%20Times (Accessed January 6, 2024).

422 National Library Board Singapore, 'Singapore's First Television Station,' National Library Board, October 9, 2023 at https://www.nlb.gov.sg/main/article-detail?cmsuuid=f84fe603-7339-4629-b781-50b75fa3d21f (Accessed December 6, 2023).

423 *Ibid.*

424 'Fact Sheet - MDA to Work with Industry to Put Together National Data on Media Consumption Across All Audio-visual Content Platforms, Including Broadcast TV, Online and Mobile, Beginning with a Trial in 2015,' Infocomm Media Development Authority, August 28, 2023 at https://www.imda.gov.sg/resources/press-releases-factsheets-and-speeches/archived/mda/press-releases/2014/fact-sheet—mda-to-work-with-industry-to-put-together-national-data-on-media-consumption-across-all-audiovisual-content-platforms-including-broadcast-tv-online-and-mobile-beginning-with-a-trial-in-2015 (Accessed December 6, 2023).

425 National Library Board Singapore, no. 416.

426 Magazine, Adobo, "ABS-CBN Maintains Lead in SG-TAM Ratings for Filipino Channels in Singapore with TFC" *Adobo Magazine Online*, October 17, 2022 at https://www.adobomagazine.com/press-release/abs-cbn-maintains-lead-in-sg-tam-ratings-for-filipino-channels-in-singapore-with-tfc/ (Accessed December 6, 2023).

427 National Library Board Singapore, 'Radio Broadcasting in Singapore (1924–46),' National Library Board, October 9, 2023 at https://www.nlb.gov.sg/main/article-detail?cmsuuid=08626775-37d3-4bac-8819-c36421e79271 (Accessed December 6, 2023).

428 Chua Ai Lin, "The Modern Magic Carpet': Wireless Radio in Interwar Colonial Singapore,' *Modern Asian Studies*, 46 (1), 2012, pp. 167–191.

429 'Mediacorp Remains SG's Top Audio Network, Reaching 88% of Adults & 9 in 10 Digital Listeners Through Its FTA Radio Stations & Digital Radio Network,' Mediacorp, December 15, 2021 at https://www.mediacorp.sg/corporate/news-release/media-releases/mediacorp-remains-sg-s-top-audio-network-reaching-88-of-adults-9-15471012 (Accessed December 6, 2023).

430 *Ibid.*

431 Sue Howe, 'Social Media Statistics in Singapore,' Meltwater, April 14, 2023 at https://www.meltwater.com/en/blog/social-media-statistics-singapore (Accessed December 6, 2023).

432 *Ibid.*

433 'University of Minnesota Human Rights Library,' Human Rights Library-University of Minnesota, September 16, 1963 at https://hrlibrary.umn.edu/research/singapore/singapore-constitution.html (Accessed January 7, 2024).

434 'Chee Siok Chin and Others v Minister for Home Affairs and Another,' The High Court of Singapore, December 18, 2023 at https://www.elitigation.sg/gd/s/2005_SGHC_216 (Accessed January 7, 2024).

435 Emmy Sasipornkarn, 'Why is Singapore Falling Behind in Press Freedom?,' Dw.com, September 25, 2020 at https://www.dw.com/en/why-is-singapore-falling-behind-in-press-freedom/a-55056720 (Accessed January 7, 2024).

436 'Singapore,' Reporters without Borders, 2023 at https://rsf.org/en/country/singapore (Accessed January 8, 2024).

437 'Commencement of the Sedition (Repeal) Act 2021,' Ministry of Home Affairs, November 1, 2022 at https://www.mha.gov.sg/mediaroom/press-releases/commencement-of-the-sedition-repeal-act-2021/.

438 'Protection from Online Falsehoods and Manipulation Act,' POFMA Office, January 9, 2024 at https://www.pofmaoffice.gov.sg/regulations/protection-from-online-falsehoods-and-manipulation-act/ (Accessed January 8, 2024).

439 'Singapore,' no. 430.

440 National Library Board Singapore, 'Formation of Singapore Press Holdings,' National Library Board, October 9, 2023 at https://www.nlb.gov.sg/main/article-detail?cmsuuid=34789177-5f5e-468d-9a77-db3680ce4161 (Accessed January 7, 2024).

441 "Singapore Media Guide" *BBC News*, May 23, 2023 at https://www.bbc.com/news/world-asia-15966553 (Accessed January 7, 2024).

442 *Ibid.*

443 Simon Casady, 'Lee Kuan Yew & the Singapore Media: Purging the Press,' *Index on Censorship*, 4 (3), 1975, pp. 3–6. https://doi.org/10.1080/03064227508532442.

444 'Singapore,' no. 430.

445 'Singapore,' Reuters Institute for the Study of Journalism, January 9, 2024 at https://reutersinstitute.politics.ox.ac.uk/digital-news-report/2022/singapore (Accessed January 8, 2024).

446 "Singapore Media Guide" no. 435.

447 Drew & Napier LLC, 'In Brief: Media Law and Regulation in Singapore,' Lexology, August 5, 2020 at https://www.lexology.com/library/detail.aspx?g=bad6a3ed-7528-435a-93cf-0c2bdaa9cca9 (Accessed January 8, 2024).

448 Joshua Lee and Belmont Lay, 'States Times Review to Close Down After Getting Blocked in S'pore by Authorities,' Mothership, November 9, 2018 at https://mothership.sg/2018/11/states-times-review-closed-down/ (Accessed January 8, 2024).

449 'Singapore Suspends Independent Website, Threatens It with Closure,' RSF, October 15, 2023 at https://rsf.org/en/singapore-suspends-independent-website-threatens-it-closure (Accessed January 8, 2024).

450 Joshua Lee and Belmont Lay, no. 442.

451 'Singapore Suspends Independent Website, Threatens It with Closure,' no. 443.

452 Howard Lee Kwai Hou, "Media Governance in Singapore – Efficacy and Challenges," PhD dissertation, Murdoch University, 2021. ProQuest at https://researchportal.murdoch.edu.au/esploro/outputs/doctoral/Media-governance-in-Singapore—efficacy/991005541062107891 (Accessed January 8, 2024).

453 *Ibid.*

454 Howard Lee Kwai Hou, no. 446.

455 Pauline Estella and Martin Löffelholz, 'Philippines,' Media Landscapes, 2024 at https://medialandscapes.org/country/philippines (Accessed January 11, 2024).

456 *Ibid.*

457 Yvonne T. Chua, 'Philippines,' Reuters Institute for the Study of Journalism, June 14, 2023 at https://reutersinstitute.politics.ox.ac.uk/digital-news-report/2023/philippines (Accessed January 11, 2024).

458 *Ibid.*

459 'Philippines,' RSF at https://rsf.org/en/country/philippines (Accessed January 12, 2024).

460 Media Ownership Monitor at https://philippines.mom-rsf.org/ (Accessed January 12, 2024).

461 Pauline Gidget Resterio Estella, 'Digital Populism, Digital Newswork and the Concept of Journalistic Competence: The Philippine Condition,' Media International Australia, April 2021 at https://www.researchgate.net/publication/350610336_Digital_populism_digital_newswork_and_the_concept_of_journalistic_competence_the_Philippine_condition (Accessed January 12, 2024).

462 Media Ownership Monitor, no. 454.

463 'Philippines,' no. 453.

464 Yvonne T. Chua, 'Philippines,' Reuters Institute for the Study of Journalism, June 14, 2023 at https://reutersinstitute.politics.ox.ac.uk/digital-news-report/2023/philippines (Accessed January

11, 2024).

465 'TV Outlets Philippines,' Media Ownership Monitor at https://philippines.mom-rsf.org/en/media/tv/ (Accessed January 12, 2024).

466 *Ibid.*

467 Pauline Estella and Martin Löffelholz, no. 449.

468 'Hope Channel Philippines,' Russel Wiki at https://russel.fandom.com/wiki/Hope_Channel_Philippines#:~:text=Hope%20Channel%20Philippines%20is%20a,owned%20by%20Digital%20Broadcasting%20Corporation (Accessed January 12, 2024).

469 'The 1987 Constitution of the Republic of the Philippines – Article III,' Official Gazette of the Republic of the Philippines at https://www.officialgazette.gov.ph/constitutions/the-1987-constitution-of-the-republic-of-the-philippines/the-1987-constitution-of-the-republic-of-the-philippines-article-iii/ (Accessed January 12, 2024).

470 'Philippines,' no. 453.

471 *Ibid.*

472 Teresa R. Melgar, "The Political Economy of Power in Contemporary Philippines: Patterns of Continuity and Change", in Hans-Jürgen Burchardt and Johanna Leinius (eds.), *(Post-)Colonial Archipelagos: Comparing the Legacies of Spanish Colonialism in Cuba, Puerto Rico, and the Philippines*, University of Michigan Press, 2022, pp.142–168 at http://www.jstor.org/stable/10.3998/mpub.11747103.13.

473 *Ibid.*

474 'Economy and Media Philippines,' Media Ownership Monitor at https://philippines.mom-rsf.org/en/context/economy/ (Accessed December 30, 2023).

475 *Ibid.*

476 *Ibid.*

477 Rene Guioguio, 'An Overview of the Mass Media Situation in the Philippines,' Media Ownership Monitor, 2015, pp. 1–7.

478 Sarbananda Sonowal, "India Rises to Fourth Largest Economy in the World, Powered by the Astute Leadership of PM Narendra Modi ji" *Press Information Bureau*, Ministry of Ports, Shipping and Waterways. Govt. of India, May 25, 2025.

479 Jack Donnelly, "Realism and International Relations," Cambridge University Press, Cambridge, 1st ed. 2000, p. 12.

480 Nico Meissner, 50 years on: Galtung and Ruge's news values factors revisited in online audience building for independent films, First Monday, 26 January 2015, at https://firstmonday.org/ojs/index.php/fm/article/view/5850/4408. (Accessed 8 November 2025)

481 Nasrullah Mambrol,. "Analysis of Stuart Hall's Encoding/Decoding." Literary Theory and Criticism. Last modified November 7, 2020, at https://literariness.org/2020/11/07/analysis-of-stuart-halls-encoding-decoding/. (Accessed 8 November 2025)

482 Joint Statement on India – Malaysia Comprehensive Strategic Partnership, Ministry of External Affairs, Government of India, 20 August 2024, at https://www.mea.gov.in/bilateral-documents.htm?dtl/38187/Joint_Statement_on_India__Malaysia_Comprehensive_Strategic_Partnership. (Accessed 8 November 2025)

483 "Shannon and Weaver Model of Communication," Communication Theory, 10 July 2014, at https://www.communicationtheory.org/shannon-and-weaver-model-of-communication/. (Accessed 8 November 2025)

484 S. Priyadharma, Theoretical Framework, In: Internet and Social Change in Rural Indonesia, Springer VS, Wiesbaden, 2021. https://doi.org/10.1007/978-3-658-35533-3_3

485 Xi.Cui, "Nick Couldry and Andreas Hepp, "The Mediated Construction of Reality," *Mass Communication and Society,* Polity Press, Cambridge, UK, Vol. 21 (1), 2017.145–47.

doi:10.1080/15205436.2017.1407584.

486 Lilie Chouliaraki, "The Spectatorship of Suffering," SAGE Publications, London, January 2006, p. 105. DOI: 10.4135/9781446220658

487 D.K. Thussu (Ed.), Media on the Move: Global Flow and Contra-Flow, Routledge, London, 1st ed. 2006. https://doi.org/10.4324/9780203001233

488 Philip Seib, 2010. "Transnational Journalism, Public Diplomacy and Virtual States," *Journalism Studies*, Vol. 11 (5), pp. 734–44. Doi:10.1080/1461670x.2010.503023.

489 Michael Curtin, "Playing to the World's Biggest Audience: The Globalization of Chinese Film and TV," University of California Press, Berkeley, 2007.

490 Om Prakash Das, 'How ASEAN Media Portrays India: Insights into the Construction of Media Text,' MP-IDSA Occasional Paper, no. 63, 2024.

491 *Ibid.*

492 *Ibid.*

493 Edward S. Herman and Noam Chomsky, *Manufacturing Consent: The Political Economy of the Mass Media,* Pantheon Books, New York, 1988, p. 1.

494 Robert W. McChesney, *The Political Economy of Media: Enduring Issues, Emerging Dilemmas*, Monthly Review Press, New York, 2008, p. 3.

495 John Pilger, '9 Quotes from John Pilger on Media and Power,' Real Media, June 16, 2015.

496 Noam Chomsky, *Media Control: The Spectacular Achievements of Propaganda*, Seven Stories Press, New York, NY, 2002, p. 29.

497 Noam Chomsky, *Chronicles of Dissent,* Penguin, UK, 2022, p. 6.

498 Herbert I. Schiller, *Communication and Cultural Domination,* Pantheon, New York, 1976, p. 9.

499 *Ibid.*

500 *Ibid.*

501 Raymond Williams, quoted in *Media Studies: A Reader,* NYU Press, 2nd ed. New York, 2001, p. 410.

502 Edward Herman, 'The Propaganda Model Revisited', *Monthly Review-New York*, 48, 1996, pp. 115–128.

503 Edward S. Herman and Noam Chomsky, p. 2, no. 474.

504 Selda Bulut, "The Political Economy of News Production", in Ozgul Kocak (ed.), *Handbook of Research on the Political Economy of Communications and Media*, IGI Global, Hershey, 2020, p. 17.

505 Cherian George and Gayathry Venkiteswaran, p. 12, no. 376.

506 *Ibid.*

507 Sofie Syarief, 'The Media in Indonesia: Journalism between the State and Oligarchs,' Perry World House, April 25, 2025 at https://perryworldhouse.upenn.edu/news-and-insight/the-media-in-indonesia-journalism-between-the-state-and-oligarchs/ (Accessed on May 27, 2025).

508 *Ibid.*

509 Mumtaz Aini Alivi, Ghazali Ahmad Akmar, Ezhar Tamam and Mohd Nizam Osman, 'A Review of New Media in Malaysia: Issues Affecting Society,' *International Journal of Academic Research in Business and Social Sciences*, 8, 2018.

510 'Thailand | RSF,' Rsf.org. 2024 at https://rsf.org/en/country/thailand (Accessed May 27, 2025).

511 *Ibid.*

512 'Thailand: UN Experts Seriously Concerned about Dissolution of Main Political Party,' OHCHR, 2024 at https://www.ohchr.org/en/press-releases/2024/08/thailand-un-experts-seriously-concerned-about-dissolution-main-political (Accessed May 27, 2025).

513 Martin Albrecht Haenig and Xianbai Ji, 'A Tale of Two Southeast Asian States: Media Governance

and Authoritarian Regimes in Singapore and Vietnam,' *Asian Review of Political Economy*, 3 (4), 2024. https://doi.org/10.1007/s44216-024-00024-6.

514 *Ibid.*

515 Pauline Estella and Martin Löffelholz, no. 449.

516 *Ibid.*

517 Om Prakash Das, 'How ASEAN Media Portrays India: Insights into the Construction of Media Text,' MP-IDSA Occasional Paper, no. 63, 2024.

518 Om Prakash Das, 'How ASEAN Media Portrays India: Insights into the Construction of Media Text,' MP-IDSA Occasional Paper, no. 63, 2024.

519 Denis McQuail, and Mark Deuze, McQuail's Media and Mass Communication Theory, SAGE, Thousand Oaks, 7th ed. 2020, p. 640.

520 Jennifer Ostini, and Anthony Fung, "Beyond the Four Theories of the Press: A New Model of National Media Systems," *Advances in Foundational Mass Communication Theories,* 5 (1), 2018, pp. 41-56. doi:10.4324/9781315164441-5.

521 Jayati Bhattacharya, "Ties that Bind: India and Southeast Asia Connectivities," *Association of Asian Studies,* Winter 2020, at https://www.asianstudies.org/publications/eaa/archives/ties-that-bind-india-and-southeast-asia-connectivities/. (Accessed 9 November 2025)

522 Om Prakash Das, 'How ASEAN Media Portrays India: Insights into the Construction of Media Text,' MP-IDSA Occasional Paper, no. 63, 2024.

523 S. Jaishankar, *The India Way: Strategies for an Uncertain World*, Harper Collins, New Delhi, 2020, pp. 110–112.

524 Adrian Athique, 'Soft Power, Culture and Modernity: Responses to Bollywood Films in Thailand and the Philippines,' *International Journal of Cultural Studies,* 22/ (4), 2019, pp. 5–23.

525 S. Tharoor, *Pax Indica: India and the World in the Twenty first Century*, Penguin Books India, New Delhi, 2012, p. 278.

526 A. Mazumdar, 'India's Public Diplomacy in the Twenty-First Century: Components, Objectives and Challenges,' *India Quarterly*, 76 (1), 2020, pp. 24–39. https://doi.org/10.1177/0974928419901188

527 S.Y. Kumar. 'The Limits of India's Soft Power in South Asia,' *Journal of Contemporary Politics,* 2 (1), 2023, pp. 15–25. doi:10.53989/jcp.v2i1_1_surendra.

528 Alister Miskimmon, Ben O'Loughlin and Laura Roselle, pp. 1–22, no. 55.

529 *Ibid.*, pp. 23–55.

530 Alister Miskimmon, Ben O'Loughlin and Laura Roselle (eds.), *Forging the World: Strategic Narratives and International Relations*, University of Michigan Press, Ann Arbor, MI, 2017, pp. 1–22.

531 Dr. Zeba A. Mughal and Prof. Juan Martínez, 'Public Discourse and Local Media,' *Advance Social Science Archive Journal,* 2 (1), 2024 at http://assajournal.com/index.php/36/article/view/29.

532 Gayatri Chakravorty Spivak, 'Scattered Speculations on the Subaltern and the Popular,' *Postcolonial Studies,* 8/ (4), 2005, pp. 475–486.

533 Deepika K. and Kuber Nag, 'Analyzing Subaltern Narratives in Indian Social Media Using Machine Learning,' *Journal of Informatics Education and Research*, 5 (2), 2025. doi:10.52783/jier.v5i2.2725.

534 Roger Silverstone, *Media and Moral Order*, Routledge, London, 2007, pp. 19–31.

535 Nancy Fraser, 'Rethinking the Public Sphere,' *New Left Review,* 181, 1990, pp. 56–60.

536 Karen Lollar, 'Strategic Invisibility: Resisting the Inhospitable Dwelling Place,' *Review of Communication,* 15 (4), 2015, pp. 298–315. doi:10.1080/15358593.2015.1116592.

537 David Altheide and Robert P. Snow, *Media Logic*, SAGE Publications, Beverly Hills, CA, 1st

ed. 1979, pp. 15–30.

538 Katarzyna Molek-Kozakowska, 'Towards a Pragma Linguistic Framework for the Study of Sensationalism in News Headlines,' *Discourse & Communication*, 7/ (2), May 2013, pp. 173–197.

539 David Altheide and Robert P. Snow, no. 512.

540 Kevin Munger, Mario Luca, Jonathan Nagler and Joshua Tucker, 'The Effect of Clickbait,' Center for the Study of Democratic Politics, Princeton University, September 26, 2018.

541 David M. J. Lazer, Matthew A. Baum, Yochai Benkler and others, 'The Science of Fake News,' *Science,* 359 (6380), 2018, pp.1094–1096.

542 David Altheide and Robert P. Snow, no. 512.

543 Katarzyna Molek-Kozakowska, pp. 180–185, no. 513.

544 David M. J. Lazer, Matthew A. Baum, Yochai Benkler and others, no. 516.

545 Jarno Lang, "Media Freedom in Southeast Asia Remains An Issue" *Fair Observer*, March 29, 2015 at https://www.fairobserver.com/region/asia_pacific/media-freedom-in-southeast-asia-remains-an-issue-21378/ (Accessed June 11, 2025).

546 '2024 World Press Freedom Index – Journalism Under Political Pressure,' RSF at https://rsf.org/en/2024-world-press-freedom-index-journalism-under-political-pressure (Accessed June 11, 2025).

547 Andreas Harsono, 'The Rocky Road to Press Freedom in South East Asia,' Human Rights Watch, February 22, 2023 at https://www.hrw.org/news/2023/02/22/rocky-road-press-freedom-south-east-asia (Accessed June 11, 2025).

548 '2024 World Press Freedom Index – Journalism Under Political Pressure,' no. 521.

549 Tommy Walker, 'Most Countries in Asia See Decline in Press Freedom,' *Voice of America*, May 3, 2024 at https://www.voanews.com/a/most-countries-in-asia-see-decline-in-press-freedom/7596795.html (Accessed June 11, 2025).

550 Sebastian Strangio, 'Press Watchdog Paints Grim Picture of Southeast Asian Media Freedoms,' *The Diplomat,* May 6, 2024 at https://thediplomat.com/2024/05/media-watchdog-paints-grim-picture-of-southeast-asian-media-freedoms/ (Accessed June 11, 2025).

551 Jarno Lang, no. 520.

552 Andreas Harsono, no. 522.

553 Bruce, 'The World's Not One Size. Why Have a 'One Size Fits All' Communications Approach?,' Marmalade Box, September 4, 2017 at https://www.marmaladebox.com/comms/one-size-fits-all-communications/ (Accessed June 11, 2025).

554 Sofia Syarief, *no. 534.*

555 *Ibid.*

556 Wisnu Prasetya Utomo, 'Media Oligarchy and the Shaping of News in Indonesia,' The Conversation, December 20, 2017 at https://theconversation.com/media-oligarchy-and-the-shaping-of-news-in-indonesia-89094 (Accessed June 12, 2025).

557 Ross Tapsell, *Media Power in Indonesia: Oligarchs, Citizens and the Digital Revolution*, 1st ed. Bloomsbury Publishing, London, 2017, pp. 48–50.

558 *Ibid.*

559 Sofia Syarief, *no. 534.*

560 Oliver Boyd-Barrett, "Multinational News Agencies", in *Multinational Service Firms (RLE International Business)*, Routledge, 2013, pp. 107–131.

561 Denise Hsiu-wen Li, 'The Reliance on the Four Major News Agencies for International News Reports in Taiwan,' All Graduate Plan B and other Reports, 1990 at https://digitalcommons.usu.edu/gradreports/1599.

562 'The Big Four,' New Internationalist, June 1, 1981 at https://newint.org/features/1981/06/

01/four (Accessed June 11, 2025).

563 '14.2 Global News Agencies and International Reporting,' Fiveable, 2024 at https://library.fiveable.me/media-politics/unit-14/global-news-agencies-international-reporting/study-guide/Ye5EBsft42YHATfr (Accessed June 10, 2025).

564 'The Big Four,' no. 537.

565 Abida/ Ashraf, *Electronic Colonialism: Outsourcing as Discontent of Globalization*, Academia.edu, Paris, 2011, p. 135.

566 Cathleen LeGrand, Chris Paterson and Jörg Wiegratz, 'Afro-optimism and Progressive Modernity: The Fintech Story in the African Press,' *Globalizations*, 21 (5), 2024, pp. 803–820.

567 Daya Kishan Thussu, 'Communications Question: Neo Colonialism in News Media,' *Journalism Studies,* 23/ (X), 2022.

568 Aditya Sinha, "India, West, And Why 'Narrative Sovereignty' Matters" *NDTV Opinion*, December 11, 2024 at https://www.ndtv.com/opinion/india-west-and-why-narrative-sovereignty-matters-7224889 (Accessed June 11, 2025).

569 Anna K. Johnson, Joséphine Lechartre, ªehrazat G. Mart, Mark D. Robison and Caroline Hughes, 'Peace Scholarship and the Local Turn: Hierarchies in the Production of Knowledge About Peace,' *Journal of Peace Research*, 60 (4), 2023, pp. 675–690.

570 Cheryl Pricilla Bensa and Lupita Wijaya, 'Media Propaganda Techniques in the South China Sea Dispute,' *Jurnal Komunikasi Ikatan Sarjana Komunikasi Indonesia*, 2, 2017. 10.25008/jkiski.v2i1.93.

571 Bama/ Andika/ Putra, 'Fake News and Disinformation in Southeast Asia: How Should ASEAN Respond?,' *Frontiers in Communication*, 9, 2024, pp. 3–4.

572 *Ibid.*

573 *Ibid.*

574 *Ibid.*

575 Cheryl Pricilla Bensa and Lupita Wijaya, no. 545.

576 Diana ben-Aaron, "Given and News: Media Discourse and the Construction of Community on National Days," PhD, University of Helsinki in Auditorium XII, November 26, 2005.

577 Edward T. Vieira and Yulong Li, *Public Relations Planning: A Practical Guide for Strategic Communication,* Routledge, London, 2024.

578 Yan-Ching Lin, Min-Chun Hu, Wen-Huang Cheng, Yung-Huan Hsieh and Hong-Ming Chen, "Human Action Recognition, Human Action Video Retrieval," Proceedings of the 20th ACM International Conference on Multimedia, Nara, Japan, 2012, pp. 1053–1056.

579 Jianjun Zhang, 'State Power, Elite Relations, and the Politics of Privatization in China's Rural Industry: Different Approaches in Two Regions,' *Asian Survey*, 48 (2), 2008, pp. 215–238. https://doi.org/10.1525/as.2008.48.2.215.

580 Kalathmika Natarajan, 'Digital Public Diplomacy and a Strategic Narrative for India,' *Strategic Analysis,* 38 (1), 2014, pp. 91–106. doi: 10.1080/09700161.2014.863478.

581 Sarah Lee, 'The Ultimate Guide to Instrumental Value,' Number Analytics, May 26, 2025 at https://www.numberanalytics.com/blog/ultimate-guide-instrumental-value (Accessed June 11, 2025).

582 Emily Abbey, 'Triadic Frames for Ambivalent Experience,' *Studies in Psychology,* 27 (1), 2006, pp. 33–40. doi:10.1174/021093906776173199.

583 Sarita Dash, *The Way Forward. In: Cultural Dimensions of India's Look-Act East Policy*, Palgrave Macmillan, Singapore, 2023, pp. 469–472. https://doi.org/10.1007/978-981-19-3529-9_12.

584 Rohan Mukherjee, 'The False Promise of India's Soft Power,' *SSRN Electronic Journal*, 2013. 10.2139/ssrn.2246839.

585 Himanshu Prabha Ray, "Shared Cultural Heritage: Towards A Sustainable Future", in Dr Prabir De (ed.), *Act East: ASEAN-India Shared Cultural Heritage*, 1st edition, Research and Information System for Developing Countries, 2019, pp. 9–20.

586 "Press Trust of India", in *Encyclopedia Britannica*, March 26, 2025 at https://www.britannica.com/topic/Press-Trust-of-India (Accessed June 11, 2025).

587 'About PTI,' Press Trust of India at https://www.ptinews.com/about (Accessed June 11, 2025).

588 Amit Kumar, 'Indian News Agencies: 7 Prominent News Sources in India and Beyond,' *Indian Media Studies*, September 18, 2024 at https://indianmediastudies.com/indian-news-agencies/ (Accessed June 11, 2025).

589 Prasar Bharati, Public Service Broadcaster at https://prasarbharati.gov.in/ (Accessed June 12, 2025).

590 Madhavi Ravikumar and Shuaib Shafi, "Digital Opportunity and State Authority: The Case of Doordarshan News in the Provision of Public Service Journalism", in Alessandro D'Arma, Maria Michalis, Gregory Ferrell Lowe and Michael Bernhard Zita (eds.), *Challenges and Developments in Public Service Journalism*, University of Westminster Press, 2025, pp. 227–245.

591 'DD India – Prasar Bharati,' Prasar Bharati – Public Service Broadcaster at https://prasar bharati.gov.in/dd-india-homepage/#:~:text=About%20Us%2D%20DD%20India:,World% 20 including%20the%20Indian%20Diaspora (Accessed June 12, 2025).

592 'Reuters and ANI Expand Partnership,' Reuters, June 11, 2018 at https://www.reuters.com/article/idUSKBN1J705M/ (Accessed June 12, 2025).

593 'Express/ Computer, Unleashing the Power of Digital: Prasar Bharati Amplifies Its Online Presence,' September 4,/ 2023 at https://www.expresscomputer.in/features/unleashing-the-power-of-digital-prasar-bharati-amplifies-its-online-presence/103092/#:~:text=Since%20migrating%20to%20AWS%2C%20PBNS,channels%20and%20250%20radio%20stations (Accessed June 12, 2025).

594 Amrita Madhukalya, "Four Years Since Launch, Uncertainty Looms over Prasar Bharati News Service's Fate" *Deccan Herald*, June 19, 2023 at https://www.deccanherald.com/india/four-years-since-launch-uncertainty-looms-over-prasar-bharati-news-services-fate-1228852.html (Accessed June 12, 2025).

595 'Express/ Computer, Unleashing the Power of Digital: Prasar Bharati Amplifies its Online Presence,' no. 568.

596 "Union Minister Shri Anurag Thakur Launches Prasar Bharti - Shared Audio Visuals for Broadcast and Dissemination (PB-SHABD)" *Press Information Bureau*, March 13, 2024 at https://www.pib.gov.in/PressReleasePage.aspx?PRID=2014202#:~:text=Union%20Minister%20of%20Information%20and,National%20Media%20Centre%2C%20New%20Delhi (Accessed June 12, 2025).

597 "CEO, Prasar Bharati Elected Vice President of ABU" *Press Information Bureau*, December 16, 2020 at https://www.pib.gov.in/PressReleaseIframePage.aspx?PRID=1681238#:~:text=Prasar%20Bharati%20has%2 0achieved%20another,was%20forwarded%20by%20NHK%20Japan (Accessed June 12, 2025).

598 'Asiavision Awards 2025 – Celebrating the Contributions of Asiavision Members – ABU,' Asia-Pacific Broadcasting Union, May 23, 2025 at https://www.abu.org.my/2025/05/23/asiavision-awards-2025-celebrating-the-contributions-of-asiavision-members/ (Accessed June 12, 2025).

599 Amit Kumar, no. 563.

600 Nina Pološki Vokić, Ana Tkalac Verčič and Dubravka Sinčić Ćorić, 'Strategic Internal Communication for Effective Internal Employer Branding,' *Baltic Journal of Management*, 18

(1), 2022, pp. 19–33.

601 Guy J. Golan, "An Integrated Approach to Public Diplomacy", in Guy J. Golan, Sun G un Yang and David Kinsey (eds.), *International Public Relations and Public Diplomacy: Communication and Engagement*, Peter/ Lang, New York, 2014, 417–440.

602 Sarah Lee, 'Whole-of-Government Policy Implementation,' Number Analytics, May 25, 2025 at https://www.numberanalytics.com/blog/whole-of-government-policy-implementation#:~:text=Implementing%20Whole%2Dof%2DGovernment%20Approach&text=Building%20collaborative% 20relationships%20between%20government,needed%20to%20support%20collaborative% 20governance (Accessed June 10, 2025).

603 'China Goes Global: A History of Xinhua News Agency's International Expansion from 1978 to 1989,' Open Collections - UBC Library Open Collections, 2022 at https://open.library.ubc.ca/soa/cIRcle/collections/ubctheses/24/items/1.0412624 (Accessed June 14, 2025).

604 D.C.S. Mayal, 'Chinese Global Media Strategies and Their Footprints in South Asia,' *ORF Issue Brief*

737, October 2024, Observer Research Foundation.

605 Xiaoling Zhang, 'Chinese State Media Going Global,' East Asian Policy, National University of Singapore, 2009.

606 '14.2 Global News Agencies and International Reporting,' no. 538.

607 *Ibid.*

608 'AP Introduces New Customer Program on the Future of News,' The Associated Press at https://www.ap.org/media-center/press-releases/2025/ap-introduces-new-customer-program-on-the-future-of-news/ (Accessed June 15, 2025).

609 'China Goes Global: A History of Xinhua News Agency's International Expansion from 1978 to 1989,' no. 578.

610 Amit Kumar, no. 563.

611 *Ibid.*

612 *Ibid.*

Bibliography

1. Altheide, David L., *Creating Fear: News and the Construction of Crisis*, Aldine de Gruyter, New York, 2002.
2. Asia Centre, Media Freedom in Southeast Asia: Repeal Restrictive Laws, Strengthen Quality Journalism, Asia Centre, Bangkok, 2022.
3. Atkins, William, *The Politics of Southeast Asia's New Media*, Routledge, 2013.
4. Backman, Michael, *Asian Eclipse: Exposing the Dark Side of Business in Asia*, John Wiley & Sons, Chichester, 1999.
5. Baum, Matthew A., *Soft News Goes to War: Public Opinion and American Foreign Policy in the New Media Age*, Princeton University Press, Princeton, 2003.
6. Bennett, W. Lance and Paletz, David L., *Taken by Storm: The Media, Public Opinion, and U.S. Foreign Policy in the Gulf War*, University of Chicago Press, Chicago, 1994.
7. Bennett, W. Lance, *News: The Politics of Illusion*, Longman, New York, 1988.
8. Bharti, Simant Shankar, *The European Union's Role in South Asia: Development Policy and Soft Power*, Routledge, London, 2025.
9. Brady, Anne Marie, *Marketing Dictatorship: Propaganda and Thought Work in Contemporary China*, Rowman & Littlefield, 2009.
10. Brewster, David, 'India's Defense Strategy and the India, ASEAN Relationship,' *India Review*, 12 (3), 2013.
11. Bromley, Michael and Romano, Angela, *Journalism and Democracy in Asia*, Routledge, London, 2006.
12. Brommesson, Douglas and Ekengren, Ann-Marie, *The Mediatization of Foreign Policy, Political Decision Making and Global Governance*, Palgrave Macmillan, US, 2017.
13. Burkart, Patrick, *Pirate Politics: The New Information Policy Contests*, The MIT Press, 2014.
14. Burrett, Tina and Kingston, Jeffrey, *Press Freedom in Contemporary Asia*, Routledge, Abingdon, 2020.
15. Carroll, Toby, Hameiri, Shahar and Jones, Lee, *The Political Economy of*

Southeast Asia: Politics and Uneven Development Under Hyperglobalisation, Palgrave Macmillan, Cham, 2020.

16. Chambers, Paul and Waitoolkiat, Napisa, *Khaki Capital: The Political Economy of the Military in Southeast Asia*, NIAS Press / Silkworm Books, Copenhagen / Bangkok, 2017.
17. Chandra, Satish and Ghoshal, Baladas (eds.), *India and Southeast Asia: Cultural, Economic and Strategic Linkages*, Gyan Publishing House, New Delhi, 2011.
18. Church, Peter, *A Short History of South-East Asia*, John Wiley & Sons, Singapore, 2017.
19. Desch, Michael C., *When the Third World Matters: Latin America and U.S. Foreign Policy*, University of California Press, Berkeley, 1993.
20. Devi, T. Nirmala and Raju, Adluri Subramanyam (eds.), *India and Southeast Asia: Strategic Convergence in the Twenty-First Century*, Manohar Publishers & Distributors, New Delhi, 2012.
21. Elias, Juanita and Rethel, Lena, *The Everyday Political Economy of Southeast Asia*, Cambridge University Press, Cambridge, 2018.
22. Entman, R. M., 'Framing U.S. Coverage of International News: Contrasts in Narratives of the KAL and Iran Air Incidents,' *Journal of Communication*, 41(4), 1991.
23. Entman, Robert, *Projections of Power: Framing News, Public Opinion, and U.S. Foreign Policy*, University of Chicago Press, Chicago, 2004.
24. Erni, John Nguyet and Chua, Siew Keng, *Asian Media Studies: Politics of Subjectivities*, Blackwell Publishing Ltd, Oxford, 2005.
25. Fenton, Natalie, Freedman, Des, Livingstone, Sonia and Haddon, Leslie (eds.), *Media Policy and Public Communication*, SAGE, London, 2016.
26. Freberg, Karen, *Social Media for Strategic Communication: Creative Strategies and Research*, SAGE Publications, Thousand Oaks, CA, 2018.
27. Fuchs, Christian and Mosco, Vincent (eds.), *Marx in the Age of Digital Capitalism*, Brill, Leiden, 2015.
28. George, Cherian and Venkiteswaran, Gayathry, *Media and Power in Southeast Asia*, Cambridge University Press, Cambridge, 2019.
29. Heath, Robert L., *Handbook of Public Relations*, SAGE Publications, Thousand Oaks, CA, 2001.
30. Heng, Russell Hiang-Khng, *Media Fortunes, Changing Times: ASEAN States in Transition*, ISEAS Publishing, Singapore, 2002.
31. Herman, Edward S. and Chomsky, Noam, *Manufacturing Consent: The Political Economy of the Mass Media*, Pantheon Books, New York, 1988.
32. Hess, Stephen, *The Government/Press Connection: Press Officers and Their Influence on News Coverage*, Brookings Institution Press, Washington, D.C.,

1996.

33. Higgott, Richard and Robison, Richard, *Southeast Asia: Essays in the Political Economy of Structural Change*, Routledge, London, 2013.
34. Holiday, Ryan, *Trust Me, I'm Lying: Confessions of a Media Manipulator*, Penguin, New York, 2012.
35. Hutchcroft, Paul D., *Booty Capitalism and the Political Economy of the Philippines*, Cornell University Press, Ithaca, 1998.
36. Jain, B. M., *China's Soft Power Diplomacy: Myth or Reality?* Lexington Books, Lanham, 2017.
37. Kumar, S. Y. S, 'The Limits of India's Soft Power in South Asia,' *Journal of Contemporary Politics*, 2023.
38. Lim, Joanne B. Y., *Digital Media Interventions in Southeast Asia: A Decolonial Perspective*, Palgrave Macmillan, Cham, 2025.
39. Luxmi, M., *India: A Global Soft Power Leader in the 21st Century*, Anu Books, New Delhi, 2022.
40. Mattelart, Armand and Mattelart, Michèle, *Theories of Communication: A Short Introduction*, Sage Publications, London, 1998.
41. McChesney, Robert W., *Communication Revolution: Critical Junctures and the Future of Media*, The New Press, New York, 2007.
42. McChesney, Robert W., *Rich Media, Poor Democracy: Communication Politics in Dubious Times*, University of Illinois Press, Urbana IL, 1999.
43. McLuhan, Marshall, *Understanding Media: The Extensions of Man*, McGraw Hill, New York, 1964.
44. Mohammed, S., 'Strategic Communication and India's Soft Power,' *International Journal of Management and Public Relations*, 2025.
45. Mosco, Vincent, *The Political Economy of Communication*, Sage Publications (2nd ed.), London, 2009.
46. Murdock Graham and Golding, Peter, *Communications and Culture in the Digital Age: The Political Economy of Information*, Routledge, London, 2005.
47. Nayak, Babuli Chandra, 'Soft Power in India's Foreign Policy and Cultural Diplomacy,' *South Asian Journal of Contemporary Affairs*, 2024.
48. Nye Jr., Joseph S., *Soft Power: The Means to Success in World Politics*, Public Affairs, New York, 2004.
49. Oguya, Thomas and Freedman, Des (eds), *Media and Capitalism in the Twenty-First Century*, Palgrave Macmillan, Cham, 2023.
50. Page, Benjamin I. and Bouton, Marshell, *The Foreign Policy Disconnect: What Americans Want from Our Leaders but Don't Get*, Palgrave Macmillan, New York, 2008.
51. Pant, Harsh V. and Saha, Premesha, *India, South Korea and the ASEAN Middle Power Diplomacy in the Indo–Pacific*, Routledge India, New Delhi, 2025.

52. Paul, Christopher, *Strategic Communication: Origins, Concepts, and Current Debates*, Praeger, Bloomsbury Publishing, New York, 2011.
53. Phongpaichit, Pasuk and Baker, Chris, *Thailand: Economy and Politics*, Oxford University Press, Kuala Lumpur / Oxford, 1996.
54. Ranjan, Amit, Chattoraj, Diotima and A. K. M., Ahsan Ullah, *India and China in Southeast Asia*, Palgrave Macmillan Singapore, Singapore, 2024.
55. Rasiah, Rajah and Schmidt, Johannes Dragsbaek, *The New Political Economy of Southeast Asia*, Edward Elgar Publishing, Cheltenham, 2010.
56. Rethel, Lena, *The Political Economy of Financial Development in Malaysia: From the Asian Crisis to 1MDB*, Routledge, Abingdon, 2021.
57. Robinson, Piers, *The CNN Effect: The Myth of News, Foreign Policy and Intervention*, Routledge, London, 2002.
58. Rodan, Garry and Robison, Richard, *The Political Economy of South-East Asia: Markets, Power and Contestation*, Oxford University Press, Oxford, 2006.
59. Schiller, Dan, *Digital Capitalism: Networking the Global Market System*, MIT Press, Cambridge MA, 2000.
60. Schiller, Herbert I., *Culture, Inc.: The Corporate Takeover of Public Expression*, Oxford University Press, New York, 1989.
61. Seib, Philip, *The Al Jazeera Effect: How the New Global Media Are Reshaping World Politics,* Potomac Books, Washington, D. C., 2008.
62. Singh, Shailza, Varghese, Philip, Balaiah, Shalini and Sebastian, Sarish, *India and Southeast Asia in a Changing World: Exploring Relationship Prospects for a Sustainable Future*, Routledge India, New Delhi, 2025.
63. Smythe, Dallas W., *Dependency Road: Communications, Capitalism, Consciousness, and Canada*, Ablex Publishing, Norwood, NJ, 1981.
64. Srivastava, 'A Decadal Snapshot of India's Soft Power Strategies (2014–2024),' Observer Research Foundation, New Delhi, 2024.
65. Wagstaff, J., 'Southeast Asian Media: Patterns of Production and Regulation,' Independent Media Reports / IssueLab, Washington, D. C., 2011.
66. Wasko, Janet, Murdock, Graham and Sousa, Helena (eds.), *The Handbook of Political Economy of Communications*, Wiley-Blackwell, Malden MA, 2011.
67. Williams, Louise and Rich, Roland Y., *Losing Control: Freedom of the Press in Asia*, Australian National University Press, Canberra, 2000.

Index

H

I

J

L

M

N